Carrie Chapman Catt

A PUBLIC LIFE

Carrie Chapman Catt

A PUBLIC LIFE

JACQUELINE VAN VORIS

The Feminist Press
at The City University of New York
New York

99 98 97 96   4 3 2 1

Library of Congress Cataloging-in-Publication Data

Van Voris, Jacqueline.
Carrie Chapman Catt: a public life.
Bibliography: p.
Includes index.
1. Catt, Carrie, Chapman, 1859-1947.
2. Women in politics—United States—Biography.
3. Women—Suffrage—United States. I. Title.
HQ1413.C3V25 1987   324.6'2'0924 [B] 87-8533
ISBN 0-935312-63-3 — ISBN 1-55861-139-8 (pbk.)

Text design: Melodie Wertelet
Cover design: Tina R. Malaney

Photographs:
Parts I, II, and III (pages 1, 27, and 53)
courtesy of the State Historical Society of Iowa, Des Moines, Iowa;
Parts IV and V (pages 115 and 167) courtesy of the Sophia Smith Collection,
Smith College Library, Northampton, Massachusetts

Printed in the United States of America on acid-free paper by BookCrafters.

Contents

Preface

Carrie Chapman Catt led an army of voteless women in 1919 to pressure Congress to pass the constitutional amendment giving them the right to vote and convinced state legislatures to ratify it in 1920. And then, the first battle won for women, she devoted the rest of her life, more than twenty-five years, to work for peace as the basis of human rights. Catt was one of the best-known women in the United States in the first half of the twentieth century and was on all lists of famous American women. An office party to celebrate her fiftieth birthday was front-page news of the *New York Times:* her meetings and speeches were covered by the worldwide press. She had access to politicians and presidents. Today, however, her work is little known.

The first biography of Catt was written by Mary Gray Peck, Catt's devoted friend, who published *Carrie Chapman Catt: A Biography* in 1944, three years before Catt's death. Peck wrote from her own experiences in the suffrage movement and her long admiration of Catt. Many letters between Peck and Catt are in the Library of Congress and we are indebted to Peck for saving the bulk of extant Catt materials deposited there. However, some of the letters were heavily edited, presumably by Peck, and very little of a personal nature remains. There are no letters to or from Leo Chapman, Carrie Lane's first husband, or George Catt, her second. There are no papers from family members and no personal diaries. Undoubtedly, Carrie Chapman Catt herself destroyed materials of a private nature. Her life was spent so much in public she guarded what privacy she had. This book, then, is subtitled "A Public Life."

Catt was a compelling speaker, she knew how to inspire workers, and she understood the importance of education and agitation. Above all, she believed that "organization is the only assurance of final triumph of any cause." When the Nineteenth Amendment was finally approved by Congress in 1919, plans for ratification were so well made that the bill was law within eighteen months.

The story of the suffrage movement has been told several times, but never from Catt's evolving viewpoint. It consumed her time and energy for nearly half of her long life, which spanned the years when the United States emerged from a frontier society to become a world power. She was born in 1859, the year John Brown struck his blow against slavery at Harper's Ferry. Eighty-eight years later, when she died in 1947, the United Nations was formulating a human rights compact against slavery anywhere in the world.

Catt's unique contribution to the women's movement was her global view: her international work has never before been examined for its own merits. This biography traces the development of Catt's outlook from deep suspicion of all foreigners ("a regular jingoist" she later called herself) to a certainty that the world's peoples would have to live peacefully together if the species were to survive.

In 1902 Catt formalized her involvement in and leadership of the worldwide women's movement when she founded the International Woman Suffrage Alliance. Her understanding broadened as the IWSA grew in Europe, and in 1911–12 it sharply expanded during her around-the-world trip, which included Asian lands that were at the same time more backward and more advanced than any she had known. Her travel diary from this trip, freely quoted from here, is as illuminating as it is exciting.

This is an account of a life that publicly was lived with enthusiasm and faith in the progress of the human race. Catt's vision of the women's movement as an international force extended her influence and importance far beyond her own time and country; the impact of her ideas and her organization of women continues to influence the lives of millions.

EDUCATION OF AN
ACTIVIST
1859–1891

Carrie Lane Chapman in her wedding dress around the time of her marriage to Leo Chapman, 1885

· 1 ·
One of the Gifted

Carrie Chapman Catt strode across the platform in a whirl of silk, her blue eyes flashing. On the way she was tearing up the manuscript of her prepared speech to the League of Women Voters' second convention in 1921 at Cleveland. Will Irwin had just finished a graphic description of the carnage he had seen in France and how it pointed to the next war. Catt sensed an imperative for an immediate call to action. Unless women did something immediately, peace was but an interlude to prepare for war. This was her own "cross of gold" speech:

> "The people in this room tonight could put an end to war," she challenged. "Everybody wants to and everyone does nothing. It is the duty of everyone who wants the world to disarm to compel action in Washington. We are as stolid and as inactive as if we did not face the greatest opportunity in history. We are the appointed leaders. We have waited too long and we will get another war by waiting.
>
> "It is necessary that we rise out of shallow partisanship, that we act as women. God is giving a call to the women of the world to come forward, to stay the hand of men, to say, 'No, you shall no longer kill your fellow men!'"

"Toward the end, Mrs. Catt spoke against a light but steady ripple of weeping," Irwin remembered. When she sat down there was complete silence for a few seconds, followed by wave on wave of applause from the women who were again standing.[1]

Catt at sixty-two was at the crest of her fame and power as a leader of women. She had led two million suffragists to victory in the United States, which had enfranchised thirty-five million women and doubled the black vote; she had organized women in thirty-six countries all over the world; she was recognized by politicians internationally as a force to be contended with.

She was a woman from the western plains and the strong Populist streak from her Iowa years still informed her thoughts and actions. She was a suffragist born and, like the pioneer suffragists with whom she trained for leadership, saw the vote for women as the essential tool by which women could change the world for the better. Now that they had the vote, the first change she wanted was to end war.

She had persistence, tact, earthy humor, a truthful eye, and an inventive imagination for practical solutions. She was blessed with two supportive husbands, family, and friends. She cultivated her public speaking talent and organizational skills until they revealed genius; she developed tact and skill at working with and giving hope to others. Most important to the suffragists, she had the unusual ability of triumphing over defeat after defeat. Her greatest achievements were in her public life, in the changes wrought in the political arena.

Carrie Clinton Lane was born February 9, 1859 on a family farm in Ripon, Wisconsin, the only daughter and second child of Lucius and Maria Clinton Lane. Both parents had come from farms near Potsdam, New York. Lucius's grandmother had left her husband in Canada for reasons she never gave and settled on some unclaimed land with her ten children. Maria's family was well established and prosperous. In 1850, when he was eighteen, Lucius and a cousin joined the gold rush to California. By 1855 he returned, purchased a partnership in a Cleveland coal business, and married Maria Clinton. He soon found that he hated cities and within a year had sold out and bought the Ripon farm. The Lanes' first child, Charles, was born there three years before Carrie. Both children had their father's stamina and Carrie his sense of adventure and stubborn will.

Maria was quiet and bookish, very close to her daughter with whom she seemed to have an understanding that could transcend words. After high school Maria had attended a woman's school, Oread Collegiate Institute, in Worcester, Massachusetts, a city that at the time was a major feminist center. The founder and head of Oread, Eli Thayer, was so convinced that women could equal men in intellectual achievement if they had the same advantages that he had modeled his curriculum after that of Brown University. From her mother the daughter gained a love for reading as well as support for her precocious feminism.

The reticent Lanes were often flabbergasted by the direct way their daughter could make a point clear, but such assurance was certainly rein-forced by the one-room school of her time. For the child in need of skilled, personal attention, or the one who was bored or easily distracted by having other classes recite in the same room, such schools could be tedious and sometimes humiliating. The bright, independent child was often used by harrassed teachers to help other children with problems; such children gained authority, especially, if like Carrie, they could more than hold their own on the schoolground.

Once when her elder brother Charles chased her with a harmless snake in his hand she responded by squealing and running away. Then she reasoned with herself: If snakes didn't harm him they would not harm her. She picked the unfortunate creature up, and waited until Charles was unaware, then wrapped it around his neck.

Carrie Chapman Catt's first blow for her sex was struck when she was six. She and her first-grade classmates

> were lined up with our toes touching one straight crack. Suddenly, while the teacher was talking to us, one of the girls' hoopskirts became loose and slipped down to the ground. The little girl blushed and the boys all began to giggle out loud. The teacher tactfully gathered up the girl and her hoopskirt, and repaired the damage. At noontime those boys came to the girl and poked fun at her, and as they continued their annoyance, I went up to the leader and slapped his face! They had more respect for us girls after that![2]

A studio photograph taken of Carrie at this time shows a sturdy, healthy child with a determined chin. She is wearing a new dress and lace mitts that suggest an unabashed streak of vanity. The fingertips of one hand rest on a little table. She was by her own description, "an ordinary child in an ordinary family on an ordinary farm."

When Carrie was seven the family made a carefully considered move to a farm outside Charles City, Iowa. That was her first lesson in long-term planning and organization. Although Lucius was content only on a farm, his uncomplaining wife disliked the drudgery of that life. Charles City was barely a generation from the frontier, wagon trains still lurched and rattled their way west through its main street, and little of its surrounding prairie had been ploughed. However, it was a county seat of about five hundred and the railroad was nearly built to it. The Lanes planned a commodious brick house, more an urban house than the usual farm house. Maria and Carrie went by train as far as they could, and boarded in town the year the house was being built. Lucius followed with the wagon and the farm implements. Details of the move were calculated down to the fast-growing maple saplings he brought with him from Wisconsin to give shade to the house in summer and make a windbreak from it to the barn in winter.

When the family moved into the new house Carrie went to the one-room schoolhouse down the road until she went to high school in town. In good weather she rode her horse the five miles from the farm; in the winter she boarded with friends who remembered her as "livelier than a circus."

At thirteen she discovered feminism before she knew the word. During the presidential election of 1872, the Republican Lanes favored the editor and reformer Horace Greeley, who was running against Ulysses S. Grant. When Lucius and the hired man dressed to go to town to vote on the day of the election, Carrie asked her mother why she wasn't changing her clothes. She was surprised when her mother said she wasn't going. "Then how are you going to vote for Greeley?" Carrie asked. The whole family laughed at her.

The laughter rankled. Soon afterwards a young neighbor boy called at the house to see her. To make conversation Carrie said, "I think it's very unfair that women can't vote, don't you?" Then he laughed and she demanded, "What's so funny about women voting?" "Well, naturally they can't vote," he said. That did it. He writhed under her scornful rebuttal until he could make his escape.

That night after she had gone to bed, she heard her mother and father talking downstairs. "She's just scared away her first beau," her mother said. "Her last, too," her father added gloomily. They had long since given up trying to change their daughter's ways.

In her early teens she decided she wanted to become a doctor and began bringing reptiles and insects into the house where she could observe their development. Those that died she pickled in her mother's preserve jars. Her father thought animals belonged outside the house, but said little until with tender solicitude she brought an apronful of rattlesnake eggs in and they began to hatch behind the stove. Her father's patience gave out and he threw them all into the fire. To the pop of exploding eggs he laid down the law.

This cut back on her specimen gathering but her interests went on leaping here and there in the way of a bright adolescent. She borrowed a copy of Darwin's *Origin of Species* from a neighbor and although she understood little of it, as she admitted later, she was soon asking difficult questions. Why did her history book say that the universe and all people in it were made in six calendar days, whereas her geography text said the earth was millions of years old? If God made man in His image, did God look like the pictures she had seen of Piltdown man? Do angels really speak English? Is it true that only Baptists get to heaven? She got few answers but was convinced that the world was full of delightful riddles that would surely be answered in her lifetime. It was inevitable that such a speculative and interested young woman would want to go to college, and, being Carrie, she would contrive a way to get there.

Iowa State Agricultural College (now Iowa State University) had opened in 1869 at Ames. Thanks to the Morrill Act of 1862 it was offering a remarkable bargain in higher education. Tuition was free, board was $2.50 a week, and room in a college dormitory ran from $1.00 to $3.50 per term. A determined student could go to college for $150 a year. Carrie approached her father during her junior year in high school knowing that like most farmers he had little ready cash. He thought higher education for his daughter an unnecessary luxury but on the other hand knew the futility of forbidding her from going; he offered her $25 a year. She would have to earn the rest. She told him that had been arranged: She was going to teach school during the summers.

Her father was astonished but she knew the schools better than he. The majority of teachers since the Civil War were young, single women who worked for about $26 a month and were usually required to resign when they married. As country schools were rapidly growing, there was a chronic shortage of teachers, and superintendents were empowered to recruit wherever they could, briefly examine the candidate, and award a temporary teaching certificate. It was one of the few ways a respectable young woman could earn money.

When Carrie Lane entered Iowa State Agricultural College in March 1877, it was housed in a single, dignified Victorian building. Her freshman class was the ninth to enter. There were twenty-seven students; she was one of six women. During her first two years she washed dishes for nine cents an hour, and after that she worked in the library, an enviable job that paid the top student wage of ten cents. She taught in country schools during the long recess from November to March. Like most of the students she was pinched for money but joined Pi Beta Phi Fraternity [sic].

The record of her four years shows that she made respectable A's and B's and received her B.S. in the General Science Course for Women. This paralleled the general science for men but required Domestic Economy and Domestic Chemistry, two courses that gave her the basis of her first published writing.

In the *Iowa Homestead* of March 16, 1883, Carrie Lane deplored the drudgery of housework, as well as the usual neglect of nutrition and hygiene. Every woman should be taught basic chemistry and physiology. When these were understood, the status of the housewife would be raised and the nation's people would achieve a heretofore unparalleled age and prosperity. She was still preaching this doctrine when she was seventy-five.

At Ames, Carrie Lane made two innovations. The first was women's military drill. Land grant colleges offered military training for male students, and after hearing their commander extoll the virtues of such drill for health, she asked why it wasn't available for women. As a result she started the Ladies Military Company, more popularly G [Girls] Company, which drilled with broomsticks. This unlikely enterprise for a woman who was later to become a leading pacifist provided exercise and fresh air, discipline and companionship. G Company endured at the college until 1897, when physical education took over.

Carrie also won the right for women to speak for themselves in the Crescent Literary Society. To develop quick thinking and self-confidence it was the custom to call on a male member, give him a subject, and require him to speak on it for three minutes. Women members were limited to written essays and recitation until Carrie defied tradition and spoke. A debate in May of her sophomore year on woman suffrage was her doing. From then on she held offices in the Crescent and consequently learned parliamentary procedure, a rare and valuable skill that enabled her to conduct efficient meetings throughout the world for the rest of her life.

One of her speeches made at a teachers' institute when she was eighteen and in her first year at Ames caused enough comment to be reported in her hometown paper. She justified the education of women on the grounds that it would help them bring up their children well, then related this to woman suffrage, countering the common claim that women were not intelligent enough to vote. With deliberate irony she concluded, "How is it possible that a woman who is unfit to vote, should be the mother of, and bring up, a man who is?"[3]

At Ames, public speaking and debate were technically extracurricular activities. However, the nineteenth century was a great period for oratory, and the ability to think on one's feet, to hold an audience, and to articulate arguments convincingly could be of awesome importance. Students and faculty alike formed estimates of each other by their performance on a platform. Subjects were often heavily moralistic, sometimes lighthearted. Carrie Lane, as Miss Victoria Hardfist, sued Mr. Benjamin Butterface for breach of promise in a mock trial but lost the suit because he looked so pitiful next to her.

She needed more than her developing talents in public speaking and organization. She needed the conviction that society could and would get better, and she found it at Ames. The entire college, from the president to the janitor, were convinced evolutionists. President Adonijah S. Welch was a convert to Darwin and the young instructors he had recruited from Yale, Harvard, and Amherst were enthusiasts. She remembered being taught evolution in botany, zoology, geology, under microscopes, in laboratory crucibles, and in the details of queer fossils. At the time of the Scopes trial, in 1925, she wrote:

> I came forth from that college possessed by a conviction that the human race had climbed fast and far from its ancient beginning, that it was still climbing and that it would always climb higher and higher into some inestimable mature perfection; that each generation will see truth a little more clearly and comprehend the rights and welfare of others a little more tolerant'y; that the clash of opinion of our generaton is due to ignorance on both sides which in time the race will slowly outgrow. [4]

She enjoyed reading Herbert Spencer, who thought that he had found such laws for society as Darwin had for biology. She never lost her concept of evolving progress, which she correctly called a faith. Although she showed a brief interest in the Universalists in the late eighties, she was never a member of any church. Her concept of evolution as constantly improving the race leading to a free and peaceful society was sufficient to keep her going.

Carrie Lane was the only woman among the eighteen graduates at the commencement of November 10, 1880. Her achievement was remarkable and she was proving herself to be gifted in many ways. She was an energetic, enthusiastic, bright, hardworking young woman, popular and ambitious, with definite ideas of how the world should be ordered and that she was one of those who would set it right. Her next logical step was to become a lawyer. It was a new profession for women, the first Iowa woman had been admitted to the bar only eleven years before. Carrie Lane began reading law in the offices of a Charles City attorney, J. Evans Owens. A year later, in the fall of 1881, an offer came to teach high school in Mason City at $40 a month. She accepted, planning to earn enough to study law at the university in a few years. But in Mason City her joy in teaching was reinforced and she also discovered her gift for administration. After a year or two she gave up her plan for graduate work.

Mason City was another prairie town of about 4,500. It was proud of its own growth, its two flour mills, its volunteer fire department, its water works second to none in Iowa, and particularly its extravagant $30,000 high school of dressed stone that was heated by circulating hot air. Carrie Lane's abilities were soon recognized. In her second year the man who held the combined posts of high school principal and superintendent of the city schools left before the term was over. She was asked to fill his positions after the students unanimously signed a petition requesting her appointment. It was not unusual for a woman to be superintendent of schools in the educationally progressive Iowa of the 1880s; it *was* unusual that she had made her mark on the town so quickly. She continued to teach high school as well as to serve as principal and general disciplinarian. She preferred to control by her voice and manner but used a strap when necessary. Said one seventeen-year-old, "We were . . . twice as big as Carrie Lane, but we never questioned her authority."

In March 1883, the same month she was promoted, another conspicuous newcomer arrived in Mason City. Leo Chapman purchased and began to edit the weekly *Republican*. Born in Indiana in 1857, he had moved to Iowa when he was thirteen and helped on the family farm. At twenty-one he went to work in Des Moines with the *State Register*, and had risen to press reporter in the House in 1882. When he left, the General Assembly gave him a gold watch "as a token of esteem." He was twenty-six, a fastidious dresser with an erect carriage. He neither smoked nor drank, and he fully supported the temperance movement and passionately advocated woman suffrage. To the editor of the rival Democratic *Times*, Chapman was a crank, a dude, and a carpetbagger. To Superintendent Lane he was an idealist, a gentleman, and a soul mate. Before long the superintendent of schools and the *Republican*'s editor were working together on the town's Decoration Day committee and falling very much in love.

At the suggestion of the superintendent, Chapman made available a half column in the *Republican* for high school notes written by the students. In the fall of 1883 the notes reported that regular Friday afternoon meetings at the high school had dealt with a biography of Lucretia Mott and that there had been a debate on woman suffrage. The rival *Times* was quick to report criticism that Miss Lane was teaching politics in the public schools. Chapman wrote gallantly in her defense: "She only teaches truth, morality and principles. That Miss Lane teaches politics in school is hereby hurled into the lying teeth through which it first passed."[5]

The *Times* retaliated by questioning her judgment and competence. She then appointed committees to oversee the semiannual examinations. When they cleared her, she said, "It is not possible that the testimony of these

intelligent ladies and gentlemen should be impeached by the simple statement by a man who knows nothing of which he is talking."[6]

In a town of 4,500 it was no secret that the man from whom the charges
were coming was another Republican, County Auditor Henry H. Shepard.
He was a local boss of the party and the only member of the school board who
had opposed her appointment as superintendent. Probably he saw the obvious, that the new superintendent would not share those backstairs' arrangements of obligation and favoritism by which a political boss usually
maintained power. Chapman and Lane represented the opposite pole from
Shepard. He was for the conservative, entrenched members; they were
brash progressives.

Within the schools Carrie Lane was exceptionally well liked. She gave
up her spring vacation to hold special classes for high school seniors who
might otherwise have failed to graduate. By commencement in July it was
understood that she was engaged to Leo Chapman and would resign because
married women were not allowed to teach. The graduating class gave her a
copy of Poe's *Raven* with Doré illustrations, the teachers a gold brooch, and
the parents a pair of Paris-made opera glasses in mother-of-pearl and gold.[7]
They all saw her as someone rare.

Carrie Lane and Leo Chapman were married by the local Methodist
minister at her home in Charles City on February 12, 1885. In her berib-
boned gown, she looks in her wedding picture as if she could have stepped out
of a Renoir portrait. In Mason City the *Republican* carried a notice that
thereafter man and wife would act as equal coeditors. The gown and the
notice defined the marriage: It was clearly a romantic love match; it was also
an equal professional partnership.

In addition to her other duties, Carrie Chapman instituted a weekly
feature called "Woman's World," modeled on "Woman's Kingdom" edited by
Elizabeth Boynton Harbert in the Chicago *Interocean*. In it Carrie Chapman
listed conspicuous achievements of women, upheld the right of working
women to strike for better pay and conditions, harvested notes of feminist
interest from other publications, and constantly reminded readers that sentiment for suffrage was useless without organization. When suffragists met
defeat as usual, she wrote, "No step of progress was ever made but its
advocates fought dearly for victory. That women will have a voice in governmental affairs is inevitable."[8]

One series of essays in the "Woman's World" answered specific arguments against woman suffrage. To the claim that only men should have the
right to vote because they defended that right in war, Carrie Chapman argued

that by the same reasoning those men exempt from war—clergymen, teachers, physicians, editors, firefighters, legislators—should also be exempt from voting. When Horace Greeley asked Elizabeth Cady Stanton what women would do in time of war, she replied, "Just what you have done, Mr. Greeley, stay at home and urge others to go and fight."[9]

In October Carrie Chapman gave a long, enthusiastic report of a three-day congress in Des Moines sponsored by the American Association of Women and chaired by Julia Ward Howe. This was the first time Carrie Chapman had been to a woman's conference and she was dazzled. They were, she wrote, "the strongest, best-educated, most earnest, broad-minded and philosophical women in the United States." They represented the professions newly opened to women—college professors, lawyers, ministers, editors, doctors. For the first time she heard and met astronomer and Vassar professor Maria Mitchell; abolitionist-feminist Abby May; Elizabeth Harbert, Chapman's role model who was then editing the New Era; and Clara Colby, editor of the Woman's Tribune. Also at Des Moines was Ellen Foster, one of the first women to be admitted to the Iowa bar and president of the Iowa Woman's Christian Temperance Union, which was then disputing National President Frances Willard's commitment of the organization to the Prohibition Party. There also Carrie Chapman for the first time heard the great Lucy Stone speak for the equal franchise.[10]

Later that month the Republican reported on the state suffrage convention in Cedar Rapids, where a resolution was passed to circulate petitions for signatures in favor of enfranchising women and to present this evidence of popular support to the state legislature in 1886. Although Mason City had no suffrage organization, Carrie Chapman enlisted the help of friends and made a house-to-house canvass. All but ten citizens signed. She sent the results of this unusually thorough solicitation to Mary Coggeshall in Des Moines with an amusing note on the recalcitrant ten.[11] It was the first time that most of the suffrage leaders had heard of Carrie Chapman, but they were to remember her name. Meanwhile, events at home distracted her.

The fight between Auditor Shepard and the Chapmans had been renewed in the spring when Shepard initiated a ruling by the school board to discontinue special dresses and flowers at the high school graduation, ostensibly in deference to those parents who could not afford such luxuries. The ruling implied a criticism of the last commencement over which Carrie Chapman had presided. The editors of the Republican involved themselves in the brouhaha and ultimately won their point. The high school exercise went on as usual. It is conceivable that Shepard had devised his criticism as a trap to demonstrate the couple's dedication to feminism as concerned with trivia, and Carrie Chapman's anger could be taken as crass indifference to the poor.

That fall of 1885 Leo Chapman put Carrie Chapman's name up as candidate for the County Superintendent of Schools in the Republican primaries. When she lost in a 243 to 182 vote, the Chapmans broke with the party over the renomination of Shepard for Auditor and supported an independent candidate. As the November election approached, Leo Chapman's attacks on Shepard became ever more vituperative. On the eve of the election, in a desperate effort to discredit Shepard, Chapman wrote "On the Make." He alleged that Shepard had manipulated county money in such a way that warrants given to the poor for coal were decreased in value. Shepard intended to buy them and redeem them at face value but his plan did not work.[12] The article failed to defeat Shepard; it led to Chapman's ruin.

Shepherd won the election by 23 votes, 1,244 to 1,221. Thereupon he gave "On the Make" to the County Grand Jury, which indicted Leo Chapman for criminal libel. Chapman filed a demurrer, and then conveniently went to New Orleans to attend to some business and returned after the Grand Jury recessed.[13] In the meantime his coeditor published the paper.

On December 31, 1885, Leo Chapman was arrested but released on $200 bail. He was in good humor, even jaunty, and the editor of the Times thought nothing would come of the libel suit. A Pennsylvania court had dismissed a similar case and the allegations printed in the Republican seemed unexceptional amidst the rough-and-tumble, mudslinging journalism of the day. In March, however, Chapman's demurrer to the indictment was overruled by a judge and he was ordered to be ready to stand trial. Within three weeks the Chapmans had sold the Republican for what they could get and left Mason City.

In May, Leo Chapman took a train to California while his wife stayed with her parents in Charles City, planning to join him when he was settled. In August a telegram came from San Francisco with news that he had typhoid fever. She left by the first train west but by the time she arrived he was dead.

· 2 ·

Aliens and Alienated

Within a few months Carrie Chapman had lost her income, her own home, the vehicle for her work for women, the husband she loved, all hopes for their lives together, and, for a short time, her self-confidence. Nothing had prepared her for such a concentration of calamities. The year she spent in San Francisco, 1886–87, she thought of as the worst of her life, and so painful that even in later years she would discuss only a few of its details with her closest friends and always glossed over her reasons for leaving Mason City.

An aunt lived in San Francisco and helped her through the gloomy rites of death and offered her a place to live, but the lack of money was critical. Expenses had been high, she had earned nothing for six months, the forced sale of the *Republican* had left her little. She didn't have the heart to go back to teaching high school but stayed with journalism, canvassed for ads, wrote freelance articles, and became one of the estimated four million working women marginally employed, underpaid for long hours, with no job security, and vulnerable to sexual harrassment.

One evening an editor had sent her to a business office. When she did not respond to the businessman's innuendoes, he rushed from behind his desk and grabbed her. She broke away but felt the shock and indignity of an attempted rape. She remembered walking the foggy hills of San Francisco, and choking with tears of outrage. Always before people had deferred to her or at least treated her as an equal. For the first time she realized what most working women had to put up with and determined to do something for their protection.

Shortly after that she heard her name called by someone walking behind her on a downtown street. It was George Catt, whom she had known at Ames. He had been a freshman cutting lawns for money when she was a junior dazzling the Crescent Society. Since then he had become a civil engineer for a San Francisco bridge-building firm, was shortly to become their chief engineer although only six years out of college, and was demonstrating brilliance in his profession. He was trim and tanned from his outdoor work, and still had a trace of a farm boy's grin. He was unmarried, very prosperous, and still dazzled by Carrie Lane Chapman.

Probably it was he who reminded her that public lecturing at the time was a popular entertainment. A bright speaker could be influential and make a good living. Soon she had written out three lectures, hired an agent to schedule them, and after delivering and polishing them on the west coast, returned to Charles City to begin her new career.

The first of the lectures, "Zenobia," tells about the third-century queen of Palmyra whose name has come to suggest an ambitious woman. For Carrie Chapman, Zenobia was a model of worldly wisdom and cultivation. Her rise and fall before the emperor of Rome is a highly romanticized projection of Carrie Chapman's own rise and fall. She included many bravura passages to show off her oratory. She later called it a test to see if she could control an audience; "What cheek I had!"[1]

The other two lectures, "America for Americans" and "The American Sovereign," along with an article, "A True Story," show the cast of her thinking. All three condemn the way the presence of aliens perverts American institutions.

In "A True Story" she took an unblinking look behind the surface of the Gilded Age. The editor of the *Woman's Journal* who first printed it felt she had to prepare her audience by quoting Harriet Mill's admonition to her daughter, "My dear, what others endure, you can bear to know about." The article tells of a twelve-year-old Chinese girl who is sold in China, transported to San Francisco, and confined to a brothel. She is beaten whenever she resists a customer or tries to escape. Nevertheless she manages to flee to a nearby Christian mission. When her owner learns her whereabouts, the mission is served with a writ of habeas corpus. The missionaries explain to the runaway that by American law she will be taken before a magistrate, friends of her owner will swear that she is legally married to him, and the court will order her to return to him. That has happened many times before. When the little girl understands, she retires to her room and drives a penknife through her heart.[2]

In "America for Americans" Carrie Chapman argued that the floods of immigrants from paternalistic cultures were imposing their prejudices on issues that could be determined only by an informed electorate of women and men. In "The American Sovereign" she reasoned that the anti-individualism of aliens was reinforced by their cohesive ethnic groups. She saw them living in male-dominated households, frightened by the new world, and often intolerant of the rest of America. They were vulnerable to exploitation by the political boss who bought and sold blocks of their votes for favors or money. He was the real American sovereign.

Both lectures show the influence of the short-lived, localized, ineffectual American Party founded by an attorney for the Southern Pacific Railroad, P. D. Wigginton, the year Carrie Chapman went to San Francisco. Her title "America for Americans" was taken from Wigginton's statement of principles. It was a nativist party that blamed the immigrants for all the nation's problems. It drew support from those blue- and white-collar workers who felt alarmed by the anarchy of the recent Haymarket riot in Chicago, and by local riots of workers (most of them Irish-born) against Chinese laborers imported to replace them for lower wages. Unlike a former American Party, the Know-Nothings, Wigginton's was not against any particular race, or necessarily anti-Catholic. The party platform included restriction of immigration, repeal of naturalization laws, and legislation against alien ownership of real estate. It limited suffrage and governmental patronage to citizens, and the language taught in public schools to English.

A strong populist sentiment also runs through both lectures. Carrie Chapman at this time pits rural America against urban America while encouraging the urban native worker to join rural America against the aliens and their manipulators.

With a century of hindsight it is easy to see Carrie Chapman's views in the late 1880s as xenophobic oversimplifications that scapegoat immigrants. Nevertheless, both "America" lectures proved popular and were well received by audiences that included dedicated feminists. In part the attraction to these ideas came from the women's frustration with the laws that denied them the vote while offering it to any alien man who had lived in the country for six months and who had taken out first papers. Chapman's dream was of a sober, educated electorate of women and men. Her suspicion of the alien began to dissolve only when she entered international waters a decade later; her dream did not change.

In August 1887 Carrie Chapman moved back to Charles City and took a house so that her brother William could live with her in town while he was going to high school. Her professional lecturing was steady and demanding but she had time to look after him, to edit the *Floyd County Advocate* for several months so that its regular editor could take an extended vacation, and to join the Woman's Christian Temperance Union, the only organization interested in woman suffrage that had a local branch.

Her high spirits were coming back. When she took her turn as editor of the temperance column in the *Charles City Intelligencer*, she wrote an ironic article on small town hypocrisy. She knew there were five saloons in the officially dry town. She instigated some questioning of the patrons, who said they had been given milk, and wrote,

> If those men were such idiots that when they received beer to drink they thought it was milk, we women knew by the smell as we passed the doors of the places that it was beer. The president of our Union was the wife of a grocer who was superintendent of the Sunday School and frequently had temperance afternoons. He obliged his wife to resign from the Union after that, and she did. The editor of the paper disavowed any responsbility for my work. My father said I was always too strong-minded for my own good, and my mother felt that her chicken had turned out to be a duckling.[3]

Clearly the Charles City branch of the WCTU could offer only limited scope to Carrie Chapman's talents. However, she remained active and was a delegate at the state convention in 1889 when the Iowa union, after years of opposing Frances Willard's commitment of the WCTU to the Prohibition Party, broke away from the national organization. The Iowa WCTU lost influence and members, and was an important lesson to Carrie Chapman on the devastating effects infighting could have when even the most dedicated reformers wasted vital energy opposing each other.

To her Willard was a model. In later years Chapman told Eleanor Roosevelt of waiting eagerly for Willard's annual reports published in the Chicago *Interocean*. Willard had so many new ideas and such clear ways of explaining what she wanted to do.[4] She was the best administrator of a reform movement America had ever seen. Unfortunately for the suffragists she had been all too supportive of a single political party.

It was Willard's practice to include departments within the WCTU organization that would draw women interested in other reforms to temperance. Very early on she had insisted on a department for suffrage and Carrie Chapman had been heading that for the Charles City union. The entire liquor interest took this to mean that two quite different issues were essentially one movement opposed to its economic existence. Furthermore it was the weaker edge and easier to attack because it lacked the enormous organizational support of the Baptist and Methodist churches. Woman's suffrage had to oppose every bar, every brewer, every distiller, every conveyer of liquor whenever it waged a campaign.

But Carrie Chapman was not immediately troubled by such practical problems. When an Iowa suffrage leader, Martha Callahan, asked her to be organizer for woman suffrage in Floyd County at about the time that the local WCTU was breaking apart, Chapman turned her full attention to the single issue of the franchise. In October 1889 Carrie Chapman went to the state suffrage convention where she was made recording secretary. When the aging Lucy Stone heard her speak, she said clearly, "Mrs. Chapman will be heard from yet in this movement."[5] Chapman was unanimously elected state lecturer and organizer at a modest salary and within a few weeks had started a Political Equality Club in Sioux City and by the end of the year had created ten new clubs.

Nearly everyone who met these suffragists commented on their intelligence and talent. They might often be at odds with one another over issues, their numbers throughout the United States few, and their campaigns hopelessly underfinanced, but the brainy energy of their leadership could be awesome. Carrie Chapman's rapid rise to prominence reflected the leaders' instant recognition of her as one of their own, and their confident praise released a stunning energy in her.

The next January her growing popularity as a lecturer led to a short speaking tour on the east coast. She was therefore available in mid-February to be an Iowa delegate to the convention of the National American Woman Suffrage Association (NAWSA) in Washington, D.C. It was the first time in twenty years—since 1869—that the two wings of the suffrage movement had drawn together.

The suffragists had split after the Fourteenth Amendment had continued the limitation of the vote to males. Before, women had been promised by Republicans who controlled Congress that the franchise would be extended to all adults. After that failure, two laborious strategies were possible: Women could win the franchise in each separate state—the strategy favored by the American Woman Suffrage Association led by Lucy Stone and Henry B. Blackwell; or they could push for another constitutional amendment—the strategy favored by the National Woman Suffrage Association led by Susan B. Anthony and Elizabeth Cady Stanton. As both organizations would usually be represented at any public debate on the issue of suffrage, they tended to get in each other's way and to confuse the voters. In 1890 the two organizations finally recognized the necessity of using both approaches, and amalgamated themselves. The name of the new organization reflected the two strategies: National American Woman Suffrage Association.

All the major leaders of woman suffrage were there at the 1890 convention, including Stone, Blackwell, and their daughter Alice Stone Black-well, who was the person most responsible for the reconciliation of the suffragists after twenty years of working at cross purposes. The seventy-five-year-old Stanton, exhausted by the care of an infirm husband, the rearing of seven children, and a lifetime of writing and lecturing for abolition and woman suffrage, had been cajoled and prodded out of retirement to be president. Anthony was there in her black silk and red shawl; at seventy she had the carriage of a drill sergeant and was very much in charge. She was surveying the field for new talent, and her eye focused on the delegate from Iowa.

A speech was expected from Carrie Chapman, and under the title "The Symbol of Liberty" she gave a version of her trusty "The American Sovereign." When she stood before an audience, her back straight, her hair neatly parted in the middle, dressed in the well-buttoned, well-corseted style favored by the age, she had what modern actors call "presence," and what was then called "magnetism," an effortless way of commanding full attention as she spoke. Perhaps it came from her glow of health, perhaps from her extraordinarily mobile mouth that could shift in an instant from an impish smile to a rousing call for action. Perhaps it came from a carefully modulated voice that could resound through a great hall. Whatever the reason, when audiences heard Carrie Chapman speak, they listened.

After she returned to Charles City, she made another organizing trip for the Iowa Woman Suffrage Association, then left, ostensibly on a northwest speaking tour. On June 10, 1890, in a fashionable residential section of Seattle, a man looked over the back fence and saw a handsome woman walking in the garden of the neighboring house which had been recently purchased by an engineer he had not yet met. "Are you Mrs. Catt?" he inquired. "No," said the woman, "but I shall be after one o'clock today."[6] She was in the garden pacing out the plot where she intended to plant sixty rose bushes.

The privacy of her marriage to George Catt flabbergasted most of her friends including the Iowa suffragists. "I went around town with Mrs. Ankeny and begged money to keep Mrs. Chapman working," complained Margaret Campbell to Lucy Stone, "and then she went off and got married. The loss of Mrs. Chapman is very discouraging."[7] The president of the Iowa WSA was presuming that her paid state organizer had made a conventional marriage with a conventional Victorian man. She was wrong on both counts.

George Catt, thirty years old, was in charge of the Washington State operations of the San Francisco Bridge Company, the leading bridge-building firm of the west coast. He had been in Seattle for six months when fire raged out of control and destroyed most of the city. At the time he and Carrie Chapman were married he was directing the reconstruction of the piers and other waterfront structures. During the following year he built most of the bridges and trestles on the railroad lines in Washington for the Great Northern railway.

Like most effective engineers, Catt liked to be as close to his crews and work as possible and whenever he could was in the field with them. His new wife spent much of the first two months of their marriage visiting sites where mountains of earth, steel, and stone were being rearranged to make a major commercial lifeline in the northwest. Theirs was the deep love of two mature and committed people, each of whom respected the other's unusual talents.

A story circulated that the Catts signed a contract that guaranteed her two months each spring and fall to work on woman suffrage. If such a contract existed, perhaps it was one of their quiet jokes, or perhaps they drew it up to illustrate to others the nature of their private agreement.

"We made a team to work for the cause," she said. "My husband used to say that he was as much a reformer as I, but that he couldn't work at reforming and earn a living at the same time; but what he could do was to earn living enough for two and free me from all economic burden, and thus I could reform for two. That was our bargain and we happily understood each other."[8]

In August she left the cool shores of Puget Sound for South Dakota. The suffragists from the national organization went to South Dakota in response to an appeal that had been made to them at their convention in February by representatives from the Farmers Alliance and the Knights of Labor. These two organizations claimed to hold the balance of power in the state and wanted help in passing a referendum for woman suffrage that would be on their state's November ballot. The representatives did not mention the appalling condition of South Dakota roads, the calamitous drought that had hit the area, or that the heavily financed liquor industry was prepared to fight against woman suffrage. The convention had voted to support the referendum, and Susan B. Anthony set about planning a campaign and raising funds. In the meantime, however, the two state organizations had formed a new Independent Party and decided that the question of woman suffrage was insignificant and not worth a plank in their platform. Catt was disgusted with such politicians, who "are green toads when they sit on a green tree, and brown toads when they sit on a brown tree" and claimed she "never again trusted a politician's promise until she had seen it in writing at least twice."[9]

The convening suffragists had to contend as well with the searing heat, their own constricting clothing (which they felt compelled to wear to demonstrate that wanting the vote did not "unsex" them), and a plague of chinch bugs. In addition, the state suffrage committee had become preoccupied with the $8,000 Anthony had collected for the campaign. The committee would not release their plans without the money, and Anthony would not release the money until she knew their plans. In the heat tempers flared. One leader even accused Anthony of embezzlement. Angry denials and accusations appeared weekly in the press.

The $8,000 was proving miserably inadequate, and Catt was among those who were urging suffragists at home to distribute little pockets in which a penny a day might be collected from supporters. Meanwhile, for their fight against a prohibition law and the suffrage referendum, the liquor interests had a fund of $500,000.

Neither the South Dakota Democrats nor Republicans allowed the women to address their conventions. The Democrats insulted the suffragists with a large delegation of Russian immigrants who could not read English wearing great yellow badges (the color used by the liquor interests) lettered "Against Woman Suffrage and Susan B. Anthony." At the Republican convention the women were placed so far back that Catt stood on a chair and reported to the others what was going on. She was impressed when the suffrage leader Anna Howard Shaw gave a powerful speech in the five minutes allotted to the women, and outraged when three Sioux Indians were received with honor and given front seats.[10] In common with her contemporaries, Catt had grown up reading lurid reports of Indian atrocities; Custer's defeat had occurred in the Dakota Territory adjacent to Iowa during her high school years. That the native Americans who had been killing United States soldiers a few years before were now given preferential treatment baffled and humiliated her.

At one point she went to the Missouri River where on the west bank the Sioux reservation began. On the east bank she had seen college-bred women homesteading amid signs of thrifty, careful management: "On the opposite bank," she wrote, "was the Sioux reservation filled with brutal, treacherous, murderous Indians who broke treaty after treaty with the government and engaged in wholesale pillage, murder, rapine and outrage of helpless women led into captivity worse than death. The murderous Sioux is given the right to franchise which he is ready and anxious to sell to the highest bidder."[11]

Catt's attitude did not change in spite of a meeting with Elaine Goodale, one of the few whites who was trying to interpret native American life with compassion and understanding. Goodale, then superintendent of Indian instruction, tried to explain to Catt that the Sioux were suffering even more than the impoverished whites. To Catt they were aliens. Her bitter comment was that the government had "enfranchised 3000 of these Indians she is trying to civilize without once thinking of placing the same confidence in the woman who is acknowledged to be qualified to teach them in all things."[12] Like Catt's jingoism, her bigotry was modified later, but only after many years of experience.

The suffrage plan was to pepper the state with speakers. Catt was one of a dozen, her route confined to the eastern part of the state. She traveled northward from Yankton through such small towns as Hurley and Lennox, westward to Mitchell, Letcher, Woonsocket, and then continued north until by election day she was in Aberdeen. The route led her through raw frontier country with its impoverished farms whose inhabitants had her sympathy and understanding. On the way she wrote page after page for publication in suffrage papers.

"Our audiences are everywhere composed largely of farmers," she reported.

> They come from ten to twenty miles to attend the meetings. We are never able to begin before nine o'clock and the poor farmers, with their long drives home, are obliged to make an all night job of it. The people are much more enthusiastic than I expected. Indeed, with the exception of the politicians, and some classes of foreigners, who are bound by native prejudices, in the regions where I have been, there are few to convert. The bravery of the good people here surpasseth all understanding. The whole country, towns and all, are dependent upon the agricultural products of the State for support. For four years there has been a failure in crops. Drought, hot winds, hail storms, lightning, chinch bugs, have each in its turn visited the afflicted people. The farms are mortgaged, their homes are poorly built and still more poorly furnished, yet these brave men and women are forgetting all their personal grievances, and freely giving of their little, that they may help along the cause of human liberty.[13]

Again and again she was impressed by their courage and their poverty:

> At one place where I took three meals I had bread and watermelon and tea for each meal and the people themselves had not had anything else for a long time. I was once one of nine people sleeping in one room. It

was a little story-and-a-half house with one living room downstairs and the sleeping room above. There were four beds in that room, two on each side, with the ends together. I slept with a young woman who taught school and who happened to be living there at the time, and the man and his wife were in the second bed on our side of the room and the five children of the family on the other. We all went to bed in the dark.

At another place where I stopped the Postmaster met me at the station and said that I was to stop at his house, because he had the best accommodations. It was a little bit of a house with a single room, roughly built with beams across the top. He was a widower with one daughter of eighteen. We had the meeting in a small wheat elevator with nail kegs for seats, and the lamp from the Post Office with a reflector for light.

After the meeting she spent the night in the single room partitioned by a quilt hung over one of the beams, sharing a small bed with the daughter while the father slept on the settle.

> In one place I spoke standing in front of a long line of babies lying on the floor back of me. The people were so poor and they had been having such hard times that they had a stolid look. They were just at the age to have young families, and almost every woman who came had a baby in her arms. They had driven on heavy lumber wagons for miles and miles to come to the meeting, and they looked so tired sitting on those hard seats, without backs, holding the heavy babies, that I tried to make them more comfortable. The babies were wrapped up like little bundles, so that they could lie on the floor comfortably, and after I had persuaded one or two mothers to put them down all the rest followed suit. The mothers looked a little afraid at first as I stood between them and the babies but when they saw I was not very wild they grew more comfortable, and as one baby after another would send up a little squeal the mother would go and attend to it while I kept up with my talk.[14]

Early in the campaign she and Henry B. Blackwell (the only man on the suffrage circuit) were in Yankton at the same time. They found themselves in competition with a barbeque organized by the Independents to which everyone in town was going. Their meeting had been postponed without telling them. They couldn't get the Independents to share time so they took an open carriage to the front of the post office. "A boy with the big sonorous hotel bell supplied the place of a brass band," Blackwell wrote. "At his vigorous ringing the clans gathered and for an hour and a half we discoursed on the amendment. Mrs. Chapman gave a fiery speech."[15]

She herself was impressed with the women on their own. "The state contains thousands of women farmers," she reported, "young women, spinsters and widows who came here a few years ago, took up claims, improved them and are now full-fledged agriculturists. In one county I found one hundred of these independent women farmers, yet it was not the county which contained the largest number by any means."

She told of having a wheel come off the wagon in which she was being driven to a suffrage meeting by two "typical Dakota women." They repaired the damage with ingenious makeshift until they could get to the nearest house a mile away. Then, finding no one at home, they searched the barn and got a monkey wrench "which was skillfully applied and we were soon rattling on our way."

Another extraordinary woman was a widow with six children. She pitched hay all day, then got dinner, milked the cows, hitched the team, and drove them all to the schoolhouse two and a half miles away for the meeting. She was cheerful and happy although the struggle was hard, and her mortgaged quarter section was in the drought district. "She wants to vote. Is there a man so unjust he would deny her the privilege?"[16]

Catt was always publicly optimistic, but when the suffragists' executive committee asked for her assessment she took a hard look at the political realities:

> We have not a ghost of a show for success. Our cause can be compared with the work of prohibition, always remembering ours is the more unpopular. Last year the Methodist church led off in State conference and declared for prohibition. It was followed by every other church, except the German Lutheran and Catholic, even the Scandinavian Lutherans voting largely for it. Next the Republican, the strongest party, stood for it, because if they did not it meant a party break. The Farmers Alliance were solid for it. The leaders were put to work, a large amount of money was collected and representative men went out in local campaigns. It was debated on the street, and men of influence converted those of weaker minds.
>
> Now what have we? 1st.—The Lutherans, both German and Scandinavian, and the Catholics are bitterly opposed. The Methodists, our strongest friends everywhere else, are not so here. 2d.—We have one party openly and two others secretly against us. 3d.—While this county, for instance, gave $700 to prohibition, it gives $2.50 to suffrage and claims that for hall rent, the amount then not being sufficient. 4th.— When I suggested to the committee to start a vigorous county campaign

and get men of influence to go out and speak, they did not know of one
man willing to face the political animosities it would engender.

   With the exception of the work of a few women, nothing is being
done. We have opposed to us the most powerful elements in the politics
of the State. Continuing as we are, we can't poll 20,000 votes. We are
converting women to "want to vote" by the hundreds, but we are not
having any appreciable effect upon the men. This is because men have
been accustomed to take new ideas only when accompanied by party
leadership with brass bands and huzzahs. We have a total lack of all. Ours
is a cold, lonesome little movement, which will make our hearts ache
about November 5.[17]

   Her prediction about the vote proved devastatingly accurate. She was in
Aberdeen for a last-minute meeting the night before election day and stayed
over to see the action.

   I went with some of the women to sit in a polling place. It was in a
skating rink and there at one end was the ballot box and a judge or two
sat behind that ballot box, and we could do nothing but sit there and
occasionally speak to voters as they came in. There came in one by one
young men bringing with them these Russian-Germans, usually ten at a
time. The young men marked their ballots for them and handed them to
the judge, who took them in his own hand and put them in the ballot
box. Not one of them could speak a word of English or sign his name in
any language. And when they had voted they turned around and filed
out, where the leader very often to tantalize the women in the voting
place would hand over to these men one dollar and sometimes two dollars
in plain sight. Through this Russian-German element under the leadership of somebody who had money to pay to defeat woman suffrage it
went down to defeat.[18]

   It was downed by a majority of 22,790; the vote had been 45,862 against
with 22,072 for. Indian suffrage was won by 9,083 votes. The wording of the
questions was peculiar; the woman suffrage one was simply stated, but the
Indian suffrage was worded so the vote was for or against prohibiting it, hence
the negative vote "against prohibiting it" was a vote in favor.

   The work went on. Within two weeks Catt was at the Kansas State
convention with Anthony and others who had been in the campaign. There
they told their adventures and aroused fresh dedication to the cause. "Only
idiots, insane persons, traitors, Chinese, and women are now disfranchised,"
Catt repeated.

She also kept her promise to Iowa and completed her organization work for the year as well as attending the Iowa State convention.

She was exhausted when she went home to Seattle for Christmas but soon afterward wrote a major address, "Indians versus Women," that she was scheduled to give at the national convention in Washington, D.C. in February. She was en route from Seattle when in San Francisco she came down with typhoid fever. It was the disease that had killed Leo Chapman in the same city less than five years before. For the next two months she hovered between life and death. In her delirium she gave her speeches from the South Dakota campaign over and over again.

APPRENTICESHIP AS LEADER
1891–1900

Carrie Chapman Catt at a Nebraska train station on the suffrage circuit, ca. 1890

· 3 ·
Experiments in Organization

Not until the end of June 1891 was Catt well enough to work for two hours each morning in her rose garden. During her long convalescence from typhoid she published eight articles in the *Woman's Standard*. In one she argued "the whole movement for the liberation and awakening of women was begun by the suffragists and maintained by them." In another she praised Princess Angeline, daughter of Chief Seattle, in a way that makes it clear that her anger in South Dakota was directed at Sioux males who got the vote, not at native Americans in general.[1]

She also helped organize and was first president of Seattle's august Woman's Century Club, which still flourishes. She did not insist that members be committed to the suffrage movement; she wanted the club for tea, good company, and culture. Like thousands of such clubs, members read papers on assigned subjects at regular meetings, and her first was "Evolution and Women," a topic she reserved for intellectuals. All the women she had helped gather together were influential in the area; perhaps she wanted to see if they would come to her suffragist convictions of their own accord.[2] Freed from supporting herself on the lecture circuit, and freeing herself from illness, she was beginning to consider the ways in which organization could be sound but imaginative.

By fall she was once more in Iowa organizing for the state association and stressing the hard lessons she had learned in South Dakota. First, there had to be more education and it had to be continuous for all members. This was basic progressive wisdom. "The reformer," Robert M. LaFollette, the Wisconsin leader, said, "should always make sure that the underpinnings of his structure—the education of his people—was secure."[3] Catt was beginning to assemble a curriculum of suffrage studies that steadily grew more elaborate over the years. Second, she held that a successful campaign could be mounted only from a solid base of local organizations that share a common goal. The squabbling in South Dakota between the national leadership and the local clubs had been more defeating than the chinch bugs or the heat, and women could do something about it.

Meanwhile, George Catt's career took them both to the east coast. He had unexpectedly won a contract to dredge Boston harbor, and they spent the fall and winter in Boston. His invention of a more efficient dredging device was leading to other business for which the logical center was New York. They were preparing to move there at the time of the 1892 NAWSA convention in Washington, D.C.

At the convention, Harriet Taylor Upton, publicity director, noticed a young woman, very pretty, with chestnut hair and deep blue eyes, in a demure, flower-trimmed bonnet. She had made a speech but was not on the program. Upton handed her a note, "Who are you? Where were you born? Where educated? What have you done? Are you married?" The penciled reply read, "Born in Wisconsin, educated in Iowa, did newspaper work in California. Am married; he is in the back of the hall. Am not a big gun, never will be. Carrie Chapman Catt."[4]

The 1892 convention was the real beginning of a transition in which new members with fresh ideas began to replace the old guard. Susan B. Anthony, who succeeded Stanton as president, was the most conspicuous survivor of the women who had begun and led the suffrage movement.

Anthony continued the yearly ritual of testifying on the suffrage amendment at a congressional hearing, and swept Catt off with a band of women to Capitol Hill. Catt was surprised that Anthony called on her to speak first. She quoted Herbert Spencer, who accorded the same natural rights to men and women, then sat down and watched the politicians' indifference to the earnest women. She watched the amendment sink without a ripple into the great bog of legislative business to be ignored, and she decided that something new had to be done.

The incident suggests Catt's conflict between her enormous admiration for Anthony as the aging general of the woman's movement and her disapproval of Anthony's lack of organization along with her often abrasive, peremptory manner. Anthony was acquainted with Catt, of course, having heard her speak at the 1890 convention, worked with her throughout the South Dakota campaign, and followed her activities since Catt's days with the Iowa suffragists in the *Woman's Journal*. She saw Catt as an indefatigable workhorse with a keen eye for detail, having as well talent, money, time, and a supportive husband. Anthony's major change at the convention was to abolish the old executive committee and transfer its duties to a business committee chaired by Catt. Catt became responsible for recruiting and educating suffragists through a network of organizer-lecturers. She hired the speakers, planned their trips, made local arrangements, and raised money. She wrote detailed instructions for starting suffrage clubs and maintaining enthusiasm in them, made suggestions for the conduct of the meetings and broad plans for the year's work. Catt was strong on detail but never entrapped by it; she always kept her broad vision of equal rights.

After the convention, the Catts returned briefly to Seattle, sold their house, and moved to Bensonhurst, then a fashionable section of Brooklyn. There they were within easy commuting distance over the still new Brooklyn Bridge to the office they shared in the gold-domed World Building. Thereafter New York was to be their residence, though they both thought of Iowa as home.

One of Catt's innovations was calling the first Mississippi Valley Conference, which met in Des Moines for four days in September 1892. Few midwestern women were able to attend national conventions in Washington, D.C., and Catt knew the importance of these meetings to discuss mutual concerns, ideas, and experiences, as well as to make friends. She urged them to have meetings of "good feeling and jollity [which] serve well as a means of rejuvenating one's courage and hope."[5] Those the suffragists needed badly. She had spoken at a regional meeting in Boston where she found the audience somewhat reserved and the atmosphere chilly. The suffragists had drawn 1,500 participants but received little publicity, while a delegation of 200 brewers nearby "had a ringing report in the press." She attributed the difference to the men's lavish use of music, flowers, flags, and bunting. While she had omitted mentioning free beer, she had retained the sharp eye of the newspaper editor for what made good copy.

The big event of 1893 was the Columbian Exposition in Chicago, which opened with a Congress of Representative Women of All Lands. Susan B. Anthony had successfully lobbied the U.S. Congress in 1890 to amend the supporting bill for the event to include official recognition of women at what was popularly called the Chicago World's Fair. A Chicago socialite was nominally the head of the Board of Lady Managers (the organizing committee) but the actual work was done by two energetic, intelligent women—May Wright Sewall, a noted educator and president of the National Council of Women, and Rachel Foster Avery, one of the ablest suffragists of Catt's generation.

Women from all the clubs in the United States were there for the week and a large delegation of visitors from abroad spoke at the opening session. Catt had never seen internationalism on parade and she never forgot it. It changed her life.

"The great number of foreign women was a great sight to all of us young women," she remembered forty years after the event.

> In those days, every woman wore a train, and the foreign women's trains were far longer and wider than the women of this country wore. As those women went up upon the stage, we had an opportunity to see their costumes in full. But, alas, the building in which the Congress was to be held was not yet completed, and all over the platform there was dust and rubbish and shavings. So, when each woman came forward to make her little speech, she came in a cloud of dust, and upon her train were piled high the shavings that lay about. As most women spoke in their own language and most of the audience understood no language at all except their own, their attention was concentrated on the trains, their emotions divided between amusement at the queer sight and shame at the exhibit of American housekeeping. I tell that story to you because it seemed to me strange how clearly I could remember it. I can fairly see every shaving on their trains.[6]

That was all she said about the image and perhaps she never conceptualized why it had come to symbolize the occasion. It is tempting to read something of Henry James into it, in the sense of the cultured Europe and raw, unfinished America. Catt herself paid little attention to dress reform, which was a preoccupation of some nineteenth-century feminists; it was too easy to focus on the superficial costume and neglect the critical issues. She never lost sight of her basic strategy: "In matters of principle go against the current, but in matters of custom go with it."[7] The sight of those European women stirred her imagination and began to extend her empathy to the women of the world, not only to the women of her own country.

In Chicago that week there were 27 countries and 126 organizations represented with 528 delegates, plus thousands of visitors. They talked about everything: kindergartens, temperance, prostitution, dress reform, suffrage, religion, art, literature, and on and on. Each subject was assigned a place where meetings were held throughout the week. There were never fewer than seven meetings, and sometimes as many as eighteen going on at the same time. Many of them were in the Art Palace, others in the Woman's Building, a major point of interest, designed by twenty-three-year-old Sophia Hayden, the first woman graduate of the four-year architecture course at the Massachusetts Institute of Technology, who had won a nationwide competition for the honor.[8]

Catt was buoyant. "We did a whizzing business," she recalled. "Miss

Anthony, Lucy Stone, Mrs. Stanton, Miss Shaw, and many younger women spoke. It is my recollection that thirty-four [suffragists] spoke during the week." Her own major address was on one of her basic tenets, "Evolution and Woman's Suffrage." "Evolution may well be called the great discovery of our century. It is revolutionizing thought in every line of life. Evolution is not an hypothesis but an absolute proof that the 'world does move,' that it moves ever onward and upward."[9]

It was the right note for the occasion. The suffragists were the radical left of the woman's movement and relatively few of the 150,000 who attended the women's week at the exposition had declared themselves suffragists. Catt saw as one strategy that of making suffrage acceptable to the upper-income or society women who had influential friends. Suffragists were primarily educated middle-class women who had time and energy to devote to the cause as well as the indignation of their powerlessness to fight the sex discrimination they felt in the workplace and in the law courts.

Catt saw in the attitude of the press toward suffragists after the congress a marked change in their acceptance of the reformers as a normal part of the American political landscape. "The cartoonists had pictured Miss Anthony for years with a dress hanging in uneven scallops and carrying a large umbrella," Catt observed. "Other suffragists were made to look like escapers from the insane asylums. Anti-suffragists were good-looking, fashionably dressed, highly respectable women. Now the cartoonists changed their clothes. Miss Anthony never carried her umbrella in a cartoon after 1893. Suffrage clothes became more fashionable as time went on."[10]

During the exposition Susan B. Anthony was approached by a reporter from the Denver Rocky Mountain News, Ellis Meredith, who had been one of the speakers in the South Dakota campaign. She had come to Chicago with a strategy so novel and unfashionable it was nearly ignored. She represented the entire suffrage movement in Colorado—twenty-eight women (including her mother) with a total capital of twenty-five dollars. Nevertheless, with the help of a canny lawyer who had donated his time and a loyal politician, they had quietly introduced a suffrage bill into the Colorado legislature. It had been eased in so skillfully that its enemies had not noticed. The twenty-eight women had taken turns watching it through committees, seen it perfunctorily passed by both Houses, and receive the signature of the Populist governor. Ratification of the bill would be decided by voters in November. Now Meredith needed advice and money to mount a successful campaign. Would Miss Anthony help?

Miss Anthony would not. She said all national resources were pledged to a campaign in Kansas. Besides Anthony remembered Colorado with distaste as a state where suffrage had been soundly defeated sixteen years before. She bluntly asked Meredith if the opponents in the southern counties had been converted, or, she said, "Are all those Mexicans dead?"[11]

Meredith then appealed to Catt, who at first said she could do nothing. No one thought there was the slightest chance for success in Colorado and the available dollars, as usual the decisive factor, were pledged to Kansas where there was hope. It was a bad year to finance one campaign, let alone two.[12]

The very month in which the great Columbia Exposition opened, May 1893, stocks on the New York Exchange suddenly began dropping, precipitated by the decline of the U.S. gold reserve. When the stock market crashed at the end of June, a deep economic depression swept over the country that lasted about four years.

Although Catt had said she could not go to Colorado, she could not get the idea out of her mind. If the women there wanted to try. . . . She began filling pages with advice on keeping a low profile, on careful local organization with men and women working together. Her plan counted on broad, informed support with minimal opposition: "Don't get men or women who are simply suffragists," she wrote. "They must know politics and how to work a campaign. Don't make much noise about this Committee but see that in every precinct in the State a trusty *man* is found."[13]

Meredith replied that they had adopted her good suggestions, that the organization was under way, but that Catt was misinformed about the referendum. The vote was not on an amendment but on a provision of the Colorado constitution that needed only majority approval, and that Colorado used the Australian ballot (complete, printed, and secret), which made misuse of the vote more difficult, hence provided an honest election. Further, all newspaper editors had been polled and 75 percent of them had agreed to print suffrage material. There was no election that year so the fight would not be subject to national politics, but would be in the counties. The women had been given some office space, loaned some furniture; correspondence was increasing but they had run out of money for penny postcards and two-cent stamps.[14]

The letter convinced Catt and she immediately made plans to go to Colorado herself. She set about raising money; the first $100 came from the ever-generous Blackwells. Even though Lucy Stone was dying, both were encouraging and they later contributed another $200. When times are bad, Henry Blackwell said, then men will most consider change. Now is the time.[15]

Catt's next letter to Meredith was full of excitement about the campaign and with instructions about getting herself (Catt) on the road as fast as possible. She needed a keen scheduler; the campaign depended on expert timing given the relative isolation of Colorado's towns. One big meeting in Denver would open the campaign, and then she would cover the rest of the state, leaving Denver quiet until the last intense week so that the opposition could not organize. Catt could generate all the money for her expenses, but the local committee would manage the campaign. She wrote: "If possible find some other hall than a church. I know by long experience our meetings are better attended and especially by men when held in some other place." However, she was also willing to speak on Sundays and suggested a joint meeting of several churches with her speech substituted for a sermon: "I have a Sunday speech The Bible and Woman Suffrage which will not offend the most orthodox and has done some good among conservatives." The most effective were her appearances at gatherings planned by other groups. "If there should be any Chatauqua Assemblies, any Populist or Knights of Labor picnics, a meeting of Republican or Democratic clubs or anything of that sort, try to get a chance for me to speak there. I have a voice like a foghorn and can be heard in out of door meetings. I can speak twice in one day sometimes if required."

Above all, this was a local campaign and should be controlled by the Colorado people. She had been explicit in her advice because she trusted it would be useful. "Remember I am not coming to be *bossy* but only to help."[16]

Catt arrived in Denver early in September and covered over a thousand miles throughout the Rockies during the next two months. She visited twenty-nine of Colorado's sixty-three counties, speaking in two or three places in many of them. Fifty suffrage clubs were organized, the outstanding feature of which was the number of men of influence in their communities who joined. Except that Colorado was physically so different from South Dakota, the travel was equally hard, the attendance at meetings just as uncertain, and plans did not always work out as anticipated. She took it in stride with humor and ingenuity.

She often amused her friends by describing one hair-raising adventure that began when she missed the daily train that was to take her thirty miles down the mountain to the next town where she was scheduled to speak that evening. The only apparent means of transportation then remaining was a mule team too slow to allow her to keep her appointment. A large, laconic sectionhand who was lounging about the station offered to get her to Pilotsville on time. An Iowa friend reported Catt's story in the *Woman's Standard:*

"But how," she cried, "good heavens, you can't carry me."

"Handcar. Down hill all the way. Do it in forty-five minutes."

"Saved! I'll go on the handcar."

Now a handcar skidding down a mountain side is a highly uncertain sort of vehicle and was liable to jump the track any minute he took care to inform her. They often did it. There wasn't a mortal thing to hang on by except the legs of the navvy, who for the first fifteen minutes or so displayed a taciturnity of demeanor that forbade such a liberty. Her hat flew off, hairpins shot out over the landscape, she froze to the flat surface of the car as hard as she could, but remained in momentary expectation of sudden death. A thousand feet below on one side of the track flowed a river seventy yards wide with big boulders dotting its surface.

"What river is that?" inquired the traveler to keep her mind off the apparently inevitable disaster.

"That is called The River of Lost Souls."

"You don't mean it," she said with a shudder.

"On the level."

"I wish I were," she gasped, "but I'm afraid that the end approaches."

The taciturn individual at the brake deigned to smile. The car swung around a sharp curve and balanced on two wheels for an appreciable space of time. Then it righted and sped on.

Hair flying, gasping and shaken to the marrow, she got to her meeting on time, but she vowed, "I'd never ride down a mountain on a handcar again if Congress were waiting to hear me."[17]

Woman suffrage was approved by Colorado voters on November 7, 1893, the second star in the NAWSA flag. The vote was 35,798 to 29,461, a majority of 6,237 for suffrage. Of the twenty-nine counties Catt had visited, only three voted against the question.

It was the first time the women had won by their own efforts. Catt said they were "startled by their own victory. The women wanted to do something in celebration which would remain forever after in their memories. A crowd gathered in the suffrage headquarters and they talked it over, but being unable to devise any unique plan, some one started 'Praise God from whom all blessings flow,' and people passing by outside heard a great chorus of song. After which the tired workers went home quietly with praise God singing in their hearts."[18]

Catt attributed much of the success to the proximity to Wyoming and the fact that many Colorado people had lived in the state where women voted and were positive about it. There had been a few speakers who had come from

Wyoming to testify. Equal rights was no novel idea in Colorado; the sentiment was there ready to be organized.

The next largest factor was the strength of the mining unions in Colorado and their history of belief in equal rights for women. Leonora Barry Lake
had been one of the few speakers who had come from outside Colorado to
help; although she had at that time retired from active work with the Knights
of Labor, she was still identified with them. The labor unions themselves
carried a number of large mining camps in places where there were no suffrage
associations. Rapport with the miners and their unions was a new experience
for Catt. She was familiar with the farmers' part in the Populist movement,
but this was another side of it, and she said, "I believe we never have
recognized the influence of the labor organizations in this direction half so
kindly and graciously as they have recognized us."[19]

Some people mentioned the fact that the liquor interests had not
awakened to the recognition that woman suffrage was a live issue until nearly
time for the election. They managed to get out only one circular of ridicule
and abuse. While the depression of 1893 had made it hard for the bill's
supporters to raise money, on the other hand the Populists had gained
strength by the economic depression and they supported the bill.

No doubt a major element of success was the way that Catt, with a corps
of only twenty-five intelligent local suffragists who knew what to do and say
on their home ground, could galvanize support and rally women and men into
action. She was particularly pleased that more men were at her meetings than
she had ever seen before. Her detailed plans of precinct organization, honed
over the next decade and eventually used nationwide, were vital to the
strength of the movement and its ultimate victory twenty-five years later.

Catt said of herself after the Colorado campaign that she had felt like a
frog that fell into a milk pail, then struggled until it had churned "a fine pot of
butter," and climbed out.

· 4 ·
Frustrations and Plans

The first campaign of 1894 was in New York where a new state constitution was being considered, and the suffragists were demanding an equal suffrage amendment in it. The labor unions and farmers' granges were cooperating with the women. Catt gave more than forty speeches that spring and continued to organize political equality clubs. Although she was working for wage-earning women and others ill-equipped to fight their own battles, the cause also needed the help of those with power. She encouraged the suffragists to meet in the homes of fashionable supporters. The success of these "parlor meetings" attracted the attention of the *New York Times* which for the first time published an article about Carrie Chapman Catt and quoted her: "The ballot is the weapon women need for protection and advancement, whether they use it or not."[1] They would not get the option yet.

The Honorable Joseph H. Choate, chair of the biennial Constitution Convention, appointed a suffrage committee to review the amendment and carefully stacked it with opponents, including Elihu Root. Root, who was later Secretary of War under McKinley and Theodore Roosevelt, used the old argument that the franchise presumed an obligation to bear arms for one's country and so could not be extended to women. Secure in the knowledge that the suffrage amendment would be defeated, Root and Choate were elaborately courteous and held special hearings for the suffragists. They also extended the same courtesy to a new group of remonstrants based in Albany and led by an Episcopal bishop, William Croswell Doane. As evidence of popular support for the amendment, the suffragists presented the committee with a petition signed by 600,000; 211,000 came from the trade unions and 50,000 from the Granges. The bishop presented 15,000 signatures against the amendment but his arguments were deemed superior.

Remonstrants, antisuffragists, or antis, as Catt and her friends called them, were rarely visible outside a suffrage campaign. Boston was an active center for them; they seemed well financed, but by whom the suffragists were never sure. One point is clear—they did see the suffrage movement for what it was: a direct attack by women against confinement to a traditional place in the family.

To the antis, a woman's place was determined by her sex, not her personal aptitudes, hence most of the arguments against woman suffrage implied stereotyped models. To the pious, the antis claimed that woman's subordinate position was determined by the decree of God to Eve in Genesis and Saint Paul was quoted for confirmation. To the scientifically prone, they argued that the female was by nature weak and intuitive, as opposed to the strong and rational male whose natural work was to defend her and the children from the disturbing forces of the world. The world outside the female-nurtured family circle was often viewed as a paranoic nightmare, much too cruel, much too filthy in its politics for the female's delicate sensibilities. Catt's depiction of a similar chaos created by aliens has to be read in this context. She turned their arguments against them. Bad as the world is, the more reason it needs to make the most of its resources and free the woman to help set it right.

Specious as most of the antis' arguments seem, they exasperated the suffragists more than they liked to admit. Even at the climax of her Colorado triumph, Catt recalled bitterly some young men from the YMCA handing out antisuffrage literature. The one anti argument that hurt the suffragists the most, because it pointed to their small numbers, was that the women did not want the vote.

The major fight in 1894 was in Kansas. Catt had high hopes for the state; it had a strong suffrage movement and Kansas women already voted in municipal and school elections. The two key local suffragists were Anna Diggs and Laura Johns, who also represented the two major parties, Populist and Republican. In May the suffragists opened their great spring canvass; during the next two months in a marathon of conferences they expected to organize the 105 counties along precinct lines. In each place they would involve as many influential local men and women as they could.

One key element of the suffrage strategy called for persuading each political party to adopt a plank for full suffrage. Unfortunately, as the depression plummeted farm prices, tempers flared, and interparty fights became venomous. The Populists held power but were blamed for some calamitous strikes and financial losses. The Republicans were determined to win power and were therefore opposed to allowing any controversial, potential vote-losing plank in their platform. The small Democratic party wanted more power for itself and wasted no sympathy on women.

The national organizers, Carrie Chapman Catt, Anna Howard Shaw, and Susan B. Anthony, saw the issue as women first and party second; the local suffragists put party first. Laura Johns, president of both the Kansas State Suffrage Association and the State Republican Woman's Association, was insulted when Anthony suggested her loyalties were divided. The anger of some of the national board focused on Johns, and Shaw even accused her of embezzling suffrage campaign funds. Catt thought that Johns was an expert executive and a victim of "downright contrariness" but in one horrendous confrontation between Johns and Anthony, Johns felt she was about to be beheaded.[2]

The problem was complicated by old rivalries between East and West. Catt tried to bridge the gap. "I am from New York but my sympathies are with the West and my heart is with Kansas," she said.[3] Personally she was immensely successful. Nevertheless, to many she was just one more damn easterner come to tell them what to think.

The plan of getting suffrage planks in party platforms did not work. Laura Johns could not even get a hearing for the women at the Republican convention, and the tiny Democratic party actually adopted an antisuffrage statement "in the hope that the helpmeet and guardian of the family sanctuary may not be dragged from the modest purity of self-imposed seclusion to be thrown unwillingly into the unfeminine places of political strife." The Populist leaders were united in keeping a suffrage plank out of their platform, but, after elaborate parliamentary maneuvering, a minority report made the floor of the convention on June 12, and was accepted 337 to 269 with a rider, "We do not regard this as a test of party fealty."[4]

The result of the political conventions was confusion, and Catt wrote Anthony a few weeks later:

> It is remarkable the difference of opinion that is floating about. We hear of Populists who are so mad about the plank they declare they will go back to the Democratic party. Others, even those who are suffragists, are so mad at the women for putting the plank forward they say they will vote against the amendment. Democrats say there can be no fusion and that will mean death to the Populist party. Some Republicans say they will not vote for the amendment because it is now a Populist question. Again some Republicans and some Democrats say they will vote the Populist ticket because of the plank. From all these varied ideas it is impossible to find out whether we are better or worse off. At any rate, the question now has a political standing.[5]

Throughout the long, hot summer on the plains, polarization increased, with Democrats and Populists on one side, Republicans on the other. "Those two groups hated each other beyond anything I have ever seen in this world," Catt remembered. "I would arrive at a town and be met by all Populists. The meeting would be arranged by them and nobody would attend it except Populists. At the next town I would be met by Republicans and no Populists would come." Once she got off a train and there was nobody to meet her.[6]

By October and cooling weather she was publicly cheerful, writing optimistic letters that there was a chance of success. "After all the vicissitudes, hard feelings and distresses of the campaign, it begins to look as if we were going to come in 'on the home stretch.' The last two weeks have wrought wonderful changes. The Republicans are coming over splendidly and, if the Populists stand firm, we will surely come in with a fine majority. It seems as if nothing can defeat us now."[7] She was wrong, perhaps deceived by her own personal success as a speaker.

The amendment failed with 95,302 for and 130,139 against. Catt remembered it as "the most heart-breaking defeat of the suffrage struggle. The majority of the people of Kansas were earnest advocates of suffrage, yet the moral conviction of Kansas men had been utterly surrendered to imagined party advantage."[8] The suffragist treasury was as exhausted as its leaders; eleven months of speaking and arguing had gone for nothing.

Two days after the vote Catt gave the Iowa State Suffrage Association convention one of her gloomiest speeches. She sounded again the nativist bias of her American party days and even suggested that slum dwellers be deprived of the vote, although her thrust throughout her life was to expand the franchise. But she was bone tired. The financial depression was getting worse; armies of unemployed men, many of them foreign born, were said to be marching toward Washington—Coxey's army was one of them. These aimless and bewildered men haunted the national imagination and hers. Thousands more immigrants were crowding into slums to become tools of political bosses. Bitterly she repeated to the Iowa suffragists the statistics of how a blatantly sexist nation gave the vote to males. In some states an immigrant man had the vote after six months, as in Kansas, four months in Wisconsin, three months in Michigan. The suffragists had lost again, times were very bad, and the whole marvelous machinery of democracy seemed in peril.[9]

When Catt was exhausted and depressed she liked to return to her garden or her kitchen. The Catts' household afforded a cook, but Catt liked to prepare the great traditional feasts of Thanksgiving, Fourth of July, and Christmas herself. She found a serene peace in canning, transforming in a steaming kitchen piles of produce into rows of jars on her cellar shelves, each labeled neatly in her round hand, ready for a future meal. As she worked, her plans for food shifted toward plans for future campaigns, and how to prepare for them. The plans she made for the national executive after the Kansas defeat were sweeping and detailed. She wanted others, particularly the young members, to examine her ideas but they would not be revealed until the next convention, which was scheduled for Atlanta.

Two months after the Kansas defeat, Catt set off for a southern tour with Anthony beginning in Lexington, the home of Laura Clay, their foremost southern suffragist. She was one of Anthony's "bodyguards," the strong younger women close to the great old leader. For several years she had been prodding the NAWSA Executive to give some attention to the southern states. In 1894 she had helped convince her notoriously hidebound state legislature to grant married women full power over their own property and to give women limited suffrage in three cities. More important, she knew that most southern legislatures had for some time been considering ways to secure states' rights, by which they meant in part how to secure white supremacy. This thinking had begun when it became clear that with the creation of western states, the southern bloc would lose its power to control the Senate. Among the proposed poll taxes and property requirements were schemes involving woman suffrage. Henry B. Blackwell had once computed that if literacy were a requirement of suffrage, there would be more white women voters in the southern states than black voters. Legislative committees there were making the same computations.

Laura Clay's family were Kentucky abolitionists. Her swashbuckling, bowie-knife-dueling father had been Lincoln's Minister to Russia during the Civil War while her mother ran the vast farm and paid the black workers' salaries. Like most landed white families at the time, the Clays did not believe in racial equality. Anthony did. She particularly admired Frederick Douglass, Ida B. Wells-Barnett, and Mary Church Terrell. Terrell found in Catt a lifelong friend who was remarkably free from racial prejudice.[10] Both Anthony and Catt saw that, politically, states' rights and woman suffrage were two different issues.

They held meetings in Kentucky, Tennessee, Louisiana, and Alabama, occasionally separating so they could cover more meetings, but generally speaking from the same platform. There was no treasury money for the trip and Anthony's fee was $10 a speech, or a collection. As far as she was concerned, Catt was along to "carry her bonnet"; Catt thought her main job was to finish Anthony's speeches. If Aunt Susan did not get a cup of strong coffee with dinner, she would sometimes fade out within five minutes. Anthony herself said that Catt stole the show, she was "nowhere" after Catt spoke.[11] Anthony's name consistently drew large crowds but she tended to scold the men in the audience. Catt's approach was to reassure them, to presume that their motives for wanting an educated electorate were of the very highest, and then make an appeal that the best way to secure enlightened voters was to enfranchise their mothers, wives, and sisters.

Anthony and Catt were elegantly entertained in the homes of the socially prominent. In Memphis they were welcomed also in the Colored Women's Club and on a Sunday spoke in a "colored church."

Although all was calm and gracious on the surface, it was difficult to get beyond the brocade curtain draping the pedestal southern women were supposed to be on. Generally the papers were polite, but they also maintained that suffrage was a product of the strong-minded women of the East and was repugnant to southern ideas of propriety. Some clubs were formed and Catt felt "the field was in fair condition to do something."[12]

The tour ended with a NAWSA convention in Atlanta, the first held outside of Washington, D.C. Happily, a local minister denounced the suffragists so rudely that all other congregations rushed to show their hospitality and the resultant publicity increased interest and audiences.

Anthony was in her element on the stage of the Opera House. She joked, made running comments on the reports, and introduced women to each other. However, to Catt and other young women it seemed dangerous that woman suffrage depended so heavily on the wit, will, and stamina of one aging woman. In her report, therefore, Catt proposed major changes in the structure of NAWSA. "The great need of the hour is organization," she insisted. The need to introduce people to the subject had passed, the sentiment for suffrage was present; they needed to work together with a carefully planned policy. "Suffrage is today the strongest reform there is in this country, but it is represented by the weakest organization."[13] She knew what she was going to do about it.

Catt organized and then headed a new Organization Committee with a budget of $5,000 and powers so extensive that it became the center of woman suffrage in the United States. It enlarged the work she had been doing for the past few years and defined her role. Implicit in the Organization Committee was a plan to coordinate southern and western states and territories, and to build woman suffrage clubs that would last and not evaporate after every campaign.

Part of her scheme was to provide a "Course of Study" to educate women in political science. Not only would this help engage the attention of members of local suffrage clubs but it would keep up organizations in states where suffrage had been won. The real work began after enfranchisement, and voters must be educated to "worthy citizenship." Furthermore, testimony on the benefits to the general welfare gained by enfranchising women was often used as an argument for suffrage. Active organizations could provide speakers, good sound arguments, and facts. Finally, in the distant future when the time came for ratification of a national constitutional amendment, women would be ready to lobby state legislators.

In 1895 the systematic study of government had barely been recognized as a discipline by major universities and colleges. Catt proposed a challenging, pioneer course on theories of government, political institutions, and practical applications. She saw it as a three-year program, with lesson plans sent to each club, examinations by mail, and diplomas issued for successful completion. It would differ from university courses "chiefly in the recognition of the equality of rights of men and women." The committee she asked to help carry out these ambitious plans included her closest friend Mary Garrett Hay, Laura Johns of Kansas, Josephine Henry of Kentucky, Lida Meriwether of Tennessee, and Emma DeVoe of Washington.

To begin the practical work, she suggested that suffragists get tax lists and compile statistics on the amount of property taxes paid by women, a very imaginative way to start a study in 1895. The amount of taxes paid would be a revelation of taxation without representation, she predicted, and would instantly convert every believer in the Declaration of Independence to woman suffrage. After that the women should begin to study state laws, ferret out those unjust to women, and then change them.

Above all, suffragists must be visible and vigilant. They must go to all county and state political conventions, and make themselves known to all office holders and candidates to convince them that women were "valuable helpers to their friends." The press should be given suffrage material constantly, and, finally, there must be a finance committee to provide funds for the work. [14]

Anthony understood the sweep of Catt's new Organization Committee perfectly and the implied criticism that her own organization had been incomplete and slack. Her comment was magnanimous and a bit wry: "There never was a young woman yet who had just been converted, who did not know that if she had had the management of the work from the beginning, the cause would have been carried long ago. I felt just so when I was young." [15]

Ten days after the Atlanta convention, many of the delegates also attended the triennial meeting of the National Council of Women in Washington, D.C. There Anthony was presented with a $5,000 trust fund, the annual income from which would free her from constant financial worry. Rachel Foster Avery had been responsible for collecting the money from over two hundred friends in observance of their leader's seventy-fifth birthday.

Frederick Douglass paid a visit to one of the council meetings and sat on the platform at the invitation of the president, May Wright Sewall, but did not feel well enough to speak. Immediately after returning to his home a few hours after the meeting he died. The great black leader was a hero to many of the suffragists and part of their history. He was one of the few survivors of the 1848 Seneca Falls meeting where he had particularly urged that the then controversial woman suffrage item be included in their demands. At the request of his family, Anthony took part in his funeral services, paid her own tribute, and read Elizabeth Cady Stanton's eloquent memorial.[16]

The southern papers reported these encomiums with hostility. Catt had been encouraged by her January trip, "but the relation of our leaders to the colored question at the Douglass funeral has completely taken the wind out of our sails. You should see some of the clippings I have from the Southern Press and some of the letters," she wrote to a New York leader, Lillie Devereux Blake. "They were a little suspicious of us all along, but now they know we are abolitionists in disguise."[17]

· 5 ·

New Victories, Old Defeats

Catt spent much of 1895 working for her Organization Committee and sorting out the confused records of the NAWSA. Some states had not recorded the name of a single suffragist, many clubs had melted away as fast as they had been organized, and great tangles of correspondence and notes had been left by exhausted workers in the field. The new course of study needed attention, as did arranging schedules by mail for organizers and lecturers in the South and West. "We have written at least twelve letters to every engagement so you can see it is not child's play," she told Emma DeVoe. She marveled that at the end of the year her tiny staff had used up three quarts of ink.

Catt made a seven-state trip west that fall because it was increasingly obvious that in those states lay the suffragists' best hope for success. She wanted to organize the territories as well; too little attention had been paid to them. She thought equal suffrage stood the best chance of winning when a state joined the Union. The only territory pending statehood was Utah, where woman suffrage was included in the proposed constitution.[1]

Each state campaign had its own problems, and in Utah that meant dealing or not dealing with Mormons. Some of her colleagues urged her to go there, but she was uncertain that she could do any good. She tried to get more information about the situation to help her make up her mind but felt hampered by not knowing any Utah Gentiles to write to; all her Utah acquaintances were Mormons. "I am very sure I could never convert the editor of the *Salt Lake Tribune,* if he is in truth opposed to it," she wrote to Henry Blackwell. She added an insight drawn from experience: "A conversion must be a growth. I think it is almost impossible to make a friend out of an enemy."[2] She knew the work was in the capable hands of Emmeline B. Wells, a member of her Organization Committee, and wisely left the campaign to her.

A shrewd and vigorous Mormon who had written for the *Woman's Exponent,* founded in 1872 as a bimonthly journal of the Mormon Women's

Relief Society, Wells had been its editor since 1877. After attending a national suffrage association convention in 1879, she was thenceforth identified with the suffrage cause.

Women had voted in Utah Territory from 1869 until 1886, when the United States Congress took away their franchise, apparently in an effort to reduce the power of the polygamous Mormons. In 1889 the outraged women, with Wells as their president, organized the Territorial Suffrage Association. They brilliantly mobilized such support that in proportion to its population Utah had nineteen times more suffragists than New York. The result was that in Utah the constitution submitted to the electors provided for the full political enfranchisement of women as an essential part of state law rather than as a separate section to be voted on independently.[3] Victory in November was celebrated by the suffragists with great joy; Utah became the third state with enfranchised women on January 4, 1896.

A few weeks later George Catt reported on the Utah success at length to the NAWSA convention in a speech later published as a pamphlet: "It was organized public opinion which carried them to victory."[4]

George Catt had attended other suffrage meetings with his wife, but this was his only major address to the national conference and showed his pride in her work. With the ease of an imaginative engineer, he used statistical analysis, a method new to the feminists, to demonstrate by correlating figures the relation of organization to victory. To encourage other associations, the Catts offered a generous $250 to any western state whose membership first equaled 500 to each 100,000 of white [sic] population; and $100 to the first eastern association with 250 to each 100,000. The necessary memberships were only one-half and one-quarter of one per cent, indicating the tiny numbers of dedicated people active in the suffrage movement.

At home in Brooklyn, the Catts entertained with easy midwestern manners. Emma B. Sweet, a Rochester suffragist, remembered "one Bensonhurst Sunday when you sent us all away. Your mother and Mollie [Mary Garrett Hay] to the park and George and me for a bicycle ride. You had to 'born a speech' for an Ohio Chautauqua. On returning we demanded the speech. 'The speech was still-born,' you said, 'but you should see the hat I trimmed.' George whooped, Mollie looked anxious and I laughed till I cried. Your mother was very calm, evidently knowing that speeches had come out of hats before."[5]

Although both Idaho and California had suffrage referenda in November, the national association had decided to concentrate on the larger state. In California, the women who had been organized for two decades thought they were capable of handling their own campaign. The ever-present East/West resentment did not dissuade a contingent of easterners from attending anyway. Catt traveled in California for two months, shuttling up and down the state, sometimes with Anthony, usually on her own, talking for the cause with humor, logic, and effectiveness.

The writer Raymond Robins remembers her with extravagant praise:

> Clear in every detail is the scene in the smoke filled Hall of the Iroquois Club of San Francisco (then the Tammany Hall of that city and state) where you spoke for woman's suffrage against an almost unbroken wall of opposition. So you began, and then your intelligence, eloquence and charm broke down those walls of opposition and you finished with your audience of hardened politicians standing in wild applause—just for your glorious courage and the intellectual power of your achievement. Always will you remain for me the incarnation of daring intelligence and beauty.[6]

Catt recalled the campaign as the "best conducted, liveliest and most enthusiastic" of her experience. The politicians were hopeful and obliging, the press favorable, meetings were crowded and "heartily in sympathy." Even Anthony, never at her best in campaigns, rose to the occasion and went everywhere. Four days before election, "the chief Republican newspaper, the *Chronicle*, burst forth in a vituperative frenzy of hostility." The suffragists presumed the newspaper had been bought out by the liquor interests. The next disaster, according to Catt, were the lines of "Chinese voters, in 'pigtails' and sandals at the polling booths . . . who directed their votes to deny self-government to American women." The suffragists were eventually to make one of their gloomier prognostications the fact that "the better the campaign, the more certain that suffrage would be defeated at the polls."

On the other hand, there was victory in Idaho. Emma DeVoe and Laura Johns had spent months lecturing and organizing in the state in 1895 and 1896 in order to find where sympathy lay and how to exploit it. Following the successful strategy in Colorado, influential men in each community were enlisted. One of their loyal friends in Boise was William Balderston, editor of the major Republican paper, *The Daily Statesman*. Mayor E. P. Cavanah was also on their Boise committee, and on the state advisory board was James A. McGee, chair of the Democratic state central committee.

Idaho women had done much pioneer work over many years to raise public sentiment so that a woman suffrage amendment was feasible. Abigail Duniway, editor of the *New Northwest* and the leading suffragist of the area, was always very critical of National's "system of invasion into states where amendments had been submitted by the home workers and sidetracking such workers." She was not silent on this occasion, but excepted Catt.

Catt had stopped in Idaho in August on her way to California. There she addressed the four party conventions —Republican, Democratic, Populist, and Silver Republican—and successfully won endorsement from each. Duniway wrote, "Having accomplished this excellent work, she did not remain to overdo it, but gracefully retired from the state, leaving the cause in control of the people who had created it."[7]

Idaho became the fourth state with woman suffrage. Although Duniway had every right to gloat, she was very restrained. Before the election she had asked Anthony, "What would you think of the irony of Fate if Idaho wins and California loses?" and Anthony responded, "Impossible! California is managed by our trained workers from the East." Catt noted, "The campaign was simple and normal, costing only $1,800. The amendment carried without organized opposition by a majority of 5,844—12,126 for and 6,282 against."[8]

The next fourteen years brought no victories, only the drudgery of keeping woman suffrage sentiment alive year after year in the wake of defeat; "victory deferred," Catt always insisted.

Catt traveled relentlessly, organizing and revitalizing moribund suffrage clubs. There was no national policy on membership. Desperate as the suffragists were to get and keep supporters, some clubs insisted on treating the movement as exclusive and voted on new members. New York suffragists said this was not to draw social lines but to keep out the lunatic fringe. Michigan thought the "erratic people" who joined served as whetstones to sharpen the wits of the others. From conservative Louisiana, Kate Gordon reported, "We have to have applicants investigated by a committee and voted in unanimously, to keep out those who are too radical." Catt professed to see progress: "Formerly we were all cranks. Now we are the conservatives who want to keep the cranks out. This is very encouraging."[9]

She testified before the Louisiana Constitutional Convention in New Orleans early in 1898 and spoke before large audiences at other meetings there. A scrap of suffrage was won: taxpaying women gained the right to vote on all questions of taxation. This was seen as a signal victory and widely applauded as evidence the movement was progressing.

All advances, no matter how tiny, were reported with enthusiasm: in South Carolina women were invited to speak at meetings where they had never before been asked; in Vermont the persevering patience of brave workers trying to secure municipal suffrage for women taxpayers resulted in their being turned down for the eighteenth time. They cheerfully reported that there had never been such a cordial rejection.

Catt ingenuously cast about for anything that could be used to raise the suffragists' self-esteem. In 1899 NAWSA published her *Woman's Century Calendar* in which every year of the nineteenth century was documented by some event important to woman's progress.[10]

The century ended with Anthony's retirement as president of the NAWSA. She would be eighty years old in 1900 and announced that it was high time the leadership passed on to a younger woman. Anna Howard Shaw, Lillie Devereux Blake, and Catt were candidates. Shaw, the most brilliant speaker of the movement, was dependent on lecturing for a living; Blake, former president of the New York State Suffrage Association, was a witty speaker and writer, but Anthony preferred Catt as the shrewdest and most imaginative administrator. Catt also had independent means. Her election to the presidency was nearly unanimous. The last session of the convention was given over to euphoric tributes to the great old abolitionist who had come to symbolize woman suffrage in the nation's mind.

The next day when the Executive met, euphoria gave way to anger and jealousy. Catt was taken by surprise. Hour after hour of acrimonious accusations, furious reproaches, and angry resignations led to a vote to dissolve the Organization Committee that Catt had headed for five years and which had given vigor and cohesion to the national association. It is probable that the meeting would not have been so vicious had Mary Garrett Hay not been Catt's obvious successor to head the powerful committee. Hay was tireless, her loyalty to Catt was absolute, and she was shrewd and efficient, but to most suffragists she seemed tactless, prickly, insulting; "impossible" was the adjective most often used for Mary Hay. Many on the Executive felt that the dissolution of the Organization Committee was a high but fair price to pay for getting rid of her.

After the dissolution vote, Catt locked herself in her room, threw herself on her bed, "and cried for three hours." She considered resigning the presidency.[11] The next day when she met her Executive she looked drawn, a bit red of eye, but she ran the meeting with a cold; hard, deliberate care that was awesome. She would not allow the organizations to be split on personalities. She had learned from her *Mason City Republican* days the devastating cost of jealousy, plots of revenge, and slander. She accepted Anthony's motion that the officers be called an Organization Committee; it was a cosmetic device to hide the fracas from the membership. She would preside with what power she had, the suffragists would not be split over this issue or over a woman's *Bible,* or over prohibition or racism. Women must have the vote. Furthermore, the nation, though not aware of it, needed to have them as voters.

FROM NATIVIST TO INTERNATIONALIST
1900–1924

Carrie Chapman Catt during her second term as president of the
National American Woman Suffrage Association, ca. 1915

· 6 ·
New Directions

Shortly after becoming president of the NAWSA in 1900, Catt went to Anthony with the idea of forming an international woman suffrage organization. Plans had been germinating in Catt's mind since the Congress of Women in 1893. After moving to New York, George Catt's firm had rapidly expanded outside the United States. In the office she shared with him and at home the talk turned easily to foreign cities where his firm had contracts—Manila, Capetown, Hamburg, Marseilles. On her long train rides while organizing in individual states, she often found herself lulled by the click of rails and wondering what suffragists in other countries were doing. How did they meet? How did they persuade the uncommitted? How could her organization help? How could their organizations help hers?

Harriet Taylor Mill had reported on the first national convention in Worcester, Massachusetts in 1850 to Britain, Fredrika Bremer had reported to Sweden. Shouldn't the National American make such leadership formal?

By far the largest women's organization in the world was the International Council of Women (ICW), which counted membership in the millions. Catt recalled its articulate, long-trained delegates at the 1893 exposition in Chicago and their impact on the audience and the press. Unfortunately, because the ICW supported many causes—promotion of social purity, antivivisection, peace, education, dress reform, clean streets, and flower boxes in school rooms, suffrage could not be central. Many of its members were indifferent or even hostile to politics. In 1899 an affiliate, the Association of Women Stenographers proudly announced defeat of an Illinois bill that would have prevented women from being notaries public. "We were able to defeat this bill entirely with the assistance of our political friends, without that obnoxious expedient of sending representatives from our organization to lobby at Springfield."[1] Wouldn't an international woman's suffrage organization help correct the notion that lobbying was an "obnoxious expedient"?

55

To Catt's surprise, Anthony scorned the idea of international organization. Catt did not realize that Anthony and Stanton had founded the International Council of Women in 1888 to work on woman suffrage but had abandoned it when some leading English women refused to support such a radical cause. Anthony told Catt she could go ahead but that she would have to do it all herself.[2]

Rebuffed, miffed, and a little bewildered, Catt took up internationalism. It would occupy the rest of her life, long after the Nineteenth Amendment ceased to be an issue in the United States. She decided first to have an exploratory meeting of women from as many countries as possible. That meeting could reasonably coincide with the annual convention of the NAWSA in Washington, D.C. in 1902.

Before the meeting she had to get facts. But which women to query? Where were they? What was woman's status in their countries? Since almost no information was available, she designed a questionnaire for women in all the countries in the world. In those nations where she knew women were organized, such as England, France, Sweden, and Denmark, it was relatively easy to obtain information. In other countries, she sent the questionnaire to missionaries, schools, ambassadors, and consuls.

She had written twenty-eight questions, most of which required an informed essay. She wanted to know about the rights of married and unmarried women, the jobs available to women and the wages they could expect, women's educational possibilities and which women could take advantage of them, about crime and punishment, about women's rights to make a will and testify in court, about child custody rights, about age of consent, and privileges in any established church. She wanted to know if women were able to attend meetings; whether they were restricted by civil law, religion, or custom; how husbands were chosen and whether and how divorce was available. She wanted to know whether women could vote. She asked for any information that would help clarify women's legal, social, industrial, educational, religious, and political status. Catt's questionnaire was, in short, the first research on the status of women in the twentieth century. Thirty-two countries responded. Most of the answers were depressing.[3]

Her new commitment to an international alliance added considerably to her work with the national organization. Her travel and letter writing had steadily increased since she had became president, but the nation seemed to be growing ever more indifferent to woman suffrage. Muckraking disclosures in magazines such as *Collier's* and *McClure's* were demanding reform of banks and trusts, slums, and slaughterhouses. The demand for woman's rights was again thrust aside for issues felt to be more urgent. The largest national parties were preoccupied with monetary reforms. In 1900 when Catt led a delegation to the Republican convention that nominated William McKinley and Theodore Roosevelt, the suffragists were allowed only ten minutes to speak. The Democrats refused to hear them at all. The House of Representatives in Catt's home state of Iowa refused to consider any woman suffrage bill. In Oregon, where defeat was becoming a bad habit, a second campaign failed.[4]

There was one bright spot in the gloom. The International Woman Suffrage Alliance was founded in Washington, D.C. on February 12, 1902 during the thirty-fourth annual convention of the NAWSA. Seven of the eight countries with woman suffrage societies sent delegates: Australia, Denmark, Germany, Great Britain, Norway, Sweden, and the United States. There were representatives from Chile, Hungary, Russia, Turkey, and Switzerland. Canadian delegates were unable to come at the last minute.[5]

"Many changes had taken place as a result of the work of women before 1902, but there lay before them a long stretch of oppressive laws and customs to be removed," Catt wrote. "The outlook for the vote was unpromising. Four states in the United States had given the vote to women and a lively organization was pushing on with brave determination. The situation was practically the same in Great Britain and the Scandinavian countries. The women could see small advantage in uniting their efforts and those who answered the first call to joint action were brave souls indeed."[6]

Eighty-one year old Clara Barton, representing the International Red Cross, spoke to the assembled women in high-Victorian rhetoric. She told the world that this was the first time women from several countries had met to oppose the injustice of their position, which ignorant and unjust traditions "fostered and preserved through the unthinking ages, until they came to be held, not only as a part of the natural laws and rights of man, but as the immutable decrees of Divinity itself."[7]

Catt believed that one ignorant tradition that had survived for too long was the notion that woman's part in the genesis of a new life was biologically passive: that is, that women merely incubated the male seed. In her major speech at the joint national and international meetings, she spoke for the first time of her scientific hero, Karl Ernst von Baer, whose identification of the mammalian egg led to the awareness that the sperm cell and the egg cell were equally necessary in generation: "In the perpetuation of the race the function of motherhood is not the negative, insignificant thing it was once thought, but equal in importance with fatherhood. The hereditary traits of each generation come equally from the father and mother." She stressed the importance of education to eradicate sex prejudice that had its basis in the old scientific blunder.[8]

Vida Goldstein of Australia, Florence Fenwick Miller of England, and Catt were named to write a Declaration of Principles. The ten women who signed it declared their faith in eight principles beginning with: "That men and women are born equally free and independent members of the human race; equally endowed with talents and intelligence, and equally entitled to the free exercise of their individual rights and liberty." They concluded by reiterating that because the ballot was the only legal and permanent means of defending one's rights, therefore women should be voters. New educational and job opportunities that had developed over the last fifty years made woman suffrage an immediate imperative.[9]

After the exhilaration of the national and international conferences, Catt had a brief collapse following the neglect of a bad cold. But she was soon off again, organizing suffrage clubs and making several speeches. During the summer of 1902, her biggest success occurred at the annual meeting of the National Educational Association. Catt was the first woman ever invited to address the educators. More than eighty years later her ideas still have a modern ring. Education is not enough; Catt challenged the educators to find for the college woman work worthy of her college, her sex, and her race.[10]

Elizabeth Cady Stanton died on October 26, 1902. Catt had never known the much older Stanton as well as she knew Susan B. Anthony, but when she praised the great pioneer's virtues at a memorial meeting, she unconsciously listed her own: "She met personal attacks with patience, ridicule with tolerance, argument with argument." She had courage, intellect, energy and the conviction that "the world does move and women shall be free."[11]

That winter Catt helped in the New Hampshire amendment campaign, which started in December with the opening of the Constitutional Convention. Through the bitterly cold January and February she and dedicated workers aroused so much interest that there seemed to be a chance for success. Lyman Abbott, an influential Brooklyn cleric who had railed and organized against feminists for many years, was recruited to rescue the antis. He and Catt engaged in a two-day argument. The suffragists were jubilant when she "laid him out" at a jammed meeting. "He was as flat as dishwater," Catt told a friend. To Anthony she wrote, "dear and revered leader, our two meetings were a fine climax and certainly the moral effect of Brother Lyman was quite overcome. He is as blind as a bat to the real situation, but I hope he will keep on, for he is a great help to us." She scored debating points, but the suffrage amendment lost on March 10 by a vote of 14,162 to 21,788 ("less than two to one" said the positive-thinking Alice Stone Blackwell).[12]

Catt was worn down by the hard, cold weeks that ended in disappointment and was convinced that legislators and voters had been bribed. She had only three or four days at home, then set off for New Orleans where the NAWSA convention was held in March 1903.

The convention's large audiences were drawn by the novelty of women's speaking and appearing in public, wrote Anthony. They had come out of curiosity but they were attentive especially to Anna Howard Shaw and Catt. Anthony thought her successor looked "thin and pale." Catt needed rest after overtaxing herself for years. She was more anxious about her husband's health than her own. The stomach malady from which he eventually died was destroying his youthful bounce, and, though alarmed, she downplayed her concern, saying only, "He looks pretty peaked."[13]

To free Catt from many routine business details, the headquarters of the NAWSA was moved to Warren, Ohio, the home of the treasurer, Harriet Taylor Upton. To free George Catt from daily commuting, the Catts sold their Brooklyn home and took an apartment in Manhattan. She accompanied him to an engineers' convention in North Carolina, and then they sailed for a few leisurely weeks in Italy, France, and Switzerland.

This was the first of her European trips and so happy were the Catts that they made plans for another the following summer after her international conference in Berlin. But travel did not solve all problems and there was increased anxiety about her mother's health as well as George Catt's.

Catt resigned as president of NAWSA at the annual convention in 1904, but accepted a vice-presidency under the new leader, Anna Howard Shaw. Catt would continue to work with the international alliance; aside from the biennial conventions and executive board meetings most of the work was by correspondence and could be done at home. She planned to turn the organization over to a European woman as soon as it was established. She did not reckon on her steadily growing vision of including women of all nations, not just those of the western world.

The 1904 International Woman Suffrage Alliance meeting in Berlin was a stunning success. It was held under the auspices of the Suffrage Union of Hamburg, a free city. Catt explained:

> In Austria and in Germany the law forbade women to become members
> of any political society or to attend political meetings. So when in

Germany the women desired to organize a suffrage movement, it was an illegal thing to do; women did not have that much personal freedom. There was one very clever woman [Anita Augspurg] who had studied law, she was not permitted to practice, but I remember she said, with a twinkling of the eye, "Sometimes it is well to know law in order to know that there are ways to avoid the law." She organized in the free city of Hamburg and had individual members all over Germany. If Berlin or Dresden wanted to have a meeting the members of this Hamburg society called it. They had to go to the police and explain that it was a society in Hamburg. They announced when the meeting was to be held, the hall it was to be in and who would speak and preside and they usually got consent to their meeting in this way.

In Berlin there sat on the platform two policemen, one had a billy and one had a book. When the chairman came forth to call the meeting to order, she stepped up to the table and gave her name, address and status. Then she introduced me, saying that I was from the United States, representing the council of women and was only a visitor. This went down in the policeman's book. Before beginning to speak I thought it best to ask what I had better not say and they informed me that I must say nothing about the Kaiser, or his relationships, or the German history, or militarism. If I spoke on any one of these topics the policemen would have reached beneath the table for their helmets, a signal that the meeting was adjourned and if anyone showed signs of lingering, the policemen would have assisted their departure by means of their billies.[14]

Few conditions give more zest and unity to a meeting than a sense of high-minded purpose in the face of incipient oppression as symbolized by those two police officers. The delegates were alert to and relished every detail. They were impressed by Mary Anthony, the only person there who had attended the 1848 Seneca Falls meeting. They were awed by Susan B. Anthony and delighted by Shaw's remark to a friend in America who was worried about Anthony's going so far from home, "What if she does die there? Berlin is as near to heaven as is New York." They were charmed when Catt presented a gavel from the women of Wyoming who had enjoyed full suffrage longer than any other women in the world. They were amused when she told them the custom inspector's suspicion that the gavel was a weapon.

All were appreciative of Catt's skills; Shaw said: "She had the details of the plan of organization perfectly arranged. By her clearness and perfect understanding of methods, and by her tact in explaining and smoothing over difficult points, Mrs. Catt has greatly endeared herself to the suffrage women the world over."[15] Catt needed all her skill and diplomacy in dealing with such a diverse group of women, many of whom did not share the Americans' devotion to parliamentary procedure.

There were thirty-three delegates from the seven countries who affiliated with the new Alliance: Denmark, Great Britain, Germany, Holland, Norway, Sweden, and the United States; Australia had no delegates but announced affiliation. There were also representatives from countries that joined later: Hungary, New Zealand, Switzerland, and Austria.

Besides the delegates there were uncounted visitors and a large number of reporters. Early in the proceedings, a suspicious Dr. Aletta Jacobs suggested that reporters be excluded to facilitate free discussions. The Americans were quick in their defense: the reporters were particularly welcome; a free, informed electorate presumed a free, informed press.

The reporters were disposed to respond to the awe that often affected people when they first saw suffrage leadership in action. Catt herself had felt such emotion in Des Moines years before. The reporters were dazzled by the women's polish and talent, their quick and informed minds, the clarity and grace of their articulation. At a time when Europe was interested in the "new woman," page after page of superb publicity appeared in the journals of the continent.

The one sharp criticism by the press in Berlin came when the women were lavishly entertained at a garden party by Count von Posadowsky, Minister of Internal Affairs. The fact that they ate his strawberries and cream seemed hypocritical because that very day he served notice on the Reichstag that if a pending bill with suffrage for women in it were passed, he would veto it. The suffragists realized, however, that they could not afford the luxury of choosing the terms under which they would plead their cause; they would lobby any time and any place they could. "Women are learning politics," Catt remarked.

In four days of meetings, the delegates reaffirmed the 1902 declaration, approved a constitution, established a membership list, and elected officers. The delegates had no common language. As each speech was given in English, German, or French, it was translated by the learned Dr. Kathe Schirmacher into the other two languages. It was a tedious process, requiring the patience of the delegates and a dedication to woman suffrage.

Nearly all the suffrage women stayed on to attend the International Council of Women convention, which followed immediately. Most of the Americans were at a disadvantage in their ignorance of any language but their own. The outstanding exception was Mary Church Terrell.

Terrell, an eloquent, popular lecturer and writer, was the former president of the National Association of Colored Women and highly esteemed by Anthony and Catt, whom Terrell described as completely free from race prejudice. Because Terrell had studied in Berlin and Paris after her graduation from Oberlin College, she could deliver a speech in perfect idiomatic German and another in equally good French. It was a triumph for her personally and for her race.[16]

Charlotte Perkins Gilman was another well-known American delegate. Her *Women and Economics* had been published in 1898 and was widely read in the United States and Europe. Marie Stritt, the president of the German women's council, had translated it into German. In advocating the economic freedom of women, Gilman indicted Victorian attitudes and mores. Catt credited the book "with utterly revolutionizing the attitude of mind in the entire country, indeed of other countries, as to woman's place." So many people came to hear Gilman that she had to repeat her address in a second hall. Both times, the American reporter Ida Harper wrote,

> Mrs. Gilman's speech divided the audience into two hostile forces, half of the women declaring that they would never hand their children over to be cared for by professional trainers and feed their husbands on victuals from a cooperative cookery, while they used their time to aid "the larger work of the world"; the other half insisting that women in all ages had given too much time, strength, and talent to the nursery and kitchen, and that was why they had fallen behind in all great achievements. But everybody went home thinking, and that is really the essential thing.[17]

All the women who were in Berlin in 1904 went home with new ideas and new friends. All her life Catt remembered the excitement of those early meetings of the IWSA and the cosmopolitan women she met including Rosika Schwimmer from Hungary, Margery Corbett from England, Anita Augspurg from Germany, Aletta Jacobs from Holland, Annie Furuhjelm from Finland.

Furuhjelm was a newspaper editor who had come to the International Council of Women quinquennial to ask for recognition of Finnish women. She was refused by the ICW executive because her country was under Russian control. She was angry and depressed by the decision:

> It seemed to make no difference that Finland had her own constitutional rights, her own legislation separate from Russia, her own history, her own tradition. No, Finland did not count as a nation. We felt sore at heart and humiliated. Somebody advised me to turn to Mrs. Chapman Catt,

suggesting that she might perhaps take a different view of this matter of nations.

I found her standing alone in a great hall full of people, watching calmly the whirl around her. I introduced myself to Mrs. Catt, she stretched out her hand to me, and I put the case of Finland before her. She was encouraging and most sympathetic. I told her of our political difficulties, that we had no suffrage organization, and that in all probability we would not be allowed to organize for suffrage for many years. She answered that she thought Finland could nevertheless be affiliated to the IWSA. I do not believe Mrs. Catt ever realized what this meant to us, and how grateful we felt that we counted as a nation after all!

From this meeting I went home a suffragist. Not that I had to be converted. I suppose I had always been one unconsciously, but now I became conscious. And still I had not been present at the first meeting of the IWSA, because at that time woman's suffrage seemed a thing too far off to be dreamt about.

The meeting of the ICW had impressed me deeply. It was grand, brilliant, and full of interest, but there was something wanting in it to me—one big thing to bind the whole together, and give it a solid foundation, and this big thing was Suffrage—Suffrage as means to an end. [18]

Thanks to this fortuitous meeting with Catt, Furuhjelm organized Finnish women when she got home, and to the world's astonishment, within the year they were the first European women to win the right to vote.

· 7 ·
Roses and Rocks

Before the 1906 IWSA conference in Copenhagen, Catt was to lose her devoted and generous husband, George Catt, and her mentor, Susan B. Anthony. For the time being she herself seemed the fragile one. After the 1904 meetings she and the apparently indestructible Anthony briefly visited Germany and Switzerland. Catt then joined her husband for a quiet tour of the British Isles. All along she was plagued by migraines—"her troublesome head," Shaw called it.

George Catt seemed improved by the vacation but for the next two years his wife stayed as close as she could to New York. She went to Ohio for a Business Committee meeting, to the state convention in Illinois and visited her ailing mother in Iowa. For her this was limited travel.

Aletta Jacobs and her husband, Carel Victor Gerritsen, a member of the Dutch Parliament, visited the Catts in December on their way home from the Interparliamentary Peace Union congress in St. Louis. In January the Catts gave a huge reception and banquet for the Iowa State College Alumni Association of which George Catt was the national president. But events they would have taken in stride a few years before strained them. During the winter she gave six lectures at the Brooklyn Institute of Arts and Sciences on the evolution of women, then spent most of the money earned from them on osteopaths who did not seem to help her headaches.[1]

The NAWSA convention was held in Portland, Oregon, in June. Catt went but declined reelection as vice-president, and her place was taken by the social activist, Florence Kelley, National Secretary of the Consumers League.[2]

Catt visited her mother on her way back to New York. There she found news of the death of Carel Gerritsen, "a rare, brave, great, strong man," she called him.[3]

In September, George Catt was operated on for gallstones after he collapsed at his office. Surgery revealed a perforated duodenal ulcer with peritonitis. He did not respond to treatment and he died October 8, 1905, leaving his body to science and his estate for his wife to settle.

She was shattered by his death and her grief so eroded her own health that for a long time she expected to die at any moment. For weeks she lost all interest in suffrage or anything else. Unable to cope with living in the apartment filled with reminders of him, she took rooms in a hotel and asked her friend Mary Hay to stay with her because she detested being alone. Friends who remembered the spacious elegance of her Brooklyn home and her Manhattan apartment were shocked to find them working away in cramped gloom in the middle of boxes overflowing with papers.

For all her abrasive ways, Hay seemed to understand Catt's grief and needs better than anyone else. She had a solid, earthy dash of the Midwest that Catt liked and responded to. She also brought a shrewd political sense developed while helping the campaigns of her father, a minor Indiana politician. She had been for years Catt's loyal lieutenant. After George Catt's death she also became in a way Catt's partner and they lived together until Hay's death. "Mrs. Catt was essentially a statesman; Miss Hay, a politician, and together they were, in most cases, invincible."[4]

Shortly after the annual national suffrage convention in February 1906, Anthony died. "If she goes now it will be like a ripened apple falling at its full time, although we should like to keep her many years more," Catt wrote during Anthony's last illness to a mutual friend in Rochester.[5]

Catt, Hay, and Ida Husted Harper, the sharp-eyed publicist, went to Denmark in late May to make final arrangements for the third IWSA meeting scheduled for Copenhagen in August 1906. In July Catt learned that an interview had been arranged for her with Queen Louise. After many fussy instructions from protocol officers, Catt was shown into a large, pleasant drawing room of the palace. The queen had recently lost a daughter and was in deep mourning but wanted to hear about the movement. Catt told her the time had come when women should have the dignity and power of representation in government. The queen raised the standard worry about neglect of home and children. Catt answered that the movement was intended to make better mothers and give the home more influence.

As her carriage rolled through the park after her meeting, Catt realized that she had forgotten to kiss the queen's hand or to address her as "Your Majesty." It didn't matter. They were two grieving but responsible women, each in her way reassuring the other.

In 1906 four more countries joined the eight affiliated with the IWSA: Canada, Hungary, Italy, and Russia. Triumphant news came from Finland through Annie Furuhjelm. On her return to Helsinki in 1904 she had called a mass meeting on suffrage to which a thousand women came, and the following year a Central Committee for Women Suffrage was formed with Furuhjelm as president. In the meantime, a general strike in November to protest Russian oppression had gained virtual autonomy for the Finns. The Finnish Parliament on May 28, 1906 passed a bill extending universal suffrage to all men and women twenty-four years of age and older. Annie Furuhjelm was the first fully enfranchised European delegate to attend an Alliance congress.[6]

Catt contrasted Finland's generous men who knew oppression to Oregon's narrow unjust men who had full political rights but refused to share them. Others who knew repression had come to the convention. Catt welcomed the new "Union of Defenders of Women's Rights" represented by six Russian women, who had expected to have more delegates, but "the revolution, breaking out afresh, made it unsafe to leave the country." Inspired by the example of Finland, thirty liberal Moscow women organized the union early in 1905; in seventeen months, seventy-nine societies with ten thousand members had become affiliated. "It has raised and given away $50,000 for the liberation of Russia," Catt reported. "It stands for suffrage for both men and women. We learn through the press of the Russian revolution, but little does the public know of the work or influence of women there. Yet in every trial, every duty, every penalty, women have shared."[7]

One of the Russian delegates, Zinaida Mirovich, reported, "Contrary to the expectations of the skeptics, the peasant women, although undeveloped, and mostly illiterate, warmly received the great tidings of liberty and equality before the law. The objections to women's equality appeared to them to be quite absurd: they could not understand what a liberal reform meant which excluded half the nation."

This liberal period in Russia was short-lived. Reports in the Alliance journal appeared until 1913, but just before the delegation left for Copenhagen in 1906 the Duma was dissolved. Mirovich ended her report to the congress: "Progress is not stopped in Russia; we are again face to face with our worst enemies. However we shall not give up. We shall strive and work as hard as before for the great cause of progress and liberty."[8]

Delegates from other countries spoke of the growth of suffrage with optimism and humor. Catt liked the story of the Canadian woman, Mabel French, who was denied the right to practice law although she had passed all examinations with high honors. Only persons were allowed to practice law, and women were not persons. Subsequently a woman brought to court pleaded not guilty on the ground that she was not a person and therefore not accountable to the law. The court agreed, and "the magistrate ruled that according to the decision of the Supreme Court 'women were not persons, and could not be imprisoned nor fined.' This practical lesson compelled the Legislature to pass an Act designating women as persons, and so, eventually, Miss French was allowed to take her degree in law."[9]

This conference marked the first time that women from England reported on the militant tactics begun the year before that had resulted in some members of the Women's Social and Political Union being jailed. The WSPU had been organized in 1903 by a despotic and charismatic mother and daughter team, Emmeline and Christabel Pankhurst, in response to the lukewarm attitude of British political parties to woman suffrage. Their militancy had begun in October 1905, at a meeting in Manchester addressed by Sir Edward Grey, a liberal M.P. whom the Pankhursts thought made only a show of support. Grey was interrupted when Christabel Pankhurst and Annie Kenney, a feisty young Lancashire mill worker, demanded a clear answer to their question, Would the Labour Party enfranchise them? They held up a banner inscribed "Votes for Women," and were promptly thrown out. They harangued the gathering crowd in the street until they were arrested for obstruction. The two women spent a week in jail, made so many headlines, and gave such a fillip to the WSPU that militancy came to define their branch of the suffrage movement. These militant women were slurred in the press as "suffragettes," to distinguish them from the suffragists who were working sedately along constitutional lines, but the WSPU took up the pejorative appellation and turned it into an accolade.[10]

The militants' technique was to shock and exasperate the establishment into overreaction, then publicize the consequent oppression. Dora Montefiore, one of the new suffragettes, reported her protest to the Copenhagen congress. Refusing to pay taxes until she had a voice in the government, in 1904 and again in 1905 bailiffs had entered her London home and taken away enough of her possessions to cover her taxes when the goods were sold at auction. In May 1906 she had barricaded her door against the bailiffs and for six weeks her battle with them was widely publicized. She was much in demand at the Alliance meetings.[11]

The WSPU was denied admission to the IWSA on the grounds that Alliance policy recognized only one suffrage organization, or consortium of organizations, from each country. They hoped to minimize bickering on methods at the international meetings and to force cooperation within the various countries. Although Catt recognized that the militants' "irregular methods may indeed add the impetus which will bring the parliamentary suffrage to the women of England," and Millicent Fawcett, head of England's suffragists, thought the "rough methods may very probably prove their value," they stuck by their one-organization-per-country policy.[12]

Among the less controversial sessions in Copenhagen was one devoted to eulogies to Susan B. Anthony. "The stones once flung at her had become roses," Catt said. At another meeting the Alliance decided to publish a monthly paper in English with Martina Kramers of Rotterdam as editor. They also adopted a permanent badge designed by Mrs. Pedersen-Dan of Denmark. "The design is a graceful figure of Justice with her scales," Catt wrote. "A rising sun in seen in the background and the Latin words 'Jus Suffragii' [The Right of Suffrage] explain the full meaning."[13]

Catt and Aletta Jacobs went to Hungary and Austria after the convention and spoke to overflow audiences in Budapest, Prague, Brünn (now Brno, Czechoslovakia), and Vienna. Partly as a result of the interest generated, the question of granting the franchise to women was debated in the Austrian Parliament.

There were other immediate gains generated by the Copenhagen meetings. The next year Danish women were granted municipal franchise; a women's suffrage bill was carried in the Norwegian legislature in 1907, and women in Norway voted in the election of October 1909.[14]

Catt and others of the IWSA were well used to attacks on equal suffrage by conservatives, but in 1906 the Socialists, who also supported equal suffrage, joined their attackers with claims that the women of the IWSA were bourgeois and some of their bright young activists were drawn to the success, novelty, and glamour of women's issues and away from proper Socialist organizations. Catt met the attack with experienced good temper, and it was not long before the attackers were forced to take careful stock of themselves and their behavior toward women.

Clara Zetkin, the German spokeswoman and activist, made a formal, public judgment against the Alliance at the Socialist Women's Conference in 1906. She dismissed as sentimental the first three principles of the IWSA which asserted the innate equality between women and men. She was angered by the fourth, which stated that "Self-government in the home and the State is the inalienable right of every normal adult, and the refusal of this right to women has resulted in social, legal and economic injustice to them, and has also intensified the existing economic disturbances throughout the world." Zetkin interpreted this to the Socialist women as, "There it is said that the woman's right to vote is founded on the increasing prosperity which professional activity has brought to women."[15] This is a curious reading, skewed to make her point against women who, by demanding equality, were merely supporting the exploitation of the proletariat.

Zetkin scorned Catt's conception of "universal sisterhood," insisting on an antagonism between the "ladies of the aristocracy and the bourgeoisie" and the "working women" that was impossible to bridge. The strength of Zetkin's argument was directed to the fact that most suffrage in Europe was based on property. In England, for example, a bill being considered would have given the vote to women "householders," which included women who paid rent for one room. From eighty to ninety percent of those thus enfranchised would be wage- or salary-earning women. Although it was a political compromise and not an ideal bill, suffragists thought it was a step in the right direction. Zetkin's particular concern was with women who shared a room with others; single occupancy was a luxury denied even the best-paid factory workers, hence the bill was applicable only to the bourgeois and therefore undesirable.[16]

Zetkin held that Socialist women should not compromise the larger cause by cooperating with the "bejewelled ladies." She did not accept the argument that when middle-class women had the vote they would use it to help all women. Socialist women should not weaken the party by having separate organizations within it. When the day of liberation came for all workers, men and women alike would be equal.

That conclusion caused some ironic merriment among the suffragists. After the Civil War they were told to hold back because it was "the negro's hour"; in South Dakota it was "the Indian's hour," Catt observed. For some reason the reluctant clock never struck "the woman's hour." Alice Zimmern, who was making a survey of world suffrage, wrote that in 1907 the Hungarian Socialists organized a huge demonstration in favor of universal suffrage, "but the very next day an article in a Socialist paper bade the women stand aside. 'For the present,' it said, 'we must apply all our strength to wring from the class Parliament the rights of men.' After that the women might have a chance." Similarly, Austrian suffragists found themselves hampered by antiquated laws and Socialist women who refused to join them in the demand for the suffrage, Zimmern wrote. There were comparable rejections of woman suffrage in Russia and other European countries. The only exception Catt knew of were

Italian Socialists who "loyally stood by their women comrades, and initiated as well as supported efforts to promote their emancipation."[17]

Women in the Socialist movement became so vocal that in 1907 a woman suffrage resolution was adopted at the Stuttgart Congress of the Second International, with explicit instructions not to make common cause with other women: "Socialist women shall not carry on this struggle for complete equality of right of vote in alliance with the middle class woman suffragists, but in common with the Socialist Parties, which insist upon Woman Suffrage as one of the fundamental and most important reforms for the full democratization of political franchise in general."[18]

Most of the Socialist women seemed to go along with this injunction, but IWSA criticism of Socialist behavior did alert the Socialist women to look beyond the theory.

When Clara Zetkin wrote about the interviews she had with Lenin she could not avoid showing him as being ambivalent about methods of achieving women's emancipation. Should women be organized separately? The woman question was part of the social, working-class question and had to be bound firmly with the proletarian class struggle and revolution, she reported Lenin as saying to her. Therefore, there should not be separate organizations of communist women. The fact was that women had to be specially roused by means of working committees to bring them into contact with the party and keep them under its influence. This naturally required that systematic work be carried on among women. It would be silly to deny the narrow scope of the activities of peasant women and those of the lower middle class; there must be special methods of agitation and special forms of organization. "This is not bourgeois feminism but practical revolutionary expediency," he said.[19]

The most unequivocal statement came from the Marxist Rosa Luxemburg. She argued that bourgeois society abhorred and feared women's suffrage because it would immensely advance and intensify the proletarian class struggle if the female proletariat were enfranchised. In 1912 at the Second Social Democratic Women's Rally in Stuttgart, she told her audience that if they thought woman's suffrage was not urgently necessary they were deceived. She scorned any suggestion that women should be given the vote as a matter of justice. "We do not depend on the justice of the ruling classes, but solely on the revolutionary power of the working masses."[20]

Catt recognized the validity of different methods of work. It did not bother her much when some Socialist women withdrew from nonpartisan suffrage associations to work for the Socialist party in 1907. But she had long since learned to be suspicious of promises made to women in the heat of the political hunt:

> Other parties before now have invited women to withdraw from regular suffrage organizations and to labor for the party only. Women have listened and followed the command only to find that they have been employed as mere catspaws to pull appetizing chestnuts from the fire, which others ate, while burnt fingers were their only reward. In the United States, Greenback, Populist, Prohibition and Socialist parties furnish good examples of this proceeding. History has so often repeated itself along this line that I, for one, have grown skeptical. . . . Our movement is destined to end in victory, but we are not permitted to know the agencies which may be employed to bring it about.[21]

Charlotte Perkins Gilman's response was a light, intelligent verse she called "The Socialist and the Suffragist." It begins:

> Said the Socialist to the Suffragist:
> "My cause is greater than yours!
> You only work for a Special Class,
> We for the gain of the General Mass.
> Which every good ensures!"
>
> Said the Suffragist to the Socialist:
> "You underrate my Cause!
> While women remain a Subject Class,
> You never can move the General Mass.
> With your Economic Laws!"

and ends:

> The world awoke, and tartly spoke:
> "Your work is all the same;
> Work together or work apart,
> Work, each of you, with all your heart—
> Just get into the game!"[22]

Catt agreed.

· 8 ·

Amsterdam and London, Calm and Storm

In the spring before the next Alliance con-
gress in Amsterdam, the ailing Maria Lane grew worse. Catt spent most of
1907 in Charles City nursing her mother and seeing her younger brother,
home from Manila on sick leave. Will arrived in January, after having worked
in the Philippines for five years, with an unspecified "nervous affliction."
Both seemed to have improved by the end of the summer and Will prepared to
go back to the Philippines; he and his wife were in Illinois visiting her parents
when Will died in September. His death was a blow from which Maria Lane
could not recover; she died on December 3, 1907. Catt's older brother,
Charles, and his family still lived in Charles City, and his sister gave him her
share of the farm, which was the bulk of their mother's estate.

Catt stayed in Iowa until mid-January to come to terms with her grief
and to complete plans for the Amsterdam meetings. By the end of February
she was taking her own measure: "I am quite normal mentally, which is a
great improvement over my condition two years ago. Then I felt sure I could
not live long and I was not at all interested whether I did or did not."[1]

Catt spoke on the right of petition at a suffrage hearing in Albany in
February, then testified in Washington at hearings of both the Senate and
House in March. At these hearings she showed her steadily expanding vision,
stressed internationalism, and opposed provincialism. She said, "The United
States is by no means leading the world in the suffrage movement," but that
did not mean that the enemies of suffrage were winning. "Suffrage will
ultimately triumph here as a result of its triumph in other countries."[2]

In her opening remarks to the delegates of the Fourth Congress of the
IWSA, June 15, 1908, she elaborated on the same theme, that the woman's
movement could not be considered a success until woman's history becomes
an integral part of the world's history and separate studies will no longer be
necessary.[3]

The June days in Amsterdam were sunny, the city lively, the hall full of flowers, and the meetings festive. A young Dutch admirer remembered Catt as stately, tall, grey-haired, blue-eyed, with a smile on her face, a charming, eloquent, well-dressed woman of forty-nine. "The words 'woman suffrage' had not too good a sound at that time. Suffragists and Suffragettes were talked of as 'Hobbezakken,' women who would not know how to dress gracefully." But that description was wrong. "The congress opened with a march of young girls dressed in white, each holding a flag of the nation represented at this International Conference, and the prominent families of Holland had gathered there, that the young daughters of these families could join—it was the awakening of a new era."[4]

Sixteen countries were represented including the four added in 1908— Bulgaria, Finland, South Africa (Cape Colony and Natal), and Switzerland. Five were represented by fraternal [sic] delegates, making twenty-one in all. For the first time there were official government delegates from two countries, Australia and Norway, and from Utah, Colorado, and Wyoming, three of the four suffrage states. This was the first congress at which the associated press of the host country took full charge of the reports; four years earlier in Berlin the reporters had clustered around a single table, in Amsterdam one hundred places were reserved for the press. Another first was a male delegate representing the Men's League for Women's Enfranchisement in Great Britain.[5]

Many countries reported progress. Finland had elected nineteen women to the first Diet (Landstag). Most of the twenty-six bills they had proposed concerned women's status, such as the right of mothers over their children, and an increase in civil service jobs for women. During the previous year the question of woman suffrage had been brought before twenty-two national parliaments and twenty-nine state legislatures. The question had evolved from an academic theory to a practical political issue. Catt summarized, "We represent the solidarity of a sex. We oppose a common enemy whose name is not man, but conservatism. Its weapons are the same in all lands—tradition, prejudice and selfishness. We too have a common weapon—an appeal to justice and fair play."[6]

The storm center for the movement was in England. During the time the Alliance was meeting in Amsterdam, both the militant and nonmilitant Englishwomen had sponsored huge meetings in London. On June 13, thirteen thousand suffragists marched to the Albert Hall carrying banners made by the Artists' League of Women's Suffrage. The following week the first of the "monster" rallies was held in Hyde Park by the Women's Social and Political Union. Several days later a suffragette meeting at Parliament Square was marked by fighting in the crowd and the arrest of twenty-seven women. Two were so enraged by the police that they had thrown stones through the windows of the Prime Minister's house, the suffragettes' first act of intentional damage. All twenty-seven women were sent to jail for terms ranging from one to two months. All emerged as heroines and martyrs; arrest was seen as a badge of honor.

When the press sneered at the suffragettes, Catt said every new movement has been ridiculed. If it was a poor one it was laughed out of existence, if it was a good one it got stronger under attack. A movement has reached the turning point when the derision switches to the opposition. That is happening now, she said, with the laugh turning against the British government at the sight of powerful cordons of police protecting the homes of the English Ministers and the great Houses of Parliament from attacks by unarmed women.[7]

The Amsterdam conference ended in a fireworks display. JUS SUF-FRAGII blazed across the sky. The inference was clear, suffrage was inevitable. A country could have it with flowers and flags and young women in white dresses, or with broken windows, police cordons, and brutality. The choice was the state's.

After steering the report of the Alliance congress through the press, Catt went to Geneva in late August to attend the business meetings of the International Council of Women. She was planning a six-week speaking tour in Hungary, Serbia, Austria, and Germany but abruptly was called back to New York for the sale of George Catt's engineering company. The sale turned out to be more complicated than expected and it was several years before his estate was finally settled.

Frustrated in her international tour that fall, she devoted herself to New York suffrage work. She had long realized that parlor meetings and petitions were much too limited to be effective. To make a political impact, women of all social and economic groups had to be organized on precinct lines. In September 1908, she began the laborious work that finally resulted the next year in the formation of the Woman Suffrage Party.

Again, she was overworking, her health suffered, and her friends worried. To cheer her, they gave a surprise party for her fiftieth birthday in February, which was noted on the front page of the New York Times. Even that stubbornly antifeminist paper saw her as a world figure; her private life was becoming increasingly public.

A month later she went to London, checked on arrangements for the Alliance meeting, and was then off on the European speaking tour with

Rosika Schwimmer that she had canceled the previous fall. She found the women's cause had considerably advanced since her visit to central Europe with Aletta Jacobs in 1906. With her lucid prescience for shifting political winds, Catt added a plea for international peace to her usual suffrage lectures. At the end of the trip she wrote to A. B. Storms, President of Iowa State College: "I have been in Bohemia, Austria, Hungary and Germany. I found many members of Parliament in those countries far more liberal and civilized' than the Iowa legislature which seems to forget that it is a representative body and not a Russian Council of State."[8]

Meanwhile the British Parliament was behaving like the Iowa legislature. The king's speech, which presents the issues on which the government will debate that year, on February 16, 1909 had omitted any reference to votes for women. The suffrage forces seethed, and the day after Catt arrived in London at the end of the month, twenty-eight women led by Emmeline Pethick-Lawrence demonstrated at Parliament Square. Again they were all arrested, again the sentences were one and two months, and again there were more protests, more arrests.

With each militant demonstration the Pankhurst forces were growing stronger and widening the split between themselves and the suffragists. In 1906 the WSPU had asked to become a member of the IWSA; in 1909 they would not go to Alliance meetings but invited the delegates to one of their own.

Wisely, Catt went. However, in her letter of acceptance she suggested that the division would endure long after women were voters:

> When the suffrage is won in England, as it will be soon, the militant policy of your organization will divide opinion throughout the world. One class will claim that the suffrage might have been won by the usual constitutional campaign; another, that it never would have come had not unusual methods been employed. This difference of view will enter the ranks of every national association, and parties will come forward to champion and to oppose militant methods. It requires no prophet to predict the inevitable coming of this situation. Meanwhile, every fair-minded suffragist will esteem it a great and valued privilege to hear the case presented and defended by your own able women.[9]

The years have proved Catt entirely accurate.

Hunger strikes and the subsequent brutal forced feeding of the suffragettes did not begin until the summer of 1909, shortly after the Alliance had met in April and left. But militancy was accelerating and the environment was so explosive that Catt prudently set the Alliance delegates to considering their own rules and trappings. They talked at length about a seal, a banner, a hymn, and a motto, all of which were adopted. The motto suggested by Catt was in Latin for international purposes: "In necessariis unitas, in dubiis libertas, in omnibus caritas (In essentials unity, in non-essentials liberty, in all things charity)."[10] Such problems served to keep the delegates busy considering Alliance unity and to bore the press so that few reporters would be around if Catt's moderating plans went awry.

Austria, Bohemia, Belgium, and France joined the IWSA. Fifteen suffragist organizations in Great Britain were represented, including women from the newly formed suffrage leagues of artists, actors, and writers. They came from the Fabian Society, the Independent Labour Party, the Socialists, and Irish and Scottish groups. Three women who had become disenchanted with the dictatorial leadership of the Pankhursts were there, the first to leave the WSPU to form another association. Anna and Thomas Haslam from Ireland, both in their eighties, were the oldest suffragists present.[11]

An important resolution reaffirmed one that had been adopted the year before in Amsterdam: "The plain duty of women at the present hour is to secure the support and cooperation of all forces favorable to woman suffrage, without question as to their political or religious affiliations; to avoid any entanglement with outside matters; to ask for the franchise on the same terms as it is now or may be exercised by men, leaving any required extension to be decided by men and women together."

This was easier said than understood and reflects some of the basic problems of setting goals for an international federation. The terms of male suffrage varied widely from country to country; there were religious, political, and cultural differences. The most practical way to achieve woman suffrage would be to demonstrate that many women had exactly the same qualifications as the men who were voting, and therefore the gender restriction should be dropped. Such an approach does not challenge the traditional criteria of the culture except in the matter of sex. Idealists without a knowledge of practical politics demanded sweeping changes immediately, thereby compounding the difficulties. Catt stated again and again that the Alliance had never taken a position for or against any special form of suffrage, each affiliated society was entirely free to determine the kind of suffrage it would demand in its own country. Her constantly reiterated aim was to eliminate sex as a qualification for voting.

Both the suffragists and the suffragettes invited the Alliance delegates to large meetings during their congress. That of the London Society for Women's Suffrage began with a long parade of suffragists, from university women in their brilliant robes to chain makers in their overalls. There were cotton operatives, factory workers, doctors, nurses, midwives, and teachers. It was the first great show of solidarity of women of all classes and disproved the common slur that the cause was an amusement for rich women. Catt was impressed with the display and said she was "burning with desire to reproduce it in New York."[12]

The militant Women's Social and Political Union held a meeting the following night to honor the one hundred and fifty women who had been to prison for the cause. "The Government can never crush us" was the theme. The former prisoners, many in jail garb, marched across the platform to receive the "Holloway degree" (for Holloway Jail), a brooch designed for the occasion by Sylvia Pankhurst. It had the broad arrow (the mark of the prisoner) centered on a stylized portcullis. Emmeline Pethick-Lawrence, less than two weeks out of Holloway, called for all women to "stand shoulder to shoulder until the final victory is won."[13]

Almost as if the British government had planned an added attraction for the Alliance delegates, the morning after the WSPU meeting other suffragettes were released from prison. Many of the Alliance women swelled the numbers who assembled at the gates of Holloway Jail in the customary welcome to those coming out. They joined the procession to a restaurant where breakfast was accompanied by speeches. Russia's Zinaida Mirovich and Germany's Anita Augspurg especially cheered the English militants. In her enthusiasm Dr. Augspurg declared that their bravery had done more for the movement in Germany than all their suffrage work.

In spite of the differences in opinion on tactics between the English groups, both covered the IWSA meetings thoroughly and positively, especially praising Catt's skill and admirable temper. "Her illuminating smile saved many an awkward situation in the course of the week."[14]

One of the many far-reaching results of the London congress was a pledge of money from Alva Vanderbilt Belmont, the American socialite whose daughter was the Duchess of Marlborough. Catt told her that a dynamic public relations campaign was the most urgent need of the movement in the United States and named Ida Husted Harper to head a press department. Harper returned on the same ship with Belmont, and, Catt wrote, "By the time they had arrived in New York, Mrs. Belmont was ready to make a proposition of remarkable liberality. She offered to pay the rent of a headquarters for the New York State Suffrage Association, to pay the entire expenses of a National press department, and to furnish rooms for the remainder of the National work."[15]

During the annual NAWSA convention in Seattle in 1909 the delegates voted to return the national headquarters to New York City from Warren, Ohio. They agreed with Catt that "New York is the battleground of the whole nation."

· 9 ·
Women United?

Catt was clearly unwell. At the London congress in 1909 she had avoided all the social functions she could, and the voyage home failed to restore her. By neglecting almost all international work for months, she had managed to appear for the necessary speeches and legislative hearings. And somehow she had launched the Woman Suffrage Party on October 29, 1909. It was still very much of a paper plan. The national organization seemed more prone to infighting and fragmentation than ever before, and Catt made a rare complaint to Ida Harper: "My heart has been heavy all the winter with the weight of this awful situation growing more complicated and more menacing to the cause every day."[1]

The Woman Suffrage Party was an attempt by Catt to draw into a compact, active organization the various clubs that had discussed suffrage academically for years. Her strategy was to organize on the lines of the political machine, and although the Woman Suffrage Party was billed as including the whole of New York State, its officers were New York City women and it was most effective in the city. Catt herself defined it as "New York's auxiliary of the NAWSA, which has 47 other similar branches."

Catt had gratefully spent the summer of 1909 in the Catskills, resting and recuperating. Although she tried to make light of her illness, she wrote to a friend who had pressed for details: "I counted my ailments and found I had ten, but it requires a very vigorous mental effort to enumerate them all. My chief difficulty is that usual with women of *late* middle life [she was 50], only I have some inflammation, which gives me much pain and I have had so many hemmorhages that I am very aenemic, and that means no reserve of strength."[2]

She talked less about her health than the need to take advantage of the increased interest in suffrage whipped up by the English militants. She saw a tidal pattern that determined the timing for action: "Reform movements invariably move onward in waves of success followed by inevitable reaction. It is evidently now the time to increase our activities to the utmost before reaction sets in."[3]

The fragmentation of the American suffragists worried NAWSA president Anna Shaw as well. She wrote to Aletta Jacobs: "Mrs. Catt seems to be the only New York woman who can lead all the forces here, except one group who cannot be lead by anyone except the old 'Nick' himself. Mrs. Catt did a splendid piece of work in organizing what is called 'The Woman Suffrage Party,' and I think if her idea could be carried out it would be very successful; but it is a large undertaking, and needs a well woman in back of it."[4]

By the end of April 1910, Catt was confined to her bed. She joked that her doctor had told her to eat, eat, eat, consequently she had gained weight, and "It was a question of whether I should have a big waist band in this world, or wings in the next. It will be a sad joke on me if I have both." To another friend she mused on immortality, a subject she rarely mentioned. "The only thing I feel sure of is that I shall never see again those who have gone on before. The orthodox faith must be rather a consolation."[5]

She was too ill to attend the great parade in New York City on May 21, held to protest the failure of the legislature to submit a woman suffrage question to the voters. American women had paraded before but this marked the beginning of their large processions and, Catt said, a change from the days when women accepted negative legislative decisions "with silent resignation."

Her health worsened and on June 4, 1910, she underwent an operation, perhaps a hysterectomy. For several days Hay and the doctor thought she would die. Hay bemoaned Catt's weak heart and the strength she had expended on the cause.[6] Gradually her health came back.

Her doctor told her that she must spend an entire year in absolute rest in order to restore her health. "I thought a long time over a possible plan of spending a year in rest," she wrote.

> I then told my doctor that I had decided to take a trip around the world but there were three things that I had to do before I could start. I was president of the International Woman Suffrage Alliance, a congress was due soon in Stockholm, and it was my duty to prepare the program and do the correspondence with our auxiliaries. I must preside over the congress and when the congress should be over, the minutes and records had to be prepared and printed. My doctor, hearing about these three tasks, said solemnly, "Then you must rest two years, instead of one."[7]

She worked at home through the fall, going to the suffrage office only briefly when necessary. In November she presided at the celebration of victory in Washington, under the leadership of Emma DeVoe, one of her favorite organizers since they had worked together in the nineties. Catt bragged, "In point of wealth, population, and political influence, Washington is the most important state yet won."[8] It was the first state victory in fourteen years.

A week later she was "enticed" to a dinner by the "bait" of the discussion to follow: "Man's View on Woman Suffrage." She relished finding "a table full of antis and one of suffragists glaring at each other. The speakers were all men, but I was called for and had an inning at the evening."[9] She was sounding like her old self again.

Catt felt quite well when she and Hay left on the *Amerika* for Stockholm the first of April. As was her habit, she scheduled her trip to allow time to settle details of the convention on the spot, then do some sightseeing and suffrage work before the meetings began.

Catt and Hay traveled in a style that has since vanished. The trip began with a great send-off; friends had filled their stateroom from floor to ceiling with gifts—flowers, candy, fruit, magazines, books, letters. It took three hours to make a way through it, Catt said. For a week she read and answered the "steamer letters," sending advice about carrying on the work from New York to California. To Emma Sweet in Rochester she wrote hoping that proper leaders could be found for each district since it was the only way to win at the polls. She sent encouragement and money to Clara Hyde in San Francisco, with suggestions on how to get the labor vote.[10]

The *Amerika* docked at Hamburg, where Catt spent a day before she went to Copenhagen. Once there, she spoke at a large public assembly and several parlor meetings, giving six speeches in four days. She visited Parliament where the Prime Minister and other leaders assured her that the parliamentary vote for women would not be long delayed.

Then she was off for a five-day visit to Norway, culminating in an audience with King Haakon, "a very democratic sort of a King," she remarked. She praised Norway highly for its equal treatment of women and men. "One feels the difference between the enfranchised and unenfranchised countries rather in the spirit of things than in tangible form. That sex antagonism, which everywhere exists, whether we like to admit it or not, is gone, and in its place has come a comradeship on a high moral plane."[11]

The Sixth Conference of the IWSA opened in Stockholm on June 12, 1911. Catt had urged women to come "to demonstrate that the cause we represent belongs to no country and no nation or race, but is a common demand of our united womanhood." Iceland and Serbia were admitted to membership, raising the number of affiliated countries to twenty-four; fraternal delegates came from men's leagues of France, Great Britain, Hungary, the Netherlands, Sweden, and the United States. Catt adopted the boast of the British Empire and said that the sun never set upon woman suffrage activity. There were suffrage clubs from the Arctic Circle to the antipodes.

"Of the twenty-four nations represented in this Congress the women of fifteen have won more political rights than they had seven years ago. These gains vary all the way from the repeal of the law which forbade women to form political organizations in Germany, ecclesiastical suffrage in Switzerland, suffrage in Trade Councils in France, Italy and Belgium, up to municipal suffrage in Denmark, and political suffrage and eligibility in Australia, Finland, Norway, and the state of Washington." The Stockholm conference began on a note of high-minded optimism, but as the reports continued there were chilling signs that a narrow authoritarianism was becoming aggressive. Anna Lundstrom reported from Finland that "shoulder to shoulder with the men, women are striving to repel the invasion of the rights of Finland by Russia. The eastern winds have blown wilder and blacker across Finland" and the fight for the nation's survival had taken precedent over other questions.

Poland's secretary began with a gloomy understatement: "The work of reform in a land of oppression is difficult." In Hungary many of the women's friends had been defeated in "a dreadful election" and Rosika Schwimmer's long report told how Radicals, Liberals, and Democrats had shut out suffragists from political meetings because the women would not promise to drop their demands for the vote until universal suffrage was won for men.

Happily, Iceland reported successes, including a bill that gave women the right to higher education, scholarships, and to all state offices. For the first time a country with a Lutheran State Church admitted women to clerical offices. The Bishop of Iceland was quoted as saying that if St. Paul had lived in the present time he would have been the first to consent to this bill.

On the other hand, Russia, like Hungary, reported: "The emancipation of women has still many enemies, among men as well as among women." Switzerland tried hard to be optimistic, "but it needs time to dislodge the tenacious indifference of the women themselves and to influence the authorities."

Many of the younger women were coming to Catt's conviction that woman suffrage organizations should be nonpartisan. Zinaida Mirovich agreed that suffragists in Russia had found that no political party could be entirely trusted, and Rosika Schwimmer said, "Men had not only set up for themselves a double standard of morals, but also a double standard of political honesty."[12]

The star of the Stockholm convention was Selma Lagerlof, who had won the Nobel Prize for literature in 1909. She described the home as woman's contribution to civilization, her small masterpiece from which she had not excluded man. It stood as the safeguard of security and happiness, the shelter of compassion and love. The man-made state, on the other hand, with its crime and misery and menace of war had been made without woman's cooperation. It was bound to fail until man and woman joined hands to build together a masterpiece for the human race. Florence Luscomb, a young American delegate, wrote of listening to the sad voice whose words she didn't understand but sharing the emotions of men and women all over the audience who were moved to tears.[13]

Catt emphasized economic wrongs: "Modern conditions are pushing hundreds of thousands of women out of their homes into the labor market. Everywhere paid less than men for equal work, everywhere discriminated against, they are utterly at the mercy of forces over which they have no control." She denounced ill-advised legislation that would favor one group of working women over another. Some women condemned prostitution but they had no right to turn their backs on women driven by economic conditions to this last despairing effort to make a living, she insisted. "Their wrongs are our wrongs. They have been created by the very injustices against which we protest. We women demand an equal voice; we shall accept nothing less.

> To the wrong that needs resistance,
> To the right that needs assistance,
> To the future in the distance,
> We give ourselves.[14]

After Stockholm, Catt went to London. Forcible feeding of imprisoned hunger-striking suffragettes had been the government's policy for nearly two years with all the daily horrors of jaw clamps and tubes thrust into the prisoner's stomach. The official cruelty had in some ways drawn both wings of the English suffrage movement together. When Catt arrived, militants and nonmilitants alike were basking in the success of their first joint parade of June 17, 1911. Leaders of both groups were present at a Fourth of July banquet given in honor of Catt, and Millicent Fawcett boasted, "When we want a procession we raise a hand and forty thousand women come from all parts of the kingdom. The awakening of women to political consciousness is one of the greatest things the world has seen."

Catt complimented the English movement as a wonderful, powerful, soul-stirring thing; it had developed a unique quality, precious and rare, "the contagion of consecration." There was irony in the phrase; privately she thought its supporters were becoming so self-preoccupied they could not see beyond their own country. However, she held to the premise she had built into the Alliance: Each national suffrage movement must harmonize with its own nation. The Alliance was not to teach but to inspire.[15]

Catt stayed in London for two weeks and on July 22, 1911, began a trip that took her around the world in the cause of women's liberation.

· 10 ·

South Africa to the Philippines

Catt sailed around the world with her old friend Aletta Jacobs, who joined her when the ship stopped briefly at Madeira. Another Dutch woman, Mrs. Boersma, and an American, Miss Cameron, accompanied them as far as Egypt. The party first went to Cape Town, two weeks from Southampton. On the way Catt read more than a dozen books on South Africa and discussed them with her friends. Like many reformers of the time, Jacobs saw the Dutch colonists and their descendents, Boers, as heroic. Their trek into the Transvaal less than a century before was the stuff of legend. She sympathized with the nationalist aspirations of the Orange Free State and the Transvaal Republic during the Boer War (1899–1902) against the British and with those suffering in British concentration camps.[1]

Catt was ready to see the country through her friend's eyes but what most interested her were the two suffrage organizations, one in the Cape Colony and the other in Natal, which had become affiliated with the IWSA at the Amsterdam congress. She and Jacobs wanted to help realize the hope for woman suffrage in the newly formed states, and could speak for the cause in English and Dutch, the two official languages in South Africa.

Their ship docked in Cape Town August 7 and that night Catt gave her first suffrage speech there. She then went on to attend meetings, to help organize group conferences, and to meet officials for the next three months. She summarized:

> The trip from Southampton and up the East Coast [of Africa] cost about $1,200—more rather than less. We travelled 4,000 miles by train and 11,000 miles by ship, and visited 13 cities and towns. I conducted the entire correspondence arranging for the trip, engaging hotels, etc. I made a total of 45 speeches; there were 7 receptions, 18 luncheons, 14 afternoon teas, 3 morning teas, 6 dinners, 3 picnics, 12 committee meetings. I spent 36 days sightseeing and travel (11 days and 11 nights were spent on the train) which left 40 days spent with suffragists.[2]

The South Africa she saw was similar to the western United States where she had begun her work two decades earlier. "There are beautiful towns, electric lighted, sewered, asphalted and supplied with good water." Inland there were farms and frontier conditions. There were also the familiar promises made to women by politicians and not kept, familiar liberals and familiar bigots. Catt summarized the political climate in the Transvaal, the Orange Free State, and Cape Colony where women had municipal suffrage: "The leading Boers seem favorable to woman suffrage. The British are inclined to think their conviction is based upon a belief that the Boer Party (Nationalists) would profit by the votes of women, but, to the contrary, I am sure their attitude is due to their comprehension of the real value of the services of women, and they have not forgotten that promise of a previous generation."

Some British were ready to give votes to women but she found others who were "oriental" in their attitudes toward women. "Nowhere have I listened with so little patience to the picayunish objections, 'Will women marry?' 'Will they not neglect their homes?' 'Will they not cease to become mothers?'"[3]

There were also the familiar petty quarrels among the suffragists themselves. In Johannesburg she remarked on two rival suffrage clubs, "They think they have differences of tactics but what they have is a violent and narrowminded hatred of each other. It took a good deal of persuasion to get them to agree to work together." It was all very much like home.

She also found "splendid" women and with them organized a delegated convention, the first in South Africa, held in Durban in October 1911, where a Union Association of the eleven leagues was formed.[4] But while organizing suffragists was second nature, what was most exciting were the excursions and chance meetings. Catt remembered the three months as "a perpetual source of joy, I never learned so much in so short a time in my life."[5] She went to an ostrich farm (where she noted with approval that "the cock sets on the eggs from 4 p.m. until morning and does his full part of parental duty"), to the diamond mines at Kimberly and Pretoria, to a dynamite factory in Johannesburg, and to the Victoria Falls.

With Aletta Jacobs, Catt made the 1,700-mile train journey into the interior with eight pieces of hand luggage, "a bag containing my bottles, etc., which I called my apothecary shop; a bag out of which protruded three big bottles of boiled water, which I called my wine cellar; a basket of fruit, my kitchen; a basket of books, my library; a bag of toilet articles, my dressing room; a typewriter, my office; and two boxes of clothing." At the journey's end she handed these out of the train window to porters "whose dress consisted mostly of a brass plate giving his number. They set the things down in a heap of dust which seemed bottomless." She and Jacobs followed the porters to the "one-storied hotel built upon posts to prevent the white ants from devouring it. The fresh skin of a leopard killed near our hotel two days before our arrival, was a mute witness to the fact that we were in the wilds, and the story of two young men who had been camping not far away of finding a boa constrictor eighteen feet long in the tree overhanging their tent, sent the shivers down our spines."

Catt relished the joys of the tourist. She wrote pages in her diary about baobab trees and other wonders and happily copied down every story of man-eating lions told her. For the walk to the Victoria Falls from their hotel she dressed in what she considered proper safari wear: "I had bought some cavalry leggings, which I called my snake protectors, and these I put on. I wore a thin shirt waist [dress], took off my petticoat [very daring] and with my shilling hat and parasol was soon ready. We walked through the rapidly intensifying heat and dust unspeakable along broad paths."

The water was low and the falls were an anticlimax, but the trip was by no means disappointing. Once she saw the grave of a pioneer woman that symbolized to Catt the scores of women whose brave lives were unheralded:

> Before I was born, a white woman had looked upon these same scenes. A missionary she was, among the natives of that district, and no hotel sheltered her and no white man's food awaited her! Long years ago she gave up her life to the ravages of tropical fever, but all those long, hot days I experienced a strange sympathy of understanding with that heroic martyr. Mrs. Livingstone lies buried beneath a similar sun-scorched plateau, although her renowned husband sleeps in Westminster Abbey! O woman! when will the great world recognize the hidden power with you? Perhaps not until you find yourself.[6]

Catt and Jacobs went to Pretoria to pick up their work again. The wife of the Minister of Finance held a drawing room meeting; the Mayor chaired a public meeting; and they had lunch at the home of the Prime Minister, where Catt found the house, the lunch, and the wife rather ordinary, but "we were grateful for the recognition." They called upon Minister Jan Christiaan Smuts, the Boers' brilliant young war hero, and Mrs. Smuts. "He is regarded as the chief and dominating mind in the cabinet. She is called very clever with a great influence over her husband." Jacobs chatted with them in Dutch, an uncomprehending Catt smiled and was "thoroughly bored."

Happily she met a superb teller of stories about the Boer War. Mrs. Brandt had been a nurse in a concentration camp near Pretoria and part of a women's spy system for the Boers. "It was glorious to hear her tell her stories of heroism," Catt wrote. She relished accounts of the hundreds of heroic South African women.

> By the side of every man there was a woman as intrepid as he, who had turned her back upon the refinements of home life in the old world, and became a nomad in this strange, hard, new world. In times of war, and these were constantly recurring, these women moulded bullets, loaded guns, and sometimes fought side by side with the men. South African historians are generous in according these early pioneer women the undaunted pluck which kept up the spirits of the men and would not permit them to turn back from the task undertaken.[7]

Unfortunately, Catt did not see South Africa's most brilliant and famous feminist, Olive Schreiner, whose influential *Woman and Labour* was published that year. Jacobs was its Dutch translator and made the overnight trip from Port Elizabeth to DeAar to see her. In loyalty to the temperance movement, Catt gave up the pleasure of visiting Schreiner to address a meeting of the WCTU in Port Elizabeth.

Catt did see Mohandas Gandhi. She had a letter of introduction from a mutual friend, which she sent to Gandhi in Johannesburg, asking him to call at her hotel if convenient. His secretary came instead and explained that no Indian was permitted to enter a hotel to call on a guest. A lawyer friend of Catt's offered his office for an interview, so she wrote Gandhi a second time. Again his secretary came. The elevator operator refused to take him up

> and he would not so far demean himself as to walk when the European was carried. This challenged my curiosity and I told the young girl to tell him to go back to his office and that I would call upon him.
>
> Directly Miss Cameron and I, escorted by the secretary, were on our way. She took us into quarters apparently occupied exclusively by Indians. We found his office much the same as any of the less prosperous sort. The outer room was filled with Indians awaiting their turn to consult Mr. Gandhi, who was a lawyer. We found the man seated behind an American desk—a small very black man with his head wrapped in a very white turban. He was not particularly prepossessing in appearance,

but we soon engaged him in conversation and were amazed at his excellent and correct English; he was a gentleman. He told us that he had been in prison because he had evaded signing a registration paper which is made compulsory for all Indians for police purposes. He then spoke of his hope that India would be independent one day. His eyes lighted with an inner fire and he spoke with such fervor that we recognized that we were in the presence of no ordinary man. Directly he quoted from the Declaration of Independence, from Emerson and Longfellow. Proud, rebellious, humiliated, he may earn his livelihood by law, but he dreams of naught but India's independence.

When a lawyer quoting Emerson is forbidden to call upon a guest at a hotel, to ride in an elevator in a public building, and is compelled to report his movements to the police, there may be reasons for the rules that we do not know; but, said we to each other as we wended our way back to the hotel, we can at least understand that given a proud enough spirit and a long enough treatment of that kind and a revolutionist is created. If we are not greatly mistaken Gandhi is such a man. The impression that remained was that I had for the first time in my life seen a genuine fanatic.[8]

Another impressive visit was to a Kaffir kraal in Maritzburg. She and the chief had an immediate rapport, for all their obvious differences the two understood each other perfectly—both were leaders holding their own people together in the face of great power and injustice. She described the chief in great detail, his surroundings, his duties, his dignified hospitality. "He was clad in his everyday clothes which consisted of a nice square of sheep skin hanging from his waist and which always seemed to turn under him when he sat like a nice comfy rug should do." The lifelong, vehement teetotaler even went so far as to take a token sip of beer from a large calabash during a ceremony of hospitality. She talked much more about her visit to the kraal and the chief than she did about her reception by the King of Norway four months before.

Dress was always important to the suffragists, who felt it vital to establish their respectability in the eyes of the influential. Catt made wry comments about European-American ways of dressing, especially when slavishly copied in the tropics. She scorned the "fool notion" of a hostess wearing a hat in her own home, but even in the sweltering weather she herself usually wore velvet or satin, the materials of her best dresses. In Durban "for the first time I could not wear my velvet; the sweat poured off in buckets as it was." On several occasions she had lighter clothes made and often commented with a hint of envy on the trousers women wore in different parts of the world, a liberating costume she first noted in Zanzibar.

Another insight into the amount of luggage and packing involved in those days of ample and crushable dresses comes from reading about the time devoted to their care and transport. The day after the Durban convention she wrote, "The rain descended in torrents, no one interrupted, the delegates had gone, and the day was devoted to packing. I went over my papers, wrote seven letters, packed three trunks, one case of books, and ten small packages. We were all worn to a frazzle by bedtime."

From Durban the party went up the east coast of Africa to Port Said, taking two weeks and sightseeing at stops along the way. For the rest of her life Catt recollected with joy a picnic on a clove plantation at Zanzibar. From Port Said the travelers went to the Holy Land for a few weeks of the usual pilgrimages.

Catt was always skeptical of organized religions and her comments became increasingly critical. "When I had been in the 'Holy Land' three days, had made the trip to Jericho, the Dead Sea, and the Jordan, I thought every congregation ought to send its clergyman, whether Christian or Jewish, to visit this country in order to get the 'atmosphere' in which the Bible history occurred. I thought it would prove so enlightening, but after our trip to Bethlehem, my ardor oozed out gradually, and now I think congregations better keep their clergymen at home." She decided the Holy Land was unholy. The commercialization of shrines, the dirt and wretchedness of beggars repelled her. Organized religion held little interest for her and she found the antifeminism of most churches exasperating.

Although this part of the trip had its strains and irritations, it clearly shifted the direction of Catt's assumptions about women in non-Western cultures. What startled her were the varieties of attitudes and the exceptions to her preconceived notions. An Arabic-speaking leader of the American colony in Jerusalem introduced Catt to the wife of a former mayor, a Muslim. She remembered when "no man would mention public affairs in his home, but now her husband brought the papers home and read them aloud, discussing matters with his wife and children. She could not read, and she had shed tears many a time because she could not, but her daughter, sixteen years old, has always been in school and speaks Arabic, Turkish, English, French and Italian."

Catt was disturbed by what she thought was a religious requirement that Muslim women wear a veil but there was nothing in the Koran to compel them to do so, she was informed by the mayor's sister. Having been brought up in a political household, the woman was knowledgeable and discussed local events with Catt at length. Catt learned that "[wearing veils] was only custom but custom was harder to break down than religious commands. [The mayor's sister] believed women should not be veiled, but it was difficult for one woman to do much. She was intelligent and certainly a woman's woman in sympathy and understanding of the movement, of which she had never heard until that day. We had coffee as usual, and when I bade her good-bye, I begged her to do what she could to liberate her sex." Other women were shocked at the idea of discarding the veil. "A young and very pretty teacher looked especially disturbed, and said nothing could persuade her to show her face to a man!"

A few days later Catt's own nineteenth-century upbringing showed through her twentieth-century sophistication when she was at a train station in Riyaq (in what is now Lebanon) and watched a bridal group disembark from a train and mount camels for the rest of their trip. "Each camel carried two women. Not a woman spoke, or laughed or made a sound, nor did one show ever so little of her face, but all of the shoes, stockings, petticoats and drawers, including the legs nearly to the thigh, were exhibited to the assembled village! Verily, modesty is a question of religion and geography!"

From Beirut Catt and her companions sailed back to Egypt but their visit was cut short by an enforced quarantine in Alexandria because of suspected cholera on their ship. Consequently they had only a few days in Cairo but managed to form a suffrage organization there. Running through Catt's diary is a startled appreciation at discovering women who had been fighting bigotry and sex prejudice all their lives. She was gratified to find feminists everywhere: often the women were not aware that they were part of a worldwide movement.

In Egypt, Boersma and Cameron left the party and Catt and Jacobs went on together. They partly retraced their route from Port Said, back through the Suez Canal, the Red Sea, then continued southeast to India. During a brief stopover in Ceylon they visited tea plantations where they found men, women, and children working under conditions that amounted to slavery. When white plantation owners assured them the tea pickers were perfectly content and had all they needed, Catt replied acidly that she had heard the same assurances about wives but never from the married women themselves.

Her one hot argument was with Sydney Webb, the English Fabian whom she met in India, and that had more farce than force. She disapproved the Webbs' hesitation on woman suffrage; Beatrice Webb had even signed an antisuffrage petition, although later admitted she had been ill-advised and gave tepid support to the cause. By chance Catt and Jacobs shared a car with them on a twenty-mile trip from Agra to Fatqua Skri. "Among the ruins is a sort of open pagoda five stories high. We climbed to the top and sat down on a platform which commands a charming view of the country. Directly the Webbs came puffing up and seated themselves near by. Then he began to glorify those old Mohammedans and to curse modern critics who think the Indians cannot do anything great, *altho* there is nothing in the world to compare with the Agra and especially the Taj."

Impishly, Catt decided to disagree as forcefully as possible.

> When he paused for breath I began and told him that if a man today spent 11 millions of dollars on a tomb for himself and wife, the world would call him a fool, and if a government should attempt such a thing there would be a revolution, *but* if anyone had that much to spend, there were architects and artists who could do even better than those unknowns of the Taj.
>
> Well we had it back and forth. The Dr. tried to help me and Mrs. Webb tried to change the subject. At last we all arose and strode off in high dudgeon! We rode back to town together but as Sydney sat in front and Carrie behind there was no further sign of war. Now, when I think of it, all the fury of my soul rises in hatred of that man. Another [moment] I laugh and laugh at the ridiculousness of it all—that man I had never before seen and never will again! I'm sure he hates me as cordially.[9]

Catt found the Indians particularly gracious. She was invited to homes, to parties, a wedding. She went to Malabar Hill, the home of Sir Pherozeshah Mehta, a leader of the Congress party. "He is intelligent and fine, I got some information I wanted and the experience was good." Through one of the women she had met at a "purdah party" (in the secluded women's quarters) she was introduced to Mrs. S. G. Ranaday, whom Catt saw as "a genuine feminist, the daughter of a reformer, a Brahmin Samaj, who do not believe in caste of any kind. She took us to see a school for Hindu girls, where the teachers are mostly Theosophists and there were several men—all of whom *give* their time. That is due to the spirit of the new religion."

She was impressed with some of the "new virile positive sects which have arisen within the older religions." Because of the hope they held for liberating both women and men, she spoke of them at length:

> One of these is Theosophy. It is making great gains in India, and wherever it goes is holding aloft the torch of woman's emancipation.

In the school for teachers at Madras, and its schools for Hindu boys and girls at Benares, and for Buddhist boys in Ceylon some truly wonderful things are being accomplished. Twelve hundred orthodox Hindu boys in Benares are learning their old philosophy with a modern application. Among other things, they are being taught that the freedom of women is consistent with their faith, and they are setting out to correct the agelong wrong endured by the women of India. Thirty of these boys, without pay or reward, while they are themselves in school, are conducting schools for little girls, and this I thought the most significant thing I learned in India. In Bombay, too, we found men lawyers, doctors, and teachers, who were Theosophists, without pay, teaching in an overcrowded girls' school. I do not profess to understand or to endorse Theosophy. Whatever may be one's personal opinion of it, the true feminist must feel a sense of gratitude to Mrs. Besant, who has established these Eastern schools.

Catt detailed other "uplifting influences" she found "within the old religions of Asia," among Hindus, Parsees, and Mohammedans, especially the new wave of schools for girls and the example of some women who were trying to improve the position of women. She had no illusions about understanding that vast subcontinent in such a brief time, however. "I would say that India was about the last question in the world that anybody can discuss with authority with anything less than half a lifetime spent in that country. I don't know anything about India."[10]

Rangoon (where Catt was amazed to find women voters) was the last stop on the continent, from there Catt and Jacobs went to Java, touching on the northeast coast of Sumatra.[11] There they found "nice Dutch suffragists," had a meeting and organized a club of sixty women.

Aletta Jacobs had relatives in Java and an elder sister, who had been a pharmacist in Batavia for thirty years, was the leader of a group that met them, and was the chief organizer of their visit. Catt did not know Dutch so Jacobs made most of the speeches and the discussions were in that language. Catt was bored and very hot. Incongruously, she and Jacobs still dressed as if they were in the temperate zones; Catt notes going to a dressmaker for cooler clothes but in the next sentence talks of melting herself into her black satin for a meeting.

She was seldom shocked by what she saw in her travels, angered sometimes at the artificial limitations put on women, but generally amused and tolerant. She was, however, shaken by a visit to "the 'opium fabrick' as the Dutch government has taken up the manufacture of opium to get it away from the Chinese. A private person may buy and smoke all he wishes. They say the *pure* opium does no harm which is not true!"

A highlight of the trip and one she talked about for years was going to central Sumatra to see a matriarchate, the Menangkabau. She wrote at length about the visit in *Jus Suffragii* and later published an expanded version with pictures in *Harper's Magazine* under the title "A Survival of Matriarchy." It reads now as rather old-fashioned cultural anthropology, but her conclusion was sound: "The Matriarchate is as onesided and abnormal as the Patriarchate and a compromise between the two is what we all want."[12]

There were less satisfying days as well. In Djakarta she was angered to advocating militancy. At a suffrage meeting there were seventy feminists including the four daughters of the prince. The princesses talked to Jacobs at length later, and Catt sputtered about their plight: "They are in revolt of mind but poor little prisoners, they do not know what to do. They went to a Dutch school but were taken away at about twelve, for after that it is wrong for a woman to appear in public. Soon they will be married to some man they have never seen! If breaking windows could liberate our sex, we ought to smash every one in the world."

Catt and Jacobs left Java the end of June for the Philippines and it was during a stop in Makassar on the island of Sulawesi that for the first time they saw women with bound feet. They were told that the deformity was no longer considered the fashion for a bride and Catt commented: "The new woman with *feet* is at present ruling the marriage market. It is a bit hard on the woman of the pegs, but since when has progress stopped to see how her strides onward were going to affect any woman?"

The next lengthy stop was Manila, where they stayed six weeks. A great deal of time was spent visiting schools and learning about the education system. She spoke at many meetings and by the end of her stay had helped organize a suffrage association. Philippine independence was being widely discussed and the holiday called Occupation Day on August 13 prompted Catt to some musings about independence of individuals as well as nations. She sided with the Filipino nationalists and wrote: "It seems a bit cheeky to make Occupation Day a general holiday since the natives did not welcome the Americans. Alas, no man is fit to rule another and no nation is fit to rule another people."

Her biggest adventure lay before her, in China.

· 11 ·
China

Catt was fascinated by the Chinese women at first sight. Before going to Manila her ship had called at Hong Kong and for the first time she saw women manipulating their little water taxis that swarmed and bobbed about the harbor. "They were so strong minded and strong limbed, and so dexterous with their curious oar and tiller that one could not think of them as the weaker sex.'"

She saw them again from the deck of the ship taking her from Manila to Canton. There they were among the launches flying the five-striped flag of the new Republic, skittering their crafts around the junks, the merchant, fishing, restaurant, and ferry boats. Catt wrote of the Chinese women:

> They are so full of vigor, strength and self-reliance. They are always laughing and goodnatured. They don't care a flip about what anyone thinks of them, least of all men. I now understand why the coolies can go off to other lands and make money. They do not have to bother about their wives and children. The women are amply able to take care of themselves and their husbands too. The women are in business and doing hard out of door street work just like the men. Very different is the position of the real "lady." She had to lose her feet and go limping around.

Catt had arrived in China in late August 1912, an auspicious time. The years since 1900 had been marked by an upsurge of nationalism, extension of education, expansion of the franchise, and growth of societies for various reforms—including the prohibition of opium, the abolition of footbinding, and for equal rights for women. There was a general modernization of government, industry, and society. The significant shift in the position and aspirations of women had been swift and dramatic. "Girls and young women played a prominent role in the revolutionary youth movement. China's new feminism took many forms. When the revolution broke out in Wuchang, it was the boatwomen of the Canton area who went to the revolutionary front, probably the first nurses ever assigned to Chinese troops in combat."[1]

Catt and Jacobs had heard rumors that women were voting and some were even members of provincial assemblies in China. They collected all the introductions they could and went to Canton determined that if they couldn't find voters they would at least find suffragists:

> We were carried to the only European hotel in the city in sedan chairs, the only conveyance to be had in Canton, and found abundant evidence that the city was under military rule, as guards armed with rifles were stationed in every street within a few rods of each other. The manager of the hotel insisted that we must take a guide as a precaution against foul play, and in a procession of three sedan chairs, each carried by three coolies, we started forth on our quest.
>
> One by one we made our calls, presented our letters and asked questions. We knew that each province in China had been granted a provisional Assembly, with the expectation that it would later become a permanent Provincial Legislature. No one could tell us where or when the Assembly for the Province of Canton might meet, nor of whom it was composed.
>
> At last a letter from the Dutch Consul General gave us a clue, which, traced to its source, brought us to a gallery from which we looked down upon the Assembly of Canton Province in session. Lo! there below us sat the women members of whom some of the most intelligent men and women in China had never heard! How we did gloat our wondering eyes upon them! The mercury was soaring somewhere near the top of the thermometer, the humidity was well-nigh unendurable and we had been drenched twice by tropical showers, but we forgot all the discomfort and fatigue, and gazed spellbound at this manifestation of the New China.
>
> The building was an old one, hastily repaired for the use of the Assembly. There was nothing Chinese nor even oriental about it. On a raised platform sat the Chairman and Secretary, and the members sat in a semicircle before them. The whole arrangement was Western. The differences were in the people.

Neither Catt nor Jacobs understood a word but noted every detail:

> Every member carried a fan, and the men wagged theirs diligently; the women rarely used theirs. About half the men wore European dress, the other half the native gown, usually made of silk. This is so long that a gentleman must lift it when he goes up stairs or crosses a muddy street. The women, like all other women in China, wore trousers. The men all wore light-colored garments; the women were all in black except one who wore dark blue. At least two had little deformed feet. The Speaker

and Secretary wore long white silk gowns and fanned themselves leisurely.

The members did not address the chair to gain the floor, but simply arose and began to talk. Just what would happen if the spirit should move two or more to pour forth their wisdom at the same time, as with us, I did not learn, as each speaker was politely listened to, until he finished. A few, as is usual everywhere, seemed to do the talking, and one orator who made many gestures wore bracelets. All was quiet, orderly and very earnest. The vote was taken by rising. We observed that the lady members did not always vote the same way.

We went next to the Cantonese Chairman of the Tung Ming Hui (the United Sworn Society organized about fifteen years ago by Dr. Sun Yat-sen), to whom we had also been given a letter. We found him most cordial, and when he learned that we wished to speak with the women members of the Assembly, he promptly invited us to take supper at his house and promised to get as many of the women as he could.

He issued his invitations by telephone, and we shortly repaired to his house, where we met two women and two men members of the society. The ladies spoke Chinese only, but the young men had been educated in foreign schools and spoke English. While we ate our supper and put forth our first effort with chop sticks, the menu including the far-famed Chinese delicacy, shark's fins, frogs and other strange but tasty dishes, this is what we learned:

When the provisional government was formed upon the ruins of the Manchu regime, the Tung Ming Hui of Canton arranged for the election of the Assembly for that Province, the higher officials having been appointed by the provisional government at Peking.[2] Practically all men and women who chose to do so were allowed to vote for that Assembly, and it was ordered by those in authority that ten women should be elected, the whole number in the Assembly being one hundred and twenty. In reality few took interest or cognizance of the proceedings except the members of the Tung Ming Hui. The ten women were elected. One, a young woman, resigned, and is now on her way to America, where she will enter a college. In truth, her family opposed her serving, upon the ground that it was too bold and forward a position for a young woman. We saw and talked with her mother. This young lady is a Christian, but we believe the nine who accepted the charge are all Confucians. We saw eight of them.

The most curious part of the story is that the families of all of them were more or less rebellious over this sudden promotion of a female member to the dignity of lawmaker. The husbands of the married ones were quite unreconcilable to having their names made known to the world as the husbands of such prominent wives, for in China, as elsewhere, properly behaved women are supposed to be neither seen nor heard. They just said, "Very well, we won't disgrace you, we will just take our own names again while we are members of the Assembly"; so every woman is known as "Miss" although several are married.

Miss Wong Chin Cheong and Miss Lun Yin Wah are wives of officers; Miss Li Pui Lan and Miss Chong Han Kiu are wives of prominent merchants; Miss Tang Ngai Ning has been a government student in Japan; Misses Man Cheang Fong, Yik Yuet Yink and Cheong Yuen are teachers in the government Normal School for girls at Canton, and Miss Ng Kwai Sheong is a teacher.

The leaders of the Tung Ming Hui believe that women voted for the provisional Assembly in no other Province, and that there are no women members in any other Assembly, nor in the National Council. Woman suffrage was not granted by the provisional constitutional convention, so only men will vote at the coming elections. These have been postponed from time to time on account of the turbulent condition of the country, and are now fixed, but subject to further postponement, for January next.

Mr. Tse Ying Pak, chairman of the Tung Ming Hui in Canton, and at whose beautiful home we sat at table with Chinese women who had voted and with Chinese women who are members of the Assembly, is a liberal, broad-minded gentleman, in sympathy with the woman movement. He told us that the Society, which during the Revolution was transformed from a secret society into a political party, proposes to accomplish three great social changes in addition to the many material reforms on its program: 1, the complete annihilation of the practice of foot-binding; 2, the prohibition of opium smoking; 3, the elimination of girl slavery.

The first is practically accomplished, and the compressed feet have gone with the queues. The other two are more difficult. In Canton alone there are 200,000 girl slaves. Little girls from five to seven are sold by their parents for a few dollars. The buyer employs them as servants, and often treats them with great cruelty. Care enough is usually taken of them, however, to allow them to grow up in good condition, for at sixteen or seventeen they are sold again, and bring a hundred dollars for every dollar invested in them, if they are good looking and attractive. Sometimes they are sold as wives, sometimes as concubines, sometimes as prostitutes. These new Progressives realize as fully as any Westerner that a great people cannot be born of slave mothers, but cupidity, that most desperate, intriguing and successful enemy of all good causes, is set against it, and its elimination from Chinese life is not so easy as it may seem to an outsider.[3]

From Canton, Catt and Jacobs went to Shanghai and it was in the Palace Hotel there that they held their first suffrage meeting in China:

> We met nine splendid, sweet, refined, enthusiastic, hopeful, lovable young women, and three equally splendid young men. We told them about the Alliance and that we wanted to have China join it. We asked them what they had done and were doing. What a splendid story they told us. I almost had to pinch myself to make sure that I was alive. Really this day has been one of the happiest of my life—now I have shaken the hands of Mohammedan, Hindu, Buddhist and Confucian suffragists, and I've seen many a Christian missionary show contempt for the cause. How curious is the plan for the onward march of the world's army of humans! Now my dear Chinese suffragists are going to give me a recepton. And I am in China—China!!!

Catt did not use exclamation points often but in her excitement she splattered her diary with them.

During the reception given two days later, the Chinese women showed Catt the silk banner they were making for presentation to the Alliance at its next meeting in Budapest. In large Chinese characters embroidered in white on scarlet satin was the motto, "Helping each other, all of one mind." The women explained they wanted the help of foreign women, and in return they wanted to help them. Afterward,

> a long private talk with the President [of the Chinese Ladies' Mutual Helping Society which was responsible for the banner] and some of her officers cleared our minds on many points. There is no National Suffrage Association, and the women within the Tung Ming Hui have conducted the suffrage agitation in most places where it has taken place. The great distances between centers and the absence of newspapers in the interior, is the reason that the workers in one town do not even know the names of those in another, nor what has been done in any other community. In Europe and America there are no secrets concerning the National Government. Whatever Congress does one day is known the next day in the remotest little burg. Here, even the local leaders of the Republic are uncertain of the meaning of the brief despatches which come from Peking, and we are beginning to understand how it is possible for intelligent people to be so densely ignorant concerning things which are taking place under their very noses.[4]

The lack of information made an especially vivid impression on Catt whose early life had been spent on the American frontier, which everywhere was peppered with local newspapers.

She had spoken at another meeting in Shanghai, one arranged by the American Woman's Club, which was "not suffragistic in tendencies," but whose members dutifully entertained the famous American visitor. They were interested in first-hand accounts of the English suffragettes and their exploits. Catt obliged with a lecture on militancy and its occasional necessity. She said men gained attention during a labor strike when they broke windows and, "If the men could gain recognition by smashing windows, the militants argued that this was the logical thing for the women to do, and they did it and were arrested." She included a brief history of the movement in the United States and told something about the International Woman's Suffrage Alliance.[5]

Clearly her interests were with the Chinese women, not with these lukewarm Americans about whom she had little to say. She concluded her report of the exciting days, "We left Shanghai with the conviction that not the half had been told about these Chinese women, and with several clues which we must follow, and reports that we must verify."[6]

Not all of her visits were so gratifying. On the way north they stopped to see silk reeled from cocoons. The work was done by women helped by little girls who were sometimes slaves of the woman doing the reeling. "The mistress is often very cruel. One woman caught the child's hand and thrust it into the *boiling* water. But these women nearly all had bound feet. Poor things, their ungovernable tempers are proofs that they are not quite reduced to nothing." Another time she commented on the bound feet of workers in a cigarette factory, "but a compensating element is the freedom of the trousered legs." Catt's ebullience and acceptance of the Chinese women occasionally betrayed her into naiveté.

On their way from Shanghai to the capital city of Peking, Catt and Jacobs stopped in Nanking to see a suffragist and chanced to get a glimpse of famine refugees:

> I looked out from the bedroom window into a crowded nest of little straw huts with men, women and children here and there, resembling ants around their little mounds. In the foreground a woman with a baby on her hip and a little girl were grinding corn between a small "upper and nether millstone," as the women of Asia have been doing for thousands of years. It seemed a far cry to woman suffrage.
> When we found the object of our quest, Miss Wu Moh Lan, to

whom we had a letter, it was at the Headquarters of the woman's branch of the Tung Ming Hui, of which she is president, in a house of many inner courts. Here she received us, and through an interpreter we put our many questions.

The next day Miss Hui had arranged a meeting which was attended by about one hundred and fifty men and women. During the speeches Catt "noted particularly that the women present applauded with enthusiasm every allusion to their enfranchisement or expression of confidence in their abilities, while the men seemed rather patronizing."[7]

From Nanking they went up the Yangtse River to Hankow, then took the train to Peking, a week's trip. Peking was in some ways the climax of Catt's trip. She met there an ideal suffragist, Captain Sheng, about whom she wrote and spoke many times and whose autographed picture Catt treasured:

I met her at the Honan Club House in Peking one September day in 1912. She was a woman whose feet had been bound for awhile, but the order to unbind had come in time to keep her from being helplessly crippled. She was quite the greatest emotional orator I have ever heard. She spoke that day to a mixed audience of men and women and she made them laugh and cry. They were like so many children in her hands.

But more interesting by far than her oratorical gifts was the completeness of her vision of women's opportunity for service in the world. She saw it all—the equality of the sexes, the need of educational and industrial opportunity for women, one standard of sex morality, one law, one vote for all under the ideal republican form of government.

Listen to Dr. Anna Howard Shaw's most inspired utterances as they were expressed fifty years ago; turn to the pages of the *History of Woman Suffrage* and read what Susan B. Anthony had to say when the woman movement was young and what the leaders of half a century ago had to say. Their vision made clear to them what was certainly coming as a result of their own hard work and eloquent appeals. Exactly as their social philosophy was constructive and grounded in concern for the betterment of individual, of race, and sex, so was hers. Like them, she wanted women to be free and, like our leaders, her faith in woman and humanity was such that she saw clearly in freedom the liberation of what was highest and finest in her country and her people; not license, not the low and the sordid. Like them, she proposed a single standard of morality. She held firmly that men must climb up and that women must always refuse to go down.

I do not know what has become of Captain Sheng, but I do know

that the spirit of her preaching has gone into the current of influence
that is bearing the Chinese people and the world's women onward and
upward toward the haven of a better democracy than the world has yet
known.[8]

From Peking, Jacobs and Catt took an excursion to the Great Wall:

Standing on the top we looked over into Mongolia. That day we were
fortunate enough to see a caravan of at least 200 dromedaries—the
longest we had seen in Asia. For at least two thousand years these hills
upon which we stood had been mute witnesses of these dromedary
caravans bearing the products of exchange from East to West, and this
mighty wall had bounded China on the North. Now a railway will
shortly pierce these mountains, and already the glistening poles which
carry the telegraph wires may be traced as they climb over the mountains
and connect with the outside world. The view of these ancient and
modern wonders of the world side by side made more impression upon me
than anything I saw in China.

The last day of her stay in Peking Catt visited the National Council
where she noted, "Soldiers armed were in evidence there as elsewhere." It was
no wonder. Although Peking had been voted the capital of the provisional
government there were strong advocates for its being in Nanking and there
had been considerable political jockeying, particularly between the forces of
the first president of the unified Chinese Republic, Yuan Shih-k'ai, and Sun
Yat-sen. There had been a ferocious mutiny in Peking among soldiers sta-
tioned there and in neighboring areas, and large parts of Peking were looted
and burned. Mutinies were common during the years preceeding and continuing through 1912. Less than a month before Catt's visit, in August 1912,
troops devastated Tungchow, near Peking. Catt had called on the American
minister, William J. Calhoun, in Peking, and it was perhaps his suggestion
that she visit the parliament there. Calhoun was a supporter of Yuan, indeed
saw him as the only alternative to chaos.[9] Catt learned details of the situation
in Peking from Calhoun but there were no women in the National Parliament
and she was not impressed with it.

She had met several outstanding women in Peking and heard many
stories about their contributions to the new China. By the time she returned
to the United States, her exhilaration at finding so many enlightened and
able women in China had changed to indignant compassion for their position
as the revolution that these women had helped abandoned them:

When the Revolution was over many societies were organized, each had a program for the political future of the country. There was much working at cross purposes, and bitter feelings were engendered. At this juncture Dr. Sun went to Peking and succeeded in uniting five of these societies into the National Party, Kui Ming Tong [later known as the Kuomintang]. The Tung Ming Hui was the largest and the strongest, but when the others would not endorse woman suffrage, Dr. Sun, with no apparent regret, threw it out of the program of the united party. Of course the women were there to plead for different treatment, but with the usual result. A prominent newspaper correspondent told me that in an interview which he had with Dr. Sun, that gentleman told him that he would give no advice to the Government concerning woman suffrage, and that he was quite indifferent as to whether it was adopted or not. Before the Revolution his opinion was positively favorable. In other words, the Chinese women have been "sold out," as the women of the West have been many times.

We women of the West would have known this would happen, but these women of the Orient are different. They have known sorrows unthinkable, but there are others that they must know before they attain their liberty. They looked backward upon two thousand years and more of wrongs to their sex, with its bound feet, uneducated brain, and its cramped unnatural life. Ahead they saw the open door leading to opportunity, education, liberty, happiness, and they dreamed of guarding this entrance that all future Chinese women might pass through. To this end they offered their energies, their fortunes and their lives. Through that same door they now see their fellow revolutionists marching, some forgetful of their very existence, others superciliously looking back upon them with looks which say, "We have no further need of you. Go back to the place you came from."

To say that these women are desperate is to put it mildly. All of them have been shocked and surprised at the treatment they have received. Some are discouraged, some philosophically courageous, some indignantly unreconciled.

The old Revolutionary organization is following the usual course, now that its work is done, and is apparently being merged into a political party. The women's branches are being held together with a view to the formation of a national organization.

Catt discussed at length the indignation of the women who had fought in the Revolution but were now being pushed back into subservience. She saw them organizing to get the vote, to get education and job opportunities, to eliminate marriage laws and customs "which condemn a woman to slavery from birth to death," to wipe out the system of concubinage "which cheapens and humiliates women," and to abolish girl slavery. These women fought to establish a new government and "they may find it necessary to make war upon this government to get recognition. They will stop at nothing, and least of all at the possibility of death."

Catt marveled at the women's intelligence, tenacity, and courage. "Their grasp of all that suffrage means is remarkable. I can only hope that the leaders will not lose their lives in their campaign."[10]

After China, the last phase of the trip to Korea and Japan was anti-climactic. Catt held a few meetings in Japan, but her most memorable experience was going to "Yoshiwara, the famous Red Light District of Tokyo." She and Jacobs had made a survey of prostitution throughout their trip; both wrote and lectured against "white slavery" for many years:

> I shall never forget those rows of faces behind the bar, each expressive of the most unutterable sorrow! nor the hard men at the windows—a type unlike any other we have seen. Five thousand girls are there, and it is reckoned that when licensed and unlicensed prostitutes and geishas are counted there are two millions of them. The geishas, pretty girls, are trained in all the ways of coquetry, and are the real, though innocent enemies of the wife and home. She is only plying her own trade to which her parents have sold her. O Man! are you human or devil? I wonder![11]

Aside from that excursion and further research on prostitution, the trip to Japan was one of great beauty and pleasure. However, letters awaiting Catt in Yokohama convinced her she should return to the States as soon as possible. Jacobs and Catt parted company, Catt to go home via Honolulu and San Francisco, Jacobs to Vladivostok, where she would take the trans-Siberian railroad to Holland. Catt summarized their personalities and their time together:

> We joined each other at Madeira, July 20, 1911, and for one year and three months, we have been strenuously endeavoring to see the world. Our education and experience in life had been wholly different, and we therefore approached many things with a different point of view. We had many a fierce altercation. We usually put aside such quarrels each firm in the belief that she was right, but both I am confident learned much from each other because of the difference in education. We were both strong-willed, stubborn, opinionated, yet we came through firm friends, and I at least with a warm and sincere admiration for her. Her devotion to the

cause of her sex, her fund of general information on side lines, her strong memory, her calm judgment, her unceasing energy, combine to make her a truly wonderful and great woman.

Catt spent two days in Honolulu, and spoke at one meeting attended by the governor and his wife. She was eager to get home; she had articles and lectures to write but most important, she needed time to think about what she had seen. "I've had at least a million new facts poured into my brain—many of them startlingly upsetting and I really must have time to digest them. I long for solitary confinement at hard labor in my own house for a good long while but I fear I shall not get it."[12]

The trip was a crucial experience. It had broadened her vision and her goals. She recognized her growth and looked back at herself with a clear eye: "Once I was a regular jingo but that was before I had visited other countries. I had thought America had a monopoly on all that stands for progress, but I had a sad awakening."[13]

During the long days at sea Catt had almost persuaded herself she would abandon the suffrage fight and devote herself to ethnology, a latent interest that had been quickened by the trip. Realistically she knew now more than ever that dogged devotion to the cause was imperative and nothing must stand in the way. Her public responsibilities took precedence over private desires:

We have made suffrage speeches to audiences on four continents: America, Europe, Africa, Asia, and on the ships of three oceans. Our audiences have included the followers of every main religion, Christian and Jew, Mohammedan, Hindu, Parsee, Buddhist, Confucian, and Shinto, and representatives of all the main human races: Aryan, Semitic, Negro, Malay, Polynesian, Mongolian. We have left the seeds of revolution behind us, and the hope of liberty in many souls. But we have got much more than we gave—an experience so upsetting to all our preconceived notions that is it difficult to estimate its influence upon us. I sincerely pray that some degree of blessing this trip has been to me may be given to others, and especially that I may be able to convey to others the intensified conviction that the Cause of Woman cannot wait. I am tired and I would like to retire from the work and the worry, but if I can bring the result one thousandth of a second sooner by my work, I must keep at it.

· 12 ·
One Cause

When Catt arrived in San Francisco on November 4, 1912, for the first time California women were voting in a national election. Suffrage was won there in October 1911, and then in Arizona, Kansas, and Oregon during 1912, bringing the total of equal suffrage states to ten. All four successes were attributed to the soundness of organizing on precinct lines and relentless campaigning.

Catt's first task was to use these victories to build up enthusiasm and hope in the New York campaign. In the following June she planned to go to Europe to observe the militants carefully in London and then attend the large IWSA congress in Budapest. There was a global sweep about her plans; she had no way of knowing this would be the last year such plans were possible before war.

Catt's first New York meeting was on November 19, when Carnegie Hall was crowded with suffragists flushed with renewed expectation. "This battle for equal justice is not for ourselves alone," she told them, "but for the women of the entire world. Kipling says, 'The West is the West and the East is the East, and never the twain shall meet.' This may be so in men's affairs, but it is not true in women's. Our Cause is one." She was making every effort to give the New York campaign the significance and purpose of a worldwide crusade. A second welcoming meeting was held December 3 at Cooper Union, where she gave a more detailed speech on "The Awakening of Woman around the World."[1]

In the meantime Philadelphia had hosted jubilant meetings at the forty-fourth annual convention of the National American Woman Suffrage Association for a week beginning November 21. The range of interests represented by the women present showed the steadily widening base of the cause. Alva Belmont was there with her support of militancy, Alice Paul and Lucy Burns told horror tales about the forcible feeding of suffragettes in England's prisons. Jane Addams and Catt spoke on the need for political power in the hands of women to combat prostitution. Nobel Prize winner, the German Baroness

Bertha von Suttner, and Lucia Ames Mead reported on women and peace. Julia Lathrop, Chief of the National Children's Bureau, talked about the relation of child welfare to votes for women. Jessie Ashley and Leonora O'Reilly demanded votes to get working women a living wage. Capacity audiences filled the great Metropolitan Opera House. Socialist and socialite seemed for once united in one cause.[2]

After five months of work Catt glowed with health and seemed accessible to everyone. In January Anna Shaw wrote to Aletta Jacobs, "I have seen Mrs. Catt only two or three times since she returned, but it has been a joy every time I have seen her. She seems so much better in every way, so much more get-at-able. If you know what I mean by that. She is more human and in all she says has a more human touch."[3]

Before Catt left for Europe in April, she experienced for the first time some of the indignities endured by suffragettes in England during demonstrations. By London standards she was involved in a small incident but it gave her an inkling of the reasons for suffragette fury. In Washington, D.C., on March 3, the day before Wilson's first inauguration, several thousand suffragists marched down Pennsylvania Avenue in a show of strength. Catt was leading the first section, called the World-Wide Movement for Woman Suffrage. Insolent, jeering spectators began snatching flags from the women, pushing and crowding them. The suffragists felt threatened and unprotected by the police who "were totally inefficient and plainly hostile to the parade. Some one telephoned out to the fort and a troop of cavalry soon cleared the street."

At an indignation meeting immediately following the parade, Catt and others urged that Congress investigate the episode. She said that many of the men along the line were drunk enough to be locked up and she was incensed that the women of America were forced to take their appeal for the vote to such people. After a four-day Senate hearing the chief of police was fired but that brought little satisfaction to anyone.[4]

When Catt arrived in London on April 28, acts of suffragette militancy had multiplied since her last visit; arson, hunger striking, and forced feeding were common. Every newspaper brought reports of new violence against property by the suffragettes, or new acts of violence against them by police and prison guards. When she had been in London two weeks Catt wrote:

> On my first night in London I found myself at a militant meeting with Mrs. Belmont! Mr. [Israel] Zangwill [a liberal writer] made the chief speech [against forcible feeding]. It was scholarly, eloquent, thrilling and

revolutionary! The audience went wild with enthusiasm and revolt was in the air. Of late the police have pretended they could not protect the women's meetings in the Park. A young docker spoke and declared that if the police would keep away he and his friends could keep the peace there. I believe it. It is the case of the Washington parade over again.[5]

The suffrage campaign in the United States is a dull and commonplace affair when compared with the sizzling white heat of the British struggle. I chanced to arrive in the midst of a particularly interesting, and apparently crucial, period, and set to work with diligence to learn its meaning so far as I could.[6]

Three entries from her diary illustrate:

May 1, 1913. Mrs. Coit took me to an auction room where a large silver cup was sold, the article having been seized by the Government in lieu of the taxes refused by the Duchess of Bedford. In the afternoon I went to the Portman Rooms to a meeting of protest in her behalf. After that we visited Hyde Park where the Socialists were holding worldwide May Day demonstrations. After dinner I retired, fatigued and convinced that England is on the verge of a revolution.

May 2. I went to the Drury Lane theater where the Actresses League were holding a meeting and where I was to speak. Lady Willoughby de Broke presided. The most interesting thing was the disorder in a high class educated audience. Mrs. Arncliffe Sennett endorsed militancy. The house cheered and hissed. Then Miss Irene Van Brugh attempted to say she was opposed and in the confusion created by both sides she sat down. I thot about ⅓ were militants ⅓ constitutionals and ⅓ neutral. The audience talked back all the time and it was all in all the most disorderly meeting I ever saw.

May 3. I went with Miss Furuhjelm to the famous Bow St. Police Station. Miss Kenney and Mrs. Drummond were discharged as another charge was out against them. Geo. Lansbury was tried for inciting speeches. In the eve we went with Dr. and Mrs. Coit to the theater and heard *The Great Adventure* by Bennet and took midnight supper at the Carlton. It was a great day.[7]

The next day Catt went to Hyde Park where suffrage meetings "which sprung up like mushrooms all over the green [were] rushed and broken up [by the police]."[8]

During those first two weeks in London Catt attended seventeen highly charged suffrage meetings and relished them but realized that she herself was not a militant. She did not think the tactics were a substitute for constitutional methods. In the long run, certainly in the United States, she knew militancy would make more enemies than friends. The political structure made the situation different in Great Britain and it was irrational for a visitor to criticize.[9]

As Catt saw it, breaking windows and burning houses did not help woman suffrage. However, there were important questions of human rights, which transcended the acts of property damage. Militancy was focusing attention on official discrimination against women and their supporters. In the beginning the women had put questions to members of the government at public meetings in the accepted spirit and manner. They found themselves in prison, although a British man would have been permitted to act as the women had without a question. The government's discrimination against women was so blatant that it aroused more to action, followed by repeated government overreaction, and the situation grew steadily worse.

"Two wholly new and fundamental questions arose out of the matter," Catt wrote. "One, have the women of Great Britain a right to petition; the other, should these women who are manifestly political prisoners be put in the criminal division? These militants are not 'criminals,' 'hysterical fanatics' nor 'notoriety seekers,'" she insisted. When she viewed suffragettes collectively she could see them as heroic with "motives of the highest and purest and that they are swayed by loyalty and devotion to the great cause of human rights." When she saw them as individuals she was ambivalent. She considered Emmeline Pankhurst to be the John Brown of the suffrage movement: "My heart aches for that woman who is either a liberator of her sex or a serious trouble maker. Time will tell which."

The power structure was different in Britain and the United States. In the United States women depended on men to vote for their suffrage; in Great Britain their franchise depended on the Prime Minister as head of the government. Catt explained the difference: "We have to get rid of the oldest and hardest prejudice in all history: your fight is against one man, ours against a majority of men; yours is a battle, ours an evolution; yours is picturesque and very tragic, ours is commonplace but sure."

Part of her investigation was her visit to the gallery of the House of Commons. She called it a hen coop where people had to sit doubled up like half-closed jackknives. By craning her neck she could see Prime Minister Asquith, "whose anti-suffrage attitude has immortalized him." Her friends were amused that her handbag was searched for bombs by the police before she was admitted to hear the suffrage debate in Parliament.[10]

After a month in London Catt left on a stately progress arranged by Rosika Schwimmer along a route similar to their triumphant lecture tour four years before: Berlin, Dresden, Prague, Vienna, then down the Danube by boat to Budapest. At each stop there were meetings, receptions, and entertainments, and more delegates joined the entourage. There was still discrimination against women everywhere and the Alliance brought the full force of its speakers and publicity against it.

Along the way there was one unhappy reminder of the battles of the suffragette "war" in London. Emily Wilding Davison had thrown herself under the King's horse at the Derby. "She had long believed that the deliberate giving of a woman's life would create the atmosphere necessary to win the victory, and bring all the suffering of the militants to an end," explained Sylvia Pankhurst, who called it a deed of infinite majesty. Catt heard the news of Davison's sacrifice in Berlin; four days later in Vienna news came of her death. Catt arranged for a memorial service in Budapest led by Annie Cobden Sanderson, a militant who had gone to prison in 1908 for her part in the first demonstration outside the House of Commons.[11]

In her call to the seventh congress of the International Woman Suffrage Alliance in June 1913, Catt had boasted: "For the first time in the woman movement, it is expected that Hindu, Buddhist, Confucian, Mohammedan, Jewish and Christian women will sit together in a Congress uniting their voices in a common plea for the liberation of their sex from those artificial discriminations which every political and religious system has directed against them." She recognized that the Balkan War then being fought was engrossing her colleagues there but she wanted their delegates at Budapest "that the common sisterhood of the world's women may be complete."[12]

The 1913 Congress was the largest the Alliance had held. Although the official delegates were limited to twelve from each country, it was estimated that with alternate delegates, associate members, and fraternal delegates, attendance totaled about 500. The world's press had 230 representatives and for the first time the speeches were recorded—on gramophone records. The remainder of the 2,800 present were visitors, mostly from Hungary, but from other European countries and the United States as well. Catt proudly reported that standing room was filled at all the public sessions, and for one session an overflow meeting was hastily organized. All social classes participated in the meetings, from Hungarian and British aristocracy to Transylvanian peasants.

"With the exception of the Spanish American Republics, there are in the entire world only seven constitutionally organized, independent nations without an organized woman suffrage movement," Catt announced. Three were in Europe—Greece, Spain, and the Grand Duchy of Luxemburg—the others were Liberia, Turkey, Persia, and Japan. China was admitted to the Alliance, bringing the number to twenty-five nations plus two additional countries without full national rights. "The standard of the Alliance was set upon five continents."[13]

The admission of the Chinese association signaled a step toward improved status in at least part of Asia. Delegates from China had been expected but the explosive political situation at home kept them there. Aletta Jacobs presented the scarlet satin banner from the Chinese suffragists in an emotion-charged ceremony. "You cannot imagine how hard the struggle for liberty is in which these women have to fight," she said. "Many of the Chinese women have already been decapitated for the truth they told while fighting their battle for freedom, and all the leaders of the woman movement know that their life is uncertain, and that any day the men may find a reason to silence them when their eloquence and their enthusiasm makes too many converts."[14]

To the delight of the delegates and the press, several Transylvanian peasants with shawls over their heads had walked the long way to Budapest. "I thought it the most wonderful and curious thing I had ever seen," Catt said. They said they had come because they wanted to vote and they wanted to see the women of more advanced countries, especially the Americans. Five years later when Transylvania, then part of Rumania, was to have its first Constitutional Assembly elected by universal suffrage of women and men, Catt remembered the occasion and remarked, "They won the ballot before we ourselves have secured it!"[15]

In Budapest she was happy to announce that five states and the territory of Alaska had enfranchised women since the last Alliance meeting. During the convention came news that Illinois had on June 11 voted presidential suffrage to women, the first state east of the Mississippi to do so, and thus a key victory.

In her presidential address, Catt conceded some disappointments but not defeats. "When movements are new and weak, Parliaments laugh at them; when they are in their educational stages, Parliaments meet them with silent contempt; when they are ripe and ready to become law, Parliaments evade responsibility. Our movement has reached the last stage," she assured the Alliance. She spoke at length about her trip around the world, reviewing the situation of women and spluttering with indignation at their status, especially at the enforced prostitution she had found.

Jane Addams made a major speech on prostitution after which Catt proposed two resolutions requesting all governments to institute an international investigation into the extent and causes of commercialized vice. She urged the Alliance's support of the resolutions with an impassioned plea:

> When you take away from a class all its privileges, the right to earn money, the right of education, of free speech, of free publication you have made them if not slaves, economic dependents, you have placed them in a position where they may be commercialized, and it is because of this fact that we have the condition of commercialized vice. You and I may be educated, we may even have the vote, but as long as down there at the bottom there are other women, you and I are cheapened, we have not yet been emancipated. I believe the vote is the weapon we need with which to accomplish these greater ends, but the women of the world will never be emancipated until this abominable evil has been removed.[16]

The resolutions passed unanimously.

The complaint that the Women's Social and Political Union was not represented was again raised. Once again the Alliance stated its position that each country should be represented by one organization or consortium of associations. Once again they passed a resolution stating that in countries where free speech, free press, and the freedom to organize politically existed, women could best get their rights by the energetic use of those freedoms according to the laws of such countries.

Almost everyone who wrote about this conference remarked on Catt's brilliant handling of the potentially divisive issue of militancy and her diplomacy in averting an open split.[17] She was determined to give up the presidency of the IWSA but was persuaded to remain in charge for another term by an overwhelming show of support. The delegates of all the countries signed an address assuring her of their love and esteem and begging her to reconsider her intention to resign. The whole meeting rose and remained standing while the address was being read. She seemed to be the only one who could keep the Alliance together. It was the old question of infighting again, this time on an international scale—the mutual suspicion of the European continent and Great Britain.

Charlotte Perkins Gilman's strongest impression of the conference was of the growing breadth and depth of the movement: "It is no longer an academic question, a question of abstract right and justice, or a general claim of 'the ennobling influence of women.' Women are becoming very definite at last as to things they want to do, and are becoming more and more convinced that the ballot is necessary to the achievement of those purposes."[18]

Keir Hardie, British Socialist leader and M.P., attended the congress and reported that it had turned most of the labor men, Socialists, and trade unionists in Hungary into believers in woman suffrage.[19]

Catt met Dr. Alexander Geiswein, a Catholic priest and member of the Hungarian Parliament, who was almost alone among Hungarian priests in advocating suffrage for women. After the meetings his hopes for universal suffrage were much brighter. She always remembered having "a little supper" with him in Budapest when "he brought the tears to my eyes when he made a little speech and said the United States of Europe was the only way to bring peace."[20]

Budapest held a special memory for all the participants as the last Alliance conference before their world was devastated. Catt did her best during the war years to keep the Alliance together; there was inevitably deep bitterness when the women met again in 1920. They looked back at 1913 as a time of beauty and hopefulness.

Catt often spoke of the "wonderful, beautiful Congress at Budapest. It must have had a great deal to do with the movement afterwards which gave the vote to so many women. None of us think that the enfranchisement of women has brought any very great change to the world, but it might have been different if we had not had a war."[21]

ROAD TO VICTORY
1913–1920

Carrie Chapman Catt at victory celebration following ratification of the Nineteenth Amendment, August 1920

· 13 ·
New York

New York State was both the hope and the despair of suffragists. It was the home of the movement but also the stronghold of opposition. It had the biggest population of any state in the Union, the largest number of representatives in Congress. If New York were won there would probably be enough suffrage strength in Washington, D.C. to force debate on the issue. No longer could any politician say to suffragists, as Theodore Roosevelt had as late as 1908, "Go, get another State." The building, financing, and directing of an army of volunteers skillful and aggressive enough to get a suffrage amendment passed in New York was Catt's central concern for the next several years.

Meanwhile friends in other regions and states needed her advice. Would she come? A play about white slavery, George Scarborough's *The Lure*, was threatened with forced closing because its subject was deemed immoral. Would she defend it? In the NAWSA executive a crisis was beginning to crest over methods. Would she support the traditionalists? The International Alliance was polarizing as Europe moved toward war. What could be done by suffragists for peace? She received as many as twenty-five requests to speak on a single day. To all of these demands on her time she responded as she could, but the building of a New York machine went on.

It was imperative to use the momentum given to the movement in June 1913, when presidential suffrage had passed the Illinois legislature in a cliffhanging session. The state suffrage association had hit upon the idea of getting as much suffrage as the legislature could bestow—the vote for many state and local offices, and more important, the vote for presidential electors. This would eliminate the costly, long, and difficult referendum campaign. The suffragists had brilliant leadership: Grace Wilbur Trout, the state president who suggested the new strategy; Catharine Waugh McCulloch, a lawyer who drew up the bill; Ruth Hanna McCormick, later a Congresswoman, who directed publicity; and Elizabeth Booth, who ran the campaign.

Booth said that she knew nothing about practical politics but she could make people feel comfortable and talkative. She rode trains in and out of Springfield, meeting and chatting with legislators, then sat in the gallery and watched them at work. She pasted the photograph of each legislator on a card and recorded everything she could find out about political connections, business, family, interests, and foibles. One by one she began committing them to the cause. The result was a uniquely inconspicuous, personal campaign and the invention of the lobbyists' most formidable tool, the index-card file system. Booth even went to a leader of the opposition, explained that she knew he was committed to vote against woman suffrage, but understood that he was a gentleman of his word, and asked only for his word that he would not attack the suffragists' campaign. He was charmed, gave his word and from time to time excellent professional advice. In the last few minutes during the voting after the third reading of the suffrage bill, Booth discovered that seven men pledged to vote for them were missing. She fluttered a note down to her friendly enemy on the floor. The seven legislators appeared in the nick of time and the suffrage bill won.[1]

Elating and important as the victory was in Illinois, it gave women presidential, but not full suffrage. In Pennsylvania, New Jersey, Massachusetts, and New York, where referenda in 1915 were pending, women were seeking full suffrage, which required approval of all the voters, not just the legislators. Many lawmakers considered that submitting a referendum was easier for them since it passed the responsibility to the voters.

Almost all of the New York woman suffrage societies pledged to support the Empire State Campaign Committee,[2] and under Catt's leadership worked through the chiefs of the twelve campaign districts. There was a leader for each of the sixty-three assembly districts, and a captain for each of the 2,127 election districts. "Victory in 1915" was the slogan. Every worker tried to know every saloon, school, business, factory, club, and brothel, every street, lane, and highway in her precinct. Catt did not want an inch of the state unassigned or a voter who could plead ignorance of the cause. She started with a school for the basic training of the volunteers in parliamentary practice, organization, public speaking, suffrage history, and practical politics.

By the end of September there were a hundred thousand members of New York City's Woman's Suffrage Party, of which Mary Garrett Hay was president. Fifty celebrations were held in as many parks to cheer the old members and to get new ones.

At a huge Thanksgiving rally in Carnegie Hall to raise money, Catt gave a rousing speech in her old style:

Twenty-five years ago I began to work for the enfranchisement of women. They said at that time that they were afraid of the masses of women who would vote. In these twenty-five years they have admitted to these shores and given citizenship to more men—foreigners—than there were women of the voting age in this country when I first began to work for their enfranchisement. And they still say to the women, "There are too many of you." Reason will stand no more. We are going to be a government of the people or know the reason why.[3]

She no longer railed at foreigners but against the inequities of her own government.

The annual NAWSA convention in the same month was marked by controversy over the successful and widely publicized campaign of the Congressional Committee, which had been chaired by Alice Paul for the past year. This was the lobbying arm of the NAWSA but for years the only thing it had done was to arrange for the annual suffrage hearings where congressional committees "met with them in silent contempt." A woman suffrage amendment had not been voted on in the Senate since 1887, had never been voted on in the House, and had not even been reported out of committee after 1896; the hearings had become exercises in futility. At the Philadelphia NAWSA convention in 1912, three earnest young women had asked the Executive Board to appoint them to the Congressional Committee. The Board agreed. Alice Paul, Crystal Eastman Benedict, and Lucy Burns, joined by Mary Beard and Dora Lewis brought new vigor to the weary committee.[4]

Alice Paul had first come to the attention of the national suffrage association at the 1910 convention when she told of her experiences in England. A graduate student there, she had joined the Pankhurst suffragettes, sharing with them arrest, jail, and forcible feeding. She and another American, Lucy Burns, who had an even longer record of militancy and arrests, met in London. Burns stayed on, became a salaried organizer in Scotland for two years, and had come back to the States shortly before the 1912 NAWSA convention. A fiery, redheaded Irish activist, she later claimed the distinction of serving more time in jail than any other American feminist. Paul was a superb publicist and able fund-raiser. Burns was an outstanding organizer. She had been responsible for the suffrage parade in Washington in March 1913, which ended in riot; the cavalry was called out, and it made front-page news.

After that famous parade the Congressional Committee had formed a support group they named the Congressional Union; the two became inextricable. Paul had agreed to raise money necessary for the extensive plans she had for her Congressional Committee and legitimately made her appeals on behalf of a NAWSA committee. However, the Congressional Union was seen as a separate suffrage organization by the National, not just an adjunct to Paul's committee, and when the Union used money raised for the Committee, dissension flared. Paul saw it as proper, while the National contended that people had supported the Committee to help the NAWSA, not the Union. At the 1913 convention, Paul presented her report of the year's work as chair of the Congressional Committee and president of the Congressional Union, saying it was impossible to separate the work of the two.

Catt thought the Committee funding should have come from the National, and wanted clarification of the Committee-Union relationship. Lobbying was a full-time job and the chairperson should not be leading another suffrage organization as well, she contended. She and Paul talked policy together on two occasions after the convention and agreed to disagree.

While money was the immediate cause of dissension, the basic problem was the far-reaching one of method. Paul and Burns adopted the British policy of holding the party in power responsible. It was the Democratic party that was responsible for suffrage inaction in the current Congress, hence, attack the Democrats and oppose their election. The National had friends and enemies in all parties and insisted on remaining nonpartisan.

Congressional Committee members refused to be answerable to the National Board on this basic tenet and demanded freedom in adopting any action or method they saw fit. NAWSA disowned the Congressional Union and a new Congressional Committee was appointed, chaired by Ruth Hanna McCormick, who had helped lead the Illinois suffragists to victory.

Catt saw the division as inevitable and from a remark quoted by Anna Howard Shaw seemed to suspect that Paul had become overfond of publicity, an addiction to which militants are often prone. "Mrs. Catt said to me the other day that she had been looking for some time to a division among the suffragists of this country," wrote Shaw, "and that the militants and the militant-sympathizers would gather into one group while those of us who really want suffrage and not advertising would gather in another."[5]

Although animosity between Catt and Paul grew over the next few years, Catt remained on cordial terms with some of Paul's workers. Mary Beard told Catt, "I have always considered you so big because you have not considered those who differed with you as necessarily beneath contempt. You, I know, will at least give me credit for honest intent if not for good sense."[6] Catt occasionally showed a glint of envy for wilder ways—one could not work long in suffrage with male chauvinists without wanting to break something. For the time being, forbearance brought more to the cause.

Throughout 1914 the suffrage work in New York State accelerated as the Empire State Campaign was organized and agitation begun. Catt had little to do with the work of the National Association but international work continued to engross her along with the state drive. However, in June she won two significant nationwide endorsements for woman suffrage from very conservative groups.

The first came after she addressed the biennial meeting of the Federation of Women's Clubs in Chicago. The Women's Clubs as a whole had been notoriously suspicious of suffrage organizations; Catt remembered that in Iowa equal franchise associations were not allowed to join because "No club with a purpose could be admitted." Her speech was deliberately reassuring and she reiterated her basic conviction: "Women are not in rebellion against men. They are in rebellion against worn-out traditions." She appealed to her audience's sense of duty: "It is no longer a question of right for women to have a vote; it is the question of duty, duty of motherhood, to take care of the race."[7]

Another important expression of support came from the National Education Association. For years it had postponed decision by keeping a suffrage resolution in committee. Catt's address to them in 1902 had been so bold that it took them more than a decade to decide they favored woman suffrage as well as equal pay for equal work.

Catt left New York in late June for an IWSA board meeting in London. The problem they met to consider was the position of the societies in countries where suffrage had been won. They wanted to reorganize as civic leagues but did not want to cut themselves off from the worldwide bond holding women together.

Catt spent a hectic four weeks in London. Suffragette militancy had continued in spite of increased use of the Cat and Mouse Act under which hunger strikers were released from jail when their health seemed precarious but were rearrested as soon as they recovered. Cases of arson by the suffragettes were frequently reported but the emphasis shifted perceptibly from suffrage agitation to war propaganda during July 1914. On July 14 Catt and Annie Furuhjelm, the Finnish M.P., spoke to Parliament, the first time a woman legislator had addressed them. Catt's appeal was to the supporters of woman suffrage to lift the great question to a higher plane, beyond the reach of the smaller motives that agitate party politics. The world was awaiting the full attainment of this great civilizing influence, she said.

Unfortunately, the world was awaiting other things, but few people were aware how close Europe was to war. The IWSA scheduled the next congress for Berlin in 1915, and spent much time discussing publicity and press coverage. Catt went to suffrage meetings and talked with other feminists about their mutual problems. "I've tried to learn something helpful in the way of money raising," she wrote to a friend in mid-July,

> but they do not seem to know anything more than we do and that isn't much. Our plan of campaign is far and away ahead of anything here, but our plan may never get carried out, in which case we cannot boast about it. The National Union is doing splendid constructive work however. Sylvia [Pankhurst] has cut quite loose from the WSPU and has formed a separate organization and the [Pethick] Lawrences have formed another. The parent body still has women enough to burn churches and horse-whip members of the Cabinet and they still keep their big house as headquarters. They have even issued a financial statement last year and they did not have so much money as the N.U. Time was that they had more money and paid workers than the non militants.[8]

Just before Catt left London, the British government banned the display of one of the IWSA posters. Designed by a popular Hungarian artist, Willy Pogany, it gave statistics of the lower infant mortality in Commonwealth countries that had woman suffrage and depicted a mother defending her child from a figure of death. The poster was banned because "skulls make people nervous." Catt wrote ironically that ten days later "the British government voted a billion and a quarter dollars to support a war in which many a field will be sowed with bleaching skulls of 'the best we breed.' "[9]

Catt was on the *Kaiser Wilhelm II* bound for New York on July 31 when Germany and Russia mobilized and, within twenty-four hours, were at war. On August 3 Germany declared war on France and the following day German troops crossed the Belgian frontier and Great Britain entered the war. The next day Catt told reporters when she arrived in New York that "if women had had the vote in all the countries now at war the conflict would have been prevented."[10]

She was gratified to learn later that the British members of the IWSA had constituted themselves representatives of all members, offering shelter and help to German women in Britain who suddenly were "enemy aliens." *Jus Suffragii* continued to be published throughout the war and showed sympathy with the plight of women on both sides. The Alliance was "pledged to preserve absolute neutrality on all questions that are strictly national." Women's grief knew no national boundaries.

Catt had been home only a week when Fanny Garrison Villard called her to a meeting of one hundred leaders of women's organizations to plan a peace parade. Catt did not like the idea—women marching in New York could have no effect whatsoever on Europe at war. She suggested instead that they get the International Council of Women and the IWSA to support President Wilson's offer to help negotiate a peace.[11]

In spite of her protests, she helped with plans and joined the two thousand women in black who marched somberly down Fifth Avenue to the beat of muffled drums on a wet, gloomy August 29, 1914. Above them floated a white banner with a dove and an olive branch. The sight was deeply moving. Men took off their hats and many of the observers burst into tears. Even the *New York Times,* which had sneered at the plan, reported the event with awed respect. The peace parade was a symbolic funeral for all the lives, hopes, and possibilities the world war would destroy.

Although Catt was committed to the most elaborate state suffrage campaign ever fought, for the next several months she divided her time between the suffrage and peace movements. "It is votes women must demand if they would abolish the horrors, the waste, the barbarism of war, and usher in the blessings of peace."[12]

Early in September Rosika Schwimmer, who had been in London for the IWSA board meeting when war broke out, came to stay with Catt. She brought a petition that had been endorsed by women and men all over the world addressed to President Wilson urging him to offer continuous mediation to the belligerent governments. The appeal also contained plans for world reorganization that she believed would ensure permanent peace.

Catt had access to the White House by this time and arranged an audience with the president. On September 19 Wilson received from Catt and Schwimmer the first official international petition asking him to lead the movement to end war. He assured them of his interest but promised nothing.[13] Schwimmer was deeply disappointed and immediately went on a lecture tour to generate support for the peace plans.

A few weeks later Catt wrote to her, "You may well despair over the prospect of anything worth while being done for peace. Just now the whole country is alive and stirring over the raising of funds for the refugees, especially the Belgians. That is what the world has always done, it has relieved the victims of distress but never does anything to remove the cause of distress."[14]

Meanwhile, Emmeline Pethick-Lawrence was also on the peace lecture circuit that autumn of 1914, and she often shared a platform with Schwimmer. Catt valued Pethick-Lawrence as "a pioneer in the suffrage movement, introducing into it a certain spirituality which the movement has gained and retained ever since. I always have believed her to be the greatest woman suffrage editorial writer the movement has produced. She seems just as good on a peace mission."[15]

As a result of the Pethick-Lawrence and Schwimmer lectures, emergency committees for peace were formed in Boston, New York, Philadelphia, Cleveland, Nashville, St. Paul, and Chicago. By mid-December the committee members were clamoring for action. Schwimmer was back in New York staying with Catt, and with Anna Garlin Spencer's help she persuaded Catt to write Jane Addams suggesting that women conduct more demonstrations.

Catt thought the suffragists should not be the prime movers in peace demonstrations because they were pushing hard for the vote and she did not want to deflect them when victory seemed in sight. Her idea was that Addams should call for peace rallies, getting one woman in each city to take the initiative. Catt offered to undertake it in New York. She would not head the movement but, she wrote, "I will get the right people to do it and will give my assistance to it. At such meetings I think the manifesto should be a protest against the movement to increase our national armament upon the ground that we are in danger of attack." These arrangements should be carried out by women because the major peace organizations were "very masculine in their point of view."[16]

Addams replied a week later proposing they unite with a demonstration that some Washington, D.C. women were planning, rather than have simultaneous displays in several cities. She agreed with Catt "as to the masculine management of the existing Peace Societies. I have been identified with them for years, and while I believe that men and women work best together on these public measures, there is no doubt that at this crisis the women are most eager for action." Addams concluded by confiding her trepidation, "I am undertaking all this with a certain sinking of the heart, knowing how easy it is to get a large body of women togther and how difficult it is to take any wise action among many people who do not know each other well. The demand however has been tremendously spontaneous, and widespread, which should give us confidence."[17]

The gathering of women for peace was not without dissension and to her dismay Catt found herself unwillingly in the middle of it. She wrote a long letter to Addams a few days before the scheduled Washington meeting to explain her dilemma. It is worth quoting at length because it shows the complexities of what would appear to be a simple demonstration to declare for peace, and the way Catt worked her way through problems. She kept both short- and long-range goals in mind, and tried to avoid antagonizing others while maintaining her own integrity.

"I find myself in the most embarrassing position of a life time. I'd give a good deal for an honorable retreat from it. I certainly would never have consented to the use of my name had I known at the time I did so what I now know," she lamented. She had just realized that the prime movers in Washington were Congressional Union workers who supported a program proposed by Emmeline Pethick-Lawrence. Catt thought her plan impractical and had refused to aid it although she liked and admired the Englishwoman. Catt blamed herself for not being aware of the connection before and continued her explanation to Addams:

> The Congressional Union is exceedingly distasteful to most of us, not on account of its conflict with the National, nor on account of its personnel, but because it committed the stupendous stupidity of making an anti-Democratic campaign when the suffrage question was pending in eleven states and depending for success upon Democractic votes. Our politicians have heard of it and the Democrats, never friendly, have since threatened hostility. As Chairman of the New York Campaign Committee, I must not allow myself to be placed where I seem to sanction that policy. Further, people guilty of so untactical a blunder cannot be trusted to lead in so delicate a situation as the peace question in our own country is at this time. More, as President of the International Alliance, I cannot consort with militants who are extremely out of favor in the Alliance just now. The British militants have been harshly anti-German and the public does not distinguish between the Pankhursts and the Lawrences.
>
> My prayer has been that I might walk so straight a path that I could help pull that body together again at the end of the war. Especially is it important to keep my skirts clear at this particular moment, for a vote is on its round to determine whether or not we shall hold an international peace conference in Holland in April. I should lose my only hope of help in the International situation if I manage to get tangled in a press despatch with Mrs. Lawrence's peace conference.[18]
>
> Please understand that I still think a Conference is needed and that I see no objection to the Lawrence groups, nor the Congressional Union uniting with others in such a conference. My distress is that a few disconnected organizations and people have been summmoned to Washington supposedly to attend an unorganized conference, whereas they

will be mere adjuncts of a conference already arranged and with a program already adopted.

I find myself in a dilemma with four horns.

1. I am caught in a Congressional Union and militant trap in which it is uncomfortable to remain and from which it is impossible to escape. For myself I do not care, but this involves two big causes—the New York campaign and the International Alliance.

2. The peace women are vexed at a call which seems to put the responsibility of it on a suffragist, and they regard me as interfering in their field. (They regard you as one of their own and have no such feeling toward you.) If I explain how my name came to be connected with it so conspicuously, it throws the blame on you or Madame Schwimmer, and this I will not allow to happen.

3. The National suffragists are calling me to task for having joined hands with the Congressional Unionists, and this I cannot explain.

4. On the other hand the Congressional Union and militants are certain to regard me as an interloper in their conference long since prepared, and I cannot explain that.

Now, my dear lady, do you see any loophole of escape for me? I am most unhappy. If I go to Washington, I fear I cannot explain my connection with the meeting satisfactorily to the gathering or to myself. If I stay away, I am in a still more unenviable position.[19]

Although she felt damned if she did and damned if she didn't, Catt went to Washington and presided at an organizing meeting on January 9, 1915. She made the motion to form a national organization of peace, was named to a committee of three on organization, then she moved to form a committee of eleven to propose a plan of action. The next day Catt presided over a large public meeting attended by three thousand people, with hundreds more turned away. But her opening statement at the Woman's Peace Party rally was low-keyed and left its direction to the members.

The Woman's Peace Party preamble, written by Anna Garlin Spencer, demanded peace and recognition of the right of women to share in settlement of questions concerning the lives of individuals and nations. The party platform called for a convention of neutral nations, organized opposition to militarism, limitation of armaments, international police in lieu of armies and navies, education for peace, and removal of the economic causes of war. The final plank called for woman suffrage to humanize governments. This caused some discussion and Lucia Ames Mead pointed out that any woman who subscribed to the main outlines for peace did not have to accept the woman suffrage item.

The uncompromising Fanny Garrison Villard, who was present at Catt's urging, was disappointed by the flaccid platform. "Not a word was uttered against the horror of war, or of the present ideas of patriotism, or anything else of importance. Neither Jane Addams nor Mrs. Catt nor Anna Shaw have said anything at all of interest." But a week later she admitted, "The society was really organized on the basis of the sacredness of human life."[20]

Jane Addams was elected president of the Woman's Peace Party and the national office was established in Chicago. A month later Catt presided at the organizing meeting of the New York branch, but that was her only additional work with the Woman's Peace Party. She gradually unwound herself from the organization as the New York suffrage campaign increased its demands on her energy and skill.

There were times that Catt felt she was not directing a campaign but being driven by it "like a dog snarling at my heels all the time," she said. The campaign was designed to show legislators and voters the strength of women's demand for suffrage by every device that would make the cause visible. Each holiday gave a focus—on Mother's Day hundreds of churches heard appeals for the new order, on the Fourth of July the Woman's Declaration of Independence was read from the steps of fifty courthouses and the Statue of Liberty. For the first time in suffrage history a strongly organized press department got coverage in the twenty-six languages in which newspapers were published in New York State.

In New York City where the campaign was most intense

> there were barbers' days, days for firemen, street cleaners, bankers, brokers, business men, clergymen, street car men, factory workers, students, restaurant and railroad workers, ticket sellers and choppers, lawyers, ditch diggers and longshoremen. No voter escaped. There was a bonfire on the highest hill in each borough, with balloons flying, music, speeches and tableaux illustrating women's progress from the primitive campfire to the council of State. There were street dances and outdoor concerts, there were flying squadrons of speakers from the Battery to the Bronx. Bottles containing suffrage messages were consigned to the waves from boats and wharves with appropriate speeches. Sandwich girls advertised meetings and sold papers. Sixty playhouses had theatre nights, many with speeches between the acts.[21]

Suffragists quickly learned about parts of New York they had never known as they penetrated deep into what was once the alien territory of the workers. Although Catt had said when she began work for suffrage in the

1880s that her first interest was in helping working women, the suffrage organizations had attracted few of those who were most exploited. Gradually women were drawn into labor unions and came to recognize that their disfranchisement made them even more vulnerable that their male counterparts. For example, in 1911, early in the New York campaign, the public had been shocked by the horrors of the Triangle Shirt-Waist Company fire in which 146 seamstresses died because the exits were locked against union organizers. One Tammany leader, when asked why the women didn't have fire protection, responded as a practical politician, "They ain't got no votes."[22]

At the same time the suffrage movement was attracting more wealthy women and to dramatize their common cause, they were often assigned working-class areas. They went into subway excavations, into sweatshops, to building sites. One elegant woman discovered captive audiences on tenement rooftops during the summer evenings and gave speeches on one rooftop after another down the entire block.

The climax of the campaign in New York was a great parade led by Catt ten days before the November 2 election. Even a visiting Irish pacifist, who approved of militant women and thought Catt too timid, was impressed. "About 30,000 marched up Fifth Avenue in the teeth of a bitter wind, which swept down their banners remorselessly. It took them over three hours to pass any point. Some 5,000 men were also in the march. It was a great demonstration."[23]

In retrospect Catt thought the parade, which drew one and a half million spectators, might have stirred more opposition than it generated support. "In the Union League Club a group of the great men in City affairs somewhat cynically watched the procession," she wrote. "As the endless line moved on, one of the great men jumped to his feet and exclaimed, 'My God, men, I never understood the menace of this woman suffrage campaign as I do now. Here is a hundred dollars to defeat it. Who will join me?' And the dollars came plentifully, for the politically great find democracy troublesome."[24]

In spite of the 10,300 meetings New York suffragists held in the six months before the election, the seven and a half million leaflets (twenty tons of them papered the state), the $95,000 laboriously raised dime by dime, the vote for the amendment of 1915 was 553,348 against 748,332—lost by a majority of 194,984.[25] New York's neighbors in Massachusetts, New Jersey, and Pennsylvania were also denied woman suffrage.

Opponents were saying the defeats would put the suffrage movement back at least ten years, Anna Shaw remarked that night at the campaign committee office. She turned to Catt and asked, "How long will it delay your fight, Carrie?"

"Only until we can get a little sleep. Our campaign will be on again tomorrow morning—and forever until we get the vote."

The next day the office was piled high with telegrams pledging renewed support from women all over the state. "We shall never get the federal amendment until we get one of these big eastern states," Catt said, and was equally convinced that "New York is our only chance."

Two days after the election the new campaign was officially opened in a crowded Cooper Union and $100,000 was raised on the spot. Shortly afterward at the state convention Catt again called for dedication and hard work. "Roll up your sleeves, set your mind to making history and wage such a fight for liberty that the whole world will respect our sex."[26] "Victory in 1917" was the new slogan.

The four defeated amendments had polled a million and a quarter votes favorable to woman suffrage, a figure not lost on politicians. The Union League Club promptly hired an antisuffragist to lobby full time in Albany, but shrewder heads in Tammany thought that this time the slogan would be apt. They were right.

· 14 ·
War

Shortly after the 1915 election Anna Howard Shaw announced that she was stepping down as president of the NAWSA. She would go on lecturing for suffrage, but after twelve years as president she had had enough of administration, never her strong point. Catt, her obvious successor, who emphatically did not want the job, was drafted into it. She was pledged to raise money to keep the IWSA's London office open and to continue to publish *Jus Suffragii,* she was heading the second New York campaign for victory, and she didn't want to dilute her effectiveness with a third huge responsibility.

Catt found pressure put on her and the New York delegation from all sides at the NAWSA convention that opened on December 14 in Washington, D.C. Nevertheless she continued to refuse until a committee of one hundred women demanded she accept the national leadership. "As she felt the insistence of the demand closing in on her, for a moment her head drooped on [Mary Hay's] shoulder, then, with a white drawn face, she said, 'It will kill me, I think, but if the New York women will release me from my obligation to them, I will do it.' Then Mrs. Catt went up to her room, locked herself in, threw herself on the bed, and she wept as she had never wept before."[1]

Gertrude Brown agreed to lead the Empire State Campaign, Vira Whitehouse took the state presidency, and Mary Hay would stay on as the "Big Boss" in the city. The campaign was in excellent hands.

"I am an unwilling victim," Catt told the national convention. Then she thrust aside self-pity and began to make plans.

There was considerable talk about the Shafroth amendment during this convention; it was written by the Congressional Committee and introduced by Senator John Shafroth after the Senate defeat of the woman suffrage amendment on March 20, 1914. It was designed to appease states' righters and facilitate the introduction of woman suffrage to indifferent state legislatures by requiring a state to hold a referendum on woman suffrage when presented with an initiative petition signed by 8 percent of the voters at the preceding general election. It was intended to support, not to replace, the federal amendment that was reintroduced at the same time but inevitably created confusion and divided loyalties. The NAWSA executive had previously endorsed the Shafroth amendment, but at this 1915 convention reverted to supporting only the terse law for which National had been working for forty years, "The right of citizens of the United States to vote shall not be denied or abridged by the United States or by any state on account of sex."[2]

The Congressional Union, headed by Alice Paul and Lucy Burns, also wanted the federal amendment but boasted they could get it by holding the party in power responsible and using every device to block their reelection. Catt pointed out that their cause had friends in all parties, and that for a two-thirds majority in both houses a bipartisan vote was essential. The suffrage lobbies, fund-raising organizations, and publicity bureaus of the NAWSA and the Congressional Union often got in each other's way; in the public mind they were usually perceived as one although their strategies were in opposition. Catt and Paul met to try to construct a cooperative plan to get more united action in their Washington lobbying, but they could not reconcile their differences and each group continued on its own way. Catt must often have recalled her own early days in the movement when Susan B. Anthony remarked that every young woman was convinced she could have won the vote long before if she had been in charge.[3]

Catt spent six months of 1916 visiting as many suffragists as possible, feeling that she had lost touch in the twelve years since she had been president. She went to state conventions, conferences, and meetings of all kinds in twenty-three states, and members of her new Campaign and Survey Committee visited the others. Everything she saw and heard reinforced her conviction that the final push must be strong and immediate.

A woman suffrage plank in the platforms of both the Republicans and the Democrats at their conventions in June was her immediate goal. A memorable NAWSA parade of support at the Republican meeting in Chicago on June 7, 1916 was deluged by a great rainstorm but the women marched on to the Coliseum, where woman suffrage arguments were being heard. An antisuffragist was airing the old canard, "Women do not want to vote," when the doors at the back of the hall opened and thousands of bedraggled, laughing suffragists poured in, dripping water from their bright yellow ribbons and their soaking clothes. A woman suffrage plank did go into the Republican platform but was diluted by a state-rights rider added at the behest of

Senator Henry Cabot Lodge of Massachusetts and other strong antis, most of them prominent in the "preparedness" (pro-war) movement and suspicious of women's preference for peace.

Catt went to St. Louis immediately to rally her forces before the Democratic convention began on June 14. There, six thousand suffragists with yellow parasols and yellow sashes on their white dresses lined both sides of the street from the major hotel to the convention hall. All day they stood, and unless the delegates wanted to go a long way around from hotel to hall to avoid them, they trudged back and forth self-consciously through the "golden lane" with its banners and slogans and watchful eyes. A plank in favor of woman suffrage by state action was finally approved by a large majority of Democratic delegates. Catt sputtered with rage and disappointment: "The Democratics admitted that 'political exigency' demanded 'some kind of a suffrage plank,' and they thought to hoodwink the women by a jumble of words. They in no sense succeeded."

Catt was increasingly concerned with the NAWSA, which was lurching along from one defeat to another. She described the organization as a camel with a hundred humps, each with a blindfolded driver who thought she set the way. Just before the conventions, Iowa had defeated woman suffrage; after three well-publicized defeats in a single month, the incongruous beast was more confused and dispirited than ever. Catt wanted to make it into a purposeful caravan of camels, "each with one driver, and each driver knowing where she is going."[4] Those lines of loyal volunteers who sloshed through rain in Illinois and stood patiently for hours in the Missouri sun must have better direction and more hope. Something had to be done and fast.

Within a half hour after the Democratic suffrage plank was announced, the Executive Board of the NAWSA was meeting. They agreed with Catt that a crisis was at hand. Instead of the annual conference after election day, they called an Emergency Convention to meet in Atlantic City in September, the earliest possible date. They hoped that the attractions of the popular seaside resort would bring out delegates who were exhausted by the political conventions.[5]

Catt had to orchestrate the Emergency Convention with all her skill. While it would give all dissidents a forum for their grievances, and it might clear the air, it also might polarize suffragists even more. There were those, particularly in the South, who still favored the Shafroth proposal. There was a scattering of women who preferred the state-by-state method, especially a contingent from Democratic states who believed the Congressional Union had made the federal amendment hopeless. Catt saw a grave danger that

"Congress would hide behind those state rights planks and shut us out from Congress forever." The convention had to decide on a plan of action from three choices: drop work on a federal amendment and concentrate on state legislatures; drop work on state legislatures and concentrate on a federal amendment; or continue working for a federal amendment through state legislatures.

Catt was determined to overcome the lack of cohesion, and to bring organization, unity, and consequent momentum. She went to Atlantic City determined to sound a call for action so loud and compelling that it would send the suffragists straight on to enfranchisement. She wanted them to see victory as a possibility instead of a dream.

There was a three-way debate on the choices immediately after the convention opened. Catt made a long address, "The Crisis," in which she insisted the federal amendment must be gained through total cooperation from the states, and that the time to do it was now. She explained at length that procedures for amending state constitutions were varied and all were difficult. Possibilities for election fraud were endless and in state after state where women had succeeded in getting referenda they had been cheated of victory at the polls. Although political liberation of women could come only by federal amendment, nevertheless state work was necessary to gain support for the amendment in Congress and carry it through the state ratifications.

A simultaneous campaign had to be conducted in all forty-eight states. It demanded organization in every precinct; activity, agitation, education in every corner. Nothing less than nationwide, vigilant, unceasing campaigning would win the necessary ratification when the bill passed Congress, she reiterated. The time was past when a purely educational policy was desirable, they must mount an active campaign now. It was the woman's hour, she said over and over.[6]

The delegates agreed with her plan. National should continue to support the federal amendment with a nationwide campaign and continue the Washington lobby. The states would continue their work on suffrage through the legislatures or on referenda with National taking an active role in the state campaigns. A Southern states' righter, who disagreed with the emphasis on the federal amendment, muttered to her neighbor, "Flattened by a well-oiled steamroller."[7]

Money was needed as well as cooperation. Catt roused the delegates, and twenty minutes before the close of one afternoon session she announced there was "a little business." She asked for one million dollars for the year's work. More than $818,000 was pledged immediately.

Catt used every rhetorical device and personal influence she could to overcome opposition and to swing the membership to her plan. In the public meetings she was confident of success but with the Executive Council (state presidents and national officers) she aired all her repressed contempt and anger for the inefficiency and stubbornness she had found on her travels. Energy, money, years of grueling work had been squandered by women who quarreled among themselves. Fresh from the defeat in Iowa she was especially hard on that state with its "stand off" attitude toward the National Board. It held a "queer states right sentiment," she said. "Our advice was not taken at the beginning when it would have been of most value," and although the campaign gained momentum toward the end, "nothing could overcome the stupid inability of newly formed untrained committees to put speakers and workers to the best use, as has been the case in every campaign through the sheer stupidity of newly formed undisciplined committees." South Dakota and other states fared little better in her indictment.

After stunning the Executive Council with her diatribe, she produced a huge map of the United States and detailed a plan for their cooperation on a dual strategy. The major thrust of the association was to work together to achieve passage of the federal amendment. Each state was assigned an additional task: 1) the suffrage states would get resolutions from their legislatures to Congress; 2) in states where there was a chance of getting a constitutional amendment they would push for a referendum, or in states already planning referenda in 1916 and 1917 they would work for the popular vote; 3) other states would persuade their legislatures to vote for the amount of suffrage they were able to give, preferably presidential suffrage, or 4) in the South, suffrage in the primaries. Each state had to begin work at once to be ready to launch its campaign at the beginning of the next legislative sessions. This was Catt's "Winning Plan"; she also called it a "new deal."

She insisted that the National Board must have authority to act and must have cooperation from everyone. Again and again she hammered on the theme of cooperation. The National Board was paralyzed without state support; no congressional lobby, however powerful, could by itself secure the passage of the federal amendment:

A small but emphatic balance of power was held by men committed to the interests of railroads, manufacturers, big finance and the liquor powers that control them. To expect a lobby to play a successful game with such odds is babyish.

When thirty-six State Associations, and preferably more, enter into a solemn compact to get that amendment submitted by Congress and ratified in their respective legislatures, when they live up to that compact by running a red-hot, never-ceasing campaign in their own state designed to create sentiment behind the political leaders of the states and to aim both of these forces at the men in Congress, as well as the Legislature, we can get that amendment through and ratified. We cannot do it by any other process.

Catt asked for a "virile" intention by thirty-six state associations to back up a Washington lobby. She asked at least that many state presidents to commit their organizations to follow the detailed plan of work she presented, binding them to secrecy to avoid diluting the impact of simultaneous action.

"I made this promise with great faith in the suffragists but very weak in the knees when I thought of raising $10,000 in Alabama," that state's president recalled. Other presidents agreed more tentatively, saying they did not feel at liberty to pledge their states until it had been discussed at home. But Maud Wood Park, who chaired the Congressional Committee the next year, wrote, "When we filed out of the room at the close of that meeting, I thought I understood how Moses felt on the mountain-top after he was shown the Promised Land. For the first time our goal looked possible of attainment in the near future."[8]

President Wilson came on the last night of the convention; the first time a president of the United States had spoken as a suffragist to a suffrage meeting. The delegates added as much ceremony to the occasion as they could. They lined up on either side of his passageway with blue and gold sashes, they held banners with their states' names and suffrage flags. Behind the jungle of palms on the stage lurked his protective Secret Service corps, and most of the major papers in the country were represented at the press table. Wilson had asked to speak last and sat politely through the speeches of four noted public workers who discussed the improvement in working and living conditions of women and children that would result from woman suffrage.[9] Catt then introduced the president.

He was complimentary and optimistic, saying that the woman movement "has not only come to stay, but has come with conquering power." He was charming and conciliatory: "Almost every other time that I ever visited Atlantic City I came to fight somebody. I hardly know how to conduct myself when I have not come to fight anybody but with somebody." He gave them a politician's advice, "The movement was coming to full tide," and he said:

we rejoice in the strength of it, and we shall not quarrel in the long run as to the method of it. Because, when you are working with masses of men and organized bodies of opinion, you have got to carry the organized body along. The whole art and practice of government consists not in moving individuals, but in moving masses.

It is all very well to run ahead and beckon, but after all, you have got to wait for them to follow. I have not come to ask you to be patient, because you have been, but I have come to congratulate you that there was a force behind you that will, beyond any peradventure, be triumphant and for which you can afford a little while to wait.

Wilson stopped short of advocating suffrage by federal amendment.

Catt had asked Anna Howard Shaw to respond and she did not disappoint. "We have waited long enough for the vote, we want it now," she said, and turning to the president, added, "and we want it to come in your administration!" He smiled and bowed, the entire audience rose, waving their handkerchiefs in thanks as he left the hall. [10]

After the convention, Catt defined in detail the work required of every suffrage association and continued to bombard the state presidents with memos of plans, praising and scolding in turn as she saw cooperation or inefficiency.

Suffrage had a new adversary—cataclysmic war. Since the sinking of the *Lusitania* the year before, hate mongers, profiteers, and propaganda machines had been at work to involve the United States in the fighting. With splendid illogic Americans were being manipulated toward war under the lofty phrases of militarist advertising. If we are prepared for war we will have peace, was the solecism they had to sell. All other issues were being made to seem increasingly irrelevant. At the peak of war hysteria soon to come, any distraction from the war effort was considered almost treasonable.

During 1916 militarism increasingly became an accepted mode of thought under the guise of "preparedness." In January 1916 President Wilson had begun a tour of the country to urge preparedness. [11] In June the National Defense Act provided for expansion of the regular army, and establishment of a National Guard and an Officers Reserve Training Corps at universities, colleges, and military camps. In August the Council of National Defense was established as an advisory body chaired by Secretary of War Newton D. Baker. It consisted of six cabinet members charged with coordinating industry and resources of the national security and welfare.

Catt thought it politically astute to keep a low profile on peace as the country rolled with increasing speed on the war track. Throughout this time she was torn by her own conscientious objections to war, her compulsion to achieve woman suffrage in the United States, and the desire to avoid offending the national sensibilities of the women of the International Woman Suffrage Alliance to assure its continuation after hostilities among nations had ceased. She eventually tolerated the war in the cause of the greater good as she saw it.[12]

In October she wrote an exasperated letter to the *New York Times* "to explain for the thousandth time, the attitude of suffragists toward 'preparedness.'" She said, "The world needs feminizing at least to the extent that innocent men will not be ordered out to kill one another because their governments have quarreled." At the same time she reminded her readers of the work women were doing in Europe on the home front:

> The magnificent loyalty of the women, their unselfish sacrifices, their willingness to man every department of life from the cultivation of the fields to running the street cars and railroads have made the defenses possible. To charge American women with a tendency to weakly sacrifice honor to peace because some women do not love war is as illogical and ridiculous as to accuse American men of trembling with cowardice before our Southern neighbors because Mr. Wilson has not declared war on Mexico.

It was increasingly apparent that the United States would not keep out of war, and Catt concluded her letter, "What European women have done, American women under similar conditions are likely to do."[13]

In November 1916, Wilson was reelected president. He had run on his record of neutrality and the most widely quoted campaign slogan was, "He kept us out of war." A great deal of his strength was thought to come from women's groups in the West where there was woman suffrage. By the beginning of 1917 it became obvious that Wilson's successful slogan would soon be obsolete. When Secretary of State Robert Lansing in an address to Congress on February 3, 1917 announced the breaking of diplomatic relations with Germany, Catt called a meeting of her Executive Council of One Hundred to discuss their position in case of war.

The Council, consisting of officers and congressional chairs of the state suffrage associations, chairs of national committees, and certain other active suffragists, was called to meet in Washington, D.C. on February 23 and 24.

In her call to the meeting, Catt asked the members to consider the question, "Shall suffragists do the 'war work' which they will undoubtedly want to do with other groups newly formed, thus running the risk of disintegrating our organizations, or shall we use our headquarters and our machinery for really helpful constructive aid to our nation?"[14]

Delegates from thirty-six of the forty-five state organizations came to the meeting and fervently discussed a position paper framed as a letter to President Wilson. After lengthy arguments they agreed by a vote of 63 to 13 to adopt it. The next day, February 25, 1917, it was read at a public meeting by Ida Husted Harper and given to Secretary of War Baker who passed it along to the president. The letter offered the women's services to the government of the United States "in the event they should be needed, and, in so far as we are authorized, we pledge the loyal support of our more than two million members." The letter also made clear that they had no intention of laying aside work for suffrage since this was "the right protective of all other rights." The letter detailed the plan of forming a national committee representing all national women's organizations willing to aid in war work by acting as a clearing house between the government and the women "in order that service may be rendered in the most expeditious manner."[15]

The announcement that the NAWSA would stand by the government in case of war was the most widely criticized act of Catt's life. To this day, historically minded pacifists talk of her treachery in selling out to the war machine. She was immediately repudiated by the New York branch of the Woman's Peace Party and wrote to Jane Addams that she considered this as a dismissal from the whole organization.

She did not publicly defend her motives but others did. Mrs. J. Malcolm Forbes, President of the Massachusetts Woman's Peace Party, insisted that each branch was autonomous and emphasized that the action of one did not meet with universal approval. Alice Blackwell commented, "Mrs. Catt has been greatly berated by the anti-suffragists for being too much of a pacifist, and now it seems she is blamed by the pacifists as lending encouragement to war! But Mrs. Catt will continue to follow her own conscience, and to do what she believes to be best for the country and for the cause."[16]

To political Washington her performance was exemplary and needed no defense. To them she had "delivered" massive public support to the administration at a time when it was needed. She had risen far above defeats in the rigged polls of Iowa and the stubborn party conventions. She was holding her organization together and therefore could make powerful claims for political favors. The night before she sent her letters calling for the Advisory Council meeting she had dinner at the White House with President and Mrs. Wilson.[17] What was said is not recorded, probably no bargain was verbally made nor was one necessary. Each understood the other. Thereafter whenever she felt that the suffrage movement needed his personal attention he came to its assistance.

On April 2, 1917, five weeks after the NAWSA pledge of support, Congress opened a special session to begin the legislative process of declaring war. The date also marked the seating of Jeannette Rankin, Republican representative from Montana, the first woman member of Congress.

Since she had worked in the successful Washington State campaign in 1910, Rankin had been a NAWSA lobbyist and field secretary in the West. Before Congress met on April 2, two hundred suffrage women had breakfast with her at the Shoreham Hotel to celebrate her victory. Diplomatically the two leaders of the movement's major organizations were seated on either side of her—Catt was on her right, Alice Paul on her left. By accident or design the symbolism was apt. After breakfast Rankin went to the NAWSA headquarters (where she was living) and from the Moresque balcony made a short speech. A motorcade of decorated cars then drove her to the House Office Building. From there Catt and other prominent suffragists escorted her to the Capitol for the opening of Congress.[18]

President Wilson asked Congress for a declaration of war. He stated his paradoxical faith that by going to war the United States was insuring world peace, and uttered his famous dictum, "The world must be made safe for democracy." The war resolution was passed by the Senate two days later. The House concurred on April 6, with Rankin one of fifty to vote against war. The joint congressional resolution declaring a state of war was signed by President Wilson the same day.

In a circular letter to the presidents of the suffrage clubs in the NAWSA, Catt wrote about registering women for government service. No one knew what good it would do but they wanted to stand up and be counted. Catt emphasized that suffrage work must continue. "We have the chance of a lifetime to get our measure through, and concentration must be directed toward the Federal Amendment. War is a tragedy which most people in the United States sincerely regret. It however becomes our duty to waste no time in vain regret, but to ease the situation as much as possible by each doing her own share of public service in this hour of our great need."[19]

The trouble was that the women did not know how they could help and

neither did the nation's leaders. The offers to assist came as a great clutter of
pieces that needed somehow to be put together. Finding a meaningful and
conspicuous place for women in the supermasculine war society was not easy.
Secretary of War Newton D. Baker's frantic response to the problem was to
create the Woman's Committee of the Council of National Defense. Anna
Howard Shaw was the chairwoman, Catt one of the committee of ten. An
honorary committee composed of the presidents of seventy-three national
organizations of women was appointed as well as a chairwoman for each state
and territory.

The committee met in Washington the first week in May 1917 to
organize themselves and try to get a handle on the job they were expected to
do. Their portfolio was vague and as the months went by it was apparent that
they were conflicting with other organizations, government and civilian,
whose duties were as undefined as their own and with whom they overlapped.
Catt was appointed to report on what the women of other countries at war
had been able to do to help their governments. Other women were assigned
to investigate the possibilities of work in organization, finance, registration,
food, educational propaganda, industry and labor, camp morale, patriotism
and democracy, and special training for service. This was broad enough to
suit everybody but what the government was saying to the women was that
theirs was the ancient sex-assigned role: "Keep the home fires going while the
men fight for the country's defense."[20]

Catt urged members of the NAWSA to answer the government's call by
working with the forces of construction and conservation, never forgetting
their efforts for suffrage and for peace. "I am myself a pacifist, now and for
ever. War is to my mind a barbarism, a relic of the stone age, but I hold that
that belief has nothing to do with the present situation. Whether we approve
or disapprove, war is here. It is not the appeal of war but the call of
civilization which is summoning women to new duties and responsibilities."[21]

Catt's public stance toward the Great War was similar to attitudes held
by millions of Americans whose positions changed over the months between
August 1914 and April 1917. She went from pacifism in 1914 to offers of help
and support in 1917. In part this was political expediency, in part a reflection
of the powerful propaganda at work that influenced even as independent a
thinker as she.

Catt and other NAWSA leaders knew that obstruction of the war would
have meant loss of whatever influence the suffragists had built up so painstak-
ingly over the years. On the other hand, the country would need their
guidance after the war and it would have negligible effect unless they had the
political power of the vote. It is hard to see how the director of a liberal

advocacy group could have done differently and survived to be effective. George Creel, head of the Committee on Public Information, wrote of selling the war to Americans: "In all things, from first to last, without halt or change, it was a plain publicity proposition, a vast enterprise in sales-manship, the world's greatest adventure in advertising." With the aid of British propaganda he built a national infatuation with bloodshed, xenophobic platitudes, and uniformity of opinion that one observer called "as dangerous as madness and as unapproachable to reason."[22]

Catt's own perceptions were shifting, although she still considered herself a pacifist. One of the difficulties in reconciling her pacifism and her war work is due to the changes in the connotations of the word "pacifist" in the more than sixty-five years that have passed. It used to apply to all persons who hoped and worked for a world free from the curse of war. It has now come to stand for those who are opposed to war under any and all conditions. Catt's friend, Jane Addams, also a pacifist, found herself in the same situation. The irony of using Hull House for farewell dinners to honor soldiers when they left the district was not unnoticed. After the armistice, Addams wrote at length about the problem of pacifists helping the war in the hope of greater good to come.[23]

Catt did not discuss her own painful dilemma but wrote, spoke, and worked for the war effort. She dutifully gave out press statements with a high moral tone and exhortations to work hard and be thrifty, but she always said she did very little on the Woman's Committee of the Council. "It was understood very well by Miss Shaw and me that I was to keep on pushing the campaign for woman suffrage and was not expected to do much." She often talked with Shaw about the waste of everyone's time, and thought Josephus Daniels, who was Secretary of the Navy during both of Wilson's terms, was of the same opinion. "I was always rather mad at it," she said, "because Miss Shaw gave of her splendid, valuable time in which she might have been doing more to her fancy."[24]

In later years Catt was irreverently honest about what she accomplished. "The thing I remember about the Great War more distinctly than anything else is the day when some of us, representing the new Woman's Council of National Defense went to see you by appointment in order to learn what was expected of us," she wrote to Josephus Daniels. "We asked what we were to do and your answer was something like this: 'Take the women off our backs. Here is about a bushel basket full of letters from women asking what they can do. Take it away and tell those women to keep quiet till we get the war going.' As I look back on the work of the Woman's Committee, entertaining the women was the main object we performed!"[25]

· 15 ·

The Winning Plan Works

Before the Winning Plan could be implemented, suffragists had two more disappointments; in November 1916, referenda on woman suffrage were defeated in West Virginia and South Dakota. Like the recent Iowa loss, these defeats were of the old style, full of unprovable suspicions about foul play at the ballot box.

The symbol of the Winning Plan was the new NAWSA headquarters, which opened in December in Washington, D.C.—an impressive twenty-six room mansion of dressed stone on Rhode Island Avenue about six blocks from the White House. The building, called Suffrage House, declared to the nation that NAWSA was so solidly housed and so solidly financed that the women would stay until they got the federal amendment they wanted. Suffrage House held the National's expanded Congressional Committee, the "Front-Door Lobby," so called in deference to its scrupulous and formal ways of gaining influence. Catt had a permanent room for her frequent visits; others were set aside for board members, some were rented, but most of the house was used for offices and reception rooms. One office at the heart of the building held the massive, detailed files being meticulously compiled on each legislator.

War legislation had priority in 1917; both House and Senate agreed that nothing else would be considered during the special session.[1] But there were eight state referenda during the year, and in January 1917 came the first promise that Catt's Winning Plan would work. North Dakota won presidential and municipal suffrage, an event marked by an unprecedented letter of congratulations to Catt from Wilson, who wrote personally on his own typewriter of his interest in extending suffrage to all.[2] In February Ohio's legislature voted presidential suffrage for women and brought the total of electoral votes in which women had a voice to 120. In March, Arkansas women gained the right to vote in primaries, tantamount to presidential suffrage in that one-party state. It was a breakthrough in the South. There were three more victories in April, all granting presidential suffrage—Michigan, Nebraska, and Rhode Island, the first eastern state.

New York was another matter. In spite of all the women's defiant optimism after the 1915 defeat and the plans for "Victory in 1917," the New York legislature resisted putting another suffrage referendum on the ballot, probably in fear that it might pass. Leaders in both State Senate and Assembly were pledged to see that a suffrage amendment remained bottled up in committee. There it stayed until the suffragists used their growing power in Washington to suggest to the state committeemen that any hopes each might have for federal office could be severely jeopardized if they failed to produce a suffrage referendum. Only then did it pass the state legislature.

Not until August and then only with heroic effort could the machinery of the New York Woman Suffrage Party be effectively reassembled. But that meant that the suffrage movement and women's help with the war effort had to go on simultaneously. "We ask woman suffrage as a war measure as the emancipation of the slaves was a war measure," Catt said. She then drew her audience out of their seats to applaud: "The sickening horrors of these last years must never come again. When all the nations are tired, when they are bankrupt, then we need women behind every government in the world that the mother as well as the father may say something about the welfare of their common land, the destiny of their children, about the civilization under which we live."[3]

All of this was painfully expensive. Previously the women could count on free newspaper space, but in 1917 war news filled the columns, and the suffragists had to rely on paid advertisements to get sufficient coverage. Happily, financing the victory campaign had been undertaken by several wealthy women who understood money and how to get it. Helen Rogers Reid, whose husband owned and published the *New York Tribune*, was the new treasurer of the Woman Suffrage Party. With Vira Whitehouse she set a minimum of $300,000 as the amount they needed, later they added $200,000. Their realistic thinking about finance would have stunned the pioneer suffragists who counted on nickel and dime contributions. Even the previous New York State campaign had spent less than $90,000 for two years work. Narcissa Cox Vanderlip, whose husband was president of the National City Bank, was chair of the Ninth Campaign District and suggested the most effective approach to wealthy donors: "Let's get through with it now." Vira Whitehouse was not above bullying a rich but reluctant prospect: "How dare you refuse to give to the most important cause in your lifetime?"[4]

Happily at just this time Catt received a legacy from Mrs. Frank Leslie to further woman suffrage. Mrs. Frank Leslie had revitalized a bankrupt publishing enterprise left to her by her husband in 1890, and had made herself rich. On three occasions she had given checks for a hundred dollars to the suffrage movement but had otherwise not been active. Catt had invited her to receptions for donors and she in turn had asked Catt to a few of her parties, but the two women had talked together at some length only once. In September 1914, Catt was astonished when a lawyer called at her apartment and told her of the bequest. When he had gone, Catt came into the room where Mary Hay and Clara Hyde were waiting. Her face pink with excitement, she announced, "I am an heiress!"[5] The estate was estimated to be worth about two million dollars.

The bequest came with troubles; out of Mrs. Leslie's past rose claimants in swarms, each with some new legal trick to break the will. Catt spent many sleepless nights worrying about "the Leslie business," which had begun about the time she had finally settled George Catt's estate and was herself embroiled in the 1915 New York campaign. "I often worked all day in the office and then went home to spend three hours more in the evening with my attorney and the hostile lawyers and claimants," she said.[6]

Because of the publicity given the bequest, Catt was besieged with so many requests for a share of the fund that she had to hire an extra clerk to handle the mail. On the other hand, pledges upon which the suffragists had been relying stopped in the middle of the 1915 campaign when potential donors presumed Leslie money could be spent instead of theirs.

After more than two years in courts, Catt received the first installment of the legacy early in 1917, just when it was most needed. Half of the estate had been spent in lawyers' fees and court costs by then. She said that one of the happiest days of her life was the February day in 1917, when from the first receipts from the Leslie estate, she gave Vira Whitehouse $10,000 for the New York State campaign committee, and Mary Garrett Hay $15,000 for the New York City work.

Part of the legacy was in jewels, which were unceremoniously brought to suffrage headquarters in a suitcase. Catt tipped out the contents onto her desk. "From tarnished white silver settings turned black by long storage in a bank vault, emeralds and rubies, diamonds and pearls flashed forth," $34,000 worth. "She called in her assistants to gloat with her over the fabulous pile, and someone perched a diamond tiara on Mrs. Catt's crisp white hair." They fingered and marveled for an hour or so, then "the jewels went back in the cases and were sent immediately to be sold."[7]

The suffragists eventually received just under $1,000,000 from Mrs.

Frank Leslie. Since this was left to Catt personally she brought together a few friends whose honesty and judgment she trusted and incorporated them as the Leslie Suffrage Commission, charged with spending the money. Most of it went to finance the Leslie Bureau of Suffrage Education, whose director was Rose Young. It immediately became an effective propaganda machine using brochures, billboards, ads, daily news services, feature services, and research. Its professional staff soon made it the best press and publicity agent the NAWSA had ever had.[8]

Suffrage women kept their demands active and in public view by every means they could devise. Antisuffragists claimed those who worked for woman suffrage were unpatriotic, un-American, and Communistic (a recently added slur) for intruding their claims in time of war. All suffragists were under attack, particularly the mild demonstrations of the National Woman's Party (successor to the Congressional Union), which were regarded as militant.

Beginning on January 10, 1917, the Woman's Party picketed the White House, carrying banners lettered "Mr. President, What Will You Do for Woman Suffrage?" and "How Long Must Women Wait for Liberty?" They continued through the spring with varying banners and stunts. At first they were amusing and picturesque, and Wilson reportedly nodded and tipped his hat to them when he passed through the gates. But when a war mission seeking cooperation was sent from Russia, the diplomats saw a banner claiming that America was no democracy because twenty million American women were denied the right to vote. Charged with obstructing the traffic; half a dozen women were arrested during the next two days, then dismissed on their own recognizance. The third day's groups were fined $25 or three days in jail for their "unpatriotic, almost treasonable behavior." They chose jail, of course, and made headlines across the nation. The picketing and arrests continued throughout the summer; conditions in the Occoquan Workhouse were appalling to these middle-class women who had never dreamed such a place existed, and they denounced the government for mistreatment.

The trumped-up charges of "obstructing traffic" were thin and infuriating but effectively turned attention to the women. Americans never destroyed property as their English counterparts did; picketing was enough to earn them the title of "militant." From the beginning there was argument about whether they helped or hindered the movement. Catt thought their actions were "unwise and unprofitable to the cause." Most of the NAWSA agreed that they hardened the opposition and delayed victory. "To us it seemed childish reasoning to think that by standing at the gates of the White House, displaying banners which carried sentences from his speeches, they could force the President of the United States to act," wrote Catt's friend Gertrude Brown, but he "did not waver in his support of our amendment, nor did he confuse the small group of militants with our huge organization."[9] Nevertheless, like their English sisters, they brought attention to woman suffrage.

Throughout the war years both NAWSA and the Woman's Party hammered on the idea that as long as women were denied the franchise it was wrong to claim that the United States was a democracy. "The United States has no right to talk about making the world safe for democracy as long as it believes in drawing the sex line. There is nothing more illogical than to insist that men have the divine right to rule over women and say at the same time that kings haven't divine right to rule over men. Ours is not a true democracy," was the burden of many of Catt's talks that spring.[10] She and other suffragists seized happily on Wilson's phrase in his speech to Congress in April 1917 asking for war to make the world safe for democracy. This was a pithy rationale they could fasten on to and did—to stress democratic self-determination aims of the United States for all the world and emphasize that such aims depend on votes for all people.

As the months went on and there was no hope of any action on the federal amendment that war year, suffrage attention focused on New York State's campaign. Suffragists there set about to prove Catt's claim that "a million New York women want to vote." Doggedly they canvassed door to door, through slums and town houses, and collected 1,030,000 signatures of New York women appealing to men for the vote. They did everything they could think of to make the public realize the enormous force of those names, the greatest number of signatures ever on a petition. They held the usual press conferences, distributed posters and leaflets by the ton, ran ads in newspapers, and forced reluctant politicians to verify the signatures.

On October 27, 1917, the last great suffrage parade was held in New York, with twenty thousand women marching up Fifth Avenue from Washington Square to Sixty-second Street in the most forceful demonstration ever made. There were so many instructive banners the effect was like a walking speech. The million plus signature petition was dramatically presented on side strips of beaver board and on ballot boxes. Women were there in divisions of farmers, industrial workers, doctors, nurses, social workers, lawyers, actors, musicians, painters, sculptors, illustrators, editors, authors, and teachers. It took three hours for the procession to pass.

Finally, it was not the hoopla, the leaflets, the processions, or the stunts, but the control of a powerful political machine that tipped the scales for victory. A few days before election, the Executive Committee of Tammany Hall, in response to pleas from members whose wives had been made captains and assembly district leaders for the Woman Suffrage party, passed orders to keep hands off the election and give the amendment a chance.[11] For once there would be no cemetary constituencies, premarked ballots ironed together, or strange slips of the ballot counters' pens.

At suffrage headquarters in New York City on the night of November 6 as the returns "began to show that suffrage was winning in every borough in greater New York, happy trembling voices congratulated each other. Some frankly wept. 'Carrie,' said Dr. Shaw to Mrs. Catt, 'if we win I don't think I can stand it.'" The news of victory came just before midnight. "'The New York Times had flashed a white light showing suffrage has carried the state.' They cheered and shouted, laughed and cried. Mrs. Catt was jubilant. 'The victory is not New York's alone. It's the nation's. The 65th Congress will now pass the federal amendment.'"[12]

Maine had been defeated in an ill-advised referendum in September, but with the previous victories of 1917 in Ohio, Indiana, Rhode Island, Nebraska, Michigan, and Arkansas, the number of presidential electors for whom women were entitled to vote had been increased over 150 percent in the last twelve months, from 91 to 232. "The mandate from the country to Congress, which earlier suffragists had sought from the states, had been given and the way was opened, after forty years of wandering in the wilderness' as Miss Anthony had called it, for the submission of the Federal Suffrage Amendment."[13] There were to be more victories and more defeats before Congress surrendered but the way was open and clear at last.

A few weeks later, the NAWSA held its annual convention in Washington, D.C., and Catt used the occasion for some blitzkrieg lobbying. Thirty groups of delegates went off one morning to talk to their members of Congress. They reported back in the afternoon that thirty-five new House votes were pledged. Catt felt a "thrill of approaching triumph" when the Arkansas president announced that her members of Congress, with two exceptions, "say they will be *pleased* to vote for the federal amendment." Catt thought, "If the border States were coming in all would be well."[14] When enough other states reported positively, victory began to appear inevitable.

She framed her major speech to the convention as an address to Congress. She condemned the obstructionists to the federal amendment, showed the opponents' inconsistencies, the waste of time, energy, and money spent by state referenda, clarified the reasons for insisting on the federal method, and put responsibility for delay on Congress. It was a tightly reasoned resumé of hundreds of speeches she had written with confidence and brilliantly delivered. "To see her was like looking at sheer marble, flame-lit," wrote one effusive reporter. Through all her years in politics, Catt kept a touching faith that enlightened argument could sweep away all but corrupt opposition. She herself considered this one of the most important speeches of her life, the climax of fifty years' work was at hand and she tried to make it the best speech she had ever delivered.[15]

The time for submitting the federal amendment with a real chance of success had arrived. A previous triumph of the Congressional Committee, under the leadership of the intelligent, effective Maud Wood Park of Boston, had seen the establishment in September 1917 of a Woman Suffrage Committee in the House. Hitherto the woman suffrage bill had been referred to the Judicial Committee, headed by a strong and immovable opponent of the federal amendment, Edwin Y. Webb of North Carolina. Judge Raker of California was appointed chair of the Woman Suffrage Committee. He introduced a new amendment resolution, and it went automatically to his committee, which promptly reported it favorably. The House vote was scheduled for January 10, 1918.

"The wonderful day came at last and with it the vote which put us through," wrote Catt. It began with Jeannette Rankin, the first congresswoman, who opened the long debate that followed. Suspense vied with tedium as fifty-three more speeches were made during the interminable afternoon. The suffragists barely had their required number of votes and won only because at least five friends came from their sickbeds to vote. Tennessee Representative Thetus W. Sims came with a broken shoulder that he would not have set until after the vote because he was afraid the anesthetic would keep him down. In spite of excruciating pain he stayed on to encourage political friends who were less convinced than he. Henry A. Barnhart of Indiana had himself carried on a stretcher to a place near the Speaker's desk; Robert Crosser of Ohio left a sickbed and the Republican leader James R. Mann of Illinois left a hospital and came in spite of his doctor's warning he was risking his life. Most poignant of all was Frederick C. Hicks, Jr. of New York, who had left his wife's deathbed on her insistence to cast his vote for the resolution. He then went home to her funeral.

The amendment passed by a single extra vote, 274 ayes to 136 nays, one more than the required two-thirds. On their way out of the Capitol, Catt and the women started singing, as they had so long ago at the victory in Colorado, "Praise God, from whom all blessings flow."

The next day Catt wrote to each of the NAWSA state presidents and congressional chairs asking them to start to work at once to get the Senate vote. She was so sure of immediate victory she had a new dress made to wear when she stumped the states to get the amendment ratified. "We teased her about that ratification dress, as month after month went by without a vote," Park wrote, "yet she still found it hard to credit Mrs. Gardener's maxim 'You can't hustle the Senate.'"[16] Catt had ample time to realize the truth of the statement, and the ratification dress had to be remodeled by the time she had occasion to wear it.

By April the NAWSA had completed plans for the ratification campaign; as soon as the Senate passed the amendment every suffrage association knew exactly what to do and how to do it. The Senate delayed, and when the vote was finally set for May 10, it was called off at the last minute. Catt simmered with frustration; she had made more than thirty trips to Washington in six months and had been at home only three weeks in all. She was thoroughly exasperated by June when she wrote, "To deny women the vote longer in any part of the country makes of our war aims a travesty and a lie. It offers vindication to the German claim that America pretends to lofty aims but they are mere talk!"[17]

During this period of attenuated frustration, Catt called for a flood of suffrage petitions and letters which, if they did not influence the Senate, kept her organization involved. British women had been enfranchised January 10, 1918 (the same day as the House vote in Washington). With Shaw, Gardener, Park, Ruth White of the Washington office, and Rose Young, their publicist, Catt called on Wilson personally with an appeal from women of allied nations to demonstrate American democracy by giving women the vote. He acknowledged it with a letter about the debt the world owes to women, and his support of the federal amendment. They got him to revise it and to specify his desire for the Senate's approval during the present session. The Senate thought the letter untactful and responded by delaying their vote.

At one point Catt became so exasperated with aimless sparring over woman suffrage on the Senate floor that she lashed out at a friendly senator. When Park went to explain and apologize to him on Catt's behalf, Park burst into tears and had to endure the usual patronizing comments about women's emotions.

"The whole dastardly business of delay, and backing and filling, and hauling and yanking, has rasped CCC sometimes beyond endurance," Clara Hyde wrote candidly.

She has had periods of deeper depression after some of her Washington trips than I have ever known her to have. Usually she comes out of them pretty quickly, as quickly as Moll will let her. There has been some fracasing in the Washington headquarters—personalities clashing, and people getting on her nerves. But beautiful and patient Maud Park straightens them all out and they go on once more. The Chief wouldn't know where to turn without Maud's wonderful brain and her rare sense of humor. But I believe the only place where CCC is really free from contending forces is in a train *alone* with a book, suspended between somewhere and somewhere.[18]

Restlessly Catt turned her attention to other problems. She rallied the suffragists to promote Liberty Loans, work she saw as a way to keep the movement visible during war hysteria. Early in the war she had been alarmed at infractions of child labor laws and vociferously opposed the suggested repeal of the protective legislation. She used the NAWSA information service to publicize the variety of new jobs women were holding during the war, but she was outraged at their poor work conditions and low salaries. She sent a furious letter to Secretary of the Treasury McAdoo when she found hundreds of women in the government's own printing and engraving service were required to work twelve hours a day without adequate places or time for rest and meals. She took on the State Department for having sharply different pay scales for men and women, and she waged her own guerrilla-memoranda war against that discrimination. Women and men must be paid at the same rate for the same job she insisted; anything less betrayed both men and women.

The Senate continued to delay the vote on the suffrage amendment until the end of September. One of the few cheerful notes during that hot, bleak summer was the election of Mary Garrett Hay to chair the Platform Committee at the Republican State Conference at Saratoga in July. It was the first time a woman held the post, second in prestige only to the convention chair. Catt wrote to Park about this first convention in which women were permitted to take a real part. "Of course you have heard that Mollie is chairman of the resolutions committee of the Republican conference and that members of her committee are Senator Wadsworth [whose wife was national president of the antis], Senator Calder, Elon R. Brown and other distinguished politicians. We are in roars of laughter over it. It was certainly a mighty victory."[19]

Finally the Senate announced a vote would be taken on Thursday, September 26, and suffragists once again descended on Washington. "It is like pandemonium at the [Suffrage] house," wrote Catt, "every corner stuck full of suffragists."[20] Rumors flew—the vote would be postponed, it was on;

this senator was for, that one against. Catt led a delegation of thirty-five women bearing masses of data and petitions, and she presented the vice-president with a roll of manuscript a foot and a half in diameter. A similar expression of support for the amendment was left with Senator Jones of New Mexico, chair of the Woman Suffrage Committee.

A few anti-amendment senators made their first appearance in weeks. "Mrs. Catt found listening to the opponents, with no chance to reply so trying that when it became clear there would be no vote that afternoon she went back to Suffrage House," Park wrote.[21]

Catt returned to the gallery Friday and Saturday. Still the debates droned on. Although Park and Hay were not confident that President Wilson could change any votes, Catt called on him again for help. "We hope that you who have proved yourself a miracle worker on many occasions may be able to produce another wonder on Monday—the wonder of putting vision where there was none before," she wrote to him.[22] He agreed to appear.

Promptly at one o'clock, Wilson, flanked by his cabinet, came and spoke simply and directly, asking support of the federal amendment, which many of his own party opposed. After his departure, the senators went on with their bitter debate.

The following day, October 1, 1918, the vote was taken. There were sixty-two in favor, thirty-four against, just two votes short of the needed two-thirds majority. Senator Jones, just before the total was announced, changed his vote so he could move reconsideration, thus allowing the amendment to stay on the calendar for the current session.

After those agonizing days, Catt never again went to Washington when a suffrage vote was to be taken. She could do nothing and it was useless torment to be there. She did go with Park and others the next day to call on the president and thank him.[23]

Three of the four state suffrage referenda were successful in November— South Dakota, a winner after twenty-eight years and on the seventh try, Michigan, and Oklahoma. Louisiana was defeated in its only referendum. The campaigns had been difficult; continuing war fever and the decimating flu epidemic that swept the country were major events in 1918 that distracted many ardent suffragists from the old work. Catt herself had been forced by flu to cancel her plans to go to South Dakota in October but had sent a constant stream of advice and publications. She insisted on pamphlets being mailed over objections of local leaders that postage had gone up; every letter now cost two cents.[24]

On November 11, 1918, the armistice was declared. Within a few days

Catt made a public appeal urging that women be represented in the United States delegation to the Peace Conference scheduled to begin in Paris in December. Released from condoning a war she supported only for political expediency, she began at once to talk about what women could do to end all war. Women's participation in the world's work was vital to shatter the illusion of male-dominated governments that war was the means to secure peace.

But the vote for women had to come first.

· 16 ·
Victory

A second defeat of woman suffrage (by one vote) in the Senate on February 10, 1919, during the lame-duck session, destroyed all hope of friendly Democrats that the Sixty-fifth Congress would get credit for passing the amendment. Nevertheless the 1918 election placed so many suffrage friends in both houses of the next Congress that victory seemed assured.

In the interval before the Sixty-sixth Congress, the suffragists held a Jubilee Convention in St. Louis beginning on March 24, 1919. This celebrated the fiftieth anniversaries of the National and the American Woman Suffrage Associations and marked the half century of woman suffrage in Wyoming. "Jubilee" was used in its anniversary meaning; when the convention was planned the suffragists had hoped it would be in a celebratory sense as well. Because Catt expected that NAWSA's work to secure the suffrage would soon be finished, she used the Jubilee Convention of 1919 to organize NAWSA's successor, the National League of Women Voters.

NAWSA estimated its membership above two million. About seven million women had secured some kind of suffrage by 1919. The ratified federal amendment would give full suffrage to about twenty-seven million, the largest extension of the franchise by a government not in the throes of revolution. About twenty million women would have had little experience in politics, and Catt saw that before such an organization as she envisioned could be an effective, informed lobby, its first priority would be education in using the vote.

She always envisioned that organized suffragists would continue working for the liberation of women and for honest, responsive government once they had the vital tool of the vote. From the time she first became active in the movement she was appalled at how little women knew of the most elementary rules of parliamentary procedure, let alone of how a bill becomes an act. When her organization machinery was set up and working in the 1890s, her next project had been in 1897 to start a political science course. This was the first trial run of her basic concept of the League of Women Voters, which she described as "the education of women citizens, piloting them through the first years of political participation, and removing the relics of discrimination against women."[1]

Schools for her campaign workers were held intermittently over the years, the most ambitious during the New York State campaigns. A prototype of the National League was the National Council of Women Voters organized at Tacoma, Washington, in January 1914, with Emma Smith DeVoe as president. It represented women from five states and grew as more states enfranchised them. In addition to knowing how to use the vote effectively, Catt insisted everyone should know the great contributions women had made to America's history.[2]

Catt was convinced that in spite of the graft and corruption she had seen in politics, most people wanted honest government but were not sure how to make intelligent use of their citizenship. An organization of women voters would educate themselves and through them would promote active participation in government by all citizens. With unwarranted optimism, Catt thought the education of women in politics could be accomplished quickly, and after a few years the League of Women Voters would disband, although, she wrote, some people who were "in the spirit of the new movement may discover it is an organization worth perpetuating."[3]

There were fifteen full suffrage states by the time of the Jubilee Convention and concurrently with NAWSA reports and meetings there were discussions preliminary to the organization of the League of Women Voters. The tenth of eleven recommendations made by the NAWSA Executive Council and adopted by the convention was, "That an organization of women voters be formed." It was a quiet and unassuming start of a complex and influential permanent national association. For the next year it remained merely a section of the NAWSA.[4]

A special session of the Sixty-sixth Congress began on May 19, 1919. Representative James R. Mann of Illinois, a Republican of some stature, agreed to chair the low-ranking Woman Suffrage Committee.[5] Mann introduced the woman suffrage bill as House Joint Resolution No. 1 on the opening day. The next day it was favorably reported by the committee, and the vote was taken on May 21, 1919, with 304 in favor to 89 opposed. "Never was there a more splendid response to the movement for justice to women now sweeping through the world," Catt said.[6]

The Senate preliminaries for bringing the resolution to vote appeared perfunctory to the Congressional Committee. Debate began on June 3 and for two of the hottest days of the summer, suffragists crowded the galleries and forced themselves to listen while the senators talked on and on and on. Finally, late in the afternoon of the fourth the roll call began, and as in a dream they heard the words, "The ayes are 56 and the noes are 25." They had won.

Catt had stayed at home, firm in her resolution not to torture herself by listening to any more congressional debates. Hay at once phoned the news. "CCC danced all over the place and then settled down to THINK."[7] She immediately sent off telegrams to the governors of the states asking them to call special sessions for quick ratification of the Nineteenth Amendment, or to urge ratification by those states already in session or soon to meet. She also wired the women in each state who were in charge of ratification committees to set their plans in motion.[8]

Her action plan started a race to see which state would be the first to ratify—a rivalry that would have seemed millennial to the pioneers of the women's movement. Illinois and Wisconsin legislatures were in session and both ratified within the week, on June 10, 1919. Illinois won the race but forty-five minutes later Wisconsin put a special messenger on the train to be the first to reach the Secretary of State with its certificate. Michigan ratified the same day in special session.

That evening a last party was held at Suffrage House, where Catt, Hay, Park, and Gardener received members of Congress and their spouses in a quiet celebration. Her friends had never seen Catt look so contented and happy. "She spoke easily and pleasantly, no oratory, and in a heart to heart way as though we were all one family, and she was taking everybody into her heart. I have never seen Mrs. Catt in that attitude before," wrote Caroline Reilly to Anna Howard Shaw, who was ill with pneumonia and unable to come.[9]

A week later Kansas, New York, and Ohio ratified, and the month's roster was completed by Pennsylvania, Massachusetts, and Texas. Five more states followed in July and August—Iowa, Missouri, Arkansas, Nebraska, and Montana—with three more in September—Minnesota, New Hampshire, and Utah. Within the first four months the suffragists had ratification by seventeen of the necessary thiry-six states; they were 47 percent on their way.

Catt urged friends of the amendment not to allow it to come to vote unless they were sure it would pass—victory bred victory and must not be diverted by defeats that might become equally contagious. Opponents introduced the ratification in Delaware, Georgia, and Alabama by the end of September, and in each case the amendment was turned down.

The greatest exasperation was in the western suffrage states. In spite of pressure brought on the governors, none, except Utah, was willing to call the necessary special session, even when the suffragists or the legislators were willing to pay expenses. This was not due to disinclination to ratify the Nineteenth Amendment, but to put off as long as possible labor legislation, which threatened to come before any session. A general strike in Seattle in February 1919 signaled the increasing strength of the labor unions, with agitation and unrest continuing.

By fall only five of the fifteen full suffrage states had approved the amendment, so in October Catt packed her refurbished "ratification dress" and headed west on a "Wake Up America" tour. It was a propaganda trip in the old style, fourteen conferences in thirteen states in eight weeks. There were one- and two-day conventions and meetings with women; there were visits to capitals to see governors and important state officials. She stirred local organizations to demand that governors call special legislative sessions and she encouraged suffragists to use whatever influence they had on legislators. Ratification was one purpose of the trip, the other was to explain the new League of Women Voters.

Traveling with Catt were several women who represented the most immediate of the new League's concerns: Dr. Valeria Parker of the Social Morality Committee; E. Jean Nelson Penfield, Committee on Codification of the Civil Laws; Jessie Haver, Committee on Food Supply and Demand; and Marjorie Shuler, Committee on Election Laws and Committee on Child Welfare. There were eight national League committees and when possible the state's chairs were present at the conferences.[10]

At the meetings the old time suffrage workers were honored. In Salt Lake City, Catt found the ninety-three-year-old Emmeline B. Wells still going strong, as was Emily Richards, who was president of the state suffrage council begun in 1899 during Catt's visit to Utah. In Mitchell, South Dakota, where Catt had started on her first campaign by attending the searing Republican State Convention in 1890, there were twenty-five South Dakota stalwarts who had worked in the movement for the past three decades. Catt met other old friends every place she visited. (In San Francisco an old beau from Charles City high school days surprised her with a marriage proposal. She was flattered and amused but much too busy waking up America.) Off she went to Denver and Laramie. There the program for one session was typical: "The Woman Voter and the Nation's Laws," "The Woman Voter and the Nation's Morals," "The Woman Voter and the Nation's Children," followed by Catt's "Wake Up America."

California, Maine, North Dakota, South Dakota, and Colorado all ratified in November and December in special sessions. In the first six weeks of 1920, Rhode Island, Kentucky, and New Jersey ratified in regular sessions, with special sessions approving the amendment in Oregon, Indiana, Wyoming, Nevada, Idaho, and Arizona. During the same time the amendment was turned down by Mississippi, South Carolina, and Virginia.

Nevertheless, the NAWSA Executive Board called its delegates to a Victory Convention in Chicago, February 12–18, 1920. Although the name was premature it antedated final success of the Nineteenth Amendment by only six months. The conference marked the completion of the work of the NAWSA, dissolution of the national organization (except for a small board to make final disposition of assets and records), and the first convention of the League of Women Voters for which the foundation had been laid the preceding year.

In previous conventions women were called to cheer and encourage each other, to teach and learn, and to go forth strengthened in the fight for their common cause, Catt reminded suffragists in the call to the Victory Convention; however, "This time they are called to rejoice that the struggle is over and the women of the nation were about to enter into the enjoyment of their hard-earned political liberty." During their meetings she said they would honor the pioneers and their ever buoyant hope, their unswerving courage and determination; they would express the joy of the present; and they would ask what political parties wanted of women and they of the parties.

An especially moving tribute to the pioneers included a memorial to Anna Howard Shaw, who had died on July 2, 1919. She had lived to see the Nineteenth Amendment passed by Congress and the beginning of the ratification. Catt's tribute to the early workers included "glorious Susan B. Anthony, whose indomitable will kept things stirring for forty years and more; and greatest of them all, with her transcendent gifts—Anna Howard Shaw." The convention voted and began funding a joint memorial to Shaw— at Bryn Mawr College a foundation in politics, and at the Woman's Medical College of Pennsylvania, a foundation in preventive medicine.[11]

Catt presented to the seven hundred women there the plan and purpose of the League in an inspirational talk. She emphasized that the object of the League of Women Voters was not to seek power in organization but power to secure legislation. The League's constitution, with its details of membership and officers, representation, and budget was approved. Its simply stated object was "to foster education in citizenship and to support improved legislation." The keystone of the structure was that every woman was urged to become an enrolled voter and work within the party of her choice but "as an organization it shall be allied with and support no party."

Catt emphasized that "We must be nonpartisan and all partisan." It was easy to say, hard to practice. She pointed out the anomaly of the League of Women Voters being a semi-political organization doing political things, getting legislation passed, educating for citizenship. At the same time she wanted the League to lead the way, to be ahead of the political parties by at least five years. Traveling in the rear of the procession was too dusty and dirty, in the middle it was too crowded, only in the lead was the air clean and bracing.

Catt insisted she did not want to lead the new work, that was for younger and fresher women. "For thirty years and a little more, I have worked with you in the first lap of this struggle toward woman's emancipation," she said. She refused the presidency, settling for "Honorary Chairman." Maud Wood Park was elected to head the League of Women Voters.

A feature of the salute to the pioneers was the presentation of distinguished service certificates and honor roll badges. As Catt neared the end of the long presentation, Harriet Taylor Upton stepped from the rear of the platform, waved Catt aside, but kept a detaining hand on her arm, and began a presentation speech. Catt's "Distinguished Service" badge was a brooch consisting of a large sapphire surrounded by diamonds. Nickels and dimes had been collected by public subscription and the individual contributions had poured in by the thousands. The jewel was the National's parting gift to her. Some teachers asked their pupils to contribute and a favorite story among the fund-raisers was that one small boy told his mother he needed a penny to give for a monument to Charlie Chaplin's cat. This was considered a great joke and eventually it was told to Catt. She perpetuated the anecdote by inquiring, "Who is Charlie Chaplin?"[12]

After the convention, Catt wrote about the League of Women Voters to Anne Martin: "It has a pretty full program this year. The first one is its schools of citizenship which are designed to teach the women how to vote intelligently and also to get out as many women to vote as possible. The second is to secure planks in the platforms of the parties and to work for legislation in the 1921 sessions of the Legislatures. No movement to back women candidates was proposed in the National Convention. Each state is free to take that matter up if it so desires."[13]

In the spring Catt went off to Geneva and the important first postwar congress of the International Woman Suffrage Alliance. Before she left for Europe, ratification occurred in New Mexico, Oklahoma, West Virginia, and

Washington, totaling thirty-five states, just one short of the needed majority. But as those states where ratification was politically possible grew fewer, national and local opposition could be concentrated against the amendment. One of the strategies of Catt's winning plan had been to involve so many states simultaneously that national opposition was diffused. But by this time such an advantage no longer served. There was so much opposition in West Virginia that ratification had been a long cliff-hanger. Finally the House had approved and the state Senate vote was tied at 14 to 14 when Senator Jesse A. Bloch secured a place in the suffragists' roll of honor when he dashed by special train from California to break the tie in the nick of time. When Catt returned from Geneva in August, the last great political fight for suffrage was being waged in Nashville.

"I had scarcely taken off my hat at home before I was summoned to Tennessee," Catt wrote to one of her Alliance friends. She packed her overnight bag and went down for a few days just to make sure that preparations were adequate. She was appalled at the size and force of the opposition being marshaled to defeat the federal amendment. An old hand at spotting unscrupulous tactics, she decided to stay and fight on the spot. "It's awful that she has to be there in the heat but there's no other way out of it and she is ten times more satisfied being on the ground watching the machinery than being at home stewing over the possible mistakes that might be made in Tennessee," wrote Clara Hyde. To Catt herself, Hyde wrote of the satisfaction the suffragists felt to have the "Dear Chief" on the spot: "You have energized and galvanized the whole ratification machinery. We have a place in the publicity sun again. You are on the front page of the [New York] *Times* this morning. It is hard on you to be the goat in a factional fight under a torrid sun, but if there is such a thing as compensation for duty done, it is flowing to you in a wide stream of blessings from all over the country."[14]

Catt went on a speaking tour of the major cities in Tennessee, then settled in at the Hotel Hermitage to see ratification through. She herself did no lobbying at the state house, leaving this to the Tennessee suffragists who descended on the capital en masse. Sue White, Tennessee chair of the National Woman's Party, directed her organization's activities, and there were antis by the score.

On August 13, 1920, the Tennessee Senate voted approval and Catt wrote:

We now have 35½ states. We are up to our last half of a state. With all
the political pressure, it ought to be easy, but the opposition of every sort

is here fighting with no scruple desperately. Women, including L[aura]
Clay and K[ate] Gordon [two of Catt's old friends who turned against her]
are here appealing to Negro phobia and every other cave man's prejudice.
Men, lots of them, are here. What do they represent? God only knows.
We believe they are buying votes. We have a poll of the House showing
victory but they are trying to keep them at home, to break a quorum and
God only knows the outcome We are terribly worried and so is the other
side. I've been here a month. It is hot, muggy nasty, and this last battle is
desperate. We are low in our minds—even if we win we who have been
here will never remember it with anything but a shudder. Verily the way
of the reformer is hard.[15]

Catt's public summary was:

Never in the history of politics has there been such a force for evil, such a
nefarious lobby as labored to block the advance of suffrage in Nashville,
Tenn. In the short time I spent in Tennessee's capital, I have been called
more names, been more maligned, more lied about than in the thirty
previous years I worked for suffrage. I was flooded with anonymous
letters, vulgar, ignorant, insane. Strange men and groups of men sprang
up, men we had never met before in battle. We were told this is the
railroad lobby, this is the steel lobby, these are lobbyists from the
Manufacturers' Association, these come from the aluminum interests,
this is the remnant of the old whiskey ring. Even tricksters from the
United States Revenue Service were there, operating against us, until
the President of these great States called them off. They appropriated our
telegrams, tapped our telephones, listened outside our windows and
transoms. They attacked our private and public lives.[16]

Permeating all this was the unrelenting heat of the South in August.
The most dramatic session ever held in the Tennessee House galvanized
Nashville on a stifling August 18. Catt kept her resolution not to go to the
state house to listen to the roll call but through the open windows of her
rooms in the nearby hotel she could hear cheers and applause. Later she heard
the details. One man was carried from his hospital bed to vote for the
amendment; another who was on the train going home where his baby was
dying leaped off the train as it was moving out of the station. After he voted
for the resolution, another suffrage friend sent him home by special train.
The vote was tied 48 to 48 when a twenty-four year old first-term representative from the mountains of southeast McMinn County changed his vote in
deference to his mother's charge that he vote for the resolution, although he

knew his constituency was not in favor. Harry T. Burn's switch carried the day and ratification was complete.

One of Catt's sources of power was her understanding of the courage shown by friends of suffrage who often stood alone in their own small towns and risked their careers to vote for women. She never mentioned the problems Leo Chapman had in Mason City, but she never forgot the pain of small-town rivalries. Harry Burn was high on the suffrage roll of honor, representing thousands who had voted by their conscience. [17]

The suffragists waited out the political maneuverings to try to overturn the vote before celebrating on August 24, when Governor Roberts signed the certificate of ratification and sent it to Washington. To avoid delays that the opponents' lawyers were busy preparing, Secretary of State Colby had left orders to be awakened at the moment it arrived. He was called at 3:45 A.M. on August 26, 1920, and after clarifying a point or two with the Solicitor General who had sat up all night waiting, without ceremony, in his own home, Colby signed the proclamation announcing that the Nineteenth Amendment had become part of the Constitution of the United States. [18]

Catt arrived in Washington shortly after eight that morning on her way home from Tennessee. Harriet Taylor Upton and Maud Wood Park were in the room with her when she telephoned the Secretary of State to ask if the certification had been received. As Park later wrote, "She put down the telephone, turned to us and said, 'The Secretary has signed the proclamation, and he wants us to go over to his office and see it before he sends it out.' So quietly as that, we learned that the last step in the enfranchisement of women in the United States had been taken and the struggle of more than seventy years brought to a successful end." [19]

In the afternoon, Catt, Park, and Helen Gardener were received at the White House by President and Mrs. Wilson. They presented to him "a memorial of appreciation in the form of a bound volume, a page coming from each state Association, acknowledging the work he did for suffrage." [20]

A great victory meeting was held that night and the next day Catt proceeded in triumph to New York. She was met at Pennsylvania station by a mob of suffragists, and by Governor Alfred E. Smith, with official congratulations to the state's "distinguished citizen." Her favorite picture was taken just before the procession started for the celebration meeting at the Hotel Astor—she stands triumphant with a huge bouquet of blue delphiniums and yellow chrysanthemums tied with a yellow ribbon on which the Tiffany studios had painted in blue, "To Mrs. Carrie Chapman Catt from the enfranchised women of the United States." The band played "Hail the Conquering Hero

Comes," banners waved, and women split their gloves clapping. "This is a glorious and wonderful day," she said. "Now that we have the vote let us remember we are no longer petitioners. We are not wards of the nation but free and equal citizens. Let us do our part to keep it a true and triumphant democracy."[21]

Catt was home at Juniper Ledge, the new house she and Mary Hay shared in Westchester County, through the fall, "to rest, exercise and get myself back on the trolley," she wrote to her friend Mary Peck. She gardened and supervised the building of a greenhouse she had always wanted, but she did not retire. She went to the New York office several times every week, spoke at meetings and held some briefing sessions for workers in the anti-Wadsworth campaign the League of Women Voters was sponsoring. (James Wadsworth, New York senator, and his wife, president of the National Association Opposed to Woman Suffrage, were fierce enemies of enfranchisement.) She also kept up on the progress of the legal barriers the diehard opposition was trying to erect to block women's vote. "The Antis are giving me no rest. The entire anti press of the South are screeching at me and [our legal advisor] tells us that they propose 'to enjoin and mandamus' all the election boards. So, as I am not a lawyer am a bit out of my depth. I have to keep my eyes open and my nerves alert lest they do put something over on us that no one expects. So life is not yet the calm pacific thing you imagine."[22] She had foreseen much of this and had retained for the suffragists Charles Evans Hughes, the most celebrated constitutional lawyer of the time.

She herself was more interested in assuring that the United States join the League of Nations. In October she abandoned her stated position of neutrality in the presidential campaign, and in spite of the noisy disapproval of the Republican Mary Hay, Catt headed an appeal signed by sixty-five prominent women urging support of the Democratic ticket of Governor James M. Cox and Franklin D. Roosevelt. Some of the positive results that she thought would come from the international peace machinery would be the lowering of taxes and the cost of living through disarmament.[23]

Catt was gravitating toward her next cause, working for peace through international understanding and cooperation. As yet she had no definite plan of her own. "Women say they want no more war. The only way by which they can avert war is through a knowledge of world politics. Intelligence and understanding must be cultivated, and intolerance, reaction and provincialism uprooted from every mind. That is the task of the new woman voter," she wrote in a national magazine just before the presidential election. Membership of the United States in the League of Nations was the sine qua non.[24]

The election of Warren G. Harding on November 2, 1920, doomed the League of Nations, but the fight for internationalism continued in spite of growing isolationism in the next decades.

Two weeks after the election, at a League of Women Voters dinner concluding a regional conference, Catt made an impulsive speech declaring it was only because of partisanship and cowardice that representatives of the United States were not now sitting at the League of Nations meeting in Geneva with the representatives of forty-one other nations in a movement to end war. "She blew the cover off the soup pot and spilled the whole contents," Hyde described the speech and added, "The League of Women Voters won't play League of Nations principally because there are on the board some strong machine Repubs. I never saw CCC so het up over any situation. I believe she was dying for the opportunity to scourge the women on the subject and she jumped right in. Mollie [Mary Hay] feels as black as ink over the business. She was howling round that an avalanche of resignations was pouring in the LWV headquarters and stinging CCC like a wasp with the trouble she had caused."[25]

One member of the Republican Women's State Executive Committee resigned from the League of Women Voters because of Catt's "deplorable action" in making the speech that "was smeared thickly with the kind of sentimentality which kept us out of war."[26] It was not the last time Catt was castigated for her strong commitment to peace.

Catt's presence at the meeting had been by chance; she had expected to sail for London for IWSA Executive Board meetings the week before but the ship had been delayed by a strike in England. She boarded it two days later and en route wrote tongue-in-cheek to Mary Peck,

> I've done several things lately much more erratic than the cow did when she jumped the moon. At least that is what several erstwhile friends think. I elected Wadsworth by coming out for the League of Nations. I've killed the League of Women Voters dead as a coffin nail by staying out for the said L of N. What little influence I once had is entirely evaporated; new friends have left me and old friends now regard me coldly. At last I am free with no guardian but my conscience and I am rather enjoying this suddenly won isolation.[27]

So quickly was American sentiment changing that barely four months after bands had hailed her as a conquering hero, she was being denounced by former friends as an enemy. She found it bracing.

The League of Women Voters' firm stand against Wadsworth and their unsuccessful attempt to have him defeated in his reelection taught a hard lesson. This ill-advised excursion into partisan politics seemed merely vindictive to some. For a short time it seemed that the newly launched League of Women Voters might be scuttled by party machinery of which they had only sketchy knowledge and no control. In succeeding years the League stubbornly refused to support or oppose candidates and concerned itself only with issues, a policy that immeasurably strengthened public opinion and eventually gained admiration for the League's thorough study of issues before giving support to legislation.

The women had to listen to the new Republican Governor Nathan L. Miller of New York tell them at a state League convention several weeks after the election that they had no reason to exist, they were a menace to the institutions of the republic (because they were not a political party), they were evil, and he was opposed to the social welfare legislation the League advocated. There was no applause when he finished his diatribe.

Catt replied that the governor was suspicious because "The League of Women Voters constitute the remains of that army which for fifty years in the State of New York fought the battle for the enfranchisement of their sex. They stood fast until the State of New York caught up with them and until the nation caught up with them. The majority surrendered but a minority remains, still bitter because we are women." The League was going ahead with its social welfare program, using the hard-hitting tactics learned in suffrage battles. The League urged women to join existing parties but it was never intended to be a political party itself. They were out to educate the citizens and to get better government. "I do not recall one time in history when a great reform was brought about by a political party," Catt observed to the governor. "The League of Women Voters aspires to be a part of the big majorities which administer our government, and at the same time, it wishes to be one of the minorities which agitates and educates and shapes ideas today which the majority will adopt tomorrow."

It made for a lively convention. Newspaper headlines about the League of Women Voters were splashed on front pages all over the state. Catt herself dismissed the furor as being caused by ignorance and said, when the governor charged the League with being a "menace" as he did four times, "he was so far overreaching facts as to be amusingly ridiculous." Her account of the incident in the *Woman Citizen* was summed up in its headline, "A Teapot in a Tempest."[28]

The League of Women Voters was well launched in spite of the rocky takeoff, and turned its attention to important social legislation. Catt followed the League's fortunes with interest, gave money from the Leslie fund to support the League's news section in the *Woman Citizen*, gave speeches to and about the League of Women Voters for the rest of her life, but turned her primary skills to the problem of world peace.

PEACE AND WAR
1920–1947

Carrie Chapman Catt, ca. 1923

· 17 ·

The Alliance Resumes

On November 14, 1918, three days after the armistice and long before the Tennessee ratification, Catt began to plan the first postwar congress of the International Woman Suffrage Alliance. Thanks to American money, the Alliance headquarters in London had weathered the war years, keeping its doors open and publishing its impartial journal every month. Working with other organizations through the International Woman's Relief Commission, more than a thousand European and British women had been repatriated.[1]

On the other hand, the sprawling membership had been polarized by the cruelty and propaganda of war. The timing of the next congress was crucial. Some raw feelings toward recent enemies had to heal, but the delay must not be so long that women would lose their impetus for action. Catt knew that failure of the Alliance to reassemble productively could mean "the loss of a generation in the evolution of human society."[2]

Marguerite Schlumberger, leader of the French suffragists, "is terribly bitter against the German women," wrote Clara Hyde, "and I don't think will be hospitable to the idea of an early congress, or of giving them shoe-room at any congress where they expect Frenchwomen to take part. Of course no correspondence can be had with the Central Powers concerning the Congress until after the treaty of peace is formally signed, because until that is done we are technically at war yet. So we can't get at how the German women would regard a Congress. The chief has a big job before her."[3] In the end, only the Belgian women held out and refused to attend the congress in the summer of 1920.

Catt's first concern was for the women to be united to work for women. Plans were made for the IWSA to meet in Madrid in the spring of 1920 but church hierarchy opposed the feminists and Catt changed the meeting place to Geneva to avoid an open clash.

More than four hundred women met for a week in June 1920, at the Eighth Congress of the IWSA. Since the last congress in 1913 the map of

Europe had been redrawn—political boundaries changed, old countries divided, new nations created, independence restored to former dependencies. Ironically, woman suffrage had come to many as a result of the war.[4] It seemed a small gain to come from so much suffering.

Catt admitted she never thought she would see the day when women representing enfranchised countries were so numerous she had to ask them to cut short their speeches. Gaunt delegates told of starvation, runaway inflation, ruinous taxes, increasing and ever more violent crime. Broad issues of revolution, political instability, and the future peace of the world clamored for attention. Catt said, "Facing the gigantic political tasks, the newly won vote seems pitifully poor and small. Men and women are experiencing a sense of helplessness they never knew before." She searched for an apt metaphor to describe her despair of coping with the issues and came up with one as old as Aristophanes: "Each nation is like a hopelessly tangled ball of yarn, and the world is like a basket full of them."[5]

The good news was that with the extension of suffrage women had been elected to the parliaments of ten countries. As a further indication of women's growing political strength, sixteen governments had sent official delegates to Geneva.[6]

Happily the tensions before the congress had been eased by the diplomatic intervention of Adele Schreiber, a newly elected member of the German Reichstag, who arranged a small, private meeting with the French women. In neither country, she said, had women had political influence in declaring or conducting the war, and in both countries women and their children alike had suffered. She appealed to both sides to be benevolent, the cooperation of all women was needed for the maintenance of peace. The French accepted this, and many commented on the reassuring sight of Marguerite Schlumberger and Marie Stritt, a German government delegate, sitting side by side.[7]

Delegates from the new republics, Czechoslovakia, Lithuania, Ukrania, Estonia, Poland, and Latvia told of the part women were taking in forming their first governments. Schickina Javein, president of the Russian affiliate to the IWSA, was laconically reported as being unable to come since she was a fugitive from her country, but she sent her greetings to the congress. There had been no response from either the Portuguese or the Polish auxiliaries, but the Polish government sent an official representative. Four new auxiliaries were added to the IWSA—Argentina, Greece, Spain, and Uruguay.

And there were the "exotics"—women from Japan in their kimonos and from India in saris. Chinese women were on their way but the difficulties of postwar travel prevented them from getting to Geneva in time. A Turkish woman told of advances in her country. Most astounding of all was Mrs. Hanije Seidamed, wife of the Tartar president of Crimea. She reported that her country, immediately upon declaring its independence, gave suffrage to its women—Mohammedan women—and the women of the United States were not yet enfranchised! There were, in fact, five women elected to the Diet, one of whom was the vice-president. It was a great revelation to the Alliance that the Moslems were so far advanced.

Less dramatic but widely and wryly noted was the announcement that Luxembourg women had been given the franchise in 1919 and were subject to a fine if they did not vote.[8]

In her regular president's address, Catt complimented the countries where woman suffrage had come and dwelt at length on the anomaly that the United States could not yet be counted among the number. She warned her colleagues to beware of indifference to their governments and reminded them that with their votes they could rebuild Europe, emancipate their sex, and make the world a fit place to live. Democracy must be extended to world politics, and the old militarism must go.

As for the Alliance itself, the question was one that had been discussed before the war: When the ballot is won, what shall we do? Catt wanted to expand the work of emancipation to include men and women. Her goal was worldwide amity to exclude war forever through an international nexus of viable democratic institutions. She made her old appeal for education, honest elections, and high ideals in politics. She concluded her address by saying it was time for the older leaders to step down and for younger women to take over. Seldom did she end a speech so inconclusively, but she wanted to retire from the presidency, citing her age [sixty-one] and diminished energies.[9]

The delegates got up a petition asking her to stay in office and argued that if the president were a European woman, Americans would not take as large a part in the Alliance as formerly. It would be another American withdrawal from internationalism. Catt, acutely sensitive to the isolationist position the United States Congress had taken against the League of Nations, was persuaded to withdraw her resignation and was reelected by acclamation.

Many women remarked on Catt's untypical weariness and air of sadness at the meetings. Her buoyancy seemed to have been absorbed in the long fight for the Nineteenth Amendment and its ratification. There was always at the back of her mind the uncertainty of that necessary thirty-sixth state. She enjoyed greeting old friends but was distressed at the gauntness of many, reflecting the desperate food shortages in parts of Europe. There were sad tales of war and suffering. It was an emotional and enervating conference, but an ambitious program of working for women's political, personal, domestic, educational, economic, and moral rights was set in motion.

Catt left Geneva immediately after the congress; in mid-July she went to Tennessee and stayed until ratification was complete. She returned to New York in triumph at the end of August, then went to IWSA board meetings in London in mid-November.

It was her first trip to England since 1914. She found a bleak, cold country suffering from coal strikes. The London press greeted her as a natural aristocrat, a kind of Queen Mother figure:

> Mrs. Catt [is] a dominating figure of mature womanhood, alert and modern in every detail, dressed in superb taste, always in blue or black, corseted to perfection, with neck open in a deep V, edged with fine old lace and wearing, as always, her single jewel, a large clear blue stone low on her bosom. Her hair is snowy white and her eyes are bright and searching and in spite of the long struggle, barely ended, she seems to be in radiant health, with no trace of the weary sadness which distinguished her at the Geneva congress.[10]

The IWSA Board set up four committees to collect from all nations information about (1) the nationality of married women, (2) women's right to work and to equal pay, (3) the care of married and unmarried mothers and their children, and (4) moral standards, the restraint of prostitution, and the campaign to combat venereal disease. The board asked women of the enfranchised countries to help further the work in those countries without the vote: Great Britain concentrated on South Africa, India, and Egypt, and was to give special care to the women of Palestine, where the Jewish women were themselves beginning to organize the Arab women in the hope of securing political rights for them. Canada was asked to help Newfoundland, and the United States would organize women in Jamaica, Cuba, and South America.[11]

After making the commitment for U. S. women, Catt had to find out as much as she could about the only continent in the world, South America, where no woman had the vote. There were suffrage associations in Argentina and Uruguay that were affiliated with the IWSA, and organizations in Brazil, Chile, and Paraguay, as well as in Cuba and Puerto Rico.

Lavinia Engle, a member of the Baltimore League of Women Voters, suggested that a pan-American conference be held just before the League's third national convention there in April 1922. With the blessings of the State Department, invitations were sent to all the Latin American countries, plus the Philippines and Canada. El Salvador alone declined. Eighty-five women from twenty-two countries met for three days of round-table discussions about mutual problems such as social morality and child rearing. Before the meetings ended, Catt had organized the Pan American Association for the Advancement of Women (National Liga para la Emancipacion de la Mujer). Objectives included educational opportunities for women, the right of married women to control their own property and wages, and to have equal guardianship with their husbands of their children. The most controversial item was the shortest, "To secure the vote for women." It was a briefer, more succinct, and less demanding list than the Seneca Falls resolutions three-quarters of a century earlier but the essence was there. It was Catt's way to start on a low-keyed note and proceed step by step toward making drastic changes quietly. Inevitably, Catt was asked to be president and she agreed to take the office for a year, during which time she would visit South America and report on the status of women there.[12]

Catt's commitment to international suffrage led to an exceptionally wide-ranging year. She was going to Rome to make arrangements for the IWSA in 1923, then had planned a lecture tour through central Europe. After Executive Board meetings in London, she was off to South America, and then would return to Italy for her final congress as president.

Before she left, she was commissioned to write a book with Nettie Rogers Shuler titled *Woman Suffrage and Politics*. Day after day she wrote, and as the manuscript grew so did her migraines. Catt would have been well advised to put the book aside until she had more leisure. As she reviewed the old campaigns of the NAWSA, long-repressed angers and disappointments surfaced in her prose, which tended to become bitter and brittle. The book heavily emphasizes the frustrations and defeats of suffragists by the corrupt hirelings of the liquor industry but says all too little about the innovative, dedicated women who made suffrage possible. The manuscript was completed in August but came back from the publisher with a request for drastic revision. Catt worked on rewriting until she left for Europe in October, reluctantly leaving the last draft to Shuler and Rose Young. The book exhausted her, she felt like "a mere pancake" and suffered "spells of dizzyheadedness and fatigue." The sea voyage revived her somewhat but she was too jaded to enjoy it.

Rosa Manus, a Dutch woman who had been a loyal friend of Catt's since the 1908 Alliance congress in Amsterdam, was at the dock in Naples to meet her and accompany her to Rome. Following six days of meetings with the Italian women, a date for the congress had been set, a place obtained, and a press chair appointed. It had taken a world of talk to get that little accomplished. To make matters worse, Catt developed dysentery that plagued her for the next several weeks.

Meanwhile bands of black-shirted men were marching across Italy to converge in Rome not far from her hotel. On October 28 Mussolini was empowered by the king to form a new Cabinet. Catt noted in her diary that the city was under siege but in her illness these events seemed unreal: "It is just politics á la Italien," she wrote. The next day, "Rosa and I went hunting for Fascisti. They were everywhere, singing and marching with the populace looking on. I came home and took my aches to bed." On October 31 Mussolini entered Rome. The stone walls of the city were plastered with placards declaring a holiday to celebrate the triumph of fascism. Catt marveled that "the day passed with no incident to disturb its order—blue skies, marching armed men, music and thronged streets—nothing more." Later when she wrote her account for the *Woman Citizen* she made her loathing clear: "The Fascist movement is too big, too unique, too significant to be overlooked. It is a young man's movement and Mussolini is himself young. It is also a soldiers' movement. At any moment it may take on a new program, and behind it is an armed political party which overnight may become an army." She emphasized "the Fascisti are anti-feminists. Mussolini is not only an anti-suffragist but one with no open mind." She told friends that he offers "small comfort to reformers."[13] She did not want to hold the 1923 congress in Rome.

Catt and Manus left Rome on the first of November for Budapest, the beginning of a planned tour of Hungary, Austria, Czechoslovakia, and Germany en route to London and the IWSA Executive Board meetings. Catt wanted to see what was happening to the suffrage forces in a middle Europe plagued by inflation and hunger. Universal suffrage had been extended in Hungary immediately after the war but political changes were unending and by 1922 women were voting on more restricted terms than men. Hungary had been carved up by the terms of the peace treaties and traveling to the expatriated territories was very difficult: "This is just one evidence of how treaties of peace sowed fresh seeds of war."

Catt, made even more sensitive to the Jews' plight by seeing it through the eyes of Rosa Manus, was distressed at the growing anti-Semitism she saw in Hungary. They were particularly alarmed at the growth of a movement called the "Waking Magyars," which was intensely racial, nationalistic, brutal, and "patriotic." Catt saw a parallel to the beginning of the Italian Fascist movement in many ways, and anti-feminism in both: "The fate of Hungary is woefully sad but the suffrage group is still a center to carry on."

The next stop was Vienna, an economically and spiritually depressed city where no one smiled. Although Catt saw eleven women sitting in Parliament the day she visited, the Committee on Woman Suffrage no longer existed. [14]

Prague was an exception to the gloom she had felt so far. Inflation was less exorbitant than in Austria, wages were good, and the money had purchasing power. Through an Alliance friend Catt was able to talk with representatives or heads of all Czechoslovakian political parties about woman suffrage. Voting was universal and compulsory for men and women in the new republic. The only complaint she heard was from the Agrarian party chair, who thought the peasant women were more loyal to the Catholic church than to the party. She had lunch with the popular President Thomas Masaryk and his equally well-liked and famous daughter, Alice, one of sixteen women elected to the Czechoslovak Parliament in the April 1920 elections. Catt liked them both and thought the country lucky to have the wonderful, serene, big-souled man for their president. [15]

In Prague Catt's dysentery flared up. When she got to her next stop, Berlin, Rosa Manus sent for her brother-in-law, Felix Jacobi, a physician there. "He gave me opium at once to stop the diarrhea, ordered a purge and a day's fast with medicines including injections of oil," Catt wrote. Dr. Jacobi also "permitted a dose of strichnine [sic]" so she could get through a speech at the Reichstag. It was the first time a foreigner, let alone a woman, was accorded the privilege of addressing that body. There she said that women need not be modest about proposals to help their countries, "for men had made such a mess of things that no man could find a way through." After that comment, the English ambassador, Lord d'Abernon, stalked out, followed dutifully but reluctantly by his wife. [16]

Berlin was the end of her European tour in that dreary, wet autumn of 1922. She canceled scheduled visits to Dresden, Cologne, and Paris and stayed in her hotel room in Berlin for a week. Marie Stritt and a few other German women met at the hotel and organized an auxiliary to take the place of the now defunct German suffrage association.

She brooded about her trip and wrote about it for the *Woman Citizen,* concluding that "War must be effectually and forever put out of the world and the thoughts of men who occupy themselves today with navies and cannons and airplanes must be turned to the problem of making this a world for everybody with justice to all." Under the old totalitarian system there was no hope for peace and no place for women.[17]

She was still ill when she dragged herself to London at the end of November, and held meetings in her room during the ten days she was there: She felt herself beleaguered in spite of anxious and careful nursing by Rosa Manus, grew cantankerous, and ended the wretched European tour in an unprecedented fight with her Board. She unsuccessfully tried to get the congress moved from fascist Rome, and fought with the English women about the Alliance being run by a headquarters group rather than the elected officers. For over a week she was contested and voted down on every point.

When Catt and Manus left London on the first leg of their journey to Rio de Janiero, several of the Alliance women were at the train to see them off with flowers and presents. Catt's old sense of humor returned and she noted, "So I went away like a bride with wedding presents on the one hand and a family rejoicing on the other that the cross old thing was out of town."

Two American women, Elizabeth Babcock and Anita van Lennep, accompanied Catt and Manus on the South American trip, during which they visited six of the eleven republics, including those with the largest population, most stable governments, and acknowledged progressiveness.[18]

The leisurely crossing into sunshine and summer worked wonders for Catt's health. When they reached Rio eighteen days after leaving London, she had recovered her old verve.

Work began immediately with a Congress of Women of Brazil, organized by Bertha Lutz's Association for the Advancment of Women. Catt was appalled at the confusion of the meeting—women talked loudly among themselves, votes were rarely put, and there was no order. But an association was formed that affiliated with the IWSA the following year. Catt was fascinated by the "curious contrasts" in Brazil. "Very many women are held in almost harem restrictions" yet there were many physicians, dentists, lawyers, writers, sculptors, poets, painters, civil engineers, and notable scientists among them. She noted that "This advance column of women at home, coupled with the liberation of women the world around, is fast breaking down the outworn bondage and creating a new point of view in public opinion."[19]

As the deliberately temperate ambassador of international feminism, Catt was well received during her tour. In Brazil she was the first woman to be entertained by a special government committee for the reception of dignitaries, and the vice-president took her to observe the Senate. In Argentina she was entertained by the Council of Women, but was most impressed by the hospitality in Uruguay, where the government paid her hotel bill and put two automobiles at her disposal. They were met at the boat with music, flowers, and a delegation of two hundred women. "There were continuous meetings, conferences and sight-seeing" before the women were given a send-off as impressive as their reception.[20]

Catt joked about the constant presence of photographers. "I was never in a land so daft on photos as this one. The man with the camera lurks behind every bush. Somewhere there are photos of me under a breadfruit tree, a coffee tree, under the neck of a giraffe, standing by a live loose boa constrictor, with the President of Uruguay and the Directors of all sorts of institutions. I've been photo'd on every platform and the smell of brimstone is continuous. When Miss Babcock went to a movie she saw us all walk out on the sheet [in a newsreel]."[21]

In Chile she was received by President Arturo Allesandri, whom she described as a feminist. He charged her with delivering a message to the president of Peru concerning arbitration of some Chile-Peru dispute. Catt treated the task as a secret mission and savored her role as the heroine in a spy story, although she felt obliged to report the incident to the American Embassy after she had talked to President Laguia.

In Santiago she found a vigorous Council of Women and a woman's club where she met writers, musicians, and artists. In Lima she formed a Council of Women after speaking to the Peruvian women, thinking the more conservative group had a better chance of survival than a suffrage club. The final weeks of her tour were increasingly frustrating. She liked historical Lima but was disgusted by the addiction to bullfights and lotteries she found there. When she visited the museum it was empty except for a few Indians lingering sadly by the relics of their ruined civilization.

In Panama her itinerary confined her to the Canal Zone. She held a few meetings but the week was almost entirely taken up with social events.

On her way across the Atlantic to Rome she prepared reports. The main one was confidential to the Leslie Commission, which had subsidized the trip. Catt argued that North American feminists should be fully supportive of their sisters to the south but in no way aggressive or prescriptive. If the term "Good Neighbor Policy" had been coined then she might have used it.

"The women of South America are marching as straight to their liberation as those of any other continent, although the march is slow, and like all movements in Latin lands, the trail leading on is not clearly defined," Catt wrote. She detailed the prejudices, the rigid societies, the difficulties of women in the tradition-bound spheres, the role of the Catholic church, her impressions: "State, politics, church, lotteries, horse racing, bull fighting and charity are mixed up in a way utterly baffling to an outsider. The church is often too political to be altogether spiritual and the state is too religious to be altogether political." She found prejudice against North Americans, who were regarded as imperialists, although she herself was well received because she went as head of the international Alliance and of the new Pan-American Association. She decided that the Pan-American Association as begun in Baltimore was a false start because distances in South America were too great to permit the frequent meetings among representatives from the various countries that would be necessary. A better plan was one suggested by the president of the Chilean Council of Women, which proposed organization by regions. The most pressing need was a unified campaign to amend the civil codes and improve facilities for women's education. Catt doubted that suffrage would be a real issue for some time in any South American country except Brazil and Uruguay.

She emphasized as she often did: "The vote never has been the sole aim of the woman movement in any land nor is it the climax. The campaign for the vote was only one battle in the long struggle begun centuries ago." The vote was a convenient measurement to survey the woman's movement in any country and estimate its future: "The vote has been the Great Divide on the continent of tradition."[22]

South America was an enormous challenge and she concluded: "I never did a piece of work which has so interested and stimulated my desires to help as this. I would need to read a few tons more of South American history and to learn Spanish before I should be really equipped for the task."[23] With some regret she left that work to others.

After an uneventful crossing from Panama to France, Catt and Manus went on to Rome for Catt's last congress of the IWSA. As her health had returned, so had her irreverence toward arbitrary authority. She decided the Alliance could exploit the publicity of Italy's new dictator. Mussolini was the man the world was watching in the spring of 1923, and she wanted to use him in his own capital. He had agreed to speak to the open meeting that preceded the business meetings of the congress. Shortly beforehand Catt and the Italian delegates met him privately and received his permission to present to him copies of all resolutions the Alliance passed in Rome. He insisted that the women be escorted to him by Blackshirts as a guard of honor. She took his measure as half professional chauvinist and warmonger, half charlatan.

The Alliance congress was widely covered by the press throughout the world. Mussolini's speech and Catt's reply at the opening session were carried in newspapers from Norway to South Africa. In his brisk staccato style Mussolini welcomed the women and assured them his government would not offer "any preconceived opposition to the enfranchisement of women." Indeed, he promised some local franchise and uttered the usual platitudes about the moral responsibility of women. He also bowed to their contributions during the war. Catt translated his comments as, "Thank you for your help, now go home."[24]

Catt responded with a directness only thinly glazed with tact:

> We do not come to Rome as timid suppliants for small favors. Men tell us that you stand for order, for unity, for patriotism, for a better and a higher civilization in the world. These are our ideals, too. We stand for educated men and women, for schools for every child, for work and good wages for all, for better homes, for more tender and scientific care of children, that they may grow up to build a better order of things. We stand for the abolition of those old codes of law which, all the world around, kept women in perpetual tutelage and allowed them no independent individuality. These codes have made many men cruel masters, and women timid and shrinking dependents. "Male and female created He them," says Genesis, "and gave them dominion over the earth." Alas! the males took all the dominion to themselves, and we stand for getting back our half of it. We stand, too, for the principle of self-government, and for votes for men and women on equal terms.
>
> We make no political intrigues. We shall not disturb the peace of Italy. We have, however, asked all the civilized Governments of the world to endorse our plea and our program. We ask this Government to do so.[25]

Mussolini followed her speech in a written Italian translation with no apparent reaction and at the end of the congress presided over an official reception for the delegates. He also reviewed Rome's first suffrage parade, which was led by Catt and Margery Corbett Ashby, the new Alliance president. He again promised that Italian women would be given the vote (by gradual stages). This was the first form of woman suffrage ever offered by any of the Latin countries.[26]

Catt had reason to be happy at this congress. Since the first European conference the Alliance could measure real progress. In 1904, outside of the four suffrage states in the United States, there were only two places in the world that claimed equal suffrage—New Zealand and the Isle of Man. In 1923 women from forty-three countries, representing two-thirds of the world's nations, convened in Rome; women had equal suffrage in twenty-five, including the United States, the newly established Irish Free State, and six Indian states—the first from Asia to have woman suffrage. Thirteen new auxiliaries were added, including Palestine, Egypt, Japan, Jamaica, and Brazil. Brazil's affiliation and a government delegate from Chile were the first fruits of Catt's South American trip.[27]

Women were making progress in government—there were a dozen women members of parliaments in Denmark, Finland, Germany, and Poland; official government delegates from Portugal, Estonia, Rumania, China, Chile, and Finland; Dame Rachel Crowdy was there from the League of Nations Secretariat; Anna Wicksell of Sweden was a member of the League's Mandates Commission.

Pioneers of the international woman's movement came to Rome as well as fresh newcomers. Annie Furuhjelm was serving her fifth three-year term in the Finnish Diet; Norway's pioneer suffragist, the eighty-year-old Marie Quam had taken a nine-day trip to be there. Bertha Lutz from Brazil was one of the younger women on whom much hope was placed. The fiery Spanish writer, Isabel de Palencia, outspokenly contemptuous of Mussolini, had come to Rome out of admiration for Catt and her dedication to peace.

The real business of the congress was to decide the ways women could achieve their goal of equality. Women in more than half of the member countries were enfranchised and ready to use the power the vote gave them to extend their influence and to help their voteless sisters. Everything Catt worked for, everything feminists have sought at any time or place, was equality in education, government, economics, and moral standards. It all leads to respect for the individual. When the ideal of human rights is achieved through universal recognition of individual rights, there will come the greatest of all rights, a peaceful world.

The immediate causes the women addressed in 1923 were equal economic, civil, and moral standards. Committees had systematically studied the problems of women's right to work and to receive equal pay; the right of a woman who made homemaking her career to a proportion of her husband's income and benefits, and in cases of substandard income, public aid to dependent children; the right of a married woman to keep her own nationality and not be forced to take that of her husband; sex education, the suppression of traffic in women and children, abolishing state regulation of prostitution, and venereal disease education and treatment—the series of complex problems under the committee studying "moral questions" were the least understood and the most controversial.[28]

Catt said she thought the issues were too broad and insisted that political activism was the most profitable use of the Alliance's time and energy. She was cautious about diluting the resources of any organization, knowing that results were achieved by concentrating on limited objectives and then moving on. "Civilization is not produced by a single movement. It is rather a fabric woven of many threads, each of which is necessary to its perfection. I do not feel that I want to pull on every thread," she wrote.[29] Each person must work for personally important causes, no one person or organization could accomplish everything.

A tearful delegation of two dozen women tried to persuade Catt to change her mind about retiring from the presidency, but she stood firm. She made a graceful speech of appreciation to all the workers and said goodbye.

By the first of June she was home after eight months of constant travel and meetings. From then on, almost all her speeches had a single theme: peace. Interviews, League of Women Voters meetings, conferences, big meetings and small ones, they were all variations on the topic.

Within a week of her return she was welcomed back by eight hundred women at a Hotel Biltmore lunch, and made her first radio talk, which was broadcast to three states by station WEAF. "I have decided to use the few years remaining to me to help the men. The woman movement is safe. It is the one place in this troubled world where no armies are being raised and where victory is certain, but the men worry me," she said. Later she wrote to Mary Gray Peck, "I've moved on this summer and left all interest in them [women] with my sluffed off first life. I'm buckling on armor for another lap."[30]

This was not strictly accurate; she did one more task for the international woman suffrage cause the following January when she visited Cuba as acting president of the committee on pan-American organization. She spent a crowded ten days with Mary Hay and Mildred Adams as the guests of the Cuban women's groups.

The more she learned the more convinced she was that working for peace was the most vital thing she could do. Her Committee on the Cause and Cure of War with its annual conferences beginning in 1925 was her answer. She continued to use her influence in other organizations as well as she could. When the International Alliance congress occurred in Paris in 1926 without her for the first time, a Peace Committee was set up, partly in response to a letter from her. She declared that women's highest duty, once they had obtained their civil rights, was to stand in unity for the peace of nations. A close friendship between the Alliance and the League of Nations developed that continued until World War II.

In November 1927, the Alliance Peace Committee held its first study conference in Amsterdam, and Catt went. It was her last appearance at Alliance meetings although she regularly sent messages and planned to attend some succeeding conferences but each time she was prevented from going. She was especially disappointed when she became ill at the last minute and could not go to Istanbul in 1935. Her message urged women to continue their work: "The campaign for woman suffrage is about over, but the world problems that need the support of women's votes are grave and numerous. The greatest of all is War—how can we persuade men to end that cruellest and most barbarous of all human customs? By telling the truth about it, I think. There is joy in work for good causes. In the long run, when the cause is good, one can win that for which she works. Have faith in progress and lead it."[31]

The 1939 Congress in Copenhagen was darkened by the coming war. Once again the Alliance survived world war although there were heavy casualties among its members: women murdered by Nazis, interned in concentration camps, or lost in the long lines of refugees. Leaders of the Czechoslovakian Alliance were persecuted by the Communists and by the Nazis and at least one of them was murdered in 1946.

The first postwar congress took place in Interlaken in 1946. Catt again sent a message of peace, still the largest task. She urged them to continue their work because women united and determined could compel the cessation of war. "I am now a very old lady," she wrote, "but your organization is very dear to me." For her final words to the Alliance she quoted the same ones she had used thirty-five years earlier when she ended her 1911 speech at Stockholm with the verse: "There are causes that need assistance/ And wrongs that need resistance/ And therefore, work for you to do." Her own battle cry was a fitting injunction to a generation facing world in chaos.

The Alliance found its cause in the United Nations and has served as one of the advisory groups (a non-government organization) since the founding of that association after World War II. At that time 30 of the original 51 countries forming the United Nations had equal suffrage; in 1979, 143 of the 151 nations had it, leaving 8 nations still without woman suffrage.[32]

The principle of human rights toward which Catt was always working is now recognized as a universal desideratum by people of conscience. The charter of the United Nations in 1945 stated the lofty aspirations of the larger freedom, and the Universal Declaration of Human Rights adopted in 1948 further codified them. The United Nations Decade for Women, 1976–1985, had as its objectives the same program Catt wanted: equality, development, and peace.

· 18 ·
Decision for Peace

After the ratification of the Nineteenth Amendment, Catt took to waking in the middle of the night pondering what to do next. Politicians expected her to run for office, as U. S. senator from New York, perhaps. Her name was appearing regularly on all the media lists of the ten most famous American women, her knowledge of practical politics was formidable, and hundreds of thousands of new votes could be hers for the asking. But the day she walked out of the Senate unable to stomach its suffrage debate she abandoned any thought of an elected career within a legislature. More important, she was tired of "having to dodge problems for years to avoid losing votes." As more information about the shabby manipulation of public opinion toward war became known, she grew increasingly angry that she had been led to accept American participation even as a political expediency. Furthermore, her experience in Europe made her more aware than ever that woman suffrage depended on peace and democracy. And there was the immediate consideration that only a fraction of the two million women she held together in the NAWSA had joined the new League of Women Voters. How could "the scattered forces be rounded up in support of a common problem of action and propaganda?"[1] Her answer was a woman's organization supporting peace.

Catt's famous speech to the League of Women Voters at their second convention, when she brought her audience to their feet in wave after wave of applause, was the beginning: "The people in this room tonight could put an end to war."[2] Behind the moment lay her lifelong hatred of war.

In her youth in Iowa and throughout her experience in the suffrage movement she found nothing to counter the Victorian assurance that females generated and nurtured life while males were aggressive. Her father had taken no part in the Civil War; it held no glamour for her. Custer's annihilation at Little Big Horn in June 1875 and the subsequent defeat of Chiefs Sitting Bull and Crazy Horse in October 1876 were covered in detail by the Chicago *Interocean* and the Charles City *Intelligencer*, both newspapers read in the

Lane household during Carrie's high school years. Invariably these battles were depicted as barbaric Indian uprisings against the civilized and enlightened.

She was astonished when a college classmate told her he was going to be a career soldier. He was always going to have a job because there was always a war someplace, he said. She was distressed when she learned that he was killed on a battlefield in Egypt within a year after their graduation.

A year later, her intellectual mentor, Herbert Spencer, was touring America, taking issue with those social Darwinians who presumed that war weeded out the unfit, thus improving the species, and that humans were by nature fighting animals. Spencer and his American interpreter Lester Ward acknowledged that that may have been true in primitive societies, but in an industrial society it was the most fit of the adult males who fought. The brutality in human nature was kept alive when force was used to solve disputes; social progress depended on finding non-violent solutions.

The suffragists regularly heard reports on peace meetings at their annual conventions. Catt said in 1904, "Sometimes the cause of peace and arbitration seems to me the greatest of all." Behind all reforms is the ballot and we "are chained to the work for that until it is gained."[3]

Peace movements from the turn of the century up until the war tended to be dominated by businessmen and government officials whose profits in foreign trade depended on international stability. "Dead men buy no clothes," said the president of the National Association of Manufacturers.[4] These organizations stressed arbitration and law to settle disputes among nations.

Catt was a director in the short-lived Women's Peace Circle of 1905, which aimed to bring women into positions of leadership in the peace movement. George Catt's death and her illness prevented her from any real work with it. The organization faded into obscurity within a year or two.

Of more significance to her was the First National Arbitration and Peace Congress held in April 1907 at Carnegie Hall. She was a delegate from the NAWSA at these meetings, which had been called to plan the Hague Conference. Again personal loss forced her to put public affairs aside. In September 1907 her brother Will died, and in December her mother died after Catt had spent many months in Iowa nursing her.

Peace organizations were entering a new phase in 1914 and 1915 when Catt helped found the Woman's Peace Party and persuaded Jane Addams to head it. With the war in Europe, businessmen realized that immense profits could be made by supplying armies, and most of their peace associations were either abolished or became enthusiastic about "preparedness." Women became central in the peace movement partly by default and partly because those drawn to it were suffragists, social workers, reformers, and radicals who knew how to promote their cause.

In 1915 Catt was caught up in the crucial New York suffrage campaign, and then drafted as head of two million fractious members of the NAWSA. Alice Paul led at most fifty thousand and could more or less disregard the war. Catt had no such options and she also had Cassandra's unhappy talent of seeing unpleasant truths clearly. She was certain that once a major war had started, no high-minded statements could stop it. NAWSA's acceptance of limited war work kept Catt's forces together; she continually reminded Congress of the suffragists' patriotism. When President Wilson advanced his fourteen points as the only possible program for peace, she strongly supported him.

On November 18, 1918, one week after the armistice, Catt called a meeting of the women's organizations of New York to discuss what women should and could do to establish a peaceful world. Their immediate goal was to have women present at the peace talks. "Wherever women are subordinated to men, where their rights are disregarded, there is a fertile field for militarism to thrive," Catt said. "The rights of women must enter into the treaty which is to be made."[5] They requested President Wilson to appoint women to the treaty delegation, as did other women's groups in the United States, England, and Canada. In spite of all their efforts, no woman was present.

During the next two years, Catt pulled together the International Alliance and organized its first postwar congress in Geneva. There her loathing of war and those who advocated it were reinforced. She saw that in the Treaty of Versailles "the seeds of new wars" were planted and "waiting for a chance to spring to life."[6] The one hope to abort their growth was the League of Nations.

On April 12, 1921, the League of Women Voters annual conference in Cleveland was going smoothly. Eleanor Roosevelt, a delegate from New York, wrote her husband about the "really good speeches" that morning and praised Catt's "clear cold logic."[7] Catt was scheduled to talk again in the evening with other speakers who supported the League's campaign to reduce armament. In quiet moments during the convention she brooded on President Harding's myopic foreign policy. The morning papers had blared the depressing news that the United States had again refused membership in the League of Nations. President Harding had made that position clear in his state of the union message.

At the evening meeting, Judge Florence Allen spoke about women using their votes to assure "righteous" international law. She was followed by Will Irwin, whose recent book, *The Next War*, forecast the horror to be expected if war were not abolished. Maud Wood Park, League chair, realized Irwin was going beyond his allotted time and began to rise to stop him. She was startled to have her skirt grasped from behind by Catt's strong right hand and to be pulled firmly back into her chair. Irwin realized he was running overtime, quickly finished his talk, and turned back to his seat. Irwin wrote, "Mrs. Catt passed me. She was taking the floor without introduction—and as she walked, she was tearing up her manuscript. As soon as she could get a hearing—for the house had risen with her—she swept into such a fiery, eloquent denunciation of war and all its works as I had never heard."[8]

"The people in this room tonight could put an end to war," she challenged. "It is the duty of everyone who wants the world to disarm to compel action in Washington. Let us consecrate ourselves to put war out of this world. God is giving a call to the women of the world to come forward, to stay the hand of men, to say, 'No, you shall no longer kill your fellow men!' "

The stenographically recorded speech now reads as a florid call to action. War could be stopped. The women could stop it. It was spoken from the heart of one of the great orators—a woman who knew her subject, her craft, and above all, her audience. Many of the women there had lost sons, husbands, brothers, lovers in the war. They had been stunned into apathy and suddenly they had a chance to strike back. "We went out of that meeting sure of ourselves, of women once more. We would start something."[10]

When Catt returned from the IWSA Rome congress in 1923, she prepared for an extended trip to talk about peace to American women. The lecture tour was a test of her own endurance and to sample public opinion. "I've written a safe and sane speech and taken out all the cynicism and dumped it together with reasonableness,'" she wrote to Mary Gray Peck. "I've omitted the most controversial points and will try this on the unsuspecting public."

Catt found the trip lonely work: "I'm representing no organization [but] when I get home I'll know more than I did when I left as to what the people are thinking." The lectures were variously sponsored, many by local Leagues of Women Voters, some by individual women, some by organizations such as the Cleveland Women's Council for Prevention of War, or by other associations. Midway in her tour she bragged about her stamina: "I visited seventeen cities and made twenty-five speeches; I have ten towns more to visit and at least three extra speeches. That's not bad for sixty-plus is it? I have been making calculations tonight and I think a moderate estimate would be that I have spoken to twenty-five thousand people."[11]

"I came home from the trip convinced that the sentiment for peace per se is overwhelming, but the general mind is terribly bewildered by the political confusion and I may say misinformation carefully distributed," she wrote Judge Florence Allen in December. They had talked together when Catt spoke in St. Louis in November and subsequently discussed strategy by mail. Catt continued:

> Big and bold propositions are bound to be whittled down by the con-servatives to the least possible forward step. War exists and the trouble is that most people think it always will. To get any bold action on the Outlawry of War would at this time be impossible, but agitation of that idea will convince them that they should do something if they cannot do the whole thing. I believe very strongly in the psychology of making a bold appeal. Eventually it wins.
>
> I think your plan of proposing that the United States offer arbitra-tion treaties to all the world is a good thing. I have also been proposing that [but] I do not think that peace can be eventually secured without an International Assembly. I am wondering if a really active, progressive and yet moderate national organization of women for world peace might win the day.[12]

Jesse Jack Hooper, head of the Wisconsin League of Women Voters, suggested that the League sponsor the kind of organization Catt visualized, but the national board turned it down. Josephine Schain, who served the National Committee on the Cause and Cure of War throughout its existence, said "They feared such a grandiose affair would swamp the regular League program—the tail would be wagging the dog."[13]

Catt suggested another possibility: organization by the Woman's Joint Congressional Committee, a consortium of women's groups (including the League in Washington) that served as a clearinghouse to keep its members informed on federal legislation. Eleven WJCC representatives agreed to call a conference "to consider the present peace situation especially as it concerns the duty of women." During the fifth annual convention of the League of Women Voters in April 1924, Hooper explained the proposed conference and

asked Catt to head it. Catt agreed, assembled a committee, and a conference
on the Cause and Cure of War was scheduled for January 1925.[14]

"I am a pacifist. A pacifist is one who prefers peace to war and that is all,"
she said.

> A pacifist usually believes in defense. Aggression and defense may be
> interpreted to mean the other. Patriotism, that reverential love of home,
> flag and country, is flaunted to cover the fact that young men must kill
> other young men in its name. There is no book on defense that reveals
> the truth; a book that will clearly define when defense is defense and
> when it is aggression is needed. Apparently, no one yet knows the facts
> clearly enough to write that book. Did we know the true definition of
> defense and patriotism, the peace versus war controversy would move
> forward with more clarity and speed.[15]

As soon as Catt began to work against war, she was denounced by the
Daughters of the American Revolution as a secret agent in a web of feminist
organizations acting on orders from Moscow. She had been vilified so often by
antisuffragists as a defiler of the American family and an advocate of free love
that she was prone to regard personal abuse as "no more than a fly on my
nose." But these new attacks were somewhat different. They were monoto-
nously persistent and at their most virulent, between 1924 and 1928, they
claimed some authority from U.S. government documents and they smeared
many women Catt much admired such as Jane Addams and Florence Allen.
The attackers assumed that any attempt to establish social welfare programs,
to reduce armament, or to improve international relations was subversive and
communistic. In short, it was a resurgence of the "Red Scare" of 1919–1920.

The jingoistic patriotism extravagantly heightened by government propaganda during the war served to increase fears of anyone seen as alien and to
reaffirm many kinds of racial prejudice. One such prejudice common among
the privileged was that people of northwestern European ancestry—the
Anglo-Saxon race they sometimes called themselves—had a unique capacity
to govern and create industrial wealth as well as military might. When the
Bolsheviks won control of Russia, severed Western alliances, and secured a
controlling position in eastern Europe, the only explanation that seemed
valid was that the Reds had won by stealth and the manipulation of the
masses. When Western military attacks against the Red revolution failed, it
seemed as if Western arms had been turned against their creators. The same
calamity could befall the United States. One must be ever-vigilant, ready

with arms and alert to the dangers within the country; all those dark-skinned people in sweatshops speaking unintelligible languages were suspect. So eager were the believers of this melodrama to get verification that they accepted every rumor and hint of subversion. The most ambitious gathering of guesses and paranoic suppositions was made by a committee of the New York legislature. Its ten thousand pages published in four volumes in 1920 was known as the Lusk Report.[16]

Although the Lusk Report was quickly discredited as unreliable, it remained for many years as "authoritative" to the people who saw reform leaders and their plans and institutions as threats to America. One outspoken critic, Helen Tufts Bailie, called the report an "ammunition dump for persons attacking liberals."[17] The mischievous mixture of half-truths and fiction was widely used against Catt and other feminists and peace workers in the twenties and thirties.

Concurrent with the Lusk Committee investigations was the work of the United States government under the direction of Attorney General A. Mitchell Palmer. A formerly progressive reformer, he led the repressive action against the "Red Menace" in 1919 and 1920. His chief lieutenant was the twenty-four- year-old J. Edgar Hoover, whom Palmer named director of the newly created General Intelligence Division of the Department of Justice. The sole function of the G.I.D. was "to collect information about radicals and cordinate the results of its own investigations with intelligence transmitted by the Bureau of Investigation and other investigative agencies." Hundreds of raids, arrests, and deportations took place in the next several months in unprecedented, flagrant violations of the civil rights of thousands of people.[18]

In March 1920, some reason was restored when Louis F. Post became Acting Secretary of Labor and took charge of all deportation matters. Under the Immigration Act of 1917 as amended in October 1918, undesirable aliens could be arrested and deported only on orders signed by the Labor Secretary. "The whole red' crusade stood revealed as a stupendous and cruel fake," Post concluded after he read the records of the Bureau of Immigration. "Had the facts as they were then thrust upon my attention been generally known, public condemnation of the Department of Justice and its cooperating agencies would have been sure and swift."[19]

It seemed that the Red hysteria was over but the disease was only dormant. For a few years the court cases attacking the validity of the Nineteenth Amendment had kept Catt's old enemies busy but when the Supreme Court in 1922 sustained its constitutionality, many antisuffragists joined the propaganda effort against those advocating peace and social welfare legislation.

One of the silliest accusations against Catt was made by the *Woman Patriot*, organ of the National Association Opposed to Woman Suffrage, that the 1922 Pan-American Conference of Women in Baltimore was in reality the Women's Third International. She ignored the story but sensed a realignment of publicists against her and began collecting facts in an effort "to locate the source and motive of much propaganda which connects all movements aiming at international understanding or world peace with an alleged communistic campaign directed by Moscow."[20]

In many of the "War or Peace" speeches she made in 1923 Catt mentioned "the little group who seem to have got this entire country hoodooed on the question of peace and everything that concerns it is almost the same group that held woman suffrage back in Washington for ten or fifteen years, and the very man who is preparing the publicity calling everybody Red who does anything for peace is the very man who called all the suffragists Red."[21]

The first clear indication that a full-scale attack was to be made against women advocating peace came with the publication of an article, "Are Women's Clubs 'Used' by Bolshevists?" in Henry Ford's *The Dearborn Independent* on March 15, 1924, and continued the following week. The second installment was climaxed by a chart allegedly compiled from the Lusk Report and connecting many women's organizations with "socialist-pacifist" activities. The chart consisted of thirty-seven boxes, each with one or more women's names and organizational affiliation in it. Lines were drawn connecting the boxes in a complex pattern which gave the chart the name "the spider web."[22] The articles were immediately picked up by the wire services and newspapers across the country printed the attacks and counterattacks as they appeared, making the spider web chart a cause célèbre.

Catt was held up as a terrible example because she favored the Sheppard-Towner Act of 1921 which provided a system of federal aid to the states for maternal and infant health programs. Passage of the bill was the first intensive lobbying activity of the new League of Women Voters, but had been unsuccessful in 1920. By the time the bill was introduced again in 1921, the League had become part of the Women's Joint Congressional Committee, and this time the lobbying succeeded.

The spider web chart had been prepared by Lucia R. Maxwell, a librarian in the Department of Defense under Brigadier General Ames A. Fries, who distributed it from his office in 1923. The chart painted with the same red the cautious League of Women Voters, whose faith was in education and legislation; the more activist Women's International League for Peace and Freedom, whose sin it was to want a peaceful world; the Needlework Guild of America; the American Lovers of Music; the International Sunshine Society; and the American Legion Auxiliary. The burlesque side was commented on by one writer who said, "It was delightful to think of furtive propagandists sowing the fiendish doctrines at sessions of the International Sunshine Society!"[23]

Catt was aware the issue could not be laughed out of existence. The fact that a government department was "systematically discrediting [women] by the wide distribution of false and libelous charges, which, because of their source, carry abnormal influence," had to be fought. She urged all women "charged by the chart with unpatriotic behavior to take up cudgels in their own behalf. Don't get frightened; think. Don't be intimidated; act." To Jane Addams she wrote, "I hope, some day, the world will return to sanity."[24]

There was no longer the single issue of suffrage to unite women. Instead, their combined strength became diluted as diverse interests were reflected in hundreds of new organizations and causes. Many antis missed the days when they could focus on a clearcut opponent. Anything that smacked of advancement, of social or political justice, of liberal tendencies became a red flag issue. The words "radical-pacifist" were invariably hyphenated and alternated with "socialist-pacifist." Peace, social welfare, child protection—these were all subversive words to certain "professional patriots" of the 1920s.

Occasionally in Catt's usually calm, reasoned style comes a faint echo of the rough-and-ready journalism of the *Mason City Republican:* "Very subtly the gossips have woven into their tales without knowing where they got it the charge that all peace societies are composed of nincompoops who blindly follow leaders who are blindly leading them and the national to destruction. The timid withdraw from the peace movement, lest they be contaminated by association with doubtful characters, or unpatriotically hamper necessary preparations for defense."[25]

In the spring of 1924 the lines were clearly drawn with the Daughters of the American Revolution openly and clearly positioned against women's organizations of a liberal orientation, including the Women's International League for Peace and Freedom, the League of Women Voters, and even the International Council of Women, the American branch of which was considered by Catt to be "exceedingly conservative."

In May 1925 in Washington, D.C., Catt was a principal speaker at the International Council of Women congress, which was, as usual, conducted in English, French, and German, an internationalism regarded with great suspicion by the superpatriots. The women of the ICW reiterated their aims: permanent peace; equality of political, educational, legal, and work opportunities for women and men (including equal pay for equal work); an equal moral standard; suppression of the traffic in women, and of exploitation of women and children; the right of children for physical, mental, and spiritual development; international disarmament.

Catt had been determined to minimize the problems of the conference, including the difficulty of raising money for it, when the DAR refused the use of their hall, where the conference had been scheduled to take place. She insisted that their hostility and that of the National Patriotic Council [of women's organizations] were merely a series of misunderstandings and confusions that were ultimately inconsequential. "Our skeletons all managed to climb out of their cupboards and to jangle their bones for the visiting ladies, that's all."[26]

What rekindled Catt's wrath was the circulation of reprints of thirty-six pages from the Congressional Record. This diatribe, ostensibly an argument against extension of the Sheppard-Towner Act and passage of other social legislation, had been read into the Record at the request of Senator Bayard of Delaware in the last minutes before a summer recess of the Sixty-ninth Congress on the hot afternoon of July 3, 1926. The Sheppard-Towner Act of 1921 had specified appropriations to carry out the program for only six years. When it was time to consider granting more money, opposition had intensified. Some of it came from the American Medical Association, which feared that this was a step toward compulsory health insurance. Other opponents included the DAR, which had long seen it as "a pernicious piece of legislation being an entering wedge of communism."[27]

The "Petition for the rejection of the Phipps-Parker Bill proposing an extension of the Maternity Act," which Senator Bayard had read into the Congressional Record, had been submitted by the board of directors of the Woman Patriot Publishing Company. The irredentist antisuffragists were still speaking through the Woman Patriot, which carried on its masthead "Against Feminism and Socialism." Although allegedly a document demonstrating opposition to furthering the Sheppard-Towner Act, the petition was, observed Catt, "a wholesale attack upon the patriotism and honor of individual women and women's organizations." The accusers used a broad brush to smear their red paint and included "all the pacifism, internationalism and socialist legislative schemes among women in America, together with the Women's International League, the National Women's Trade Union League, the International Federation of Working Women, the United States Children's Bureau and the United States Women's Bureau." It singled out Florence Kelley, social reformer and secretary of the National Consumers' League, as the source of most of the mischief, but "the second-hand radicalism of Miss Addams, Mrs. Robins, Miss Lathrop, Miss Abbott, Mrs. Catt, etc. is none the less important to show, because they build communism with noncommunist hands' in working for Mrs. Kell[e]y's program."[28]

A major appeal of the Patriots was states' rights. Massachusetts was one of the states that voted against the Sheppard-Towner Act, and the home of some of the Woman Patriots. The head of the Children's Division of the Massachusetts Department of Public Health said that he would rather see babies die than have the state's local government taken over by the federal government. A Massachusetts legislator (male) is locally famous for allegedly declaring during a debate on the subject, "Maternity is not women's business." The gist of the antifederalist arguments was, "No plan of centralization has ever been adopted which did not result in bureaucracy, tyranny, inflexibility, reaction, and decline."[29] Nowhere in the state rights arguments was there a suggestion that the army and navy be administered locally.

By the spring of 1927 reprints of these Congressional Record pages had been widely circulated, often along with a pamphlet distributed by the DAR, "The Common Enemy," which sounded the old alarm against the "poison of liberalism" that was working through two hundred organizations. Catt thought the time to speak out again had come. These slanders struck at her friends and women she admired. They were women of accomplishment who were improving the lives of those too young, too weak, too unsophisticated or uneducated, too poor to fight for themselves. It was not charity they were seeking—everyone had a right to expect the opportunity to achieve a decent standard of living in this richest country in the world.

Catt's "Lies at Large" was published in the *Woman Citizen* in June; in it she tried to point out the lie vendors and to ascertain their motives. "They are either terribly scared and badly duped, or they are not scared at all and are deliberately organized to dupe others." The second article in the series, "An Open Letter to the D.A.R.," published in July and reprinted by the Women's International League as a leaflet, was one of the most widely read articles Catt ever wrote. National publicity was given to it, helped along by her being on the west coast when the article was published. She was in San Francisco en route to the Institute of Pacific Relations in Hawaii to which she was a delegate, and the California papers added to the circulation of her ideas by personal interviews.

The "Open Letter" refuted the DAR's attacks on patriotic American women and organizations. She took the DAR to task for lumping together communism, Bolshevism, socialism, liberalism, and ultra-pacifism in a "world revolutionary movement which proposed to destroy civilization and Christianity." She spoke with admiration of Jane Addams, Florence Kelley, and Rose Schneiderman, president of the National Women's Trade Union League. Catt acknowledged it was everyone's privilege to oppose inimical views but "What does stir criticism is the fact that you impugn the motives, assail the honor, question the intelligence, malign the representatives of honorable organizations, and by wholesale call advocates of these measures dupes and Reds." When she was writing the article, Catt had said, "I should pronounce it an impossibility to make a real conservative understand a radical or even a liberal, what I am hoping to do is to stir the liberals inside of the DAR to take some action."[30]

Not only did Catt's "Open Letter" stir up the liberals, it was so successful it brought increased attacks on her. These included a pamphlet called "The Strange Case of Mrs. Carrie Chapman Catt," by Hermine Schwed, who had been a lecturer for the Better America Federation and other superpatriots. Her method was to quote from Catt's own writings, string the out-of-context words together, and give a twisted interpretation. Catt ignored her.[31]

The most spectacular result of increasing national attention on the Red menace was a dramatic increase in charges and particularly the issuance of "blacklists" of prominent women, men, and organizations that the DAR and other patriots should shun. There were several lists, most of them similar; one spawned and produced in Boston made its appearance early in 1928. Catt was on the roster and was in excellent company. The list of nearly one hundred women began with Grace Abbott, Jane Addams, Florence Allen, Mary Anderson, went on with the names of distinguished American women including Zona Gale, Charlotte Perkins Gilman, Julia Lathrop, Lucia Ames Mead, Margaret Sanger, and ended with Mary E. Woolley. The men's blacklist was equally notable.

The lists were an immediate sensation and aroused widespread protest, amusement, or indignation according to the lights of the individual and the journal that publicized the emotions. Devere Allen, editor of the *World Tomorrow,* pointed out that when the DAR had presented a peace flag to Andrew Carnegie in 1907 "the roof did not fall, nor did the DAR suffer any danger from apoplexy, unless indeed from their abundant enthusiasm." Oswald Garrison Villard, editor of the *Nation,* remembered that the DAR had contributed to the cost of the great August 29, 1914 women's war protest parade down Fifth Avenue, yet "A little more than a year later the Daughters

took the position that to be a pacifist is to be a pro-German, or a pro-
Bolshevik, or a pro-somehing else which they do not like." Both he and his
mother Fanny Garrison Villard, were on the lists.[32] The *Nation* also com-
mended a series of articles published from March 19 to 26, 1928, in the
Springfield Republican that asserted that the blue [superpatriots] menace was
more dangerous than the Red, and Villard picked up the phrase in "What the
Blue Menace Means," which he wrote for *Harper's Magazine* in 1928.

Some writers such as the influential William Allen White, editor of the
Emporia Gazette, who was among those blacklisted, thought the best way to
handle the situation was through ridicule. He had "laughed the Ku Klux Klan
out of Kansas" and thought the DAR should be handled the same way. DAR
president Grace Brosseau was not "a kamelia of the Klan," but White thought
there was KKK influence on the DAR, and Brosseau "in her enthusiasm has
allowed several lengths of Ku Klux nightie to show under her red, white, and
blue." To Helen Tufts Bailie he wrote, "let in the light. Two thirds of the
success of your fight will be publicity. They cannot stand the light."[33]

Bailie was one of the DAR members whom Catt had stirred to action. In
April 1928, she published a pamphlet titled *Our Threatened Heritage,* which
was produced by the DAR Committee of Protest of which she was Executive
Secretary. She reviewed the involvement of the DAR in the controversy since
1924, its increasing use of slanders and misinformation, and urged the
members to call a halt. She was expelled by the DAR in June, and although
she appealed the decision she continued her denunciation of DAR tactics,
and her reinstatement was voted down in 1929.

By then the spider web had begun to be worn thin but its sticky strands
continued to attract a few militarists. As late as 1934 most of the same
organizations listed in the 1920s appeared in *The Red Network.* This self-
proclaimed "Handbook for Patriots" was occasionally called into play in the
next decade but it was laughed out of the game by the distinguished roster
included as "Who Is Who in Radicalism," who were, Eleanor Roosevelt wrote
in 1939, "rather a fine group of people."[34]

There is no doubt that the Red scare contributed to defeating some
social legislation. William Shirer remembered that in his student days in Iowa
he wrote an angry protest editorial in his college paper when the Child Labor
Amendment was rejected by thirteen states as a Bolshevik scheme. In a
Massachusetts referendum the amendment was defeated partly as a result of
charges that it originated in Soviet Russia and was designed to "nationalize
the children." This canard was allegedly put out by manufacturing interests,
among them an organization called Sentinels of the Republic.[35]

Some protests against the DAR leadership continued, there were flurries of resignations and recalcitrant local chapters, but by the end of the 1930s the Red hunters were temporarily at bay.

Catt thought the best answer was a large, informed group of women determined to live in a peaceful world. To that end had she organized the annual conferences on the Cause and Cure of War.

· 19 ·
Cause and Cure of War

The first Conference on the Cause and Cure
of War held in Washington, D. C., January 18–24, 1925, had 450 delegates
who represented five million women members of the nine sponsoring organizations. [1] By the end of the meetings Catt had identified 257 causes of war and
was wondering if the effort to list them and to find cures had been "a tragedy
or an experiment." To nearly everyone's surprise it turned out to be a brave
beginning for a consortium that carried on until the United States became
involved in World War II. No series of talks could cure that war, but the
organization's successor, the Women's Action Committee for Victory and
Lasting Peace, insured that women helped organize the United Nations.

The program of the opening conference was so ambitious that a week
before the meetings began only half of the thirty-eight speakers had agreed to
come. With the meetings came "confusion, suspicion and hostility inside and
outside the hall," Catt wrote. "Congress clearly viewed us with suspicion and
military groups outspokenly pronounced us a menace. Later it was whispered
that our meeting had received money for its expenses from Moscow. Some of
the presidents of the organizations were kept busy placating delegates who did
not like the conference nor anything that any speaker had said. Our conference was followed by another woman's meeting addressed by military men
favoring war and impolitely condemning our conference. We felt hostility
everywhere about us."[2]

The first day Catt set the ground rules. There would be no discussing the
horrors of war or arguing the possibilities of abolishing it: "The Conference
opens with the conviction, firmly fixed, that war is a relic of barbarism whose
abolition should have been achieved years ago." No time would be spent in
useless vilification of those who disagreed.

The first aim of the conference was the education of members on why
war continues and then what can be done to bring about peace. The main
task of the delegates was to carry back to their organizations all theories and
plans for the guarantee of national security and methods proposed for drawing

peacemakers into closer association. She relied on old formulas from the suffrage movement: "Agitation for a cause is excellent; education is better; but organization is the only assurance of final triumph of any cause in a self-governing nation."

She held it was women's duty to end war: "Women as a whole quite outdistance men as a whole in the psychology of nations. Men have been taught that physical courage is a man's chief virtue." When a man objects to physical conflict, "some one is sure to call him a coward. We women have no such obstacle in our way."[3]

Catt liked to orchestrate surprises into conferences; the first speakers on peace were two professional soldiers: Brigadier General Christopher B. Thomson, former Secretary of State for Air in the British cabinet, and Major General John T. O'Ryan, who commanded the United States 27th Division during the war. Both argued that preparedness could set up the conditions of self-fulfilling prophecy and evoke war by fear.

The generals were followed by Florence Allen, judge of the Supreme Court of Ohio, who spoke on international law and told the delegates that is was up to women to teach the world that there was no situation "in which the law of justice can not and does not function if applied" between nations and individuals. She supported the Borah resolution for the outlawry of war, then pending in the Senate, and thought a World Court with powers of enforcement was also needed.

Catt seconded her and as a point of agreement for all delegates, asked the conference to support the World Court, a step most of the cooperating organizations had already endorsed. The Republican and Democratic parties had pledged themselves to it, and President Coolidge had recommended it. She did not see much credit in approving it because it required no moral courage to endorse a policy that was already popular. She looked for the next step and hoped the conference would have the "collective courage to march ahead of the mass sentiment of our nation."[4]

One of the speakers on the League of Nations was George W. Wickersham, Attorney General under President Taft, who analyzed the League and succinctly reaffirmed many delegates' faith in international law. "War can not be prevented by pious resolutions. It can only be prevented by nations subjecting themselves to some form of agreement controlling, restricting, restraining their action. Just so long as a nation is unwilling to subject itself to some sort of restrictive agreement, just so long its protestations of love of peace, of willingness to aid in ridding the world of the terrible scourge of war, amounts to nothing more than the hollow mockery of empty promises."[5]

One of the most impressive speakers was John Foster Dulles, an international lawyer who had been a major in the war and served as counsel to the American Peace Commission from 1918 to 1919. His subject was the economic motives of war, and he emphasized that resistance to change rather than aggrandizement was the economic cause of war. He suggested that peace plans failed because they did not proceed from the premise that change is inevitable and that the problem was "to remove the resistance to change, which creates the friction from which flow the sparks that ignite wars."[6]

Other causes of war were considered, including "Overpopulation and Migrations of Peoples," "National Insecurity," "Competition in Armament," "Imperialism," and "Psychological Factors in the War Spirit." In considering the cures, the speakers ranged over the world and through history. The existing international organizations were discussed, as was the work of such government agencies as the Postal Union, the Rhine Commission, the League of Nations Committee on Opium, and others.

Grace Abbott, director of the Children's Bureau, urged international cooperation and organization as essential for the welfare of women and children.[7] Other women discussed non-political agencies and their role in international understanding: Mary E. Woolley, President of Mount Holyoke College spoke on education; Anna Garlin Spencer on women's organizations; Dr. Alice Hamilton of Harvard Medical College on medicine; Mrs. Thomas Nicholson, president of the Women's Foreign Missionary Society on the missionary as an agent for world peace.

Eleanor Roosevelt, a delegate from the General Federation of Women's Clubs, spoke twice from the floor. She held apathy as a cause of war, deplored the difficulty in getting people aroused out of their everyday concerns, and asked if others had found answers to the problem. She took issue with Wickersham, who approved of "righteous war," and later added her voice to the general consensus of the necessity of outlawing war and founding a World Court that treated war as murder.

Considerable talk throughout the conference focused on "outlawing war," a phrase that had been current since the turn of the century. Jeannette Rankin, former congresswoman from Montana, a delegate from the American Association of University Women, summarized the concept when she commented, "As long as war is the legal method of settling international disputes, it will at some time be used for that purpose. If we as a people recognize war as a crime, as the greatest crime against humanity, we can arouse the spiritual power of the nation."[8]

Catt, the compulsive organizer, suggested that a Department of Peace be created with a secretary in the cabinet. The office of Assistant Secretary of Peace in the State Department had functioned briefly in 1909 at the outset of Taft's administration and Catt thought it should be restored. Rabbi Stephen S. Wise took the proposal a step further and advocated that the State Department be made the Peace Department. The first Conference on the Cause and Cure of War recommended Catt's less radical plan.[9]

Into such wide-ranging discussion Catt introduced the question of race prejudice as a cause. It was a question she had held back on during the suffrage movement because it was divisive, and she was focusing on the issue of sex. She resented the fact that there were no black delegates at this conference because "the so-called first class hotels have an agreement that no colored person shall be accommodated either by room or in the dining room." She drew on her recent trip to South America: "We do not in our own country face the color question fairly and squarely and find some kind of a decent solution for it, and that failure is used against us throughout this Western Hemisphere."

She condemned expansion by force and the nations who "have stolen everything they could stick a flag on and feel insecure lest some other robber will take it away." She told the conference: "Sooner or later the white races must disgorge some of their spoils and give a place to the other races of the world. We stole land—whole continents; we stole it at the point of swords and guns; and we might as well understand that we must not have an acre to a man while they have an inch to a man. We must leave the door open to whatever arrangements we may make for peace in order that justice can be done to all the races on all the continents."[10]

At the end of the conference, a committee summarized the meetings. The forty-two causes were listed in four divisions: psychological, economic, political, and social. It recommended the support of the outlawry of war, the addition of an Under Secretary of State for Peace in the cabinet, the reduction of armaments, and the adherence of the United States to the Permanent Court of International Justice (usually called the World Court). To emphasize the urgency of internationalism, the delegates passed a resolution calling for immediate action by the Senate to provide for United States membership in the World Court. It was presented to the Foreign Relations Committee by Senator Key Pittman, one of its members who was the final speaker of the conference and Catt's friend from the suffrage campaign.[11]

The conference adjourned and the 450 delegates went to the White House where they were received by President and Mrs. Coolidge. The president's secretary, C. Bascom Slemp, was terrified by the thought of all

those women led by Catt converging at the White House and had sought
advice from the State Department. Secretary Hughes assured him that the
president could just make some general observations about his interest in
preventing war and said that it would be difficult for the president to refuse to
meet the distinguished delegation. Coolidge then scrawled across the top of
the communication, "Let 'em call."[12]

When he met them in the East Room he acknowledged their World
Court resolution in a flabby statement high in moral purpose but low in
substance. He talked about a World Court but seemed willing to have the
discussions go on indefinitely.

The conference closed with a strong organization. Each of the nine
cooperating women's groups was pledged to develop a program of education
and action based on the findings; the nine presidents had formed a Continuing Committee for mutual help and support that would meet during the
year; petitions, resolutions, and letters to lawmakers were being drafted.

Catt was "deeply impressed with [the] fundamental greatness" of the
National Committee on the Cause and Cure of War and did not wonder that
it frightened the uninformed. She believed that when opposition to a movement became violent it meant that it had become strong and feared by its
enemies. Furthermore, when large groups of conservative people worked for
reform that had previously been left to the more radical and prophetic, such
work was nearing a successful end. She was not surprised, therefore, when her
appeal to the army, navy, and American Legion to join in the cause of peace
was ignored, nor alarmed when the Military Order of the World War reported
on "the atmosphere of 'pacifism,' 'non-resistance' and 'internationalism' that
pervaded it and sinister ideals that apparently dominated were expressed."[13]

Some conservatives in the audience thought the speeches were too
radical and a few of them left, but in general the meetings accomplished their
objective of instigating peace sentiment in associations not exclusively pacifist.

Catt's goal was to reach those uncommitted to peace and she had not
asked any of the scores of pacifist organizations to send delegates. Some were
enraged they were not invited but most, such as Mildred Olmsted of the
Women's International League for Peace and Freedom, assumed it was because they were too radical. It was easy enough to go a Cause and Cure
conference as a delegate from one of the eligible organizations. The sharpest
criticism from within the peace movement came from Rosika Schwimmer,
who complained that Catt's organizing genius was being wasted in work with
such limited aims among women who were not pacifists as she understood the

word.[14] Patiently Catt explained that the enterprise was not aimed toward those already convinced, but to edge the millions of uncommitted American women into taking a stand against war.

In the twenty-one months before the second conference, convention delegates and other concerned women led hundreds of local discussion meetings and held conferences in every state. Catt cheered them on with reports in the *Woman Citizen* and with optimistic statements in the national press: "United action will mean the greatest mobilization for peace this country has ever known."[15]

Rosika Schwimmer had more reason for outrage when the second Conference on the Cause and Cure of War met in December 1926, and all thirty lecturers were men. She still chafed from the first meetings when delegates were put down when they advanced their own logical arguments. She remembered that when Eleanor Roosevelt challenged George W. Wickersham's support of "righteous wars," sure of his intellectual superiority, he smugly replied, "I think if I had an opportunity to confer with Mrs. Roosevelt a little she would not be so absolute in her statement." Schwimmer loathed such patronizing attitudes of the "experts" and the sterile absorption of information they expected of the delegates. Even the temperate Mildred Adams commented with dry irony about "woman's traditional role of listening at the feet of masculine sages."[16] Catt said nothing; she engaged the speakers she considered best for the subjects outlined and did not regard their sex.

In her attempts to bring the conservative women into the peace movement she was anxious to squelch any charges of radicalism, and replied to a slur in the *Washington Star* that no delegate was any redder than President Coolidge. She had heard it all before in the suffrage years: She was too radical for the conservatives and too conservative for the radicals, and only occasionally flared forth with a volley of her own.

Even the pacifist editor Devere Allen approved the occasional "flash of originality and fresh approach to an old question" he heard at the second conference. Alfred Zimmern, for instance, emphasized that pacifists were realistic while those who thought conflict normal were unscientific, romantic dreamers.

Bruce Bliven, of the *New Republic*, took a different tack and gave a modern interpretation of Hobbes, saying, "Peace is as abnormal as electric refrigeration while war is as natural as is the heat of midsummer. If power is not continuously applied you do not get your refrigeration and the midsummer heat wins."

Norman Angell, Catt's favorite spokesperson on war and peace, crit-

icized the concept of defense as the right of a great state to be its own judge of
the national interest "in the multifarious questions that arise between nations." All of America's wars were fought to defend that idea, as were all
major wars. As long as that meaning was accepted, war was inevitable because
"it means asserting for ourselves a right which by its very terms we deny to
others."[17]

The focal speech was made by Carleton Beals who condemned American policy in Mexico, particularly the disregard by 17 percent of the oil
companies of new laws that required the return to the Mexican government of
many of the subsoil rights that had been granted to foreigners, mainly for
exploration and extraction. It was in their interests, he charged, that war was
in the making, that "the State Department is threatening the Mexican
Government at the present moment." His speech gave the delegates a unity
and a focus for action that students of the period credit with being a major
influence in stopping what seemed to be an inevitable war between Mexico
and the United States.[18]

At the close of the conference the women added two resolutions to their
steady support for the World Court. One urged the Senate to take favorable
action on a protocol prohibiting the use of poison gas and bacteriological
weapons in war (which had been discussed by several speakers), the other
asked the president to resolve the difficulties with Mexico without bloodshed.

Armed with these resolutions, Catt led her six hundred colleagues to the
White House on December 10, 1926 to present the request for conciliation
and arbitration. This was one of the first links in a chain of events that led to
settlement of the Mexican-American quarrel within a year.

Five weeks later, on January 18, 1927, the Democratic floor leader,
Senator Joe Robinson of Arkansas, offered a resolution proposing arbitration
over the threatened confiscation of oil fields and other landed properties
owned by American citizens. Pressure was brought to bear to insure a
favorable vote on the resolution: seventy-five thousand ministers of the
Federal Council of Churches of Christ in America urged their congregations
to support the resolution and letters poured into Washington; other important organizations made declarations for arbitration, including the American
Federation of Labor and the World Peace Foundation.

The widespread declarations for arbitration reflected a nationwide reaction against the administration, and on January 25 the Senate by unanimous
vote declared for arbitration. Although the president was not bound by the 79
to 0 vote, he noted it, and public agitation went on. Most of the member
organizations of the Committee on the Cause and Cure of War were among

twenty-five groups constituting the Committee on Peace with Latin America which continued the pressure throughout the spring and summer. Success seemed assured in September when Dwight W. Morrow was appointed Ambassador to Mexico, replacing the less sympathetic James R. Sheffield. Morrow's conciliatory efforts quickly produced results and by the end of the year the two countries were on friendly terms.

During that summer Catt attended two widely separated peace meetings. In July she was in Honolulu for the second biennial Institute of Pacific Relations. There she was reminded of the wide varieties of people of the Pacific and of American and European aggression against them, and she felt a sense of foreboding about the chance of war with Japan. After this eighteen-day colloquium she said, "All went away with smaller racial and national vanity." In November she was in Amsterdam for the first Peace Conference sponsored by the International Woman Suffrage Alliance. There she heard sharp complaints against American immigration and tariff policies. She admitted she knew "numerous Americans who would shed other men's blood to the last drop before yielding on either point."[19]

In her major speech to the Third Conference on the Cause and Cure of War in January 1928, Catt spoke of six personal axioms that helped her to get an overview. She thought they were better phrased than the usual peace treaty, which had "gaps big enough for the wardogs to crawl through."

One, war can be abolished when civilized nations will it so, the basic premise of most peace movements. She was pleased at the way America's blundering toward war with Mexico had been turned about by public opinion. As a shrewd and experienced publicist she warned her audience that the propaganda that shaped the will of a nation was conditioning America and Europe to expect "the next war."

Two, the problem of war must be isolated from all other problems and so treated. On this point she had differed from her European friends at the Amsterdam meeting who insisted feminism was a necessity for peace; Catt saw peace as the basis for a successful feminist movement. If the world waited to establish economic, political, and social justice before extirpating war itself, it would be drawn off into a maze with no way out. The extravagance of war inhibited such justice; in 1927, 82 percent of the federal expenditures went for past and future wars. War was a concrete evil, just as slavery was concrete, the former could be abolished as the latter had been.

Three, wars have no causes, they have excuses. Wars go on because nations have the habit and move by precedent. She spoke strongly against the underlying assumption of all war propaganda, the watchword of every war college and training camp: "The way to maintain peace is to prepare for war." It was a fallacy that gripped the minds of everyone. The only reason for the existence of military organizations that she accepted was the premise in the Constitution of the necessity to "provide for the common Defence." There was no consensus on the meaning of the phrase, although it was used as justification by the "preparedness" advocates.

Four, wars cannot settle anything. The strong nation, not necessarily the just nation, wins. The Honolulu conference had reaffirmed her conviction that imperial wars of aggression begat other wars of resistance.

Five, current problems are too momentous, too crucial to be irrationally approached. Reason and conciliation are the rational means, through such agencies as the League of Nations and the World Court. "Which is the better way, to offer the lives of men on battlefields, or wreck the tempers of statesmen in a series of round tables where talk is the equipment and reason the decisive influence?"

Six, compacts between and among all civilized nations to proscribe war constitute the only possible substitute for war. She supported all treaties that limited armaments and sought cooperation, particularly the Kellogg-Briand proposals that outlawed war.[20]

A few days before the opening of this third conference, the latest in a series of proposals for outlawing war had been published by Secretary of State Frank B. Kellogg. The idea had been around for several years and had been touched upon at previous Cause and Cure conferences. Serious talk about outlawing war had begun nine months before when, on April 6, 1927, the French Foreign Minister Aristide Briand had announced that a treaty "outlawing war" between France and the United States would be agreeable to France. Catt was enthusiastic about "the remarkable proposal to the American people" and immediately wrote to all of the delegates of the second Cause and Cure conference to urge them to publicize and lobby for it as concerned individuals.[21]

Kellogg suggested a multilateral treaty that France and the United States would together propose to the principal powers—Germany, Great Britain, Italy, Japan, France, and the United States—"to renounce war between themselves as an instrument of policy." The counterproposal Briand made on January 5, 1928, was that the six powers should not agree to renounce all war, but only wars of aggression. It was there matters stood at the opening of the third conference on the Cause and Cure of War, which discussed at length a definition of aggression and the idea of renouncing war.

A major change in format in this conference was the introduction of more discussions in which both the "experts" and the audience participated. Thanks to the new system, the Kellogg and Briand proposals were thoroughly considered. Finally the delegates passed a resolution approving a multilateral treaty for the renunciation of war as an instrument of national policy.

By April Catt and the Committee on the Cause and Cure of War had detailed a plan of educating and lobbying for a treaty renouncing war. Forty-eight state conferences marshaling twelve million women members of the nine sponsoring organizations would demonstrate to the Senate that public sentiment favored the treaty. Catt announced positively, "War will disappear from the earth when women decide the time has come." This was at last "a cause worthy of our united sacrifice and devotion." They adopted the slogan, "Build friendships, not warships," and under that banner thousands of meetings were held. "That yearning of the human race for peace has found its expression in the Briand Kellogg treaty," she proclaimed.[22]

She devoted herself to arousing public opinion toward favorable action on the treaty and to develop a peace institution under the State Department. The treaty would go far to prepare the way for disarmament and the peace department would insure an active, positive power. "Give the new peace institution some of the eighty-two cents per dollar now going to the war institution and set up as lively a publicity section for arbitration as there is for a big navy. Keep the building going until confidence in the positive aggressiveness of peace produces in all the advanced countries the sense of security, as it certainly will."[23]

Major criticism of the treaty concerned its lack of a means of enforcement. Franklin D. Roosevelt commented on this and added: "Secretary Kellogg's plan fails in two points. It leads to a false belief in America that we have taken a great step forward. It does not contribute in any way to settling matters of international controversy."[24]

Various refinements were suggested and countered by Kellogg and Briand. Finally, on August 27, 1928, the Pact of Paris was signed in the Salle de l'Horloge. William Allen White concluded his report on the ceremony, "Business conjured with an ancient wand to witch away the war monster. So the false dawn of a new epoch, the pale peace pageant of the Coolidge bull market came to mankind."[25] For Catt and supporters of the treaty, the task was now to get it ratified before it could be pigeonholed by the Senate.

The first thing Catt did at the fourth Cause and Cure conference in January 1929 was to praise the workers who had organized more than a thousand meetings a month over the course of the year that had produced in more than ten thousand resolutions endorsing the treaty. The next morning,

January 15, forty-five delegations of women went by states to carry their state resolutions to their senators. That afternoon the Senate approved the treaty with a vote of 85 to 1. Two days later President Coolidge signed the American instrument of ratification. [26]

The Committee on the Cause and Cure of War was not alone in promoting the pact. The Women's International League for Peace and Freedom, the Carnegie Endowment for International Peace, and the American Peace Society were only a few of the national and local organizations working for its ratification. However, Robert H. Ferrell noted in his detailed analysis of the pact, "In this strenuous campaign for ratification, Mrs. Catt's cause-and-cure committee was especially effective. Battle-hardened in the fight for women's rights, Mrs. Catt knew how to exert pressure on the American Government." [27]

The year 1928 that moved toward political triumph had been one of personal grief and pain for Catt. It had started well—in the spring she and Mary Garrett Hay had moved to New Rochelle and a few months were spent in happy confusion while they arranged, decorated, and landscaped their new home. But on August 29, her seventy-first birthday, Hay suddenly died. "The two friends were in their rooms, talking back and forth through the open door when luncheon was announced," Mary Gray Peck recounted.

> Mrs. Catt left her room to go downstairs, calling to Miss Hay as she passed her door. There was no reply. When she was partway down the stairs, something made her turn back and go to Miss Hay's room. There she saw her friend fallen back across the bed on which she must have been sitting when overtaken with cerebral hemorrhage. She never regained consciousness, and died twelve hours later.
>
> Although she had been gradually failing in health for some time past, her condition had not been considered critical, and she had been in specially good spirits on her birthday. This sudden and utterly unlooked-for bereavement shook Mrs. Catt to the soul. [28]

The two friends had shared their home since George Catt's death twenty-three years before. Catt was devastated. During that fall and winter, loss, age, and overwork brought attacks of shingles and other illnesses. By the end of November she seemed to be getting well and Clara Hyde noted happily, "The Chief is coming back at a stronger pace now. She slept five consecutive nights without resort to dope. A week ago she spoke at a multilateral treaty meeting—a good deal in her old powerful manner. It was good to see the improvement."[29] More than fifty friends gathered for a party on her seventieth birthday in January, and a few days later she went to Washington for the fourth Cause and Cure conference.

Soon after the meetings opened she suffered a heart attack followed by fierce pains from shingles. By chance Rosa Manus had come for a visit and to attend the conference. "Rosa has been faithful," wrote Hyde.

> She was up with her nights and stayed by her days. She was the bulldog who kept off the crowd. She told me the Chief had screamed all night with pain from the shingles. I got her to revise "scream" to "groan" for ordinary consumption. I don't know what she would have done without Rosa.
>
> She presided at the opening banquet and everyone remarked how bad she looked. She did her part as Mrs. Public Opinion on the night of the International Conversation. She also read her "Monroe Doctrine" speech the last night of the Conference. She read like a racehorse which I had never seen her do before—no doubt due to the ragged state of her nerves. While she was on show she carried on. Behind the scenes she let go.[30]

The 1929 conference passed three resolutions: the perennial one urging participation in the World Court, another supporting the ratification of the Paris pact (which Coolidge signed while they were in session), and the third protesting the increase of naval armaments. They passed no resolution on specific countries but had discussed at length Mexico, Nicaragua, China, and Japan, in all of which United States foreign policy seemed to be unusually complicated.

In spite of her physical pain, Catt had flashes of her old spirit. During the Round Table on Foreign Policy there was discussion about General Augusto Sandino's revolt that began in 1927 against the United States marines' occupation of Nicaragua. "Might it be possible that Sandino is not a bandit but a patriot?" Catt asked.[31]

With enormous effort she managed to last out the conference but it left her energy reserves depleted and for the next several months she lived quietly at New Rochelle. She wrote comparatively little, lectured not at all, and left the planning of the next Cause and Cure conference to the efficient staff headed by Josephine Schain and Ruth Morgan. The World Court had become an active issue again, but she could take little part in the discussion.

She roused herself during the summer to write a few articles for the *Woman's Journal*, reiterating her old plea for education and action. "The people must speak, and before speaking they must be informed."[32] She chaired a National World Court Committee organized in July to educate and lobby, but took only a small part in its work. At the moment it seemed that support of the scheduled 1930 Naval Conference on disarmament was more urgent.

Basic to all peace schemes was armament control; if the weapons of war were minimal, the chances of keeping the peace were optimal. At the Washington Armament Conference in 1921, Great Britain, France, Japan, and Italy had agreed to limit their navies and to accept a ratio based on tonnage of capital ships. In 1927 a Geneva conference discussed limitations of cruisers, destroyers, and submarines but no agreement was reached; another meeting was arranged for 1930 in London.

Each conference was preceded by many meetings that produced a flurry of discussions, letter writing, telegram sending, and petitions by peace people (as well as militarists). With each announced international conference hope flared again that maybe this was the time something would be accomplished if only enough people showed interest; if the petitions reached massive proportions the politicians of the world might pay less attention to narrow interests and more to the broader issues of sanity and humanity.

It was against this background of hope, hope deferred, set up again, and then down again through the 1920s and 1930s that the Conferences on the Cause and Cure of War continued. Each had its discussions of disarmament, each passed resolutions supporting reduction of armaments. The issue was hot or only warm depending on what was happening in the political world. After October 1929, everything was colored by the stock market crash and the Great Depression.

· 20 ·

The Shadows Darken

Catt had thrown all her energy and craft as a publicist into rousing massive public support for the Kellogg-Briand pact. Only after its ratification did she admit its obvious weaknesses: its lack of an enforcement procedure and its failure to limit arms and arms races, hair-trigger international crises, or the vast profits made from war. "A pact to renounce war is a poor dike with which to hold back the flood," she said.[1]

Her strategy was to use the momentum of the successful pact ratification campaign and with other peace organizations at home to apply pressure on Congress to accept the World Court. She also wanted the Committee on the Cause and Cure of War to join with international peace groups to support the Conference on Naval Disarmament scheduled for London in 1930. Unfortunately, within two years the inadequate dikes against war were crumbling under global depression and increased militarism.

At the fifth Conference on the Cause and Cure of War in January 1930, once again Catt led delegates up Capitol Hill to present petitions urging Senate ratification of the World Court protocol. Once again the women met the president (this time Hoover), to declare that by supporting the World Court the United States would give evidence of the "sincere purpose of our government to uphold its commitments made through the Paris Pact."[2]

At the conference, delegates from England, Germany, France, and Japan held a forum on the effectiveness of peace movements. The stars of the conference were Uta Hayashi and Tsune Gauntlett, Japanese peace leaders who were on their way to London with 180,000 signatures on petitions to reduce naval armament. These they exhibited in handsome oriental hampers. Catt had taken up their idea, and before the conference the Cause and Cure organizations circulated similar petitions and had collected twelve million signatures. She also urged English and French women to demonstrate with the Japanese and Americans in London. There, with high ceremony, women from the four countries presented the petitions to Prime Minister Ramsay MacDonald.[3]

211

At the close of the Conference for Naval Disarmament in London on April 22, 1930, the United States, Great Britain, and Japan adopted a program of cruiser limitation, with treaty expiration set for the end of 1936. But even while these 1930 debates were going on, the United States announced that it would build the greatest battleship in the world. Catt was disgusted and when asked if a protest petition should be circulated, she replied it "would probably have as much effect as a lone ladybug sitting on a cabbage rose while she longs for rain." She saw "the chief benefits of petitions [as] the education which their circulation carries into homes, clubs, churches, and all varieties of community gatherings."[4]

When the Conference on the Cause and Cure of War opened for the sixth time in January 1931, the "Never again" public attitude in Europe as well as in the United States had become "Let's be ready next time." James G. McDonald attributed the alarming shift in outlook to ignorance. The horrors of war receded with time but the "glories" remained.[5]

The sixth conference was gloomy. Jane Addams spoke of "fears at the elbow of national policy," among them fears of the extending economic depression. The conference was well attended by 561 delegates but the pep talks were repetitive and dreary. The élan was gone. Some of the delegates left early. Even Catt's enthusiasm flagged, "It is very tiresome, these conferences."[6]

Still again the conference sent President Hoover a resolution on the World Court but Catt and her colleagues did not go to see him themselves. Once again resolutions showed continuing concern for the Kellogg-Briand pact and disarmament. The only new one was about abolishing military training in the schools and and making it elective in colleges and universities.

In her closing speech, Catt showed doubts for the first time about the effectiveness of their movement. Maybe, she mused, civilization would not be ended by the next war; maybe it had ended with the last. Maybe "we have not done our duty in spreading our influence, our information."[7]

When the next conference opened in January 1932, no one could remember when times were worse. The World Court was stalemated, and although another disarmament meeting was scheduled to begin in Geneva in February, there was little hope that it would succeed. James G. McDonald, chair of the Foreign Policy Association, surveyed the past year, saying, "1931 closed in a deep, enveloping gloom." The Japanese army had occupied most of Manchuria, India was faced with riots that were met with repression with the government, South America floundered in deep depression and was ripe for revolution, the idea of a "United States of Europe" was stillborn, and

Hitler was gaining power in Germany. McDonald concluded his jeremiad with the prophecy that if war is not eliminated "the blind forces of nationalism, the fear of war, and eventually war itself, utilizing modern science, will destroy us."[8]

All the member organizations reported attacks by superpatriots. The Home Missions and the WCTU were criticized by those who "felt the peace movement did not have anything to do with churches" and that the Bible favored wars. Business and Professional Women were busy answering charges that they were "Red" and unpatriotic. Maud Swartz of the Women's Trade Union League reported opposition to peace from workers who thought they would prosper from "a good rousing war." A number of workers had said, "It is better to be on the firing line with something in your stomach than to be walking the streets hungry."[9]

In her summing up at the end of the conference, Catt sounded like the old veteran leader telling her troops how to survive: "A reformer always knows that he is going to win, but he never does know whether it is in his day or that of somebody else. He is completely satisfied that victory will one day crown his labors."[10]

She resigned as chair of the Committee on the Cause and Cure of War at this conference but continued to attend meetings, to speak, and to circulate petitions urging disarmament. But she looked forward to new Geneva talks "less with expectation than curiosity. How can we account for the absurdity of nations promising on one hand never to go to war and on the other piling high the fighting equipment?"[11] Six weeks later Mary Woolley wrote that the Geneva meetings had recessed during the German elections. Hitler won.

Catt tried to enliven the next conference with an "interlude," a didactic fantasy she called "Mars Takes a Sabbatical." Although she was ill and missed most of the meetings, she took part in the skit. It was set at a Cause and Cure convention that is interrupted by Mars and ten women warriors who have denounced their past and declared for pacificism. He agrees to take a sabbatical of 142,857 years (one for every seven years he has been in charge) and give the peace women the $33,261,176,719.57 spent in the last war. They decide to spend it on two federal departments, one for peace, one for education, and for social programs that include old age security; maternity and infancy benefits; mental health programs for children and adults; and help for dependent or delinquent children, the sick, and the unemployed. Research would be financed to establish the cause and cure of crime, mental retardation, insanity, drug and alcohol abuse, and cancer. All these social problems could be solved with money spent on war. Never had Catt spelled out so clearly her ideas of the essential social programs that were neglected to pay for war.[12]

From the beginning of the Third Reich, Catt was alarmed by the militarist spirit it engendered. On the one hand it tended to reaffirm anti-German prejudice so effectively implanted by propaganda during the Great War, and on the other it justified American militarism. And there was a new dimension: the horror in Hitler's policy of persecuting Jews. Rosa Manus in Holland was helping Jewish refugees and had become Catt's best informant.[13]

Manus brought frightening details when she came in July 1933 to visit Catt for several weeks. Together they went to the International Congress of Women in Chicago and while there they sought advice from prominent Jews who were already organizing to relieve the desperate plight of the German Jews. Catt saw a way to extend the range of humanitarian agitation and formed the Protest Committee of Non-Jewish Women Against the Persecution of Jews in Germany, which mounted a drive for signatures to a letter protesting the German pogrom. "We cry out by this method to all the nations our horror over the mistake the German people have permitted to be made," she said. Within a month she had over nine thousand signatures.

Copies of the protest were sent to women's organizations in all countries, except Germany, and to the League of Nations. It was given widespread publicity in American and foreign newspapers as well as in the journals of women's associations. "We intend to string it all around Germany and open channels for it to leak in, but we will not send it directly to the German government, because this is an unofficial expression of sentiment and we are not asking our government to indorse it."[14]

For this enterprise, in November Catt received the American Hebrew Medal for 1933 given for the promotion of better understanding between Christians and Jews, the first time it was given to a woman. The award ceremony was presided over by Henry Morgenthau, Sr. Eleanor Roosevelt presented the medal; among the congratulations came those of President Roosevelt, Governor Lehman, and Albert Einstein.[15]

Catt and nine other women then formed a Committee of Ten to ask President Roosevelt to ease immigration restrictions and permit entry of refugees suffering under persecution. They published a carefully researched pamphlet on precedents and current views on asylum. Included was a letter to the president in which they urged that American consulates and embassies act as sanctuaries.[16] Roosevelt expressed sympathy but did not act. Catt continued her work for refugees until her death.

Meanwhile her work for peace went on. The president spoke to the delegates of the January 1934 Cause and Cure of War conference. He congratulated them on their excellent work in education on the problems of peace and war, and urged the necessity of translating this education into policies for governmental action, but said nothing of substance.

The tenth anniversary conference in 1935 was marked by the publication of a book, *Why Wars Must Cease,* which summarized the decade of work of the Committee on the Cause and Cure of War.[17] Catt headed the five-woman book committee and received the first copy on her seventy-sixth birthday, January 9, 1935. Each of the ten chapters argued a reason against war, each was written by a prominent woman, including Eleanor Roosevelt, Florence Allen, Mary E. Woolley, Jane Addams, and Dorothy Canfield Fisher. The *New York Herald Tribune* carried excerpts from each chapter, the book was well publicized by the press and at the 1935 conference.

Catt stayed at the White House during the conference. At a supper party there she sat next to the president, who talked about the pending vote on the World Court. Catt remembered him saying that if peace were to be preserved, America would have to build a navy second to none and do it as fast as possible. Catt reportedly said, "The President is a sincere friend of organized world peace, he would like to see the country in the League and the World Court, but what he really relies on to preserve the peace is our navy! He was in the Navy Department in the last war, he believes sea power is the ulimate force. And if I were in his shoes, I would want the biggest navy in the world!"[18] Nothing in her letters or speeches corroborates that statement, allegedly made to Peck. The Roosevelt charm could be formidable; perhaps all she meant by her comment was that under the circumstances she tried to understand his views and did not counter with her own.

When the Cause and Cure conference opened in 1935 a Senate vote on the World Court was imminent after ten years' delay. On January 16 Senator Borah's decade of opposition succeeded in scuttling the internationalists' dream. The resolution was defeated by a vote of 52 for and 36 against, seven short of the necessary two-thirds. Catt commented that the first duty of all reformers in a defeat was to search for flaws in their own campaign. She thought the fault lay in there having been no authoritative coordination of efforts of the many organizations working for it, no single group whose business it was to have a reliable lobby with a dependable congressional poll.[19]

Throughout the years of peace work, Catt was affiliated with other organizations, sometimes as an individual—in the League of Nations associations and the League to Enforce Peace, for example; sometimes as representative of the NCCW—on the Disarmament Committee of the Women's International Organization and on the People's Mandate Committee under the leadership of Mabel Vernon of the Women's International League. For Vernon, Catt agreed to sign the mandate to governments to fulfill their pledges under the League of Nations Convenant and the Kellogg pact but thought the time was past for it to be effective: "Now it happens to be in a very unfortunate time since the general opinion prevails that another war is imminent."[20]

She was one of the speakers at the official launching of the American campaign in September 1935, where she reiterated her conviction that before the world could be reformed, war must be stopped. By February the American campaign had grown so rapidly that the Women's International League relinquished its control to a combined People's Mandate Committee for the Western Hemisphere and the Far East chaired by Mary E. Woolley (with Catt as honorary chair) and Mabel Vernon directing. In March, Woolley and Congresswoman Caroline O'Day reported to President Roosevelt they had one million signatures; by Armistice Day the number had grown to fifty million.[21] In spite of the formidable figures, Catt was right—the mandate did nothing to stop the coming of war.

Catt counted 1936 as marking her half-century of work for women. The Cause and Cure conference celebrated her Jubilee with a banquet. The next day President Roosevelt gave her a letter of handsome praise. Her health was good and she was enjoying the adulation. In May she made "a sentimental journey" to Iowa for the unveiling of a bas relief at the Capitol honoring the pioneer suffragists, then went to her birthplace, where Ripon College awarded her an honorary degree.[22] She felt that would have pleased her parents.

By midsummer she was home in New Rochelle and characteristically making plans for change. She had decided that the CCCW should disband: "By long continuance we go contrary to our original promises."[23] The conferences had been designed to educate many for a few years, not to be perennial.

Josephine Schain, her successor, was appalled. The organization was growing as the world waited to see if Hitler's next move would trigger a massive continental conflict. Many of those who had been reluctant to join peace organizations were joining them. Catt saw the growth as too late and futile. At the 1937 conference she listed three weaknesses of the peace movement that allowed it to be blocked, frustrated, and ineffective. First, there was no common emotive name to define "who and what we are";

second, the movement lacked a positive aim, defining itself negatively in terms of the absence of war; third, it lacked a common method or policy.[24] She was beginning to formulate the view that the women should be building toward some new version of the League of Nations, an effective political world organization in which they would play an equal and active part.

The 1938 Cause and Cure conference bogged down in discusssion of a proposal to boycott Japanese imports and how it could be made effective if American women refused to buy silk stockings. In disgust Catt pointed the way back to essentials. "The true symbol of man's four millions of years of evolution is a single figure, a university graduated statesman with several added degrees and decorated with the key. Now he is wearing a gas mask, and is scurrying into a hole in the ground hoping to escape the war he does not know how to stop!!"[25]

An admiring reporter observed Catt at age seventy-nine: Mrs. Catt talks peace now instead of the vote. She reads her speeches because she doesn't quite trust her memory. But the laughs still topple all over each other, eyes get moist when she gets serious, and her lusty voice needs no public address system."[26]

Catt celebrated her eightieth birthday in January 1939 with so many enthusiastic friends that she was exhausted and unable to attend the Cause and Cure conference, the only one she missed. Before the next one, England and France had declared war on Germany, and Catt had grown increasingly impatient with talk about peace but no action. At the 1940 conference she said, "We can't settle a battle with tears—that has been tried. We might settle it with humor if we are smart enough." At the end her patience snapped, "I, for one, am tired of all this talk about causes, effects, et cetera. I think that war is bunkum and if we had the intelligence and the backbone and spiritual strength we could destroy war."[27]

By 1941, when it was clear that the United States would soon enter the war, the Committee on the Cause and Cure of War fell apart. Five of the member organizations had withdrawn and the annual conference was can-celled for lack of funds. As in every crisis, Catt seemed to renew her strength and optimism; she wanted a complete reorganization and was determined to give it a chance. "It may go on the rocks due to the situation which faces the world," but she wanted to see what it could do. Her goal was that women should take their places alongside men at the peace and be neither subser-vient nor invisible.[28] Finally, in the spring of 1943, the CCCW was dissolved and was succeeded by the Women's Action Committee for Victory and Lasting Peace, which was dedicated to giving support to the United Nations ideal. When World War II was drawing to a close and politicians and statesmen met in San Francisco to define the United Nations Organization, Catt wrote long and thoughtful letters to delegates pointing out the inherent weaknesses she saw developing and suggesting strong programs "to teach the truth of the immorality of war and the morality of Peace, the only policy for civilized people to follow and the only salvation for the world."[29]

During the war years Catt, although confined more and more to home, continued work for Jewish refugees and cooperated with the remnants of international women's organizations in exile in England to publicize protests against "the crimes that are being committed" as the policy of governments. From her study in New Rochelle she sent forth letters to important people, pamphlets, press releases, resolutions, and petitions. She circulated to the U.S. officials the first factual account in English of the horrors of the Warsaw ghetto, which epitomized all she detested. She lost several dear friends to the concentration camps; closest to her was Rosa Manus, murdered at Auschwitz, in 1942.[30]

Catt, eighty-six in 1945, looked back over the previous century with its battle for freedom and its gains by the women of the country. By 1945 the rights to equality demanded by the Seneca Falls convention were nearly achieved, she said. The gaps in the completion of the plan were due "to the leftover tradition and customary thinking which holds that men are the natural earners of money, the natural holders of jobs, and the political and economic leaders, while women are the natural supported housekeepers and caretakers of children. Women, thus, will have to find the way through this dilemma before the gaps can be filled."[31] Another woman's crusade was her answer but she was premature; it would be another generation twenty-five years later that would respond to her call to fill the gaps of sex discrimination.

Death came quietly to Carrie Chapman Catt in the early morning of March 9, 1947. She had been at home in New Rochelle on March 8 all day and evening as usual, receiving a friend in the afternoon, writing a little, reading. Sometime after midnight she had a heart attack. Alda Wilson, who had lived with her since Hay's death nearly nineteen years before, called Catt's doctor, who arrived shortly before she died at 3:30 A.M.

She had told Wilson that she wanted her funeral as simple as possible. Services were conducted in her living room by a colleague, Dr. Walter Van Kirk, the secretary of the Commission on Just and Durable Peace of the

Federal Council of the Churches of Christ in America. Sixty old friends, mostly from suffrage and peace organizations, were there. She was buried alongside Mary Garrett Hay at Woodlawn Cemetary, where Catt had erected a monument shortly after Hay's death: "Here lie two, united in friendship for thirty-eight years through constant service to a great cause."

Notes

Key to abbreviations used in the notes:

LC: *Library of Congress*
NYPL: *New York Public Library, Manuscript Division*
SL: *Schlesinger Library, Radcliffe College*
SSC: *Sophia Smith Collection, Smith College*
SCPC: *Swarthmore College Peace Collection*

CHAPTER 1. ONE OF THE GIFTED (pp. 1–13)

1. Will Irwin, "Talking War to Death," *Our World*, May 1922, pp. 4–5; *New York Times*, 14 April 1921, p. 16; *Woman Citizen*, 23 April 1921, p. 184. Elizabeth J. Hauser, "Eight Months' War against War," *Woman Citizen*, 17 December 1921, p. 23.

2. Mrs. William Dick Sporborg, "Mrs. Catt, Nearing Seventy-seven, Looks Back on Fifty Years' Service to Women," *New York Herald Tribune*, 5 January 1936.

   Most of the Lane and Clinton family history is from material in the Charles City Historical Society archives. This includes an account Carrie Chapman Catt wrote in 1943; correspondence with Matie Lane, the wife of her nephew, Warren Lane, who lived in Charles City; a Clinton family genealogical chart and data from the family Bible; a copy of Lucius Lane's will; correspondence of Catt with her brother Charles regarding her financial status and arrangements she had made for relatives who needed help in the 1930s and 1940s; 1902 correspondence with a California lawyer about her Aunt Myra Miller's estate; other correspondence, mostly about family relationships.

   The Lane family Bible is in the Potsdam Museum in New York as is other memorabilia, including details of several real estate transactions made by Lucius Lane's father, Benjamin Lane, from 1828 to 1860.

   The 1860 Wisconsin census recorded that Lucius Lane's real estate in Ripon was worth $6,000, his personal estate $100.

   At the Schlesinger Library, Radcliffe College, there are a few letters Catt wrote in 1944–45 to Constance Burnett, who was writing an article for the Girl Scout magazine *The American Girl*, that contain some details—for example, Catt's comment that her mother did not like living on a farm.

   In Catt's papers in the Library of Congress there is a typescript, "Carrie

Chapman Catt and Charles City," which Mary Gray Peck attributed to G. I. Goddard, a neighbor in that town. The account was published in the *Charles City Daily Press* about the time the Lane farmhouse was marked with a bronze plaque in Catt's honor—October 7, 1938. The memoir has information about the Barnes family, with whom Carrie Lane lived during the winters when she was in high school, 1873–77. (In the summer she rode her horse the five miles to school.) "It was as good as a circus to have Carrie Lane about," Mr. Barnes used to say, remembering her high spirits and sense of fun. The Goddard article also includes the remarks of some of her pupils as well as anecdotes about her after she moved back to Charles City in 1887.

Charles City High School has limited records for the 1870s although an enrollment book shows her name during each year from 1873–77. In the State Department of History and Archives, Des Moines, there is a school attendance book of the Independent District of Mandville, West Point Twp., Butler Co., that includes the December 2, 1878 through March 20, 1879 term taught by Carrie C. Lane. She had from nine to sixteen pupils, from ages five to eighteen, and was paid $120 for the sixteen-week term.

Information about Carrie Lane's college years is from the archives of Iowa State University, Ames.

3. *Charles City Intelligencer*, 28 June 1877, p. 2.
4. Catt, "Evolution—Fifty Years Ago," *Woman Citizen*, 11 July 1925, pp. 7–8, 29–30; "Why I Have Found Life Worth Living," *Christian Century*, 27 March 1928, pp. 406–8.
5. *Mason City Republican*, 28 September 1883, p. 1. In this issue there are several items about Carrie Lane. Without consulting her, the Democrats had nominated her County Superintendent of Schools (an elective position, the city superintendent was appointed by the School Board). She refused to be a candidate. Leo Chapman made several laudatory remarks about her, including, "Three cheers for Carrie C. Lane! All the boys are in love with her—or ought to be. No Saloonocrats can capture her."
6. Ibid., 28 February 1884, p. 4.
7. Ibid., 3 April 1884, p. 3.
8. Ibid., 10 July 1884, p. 3.
9. D. P. Livermore, *The Arguments against Woman Suffrage Carefully Examined and Completely Answered* (Melrose, Mass.: William L. Williams, 1885), p. 39; Thomas Wentworth Higginson, "War and Women," *Woman's Journal*, 29 October 1898 (reprinted from *Harper's Bazaar*, 22 October 1898) said the occasion was when Stanton was testifying before a New York legislature committee chaired by Greeley.
10. *Mason City Republican*, 15 October 1885, p. 5.
11. Ibid., 10 December 1885; Catt to Mary A. Hunter, 2 February 1959, Catt papers,

Woman's Suffrage Collection, State Department of History and Archives, Des Moines, Iowa.

12. *Mason City Republican*, 29 October 1885, p. 1.

13. Official records of Leo Chapman's indictment for "the crime of a malicious libel" and subsequent details are from the Cerro Gordo County District Court. The case was dismissed October 18, 1886 (DC Rec F, Entry 364, p. 473). It was also extensively covered in the local papers. Louise R. Noun, in her *Strong-Minded Women*, pp. 231–32, was the first writer to give the reason for the Chapmans leaving Mason City when they did. "A funereal departure," she described the result of the action of the auditor and his friends, whose intention was to run Leo Chapman out of town.

CHAPTER 2. ALIENS AND ALIENATED (pp. 14–26)

1. Catt to Mary Gray Peck, 26 March 1920, Catt papers, LC. Carrie Chapman's first three lectures are handwritten in a notebook in Catt papers, NYPL. What appears to be an earlier version or draft of "The American Sovereign," also handwritten in a notebook, is in the University of Rochester Library.

2. *Woman's Journal*, 19 September 1891, p. 304; NAWSA also published this lecture as a "Woman Suffrage" pamphlet. It was reprinted in the *Woman's Journal*, 16 March 1901, p. 87, and again 25 January 1913, p. 26. "Another True Story," in the same vein, was in the *Woman Voter*, January 1914.

3. *Charles City Intelligencer*, 13 December 1887, 22 May, 29 May, 5 June 1888; *Woman's Journal*, 1 November 1913.

4. Catt to Eleanor Roosevelt, 5 December 1938, Eleanor Roosevelt papers, FDR Library, Hyde Park, New York.

5. *Woman's Journal*, 9 November 1889, p. 356.

6. *Seattle Times*, 10 March 1947.

7. Margaret Campbell to Lucy Stone, 30 July 1890, quoted by Noun, *Strong-Minded Women*, p. 235.

8. Catt, "A Suffrage Team," *Woman Citizen*, 8 September 1923, pp. 11–12. *Engineering News*, 12 October 1905, pp. 384–85 has details of George Catt's professional career.

9. Catt, "The Worth of an American Ballot," *Woman's Journal*, 28 May 1892, p. 174.

10. Susan B. Anthony and Ida H. Harper, eds., *History of Woman Suffrage*, 4: 555–56. Catt spoke and wrote about the South Dakota campaign many times. "Because I was young and all the experiences were new, every event in that campaign stands out in my memory with a vividness which does not mark later and even more important events," she said. Her comments here are from "The

Crisis," 7 September 1916, *Proceedings of the Forty-Eighth Annual Convention* (New York: NAWSA, 1916), p. 59.

11. Newspaper clipping in minutes book of the New York State Woman Suffrage Association 1869–92; neither name nor date of paper given, probably Catt's speech at the State convention at Syracuse November 16, 1892. League of Women Voters Collection, Rare Book and Manuscript Library, Columbia University. The *Woman's Journal* report of the convention, 19 November 1892, p. 375, notes "spirited addresses" made by Mary Eastman, Carrie Lane Chapman, Lucy Stone, and Susan B. Anthony, adding, "The admission fee of 25 cents at the evening sessions did not prevent a large audience."

12. Elaine Goodale was a New England woman who had gone to Dakota Territory in 1886 as the first government teacher at White River camp on the Sioux reservation. At about the time she and Catt talked together, Goodale met her future husband, Dr. Charles Eastman, a Sioux educated in Boston who had recently returned to be physician to his people. She helped him care for the victims of the Battle of Wounded Knee in December 1890 (Kay Graber, ed., *Sister to the Sioux*). Catt and Elaine Eastman met again in Northampton, Massachusetts, in 1913 when Catt spoke there in the suffrage cause. The last time their paths crossed was in the 1920s when Eastman, a member of the Northampton chapter of the Daughters of the American Revolution, led a local fight against the Washington Executive DAR blacklists which included Catt's name.

    Catt's comment on enfranchising Indians is from "South Dakota Women," *Woman's Standard,* November 1890.

13. "From the Field," *Woman's Standard,* October 1890.

14. *New York Times,* 19 March 1911, part V, p. 8.

15. *Woman's Journal,* 8 November 1890. Catt's own memory of the occasion fifty years later differed only slightly: "Mr. Blackwell rang a dinner bell and introduced me. Then I rang it and introduced Mr. Blackwell. Then he rang it and introduced me. That is the way we kept people listening." (Catt to Justina Wilson, 9 October 1940, Catt papers, LC).

16. "South Dakota Women," *Woman's Standard,* November 1890.

17. Ida Husted Harper, *The Life and Work of Susan B. Anthony,* 2: 693–94.

18. Catt told the Aberdeen story as often as she talked about the South Dakota campaign. This quotation is from a fragment of an undated speech (probably to the League of Women Voters in the early twenties) in the Schlesinger Library.

CHAPTER 3. EXPERIMENTS IN ORGANIZATION
(pp. 29–37)

1. "Why the Daisy" and "An American Princess," *Woman's Standard,* February 1891 and October 1891. These were both signed C.L.C. [Carrie Lane Chapman]. For

the first few years after her marriage to George Catt, she generally used the name under which she had become known, Carrie Lane Chapman. When the Catts moved to New York in 1892 she began using Carrie Chapman Catt, partially perhaps because she was not as well known in the East and it was a propitious time to use her new name, and perhaps also because Mariana Chapman was an active suffragist in New York and two Mrs. Chapmans would be confusing. She often signed her articles CCC, and the alliteration was vivid with an identity and a significance of its own to all the reading, campaigning, speech-making woman suffrage world. She was called Mrs. Catt or Mrs. Chapman Catt; we have accepted contemporary practice and have dropped the "Mrs."

2. *Seattle Times*, 24 September 1933 and 10 March 1947.
3. Russell B. Nye, *Midwestern Progressive Politics: A Historical Study of its Origins and Development 1870–1950* (East Lansing: Michigan State College Press, 1951), p. 150.
4. *Woman's Journal*, 27 September 1913, p. 307.
5. *Woman's Standard*, July 1892; reprinted in *Woman's Journal*, 7 July 1892, p. 226.
6. "Only Yesterday," in the National Council of Women, *Our Common Cause— Civilization*, pp. 235–36. Also typescript of speech (incomplete), Catt papers, SSC. The Fine Arts Building where this meeting was held is now the Museum of Science and Industry.
7. *Woman Citizen*, 2 June 1923, p. 8. Catt was critical of reformers who did not make the distinction between what is fundamental and what is law or custom. "This fact has in the estimate of the conservative discredited all efforts of women to free themselves from the genuine bondage imposed by the established order." Catt knew that in the nineteenth century, public attention was deflected from women's basic wrongs when feminists began to wear the loose trousers gathered at the ankles called "bloomers" after the journalist, Amelia Bloomer, who popularized them. It was easy to ridicule bloomers, and most of the leaders of the woman's rights movement realized very quickly that this dress reform was doing the cause more harm than good. The same thing has been demonstrated in the contemporary feminist movement when an incident of women discarding brassieres was seized as a symbol of the new freedom from artificial restraint. It has been used against them by the lazy who find it convenient to use "bra-burning" as a pejorative description. Thus are real issues made to seem superficial and easily overlooked by those who do not want to see.
8. Susanna Torre, ed., *Women in American Architecture* provides the history of the building, exterior and interior pictures, and Sophia Hayden's plans for two floors. Madeleine B. Stern, *We the Women*, pp. 67–76, discusses Sophia Hayden and her work in more detail.
    May Wright Sewall, ed., *The World's Congress of Representative Women*, a detailed report of the proceedings, is an extraordinarily interesting document of woman's history on several counts. It is a Who's Who of the women of the

western world at the time, and more importantly, it details women's concerns of a hundred years ago.

9. Catt to Lucy Anthony, 20 June 1933, and unpublished manuscript, Catt papers, NYPL.

10. "Only Yesterday," typescript (incomplete), Catt papers, SSC.

11. Anthony and Harper, *Woman Suffrage*, 4: 513–14.

12. Catt to Ellis Meredith (Stansbury), 23 June 1893, Ellis Meredith papers, Colorado Historical Society, Denver.

13. Ibid.

14. Meredith to Catt, 30 June 1893, Meredith papers, Colorado Historical Society, Denver. The secret ballot was adopted by Kentucky in 1888 with other states following suit in the next decade, hence Colorado's use in 1893 was an important point to the suffragists. In the nineteenth century, elections were usually celebrations of noise, parades, fistfights, and shouting matches encouraged by free drink. The parties themselves printed the ballots and distributed them on election day. Since they were usually printed on differently colored paper, they were quickly distinguishable and it was easy to keep track of the votes. To curb the widespread bribery, intimidation, and fraud that were features of the day, the secret ballot was introduced.

15. Catt to Meredith, 5 July 1893 and 16 July 1893, Ellis Meredith papers, Colorado Historical Society, Denver; Blackwell on change, *Woman's Journal*, 23 September 1893, p. 300.

16. Catt to Meredith, 16 July 1893, Ellis Meredith papers, Colorado Historical Society, Denver.

17. *Woman's Standard*, October 1901.

18. Carrie Chapman Catt and Nettie Rogers Shuler, *Woman Suffrage and Politics*, p. 119.

19. Catt's analysis of the Colorado campaign was given in detail at a Massachusetts Woman Suffrage Association meeting in Boston on December 16, 1893, and reported in *Woman's Journal*, 23 December 1893, pp. 401, 404.

CHAPTER 4. FRUSTRATIONS AND PLANS (pp. 38–45)

1. *New York Times*, 14 January 1894, p. 12.

2. Catt to Mrs. Charles Felix Burke, 2 February 1932, Catt papers, NYPL.

3. *Woman's Journal*, 24 February 1894, p. 57.

4. Harper, *Susan B. Anthony*, 2: 789; Anthony and Harper, *Woman Suffrage*, 4: 646. The Kansas referendum is discussed from another viewpoint in W. P. Harrington, "The Populist Party in Kansas," *Collections of the Kansas State Historical Society 1923–1925*, vol. 5, no. 16, pp. 403–50.

5. Harper, *Susan B. Anthony,* 2: 792.
6. Catt to Mrs. Charles Felix Burke, 2 February 1932, and Catt to Zara B. Hollandsworth, 17 November 1944, Catt papers, NYPL.
7. Harper, *Susan B. Anthony,* 2: 796.
8. Catt and Shuler, *Woman Suffrage and Politics,* p. 122.
9. *Woman's Journal,* 15 December 1894, p. 395.
10. Paul E. Fuller, *Laura Clay and the Woman's Rights Movement,* pp. 1–72 details Clay's life up to about the time of Anthony's and Catt's southern trip. Mary Church Terrell, *A Colored Woman in a White World,* p. 145.
11. Anthony and Harper, *Woman Suffrage,* 4: 254; Anthony and coffee: Mary Gray Peck, *Carrie Chapman Catt,* p. 82.
12. Catt to Lillie Devereux Blake, 7 March 1895, Blake papers, Missouri Historical Society, St. Louis.
13. *Woman's Journal,* 23 February 1895, p. 58; Catt to Abigail Scott Duniway, 14 March 1895, David Duniway personal collection, Salem, Oregon.
14. *Woman's Journal,* 23 February 1895, p. 58; Catt to DeVoe, 13 March 1895, DeVoe papers, Washington State Library, Olympia.
15. *Woman's Journal,* 9 February 1895, p. 41.
16. Harper, *Susan B. Anthony,* pp. 814–15.
17. Catt to Blake, 7 March 1895, Blake papers, Missouri Historical Society, St. Louis.

CHAPTER 5. NEW VICTORIES, OLD DEFEATS (pp. 46–54)

1. The sample is too small to prove or disprove her theory but it is of some interest. There were ten states admitted to the Union after Catt became active in the woman suffrage movement in the 1880s; the first since Colorado in 1876 were the so-called Omnibus States in 1889–1890:

1889—Montana, North Dakota, South Dakota, Washington
1890—Idaho, Wyoming (woman suffrage included in constitution)
1896—Utah (woman suffrage included in constitution)
1907—Oklahoma
1912—Arizona (woman suffrage included in constitution), New Mexico.

In only three had there been organized campaigns to include women in the electorate as defined by the new state constitution. The campaigns succeeded in Utah and Arizona, but failed in Washington.
2. Catt to Henry B. Blackwell, 20 April 1895, Catt papers, LC.
3. There was also an advantage in that it was not a new idea: Women had a seventeen-year voting record in the state. However, it is generally thought that

the most telling reason for voting for women's franchise was to reinforce the strong political base of the Mormons and to guarantee their majority vote.

4. *Woman's Journal*, 15 February 1896, pp. 49–50.
5. Sweet to Catt, 7 January 1934, Sweet papers, University of Rochester Library.
6. Robins to Catt, 15 August 1945, Catt papers, NYPL.
7. Catt and Shuler, *Woman Suffrage and Politics*, pp. 123, 130.
8. Abigail Scott Duniway, *Path Breaking*, pp. 205–6.
9. Ibid., p. 204; Catt and Shuler, *Woman Suffrage and Politics*, pp. 122–23.
10. *Woman's Journal*, 7 April 1900, pp. 106–7.
11. *The Woman's Century Calendar* was later translated into Turkish by a Mohammedan woman in Constantinople.

   There are many modern notes in the *Calendar*. Catt was always sensitive to public opinion and particularly to the way it was expressed. She wrote, for example, under the year 1858, "In the early part of the century, higher education, good health, common sense, were called 'indelicate'; now higher education, public speaking, self support, are accounted 'unwomanly,' and the word 'unsexed' is being freely used by the opponents." In 1865: "The Woman Suffrage Societies of the United States were vigorously undertaking at this time to educate public taste to use the word woman in speaking of the sex, instead of female. The attitude of an individual toward the woman question' could be detected by the word he used, the friends of the advancement of the sex speaking of them as women, the opponents as females." Later twentieth-century feminists were even more concerned with nomenclature; the use of "woman" instead of "girl" has taken a long time to popularize.

12. *New York Herald Tribune*, 24 April 1925, p. 7, reports on the closing ceremonies of the NAWSA, although in fact, because of some pending legacies, the organization was in existence until 1950. Catt told about her crying bout, saying it was an incident she had kept secret for twenty-five years.

   Half a century after the convention, when all of the principals and most of the participants were dead, Mary Gray Peck wrote candidly in a personal letter to Edna Stantial: "Another element was the resentment aroused by Mary Garrett Hay's closeness to CCC on the Organization Committee. Miss Hay was like a red rag to a bull to many suffragists. She and Anna Howard Shaw hated each other devotedly all their lives. Miss Hay confided in me tales about Miss Shaw that would delight a criminologist. Miss Shaw told me similar ones about M.G.H.!" (28 February 1951, NAWSA papers, LC).

CHAPTER 6. NEW DIRECTIONS (pp. 55–63)

1. May Wright Sewall, ed., *National Council of Women of the United States, Report of Its Tenth Annual Executive and Its Third Triennial Sessions*, p. 1894.

2. Catt to Mary A. Hunter, 2 March 1939, Iowa State Department of History and Archives, Des Moines.
3. *Report First International Woman Suffrage Conference, Held at Washington, U.S.A., February 11, 13, 14, 15, 16, 17, 18, 1902* (New York: International Woman Suffrage Headquarters, 1902). This was the first research on the status of women in the twentieth century. Summaries of the answers were read at the conference, and Catt reported for the United States: "American women are less bound by legal and social restrictions than the women of any other country, unless we except progressive Australia and New Zealand."

   Property rights for men and women are more or less unequal in most of the states, she noted, but had been vastly improved during the last half century. She thought the new laws reflected rapidly changing public sentiment, which increasingly approved married women having these powers. "Men are usually proud of their wives' business ventures which are sometimes quite as successful as their own. Vast amounts of property are now held in the hands of women. In New Orleans, a conservative city, it was recently discovered that three-fifths of the taxpayers were women."

   She went on to discuss education, professions, and wages. In California and Utah there were laws giving equal pay for equal work in the public schools, while in Wyoming a law equalized the wages of men and women employed by the state. She recognized and commented on a problem that still vexes women, the difficulty in overcoming the tradition of being relegated to special employment, and the widely held opinion that women's work is inferior in quality and their needs not as pressing as men's.

   Given the interest today in the trend to consider carefully the equal claims of parents over custody of children instead of regarding the mother's claim as stronger, it is surprising to be reminded how recent an assumption that is. In 1902, except for twelve states that gave the mother equal custody with the father, he had complete control over the child. Women had been fighting this for years, and Catt noted that Massachusetts had granted equal control only after fifty-five years' endeavor by women of that state (*Report*, 1902, pp. 39–44).
4. Oregon and South Dakota vied in the frequency and monotony of referenda campaigns. Oregon was successful in 1912 after six campaigns, South Dakota in 1918 after seven.
5. It is impossible to be precise about the number of countries with woman suffrage societies at the turn of the century. Many had women's associations whose primary object was to improve educational opportunities for women. These sometimes included suffrage as part of their program. In 1909 Alice Zimmern published *Women's Suffrage in Many Lands*, which gave a brief review of the history and current status of the movement. It is on the basis of her study that the statement is made that eight countries had suffrage societies.

   Others had women's clubs organized to make various improvements. Many of these formed suffrage organizations later. In Iceland in 1895, for example, the Icelandic Women's Alliance was founded with the aim of improving the general condition of women. Its work was largely directed toward the extension of the existing franchise and eventually getting parliamentary suffrage. However, a women's suffrage association was not founded until 1906 (Zimmern, pp. 56–57). In Hungary a society for the improvement of education of girls was started in 1867, while suffrage agitation began in 1903 (Zimmern, pp. 102–3).

The work in France was more complicated. An association for women's rights was formed as early as 1870. A suffrage society was started about the same time to obtain the vote for unmarried women and widows who paid taxes. In 1878 the first French feminist congress was held. It was not until 1909, however, that the National French Union for Women's Suffrage was affiliated with the International Woman Suffrage Association (Zimmern, pp. 112–19).

As early as 1886 New Zealand was working for suffrage through the franchise department of the Woman's Christian Temperance Union. Suffrage was granted in 1893. Although suffrage activity was no longer necessary there, New Zealand affiliated with IWSA to help the world's women. At the turn of the century, the Isle of Man and four of the United States (Wyoming, Colorado, Utah, and Idaho) were the only other places where women had suffrage on the same terms as that granted men.

Catt wrote a brief foreword to Zimmern's book in which she described the movement as having "crept slowly upon its way, and so silently and unobtrusively that many people have not been aware of its existence, now all the world is talking of it, and is asking questions concerning its past, its present, and its future aims" (Zimmern, p. i).

An important survey of the conditions affecting women was written in 1905 by Dr. Kathe Schirmacher; the second edition in 1912 was translated into English by Carl Conrad Eckhardt. *The Modern Women's Rights Movement* is a valuable international study of pre-World War I rights (and wrongs). Dr. Shirmacher divided her discussion into four sections: the Germanic countries, the Romance countries, the Slavic and Balkan states, and the Orient and the Far East.

The Zimmern and Schirmacher books were used as quasi-official handbooks for the IWSA. In the *Report of the Congress of 1911*, p. 34, "Mrs. Catt explained, in reply to the question of the Netherlands concerning the proposed handbook, that it had not been found feasible to publish such a book. She drew attention to the books written by Miss Zimmern and Miss Schirmacher, which fulfilled the purpose."

Another widely distributed book was the International Council of Women, *Women's Position in the Laws of the Nations*. It covered much of the same information that Catt had collected in 1902 but was updated and translated. The single volume includes German, French, and English versions.

Some books have been written about the woman's movement of individual countries. An excellent one is Richard J. Evans, *The Feminist Movement in Germany 1894–1933*. Germany is an example of a country that was encouraged by the 1902 Washington, D. C. meeting to organize a suffrage association. In that year the German Union for Women's Suffrage (Deutscher Verband für Frauenstimmrecht) was founded by thirteen radical feminists. One of the reasons they founded the Union, Evans says, was "the fact that Germany was to be unrepresented at the first international women's suffrage congress in Washington in February 1902 persuaded Augspurg to found an organized suffrage movement in Germany; the lack of one was clearly becoming an embarrassment to the German radicals in their relations with international feminism" (pp. 71–72).

6. "The Early Days of the Alliance," *The International Women's News*, April 1935, p. 54.

7. *Report, 1902*, p. 21.

8. *Woman's Journal*, 15 February 1902, pp. 52–53. Her talk was also printed as a separate pamphlet, *President's Annual Address Delivered by Mrs. Carrie Chapman Catt* (Washington, D.C.: Hayworth Publishing House, 1902). Von Baer's theories influenced Catt's thought for years. In *The Woman's Century Calendar* printed in November 1899, her total entry for 1827 was:

> Von Baer discovered the ovule, the reproductive cell of the maternal organism, and demonstrated that its protoplasm contributed at least half to the embryo child. Before this time it was held that the mother had no essential share in the formation of the child, the comparison being made that man was the seed and woman the soil.' The proof of equal physical responsibility of parents opened the question of the extent of the mental and moral responsibility resting upon the mother.

Throughout her life Catt held tenaciously to her belief in von Baer as the light giver. In 1936 when she was seventy-seven years old she still identified him as the source of scientific proof of the equality of the sexes. She said his discovery was the most permanent factor in giving impulse to the woman movement. "I believe the liberation of women would have been greatly delayed were this discovery not made and accepted promptly by scientific men" (*A Message to Sweet Briar College The Woman's Century 1820–1920*, typescript, p. 5, Catt papers, SSC.

Anyone with even a minimal background in embryology would shudder at Catt's oversimplification of centuries of research by hundreds of scientists. However, it was convenient to be able to pinpoint an event and for her purposes, von Baer's discovery was dramatic proof that from life's beginning woman was equal to man.

Karl Ernst von Baer (1792–1876) was the first to see the egg within the female mammal, describing his work in *De ovi mammalium genesi* in 1827 (see Charles D. O'Malley, trans., "On the Genesis of Mammals and of Man," *Isis* 47 [1956]). Some of his predecessors, including William Harvey (1578–1657), Antonie van Leeuwenhoek (1632–1723), and Regnier de Graaf (1641–1673), had almost hit on the discovery of the egg but by mischance had not identified it. Throughout the eighteenth century various theories of mammalian egg formation had been advanced, usually with emphasis on the importance of the spermatozoa as the true agents of reproduction. Full knowledge of fertilization, inheritance, and development, along with the proof of the roles of male and female depended on continuing scientific research throughout the nineteenth century. Genetic research continues, of course, in the twentieth.

The Woman's Column, 25 September 1897, reviewed Columbia University Professor Edmund Beecher Wilson's The Cell in Development and Inheritance (New York: Macmillan, 1897), which was a basic text in the field for many years. The review began, "It has always been claimed that the woman's part in the genesis of a new life was largely passive, but later scientific study has proved the contrary." It may have been this that stirred Catt to restudy and apply her college biology courses. At any rate, although Catt seems to have been the only feminist who used von Baer's discovery as proof of woman's equality, he remained a bright beacon to her.

9. Woman's Journal, 29 March 1902, p. 100. The International Council of Women as an organization advocated the support of women from any country who were demanding the franchise on an equal basis with the men of that country. However, a national or local council was expected to support only the issues its members were ready to favor and were not bound to get behind everything International did. Many members of the Council of Women were uncomfortable with the radical notion of suffrage (Countess of Aberdeen, ed., International Council of Women, Report of Transactions of The Fourth Quinquennial Meeting held at Toronto, Canada, June, 1909 (London: Constable & Co., 1910), p. 82).

10. Report, 1902, p. 4. The Declaration was signed by the delegates to the 1902 meeting with the exception of Florence Fensham (because there had not been time to send it to her) and Sofja Friedland (who had died shortly after her return to Russia). The signatories were Susan B. Anthony, Chairman, United States; Vida Goldstein, Recording Secretary, Australia; Florence Fenwick Miller, England; Antonie Stolle, Germany; Emmy Evald, Sweden; Caroline Holman Huidobro, Chile; Gudrun Drewsen, Norway; Rachel Foster Avery, Anna H. Shaw, and Carrie Chapman Catt, United States.

11. "The Home and the Higher Education," Journal of the National Educational Association Proceedings of Forty-first Annual Meeting held at Minneapolis, Minnesota, July 7–11, 1902 (Chicago: NEA, 1902), pp. 100–110.

12. Stanton Memorial Meeting, Presbyterian Bldg., 19 November 1902, incomplete manuscript, p. 7, Catt papers, LC.

13. Catt to Emma B. Sweet, 6 March 1903; Catt to Susan B. Anthony, 11 March 1903; Sweet papers, University of Rochester Library.

14. Susan B. Anthony to Isabel Howland, 6 April 1903, Howland papers, SSC; Catt to Emma B. Sweet, 15 April 1902, Sweet papers, University of Rochester Library.

15. "College Women as Citizens," speech given at a meeting of the New York

Alumnae Club of Pi Beta Phi, 4 February 1922, printed in *The Arrow,* June 1922, pp. 613–20; and "This Changing World—Woman's Responsibility," a speech given at the YWCA, New York, 27 May 1927, typescript, Catt papers, SSC, are but two examples of her frequent recollections of the Berlin meetings.

See also Evans, *Feminist Movement in Germany,* pp. 72–73, for explication of the laws governing women's political meetings. He wrote that after this meeting in 1904 with its many delegates from abroad, dissatisfaction with the Law of Association (under which women were not allowed to attend political meetings, much less participate in them) became more apparent. Police administration of it became more lenient and by 1908 the law was changed.

16. *Woman's Journal,* 24 June 1904, p. 201. The Berlin . . . heaven anecdote "as Mrs. Catt tells the story" was recounted in Marjorie Shuler, "Women Can If They Will," *Woman's Journal,* August 1929, p. 8.

17. Ida Harper, who reported the conferences at length in the *Woman's Journal,* remarked, "Mrs. Terrell has been included in all the social courtesies extended to the speakers" (16 July 1904, p. 226). Although this comment seems a casual addition to the account, it would have been impossible in the United States. Twenty years later, when Catt was organizing conferences on the Cause and Cure of War, there were no black delegates because the hotel in Washington, D.C. where the meetings were held would not admit them.

Catt wrote "An Appreciation" of Terrell for the June 1936 issue of *The Oberlin Alumni Magazine* that so pleased Terrell she had it reprinted. Both in her autobiography and in a tribute she wrote when Catt died, Terrell commented on Catt's freedom from race prejudice and on their long friendship, which had begun in the 1890s at NAWSA conventions.

18. *Women and Economics* (Boston: Small, Maynard & Co., 1898) was translated into six other languages as well, including Dutch by Aletta Jacobs and Hungarian by Rosika Schwimmer. Catt's accolade is from the *New York Times,* 20 August 1935. She admired Gilman tremendously, and they shared an appreciation of Lester Ward's thinking, which through Gilman's interpretations had a profound effect on the woman's movement. Catt put Gilman first on her list of "the twelve greatest women" because of her "immortal books on the status of women" and her lifelong devotion to the cause, saying, "She was a great and wonderful woman." Catt epitomized Gilman's "grit" by an incident that happened during the trip to Berlin in 1904. The women were given permission by the reluctant ship captain to conduct a suffrage program, and Gilman, although prostrated with seasickness, got up and "made a capital speech." Catt always remembered it "as an evidence of tremendous will" and told the story often (Catt to Gilman, 28 May 1935, Gilman papers, SL).

Harper's quotation about Gilman, *Woman's Journal,* 16 July 1904, p. 226.

19. *Jus Suffragii,* 1 May 1914, p. 99.

CHAPTER 7. ROSES AND ROCKS (pp. 64–71)

1. The lecture series, under the general topic "The Progress Made by Women," began February 14, 1905, with "The Corner Stone," and followed on successive Tuesday evenings with "Primitive Women," "The Evolution of the Family," "The Revival of Learning among Women in the Fifteenth Century," "Women and the World's Work," and "The Past, Present and Future." Each of the lectures was reviewed the following day in the *Brooklyn Eagle*. Catt talked some about her health in her letters at the time, see for example, Catt to Laura Clay, 18 January 1905, Clay papers, University of Kentucky Libraries, Special Collections.

2. Among the reports of advances made by women during the year, Ohio was particularly proud that a Woman Suffrage Association member, Pauline Steinem, had been the first woman elected to the Board of Education in Toledo. Her granddaughter, Gloria, was to become even more famous to later feminists.

3. Catt to Rosika Schwimmer, 7 September 1905, Catt papers, LC.

4. Maud Wood Park, *Front Door Lobby*, p. 120.

5. Catt to Emma B. Sweet, 7 March 1906, Sweet papers, University of Rochester Library.

6. Annie Furuhjelm was the editor and proprietor of the paper *Nutid (The New Tide)*. She was born in Sitka during the last years of the Russian ownership of Alaska where her father was a government official. The family had left in 1867 when power was transferred to the United States. Always interested in politics, she was a member of the Finnish Diet from 1914, one of the first women M.P.'s in the world. She was a board member of the Alliance from 1909 to 1920 and attended congresses from 1906 to 1929. She died July 17, 1937.

7. Catt, "The International Suffrage Conference," *Woman's Journal*, 22 September 1906, pp. 149–51. An outstanding book on the subject is Richard Stites, *The Women's Liberation Movement in Russia*. This period is covered particularly on pages 198–237. Stites translated the new association's name as "The All-Russian Union for Women's Equality" (*Vserossiiskii Soyuz Ravnopraviya Zhenshchin*). Another excellent book from a different viewpoint is Barbara Evans Clements, *Bolshevik Feminist: The Life of Aleksandra Kollontai*.

8. The Alliance, *The Woman's Journal*, and *Jus Suffragii* spelled the name of the leading delegate to Alliance congresses Zeneide Mirovitch. Stites, *Women's Liberation in Russia*, p. 199, identified her as a well-known journalist Zinaida Ivanova; we have used his spelling of her pseudonym, Zinaida Mirovich. She and Anna Kalmanovich, another journalist and leader of the Women's Union, were two of the five Russian delegates in Amsterdam in 1908. Mirovich was a delegate in Stockholm in 1911 and was scheduled to go to Budapest in 1913 but was prevented from attending by the illness from which she died August 26, 1913, in Moscow. A brief appreciation of her life and work was published in *Jus Suffragii* (1 October 1913). *Jus Suffragii* printed her occasional articles about Russia and the

women's movement from 1908 until 1913. See also *Woman's Journal*, 22 September 1906, p. 150; Adele Schreiber and Margaret Mathieson, *Journey towards Freedom*, p. 7.

Catt never visited Russia although she made plans to do so. She was bitterly disappointed that she could not go to the great Women's Congress in St. Petersburg in 1908. The organizers had been expressly forbidden to invite any foreigners, and Catt noted that had she gone without an invitation she would not have been permitted to express even a greeting to the assembly (Catt, "Address," *Proceedings of the First Quinquennial Convention of the International Woman Suffrage Alliance, London, 1909*, pp. 64–65).

9. *Woman's Journal*, 22 September 1906, p. 150. A similar incident was reported by Millicent Fawcett at the quinquennial in London 1909. In November 1908, a case was argued before the Judicial Committee of the House of Lords in Great Britain by Chrystal Macmillan. The case for woman suffrage was raised on the plea of women graduates of the Scottish universities that they were entitled to vote in the election of Members of Parliament representing the universities. The word used in the Scottish University Act was "persons," but the appeal was unsuccessful. The House of Lords confirmed the previous decisions of the lower courts that *the word "persons" does not include women when it refers to privileges granted by the State* (*Proceedings, 1909*, pp. 103–4).

10. The word "suffragette" was first used by the *Daily Mail* in 1906. The Pankhursts were superb publicists and responded to the newspapers' constant need for diversity by providing years of copy through their increasingly outrageous actions. Whether one agreed or disagreed with their tactics no one ever questioned the fact that they changed the thrust of the sedate woman's suffrage movement and focused worldwide attention on women's demand for equality. The question of whether militancy helped or hindered the movement was argued from the beginning; no one ever doubted that they made news.

The story of the Women's Social and Political Union has been told by participants and observers over the years, and there are many books on the subject. Probably the most thorough is E. Sylvia Pankhurst, *The Suffragette Movement*. Emmeline Pankhurst, *My Own Story*, is much more personal and slanted. From reading only this book one would think she fought the battle single-handedly with a little help from Christabel. (Sylvia Pankhurst said the American Rheta Childe Dorr actually wrote it from talks with Emmeline Pankhurst, Sylvia's mother.) Ray Strachey, *The Cause*, is a standard brief history of the English women's movement. One of the best books on the subject is Constance Rover, *Women's Suffrage and Party Politics in Britain*. Her analyses of the political impact of the women's struggle are scholarly and lively.

11. Dora Montefiore, *From a Victorian to a Modern*, pp. 72–89; *International Women Suffrage Alliance, Bulletin or Monthly Correspondence*, 15 September 1906, p. 3. This is the first issue of what was afterwards called *Jus Suffragii*. The initial

number was a sixteen-page typed newsletter edited by Martina Kramers. It consisted almost entirely of summaries of the Alliance meetings as reported by the press. For some obscure etymological reason the English referred to the *women's* movement while in the United States it was the *woman's* movement. Presumably since it was Catt's brainchild, the multinational organization took the American spelling and was called the International Woman Suffrage Alliance.

12. Catt, "The International Suffrage Conference," *Woman's Journal*, 11 September 1906, p. 151. The single organization policy was never entirely satisfactory and as late as 1926 was questioned when the Woman's Party of the United States applied for membership and was strongly opposed by the League of Women Voters, successor to the NAWSA.

13. *Woman's Journal*, 29 September 1906, p. 154; Anthony and Harper, *Woman Suffrage*, 4: 817.

14. *Proceedings of the International Woman Suffrage Alliance Conference, 1908*, p. 24; Catt, "The Victory in Denmark," *Woman's Journal*, 18 April 1908, p. 61; Zimmern, *Women's Suffrage*, pp. 46–47 and pp. 152–54.

   Marie Quam was the delegate from Norway who reported on women's gains there following the reversal of the press on its position on woman suffrage, when "it then became possible for a man to advocate our cause without diminishing his good reputation." Her husband had been prime minister in Norway; she was a pioneer suffragist and active in feminist and philanthropic causes all her life. She was seventy-three years old in 1906 when she attended the IWSA congress; she went to many more international meetings and continued her work almost unabated until her death at ninety-five in 1938.

   A sequel to the 1906 Congress came a decade later when Denmark voted on the sale of the Virgin Islands to the United States. It was generally thought that the Danish women would vote against the sale because "as Mrs. Chapman Catt had made very clear during her fateful visit to Denmark, the liveliest, the most reasonable, the most intellectual women in the world were deprived by the unjust laws of the country that wanted the Islands of the right to vote." The "woman's bloc" proved as illusory in Denmark as it did later in the United States—the vote was favorable, and the sale was made. The United States took possession of the Danish islands in the Caribbean on March 31, 1917 (Maurice Egan, *Ten Years near the German Frontier*, pp. 276–79, 283–84).

15. Clara Zetkin, *Woman Suffrage*, trans. J. B. Askew (London: Twentieth Century Press, 1906), pp. 1–2.

16. Ibid., pp. 4–7; Ida Husted Harper, "The World Movement for Woman Suffrage," *The American Review of Reviews*, December 1911, p. 726. The figure used—80 to 90 percent—was based primarily on a survey conducted by forty independent Labour party branches in 1903 at the instigation of Keir Hardie, M.P. He wanted to convince the party they could press for the enfranchisement of women on the same terms as men without handing an advantage to the propertied classes. A

total of 59,920 women eligible to vote in local government elections were canvassed, and working women voters were found to number 82.45 percent. Working-class women were defined as "those who work for wages, who are domestically employed or who are supported by the earnings of wage-earning relatives" (E. Sylvia Pankhurst, *The Suffragette Movement*, p. 169).

After this survey Will Crooks was instructed to introduce to Parliament a women's suffrage bill, disparagingly termed "Bourgeois women's rights," which was despised by the Social Democratic Party (Constance Rover, *Women's Suffrage and Party Politics*, pp. 159–60).

17. Zimmern, *Women's Suffrage in Many Lands*, pp. 91–94, 123. At the 1909 IWSA Congress in London, an Italian delegate joined one from Austria in warning against trusting politicians of any persuasion. The charges the two women made were not detailed in the report but Zimmern described a meeting at Easter 1909 that had taken place shortly before the Alliance conference where Socialist women had called upon the Socialist men to redeem their pledges of genuine universal suffrage. "But the prospects are not hopeful," Zimmern remarked (p. 106).

18. Catt, "Woman Suffrage and Socialism," *Jus Suffragii*, 15 November 1907, n.p. The Stuttgart resolution of 1907 proved to be a stumbling block to some Socialist women but it was mostly an annoyance to Socialist men. There were a few attempts to pacify the women by allowing some political work among their sisters by such stalwarts as Aleksandra Kollontai and Clara Zetkin. But the main line was taken by another fiery European, Rosa Luxemburg, who saw herself as a leader of both men and women. In her view, organizing women separately to take part in the revolutionary struggle was retrogressive; it delegated them to traditional secondary roles within the party (Mary-Alice Waters, *Rosa Luxemburg Speaks* [New York: Pathfinder Press, 1970], p. 5).

19. Clara Zetkin, "My Recollections of Lenin (An Interview on the Woman Question)," in *The Emancipation of Women, from the Writings of V. I. Lenin* (New York: International Publishers, 1966), pp. 110–11. Although Zetkin's talks with Lenin were in 1920, apparently these were his long-held ideas.

20. Rosa Luxemburg, "Women's Suffrage and Class Struggle," *Selected Political Writings*, pp. 216–22. Ironically, Utah was one of the first states to enfranchise women, a move generally recognized as a Mormon maneuver to strengthen themselves, although it meant that the very conservative group acted in a progressive way in 1896. The politically radical Socialists, on the other hand, were in effect regressive and socially repressive in their attitudes toward the promotion of women's rights many years later.

21. *Jus Suffragii*, 15 November 1907.

22. *The Forerunner*, October 1910, p. 25.

CHAPTER 8. AMSTERDAM AND LONDON, CALM AND STORM (pp. 72–78)

1. Catt to Clara Hyde, 24 February 1908, Catt papers, LC.
2. *Woman's Journal,* 4 April 1908, p. 55.
3. Catt, "President's Address," *Proceedings of the Fourth Congress of the International Woman Suffrage Alliance, Amsterdam, 1908,* p. 60.
4. Anna Manus Jacobi, "Carrie Chapman Catt," *International Women's News,* April 1947, pp. 83–84.
5. Minutes of the New York State Suffrage Convention, Buffalo, New York, October 15–21, 1908, pp. 22–23. Dr. C. V. Drysdale was the Men's League delegate, his wife Bessie was a delegate from the Women's Freedom League. One of the immediate results was the formation of a Men's League for Woman Suffrage in Holland, making England and Holland the first countries to receive organized assistance from men.
6. *Proceedings 1908,* pp. 6–7, 67, 96–97. There was a total of two hundred deputies in the Landstag, hence the women's representation was just under 10 percent.
7. Ibid., p. 68.
8. Catt to Storms, 8 April 1909, Iowa State University Archives, Ames.
9. *Jus Suffragii,* 15 January 1909, p. 36.
10. The quotation is often erroneously ascribed to St. Augustine. A. Eckhof, in "In necessariis unitas," *De Zinspreuk* (Leiden, 1931), ascribes authorship to Petrus Meiderlinus.
11. The three women who left the WSPU were Charlotte Despard, Teresa Billington-Greig, and Edith How Martyn who founded the Women's Freedom League.

    The Haslams had been the leaders of the Irish women's suffrage movement since they founded the Dublin society in 1874. Anna Haslam lived to vote, at the age of ninety, in the 1918 election.
12. *Proceedings, 1909,* p. 59. Catt to Miss Lowndes, 17 May 1909, Fawcett Collection, London Polytechnic. Lowndes was a member of the Artists' League, which had coordinated the parade.
13. *Proceedings, 1909,* p. 59; E. Sylvia Pankhurst, *The Suffragette Movement,* p. 217; *Votes for Women,* 7 May 1909, pp. 633–34. Alice Morgan Wright, one of the few American women who served time in Holloway, was imprisoned for two months in 1912. She was a Smith College graduate of the class of 1904. Some of her memorabilia, including her brooch, a WSPU medal "for valour" (hunger strike), and a prison knife from Holloway, are in the Sophia Smith Collection, Smith College.
14. *Votes for Women,* 7 May 1909, p. 638.
15. Catt to Millicent Garrett Fawcett, 19 October 1909, Catt papers, LC. Alva Belmont rented for $5,000 a year the whole seventeenth floor of a new building at

the corner of Fifth Avenue and Forty-second Street. Five of the nine rooms were given to NAWSA, the other four were used by various New York City and State suffrage societies.

CHAPTER 9.   WOMEN UNITED?   (pp. 79–84)

1. Catt to Harper, 11 March 1910, Clay papers, University of Kentucky Libraries, Special Collections.
2. Catt to Clara Hyde, 15 July 1909, Catt papers, LC.
3. Catt, "The London Congress," *Jus Suffragii*, 15 May 1909, p. 69.
4. Jane de Iongh, "Letters from Dr. Anna Howard Shaw to Dr. Aletta Jacobs," *Yearbook International Archives for the Women's Movement*, 2: 91–92.
5. Catt to Clara Hyde, 30 April 1910 and Catt to Mary Gray Peck, 7 May 1910, Catt papers, LC.
6. *New York Times*, 5 June 1910, p. 20.
7. Catt, Java diary, insert between pp. 10–11, Catt papers, LC. There are eight typewritten diaries of varying lengths covering Catt's trip around the world in 1911–12. The diaries are neatly typed on standard 8½" by 11" paper. Throughout Catt pasted postcards, some newspaper clippings, and a few snapshots. Information about her trip is taken from this source unless otherwise specified. The collection consists of 589 pages as follows: 1. South Africa, 181 pages; 2. the Holy Land, 55 pages; 3. Ceylon, 31 pages; 4. India and Sumatra, 46 pages; 5. Java, 98 pages; 6. the Philippines, 39 pages; 7. China, 95 pages; 8. Korea, Japan, and Hawaii, 44 pages.
8. *New York Suffrage Newsletter*, December 1910, pp. 198–99; *International Woman Suffrage Alliance Report 1911*, p. 63.
9. Catt to Mary Gray Peck, 18 November 1910, Catt papers, LC.
10. Catt to Sweet, 13 April 1911, Sweet papers, University of Rochester Library; Catt to Hyde, 13 April 1911, Catt papers, LC.
11. *Woman's Journal*, 27 May 1911; *Alliance Report 1911*, p. 66; Catt diary, 29 April 1911, Catt papers, LC.
12. Information about the Stockholm congress is all from the *Alliance Report 1911*: Catt, pp. 61–62, 69; Lundstrom, pp. 93–94; Poland, pp. 99, 121; Hungary, pp. 108–10; Iceland, p. 111; Russia, pp. 124–25; Switzerland, p. 133.
13. *Woman's Journal*, 8 July 1911, p. 211; Schreiber and Mathieson, *Journey towards Freedom*, p. 18.
14. *Alliance Report 1911*, pp. 70–71. Catt's remark about ill-advised legislation foreshadowed debate on the Equal Rights Amendment, which began in earnest in the 1920s and has continued for more than six decades. Equal pay for equal work was never questioned but there was concern about gender regulations. Catt in her

later life believed in protective legislation for women of the trade union occupa-
tions but thought the ERA was a snare and a delusion, with its support coming
chiefly from white collar workers and professionals. She argued that the ERA
would not help women who urgently needed their work conditions upgraded. She
made a press statement through the Westchester League of Women Voters on
February 28, 1943 that was widely quoted; see, for example, *New York Times*, 1
March 1943, and *Congressional Digest*, Washington, D.C., April 1943.

   The verse at the end is a paraphrase of G. Linnaeus Banks, "What I Live
For," *Daisies in the Grass* (London: R. Hardivicke, 1865). It was very popular for
recitations in classrooms, assemblies, and Sunday Schools and was widely reprinted, sometimes under the title "My Aim." Catt used it many times.
15. *Woman's Journal*, 5 August 1911, p. 237; *The Vote*, 15 July 1911, p. 149.

CHAPTER 10. SOUTH AFRICA TO THE PHILIPPINES
(pp. 85–94)

1. In the Boer War Great Britain defeated the Boers of the Orange Free State and
   the Transvaal Republic in South Africa. An authoritative study by Thomas
   Pakenham, *The Boer War*, demonstrates that English businessmen engineered the
   war to establish British hegemony over South Africa. They wanted cheap labor
   and control over the production of gold, which had been discovered in southern
   Transvaal in 1886. The Boers stood in their way.
2. Travel diary, South Africa, p. 180. Subsequent quotations are from the travel
   diaries unless otherwise noted. See Chapter 9, note 7.
3. *Woman's Journal*, 9 December 1911, p. 385.
4. *The International Woman Suffrage Alliance Report of Seventh Congress, Budapest,
   Hungary* (Manchester: The Hotspur Press, 1913), p. 152. Years later Emmeline
   Pethick-Lawrence wrote to Catt: "Neither you nor Dr. Jacobs are forgotten in S.
   Africa. I heard of you constantly" (12 August 1930, Catt papers, NYPL).
5. Catt to Mary Gray Peck, 17 November 1911, Catt papers, LC.
6. *Woman's Journal*, 9 December 1911, p. 385.
7. Ibid.
8. "A Glimpse of Gandhi," *Woman's Journal*, 25 March 1922, p. 13. The mutual
   friend from whom Catt had the introduction may have been Emmeline Pethick-
   Lawrence, who had met Gandhi at a women's suffrage meeting during one of his
   visits to England. She is referred to only as "an English lady" in the article, and
   was not identified in Catt's diary. The lawyer who offered his office was Dr. Krause
   with whose family Catt stayed part of the time. Her host was "the best criminal
   lawyer in South Africa but the reputation does not please him and he would like
   something higher." Gandhi's secretary was probably Miss Schlesin, who later
   became a high school teacher in the Transvaal.

9. Catt to Mary Gray Peck, 13 March 1912, Catt papers, LC.
10. "Address of the President," *IWSA Report 1913*, pp. 8–10; Catt to Alice Stone Blackwell, 25 August 1922, Jeannette Marks papers, Wellesley College Library, Special Collections.
11. The islands of Sumatra and Java are part of what is now known as Indonesia. The capital, Djakarta, was formerly known as Batavia. From the seventeenth century until World War II, when the islands were occupied by Japan, the Dutch were the dominant power and the territory was known as the Dutch East Indies.
12. *Jus Suffragii*, 15 July 1912; *Harper's Magazine*, April 1914, pp. 738–47. Many of the feminists were fascinated by the idea of the matrilineal family that had been used by Lester Ward to support his influential gynaecocentric theory. The Batta people of Sumatra was one of his examples. The theory had been published in 1903 in his *Pure Sociology* (New York: Macmillan). Charlotte Perkins Gilman was one of the popularizers and wrote about it for the *Woman's Journal*.

CHAPTER 11. CHINA (pp. 95–105)

1. Mary Clabaugh Wright, ed., *China in Revolution*, p. 34.
2. The new provisional government was set up in Peking when the Chinese emperor abdicated on February 12, 1912; on April 17 the United States Congress passed a resolution sympathizing with the new government.
3. Catt, "The New China," *Woman's Journal*, 5 October 1912, p. 314.
4. Catt, "More about China," *Woman's Journal*, 2 November 1912, p. 346. The *China Press* (Shanghai), 5 September 1912, translated the organization's name as "Chinese Women Cooperative Association."
5. *China Republican* (Shanghai), 4 September 1912.
6. Catt, "More About China."
7. Ibid.
8. Catt, "The Most Interesting Person I Ever Met," 1917, typescript, Catt papers, LC.
9. Ernest P. Young, "Yuan Shih-k'ai's Rise to the Presidency," in Wright, *China in Revolution*, p. 430. Young wrote, "A spontaneous mutiny in the first year of the Republic was by no means inconceivable," p. 440.
10. "The Truth about Suffrage in China," *Woman's Journal*, 16 November 1912, p. 362. Although China was affiliated with the International Alliance in 1913, woman suffrage was thrust into the background by events of the following decades. There is no evidence that Catt heard from her Chinese friends after World War I.
11. For many years the international feminists agitated against prostitution. Catt often wrote and lectured on "white slavery," stressing that "white" was a mis-

nomer—the evil affected all women of all colors. As early as 1899 Aletta Jacobs published articles on the three most pressing problems of the day: the economic and political status of women, prostitution, and birth control. She wrote and lectured on these topics the rest of her life. Both Catt and Jane Addams, whose landmark book, *A New Conscience and an Ancient Evil*, (New York: Macmillan), was published in April 1912, spoke on the subject at the IWSA congress in Budapest in 1913.

12. Catt to Mary Gray Peck, 23 October 1912, Catt papers, LC.
13. Catt speech at the New Jersey State Suffrage Convention, Newark, November 13, 1913, reported in *Woman's Journal*, 22 November 1913, p. 371.

CHAPTER 12. ONE CAUSE (pp. 106–113)

1. *Woman Voter*, December 1912, pp. 7–8.
2. *Woman's Journal*, 23 November 1912 and 30 November 1912; Harper, *Woman Suffrage*, 5: 332–63; *McClure's Magazine*, January 1913, p. 249.
3. Jane de Iongh, "Letters from Dr. Anna Howard Shaw to Dr. Aletta Jacobs," *Yearbook International Archives for the Women's Movement*, 2: 101.
4. U. S. Congress, Senate, Committee on the District of Columbia, Hearing under S. Res. 479, 4 March 1913, Senate Report No. 53, 63rd Cong., 1st sess., Congressional Serial Set No. 6512. In the 749-page report of the investigation, there were several graphic accounts of inexperienced women baffled and frightened by the crowd's threatening acts toward them while they bravely held their positions. One woman described a group of twenty men who joined arms, and side-by-side were swinging toward the parade where she was. The young woman who was leading the section "was really terrified. She turned around and said in a very loud voice, 'Girls, get out your hatpins, they are going to rush us.' The men backed respectfully back and gave us about five feet of space on that side of the path" (p. 456).

    The march and the indignation meeting that followed were widely reported in the press, including, Philadelphia's *Public Ledger*, 4 March 1913, from which the Catt quote was taken.
5. Fragmentary notes on events during visit to London preceding Alliance Congress in Budapest, June 1913. Catt papers, LC.
6. "Parliament Fans Flames," *Woman's Journal*, 31 May 1913, p. 169.
7. Fragmentary notes, London, 1913. George Lansbury, formerly a Socialist member of Parliament, was brought up on a charge of inciting to crime and misdemeanor. This charge was based on a fourteenth-century statute that had been dredged up to use against the suffragettes and their sympathizers nearly six hundred years later.

8. George Lansbury's daughter was one of the women arrested in Hyde Park that day. *New York Times,* 4 May 1913, p. 4, and 5 May 1913, p. 1.

9. "Suffrage Militancy," 17 April 1913, four typed pages, Catt papers, NYPL. The date is typed at the heading, the words "Suffrage Militancy" are in handwriting that may be Mary Gray Peck's. There is no indication of where this was given or even if it was a speech. Catt left for London on April 19, so this may be preparation for speeches given there although the explanatory approach suggests it was given to a non-English audience. The proceedings of the 1913 Budapest congress do not include it in any speeches she gave there. It may have been a prepared statement Catt left at suffrage headquarters in case a comment on militancy was required, it may have been an unused press release, she may simply have been putting her thoughts in writing to clarify them in her own mind. At any rate it spells out her attitude toward militancy in 1913 and reflects her writing and speaking in London that spring.

10. Details and quotes are from her reports and news items: "Parliament Fans Flames," *Woman's Journal,* 31 May 1913, p. 169; *New York Times,* 6 May 1913, p. 2; *Woman's Journal,* 5 May and 24 May 1913, pp. 161–63, 27 September 1913, p. 307; *Woman Voter,* June 1913; fragmentary notes, London, 1913.

11. Davison chose the Derby, an annual race held at Epsom Downs in Surrey, for maximum publicity for her act. Since its founding in 1780, the Derby was a major social event and members of the royal family were sure to be there. Sylvia Pankhurst's description of the "deed of infinite majesty" is in her *Suffragette Movement,* pp. 467–69.

    Annie Cobden Sanderson had been brought up in a women's rights house-hold. Her father, Richard Cobden, Liberal M.P., supported the movement although his name was more commonly linked with the Anti-Corn Law League which was successful in the 1840s in repealing tariffs on grain that had made bread expensive for the poor. It was in this League that many feminists began their political education and activity. Cobden's lifelong objective was free trade with its logical complements of peace and reduction of military armaments.

12. *Jus Suffragii,* 15 January 1913, pp. 41, 53. On October 18, 1912 the First Balkan War had begun. Bulgaria, Greece, and Serbia fought against Turkey until the Treaty of London on May 30, 1913. This was followed by the Second Balkan War—Greece, Serbia, Rumania, and Turkey against Bulgaria—which began on June 29, 1913 and ended with the Treaties of Bucharest and Constantinople on August 1, 1914, at the beginning of the World War.

13. *IWSA Report 1913,* pp. 1–2.

14. *Jus Suffragii,* 1 May 1914, p. 103. The picture illustrating the report of the presentation showed the banner being held by Nina Boyle from South Africa at one end and Mrs. Briet Asmundsson with her daughter from Iceland at the other—an obvious but effective symbol of the breadth of the movement.

15. *Woman Citizen,* 21 December 1918, p. 606.

16. "The White Slave Traffic," five typed pages, Catt papers, SSC. Catt went back to London after Budapest to help establish a headquarters for the IWSA. While there she was a delegate to the International Congress for the Suppression of the White Slave Traffic.

17. "Thanks to the tact of Mrs. Catt, the Congress closed without becoming entangled in a serious controversy over militant methods," *Woman's Journal*, 28 June 1913, p. 208; "her tactful leadership," *New York Times*, 22 June 1913, p. 6; "Mrs. Chapman Catt has won golden opinions from men and women for her dignity, eloquence, and the skill with which she handled the large cosmopolitan body," *San Francisco Star*, 19 July 1913. Even Crystal Eastman, by no means in sympathy with conservative methods, called her "magnificent" and remembered the Alliance of 1913 as being "in its first strength and glory," Blanche Wiesen Cook, ed., *Crystal Eastman on Women and Revolution* (New York: Oxford University Press, 1978), p. 188.

18. "The Woman Suffrage Congress in Buda-Pest," *The Forerunner* 4, 1913, p. 205.

19. *New York Times*, 29 June 1913, part III, p. 3.

20. Catt to Schwimmer, 12 January 1924, Catt papers, LC.

21. Catt to Schwimmer, 11 June 1932, Catt papers, LC.

CHAPTER 13. NEW YORK (pp. 117–129)

1. Many writers have told the Illinois story: details are in Anthony and Harper, *Woman Suffrage*, 4: 152–61; one of the most vivid descriptions is Gertrude Foster Brown, "The Opposition Breaks," in *Victory—How Women Won It, A Centennial Symposium, 1840–1940* (New York: H. W. Wilson, 1940), pp. 83–94.

2. One that did not was the Women's Political Union founded in New York in 1907 by Harriot Stanton Blatch, daughter of Elizabeth Cady Stanton. After her marriage in 1882, Blatch had lived in England for twenty years where she was active in the Fabian Society and woman suffrage associations. Her 1907 New York organization was originally called the Equality League for Self-Supporting Women and was a pioneer suffrage recruiter among the working women of the city. By 1910 it was called the Women's Political Union and launched a state suffrage campaign. When the Empire State Campaign Committee was organized under Catt's leadership, Blatch refused to affiliate, and the Political Union continued on its own. She later joined it with the Congressional Party which became the National Woman's Party under Alice Paul.

   Although Blatch and Catt did not clash publicly, they were not friends. They had differences of opinions, ostensibly about work methods, but more likely because each of the two strong personalities was convinced of her own better understanding and ability.

3. *New York Times*, 20 November 1913, p. 2; *The Woman Voter*, December 1913, pp. 23–24.

4. Alice Paul was at the 1912 NAWSA convention as a delegate from Wisconsin's Political Equality League, as was Crystal Eastman Benedict, who had been campaign chairman for that state's recently defeated suffrage referendum. Lucy Burns was a 1912 delegate from Blatch's Women's Political Union of New York. Dora Lewis, of a prominent and active Philadelphia family, was a Pennsylvania delegate. Mary Beard, the historian, had the longest involvement with suffrage, with a particular concern for working women. She edited *The Woman Voter* for Catt's Woman Suffrage Party in 1911–12 and always admired Catt's fairness. Beard joined the National Woman's Party during the suffrage agitation but split with it in the twenties when, like most people who wanted to help working women, she supported protective legislation rather than Paul's Equal Rights Amendment.

5. Shaw to Catharine McCulloch, 19 February 1914, Dillon papers, SL.

6. Beard to Catt, 8 June 1915, NAWSA papers, LC.

7. *Woman's Journal*, 20 June 1914, p. 197; Catt, "Suffrage Straws," *Jus Suffragii*, 1 August 1914, p. 151.

8. Catt to Clara Hyde, 16 July 1914, Catt papers, LC.

9. *Jus Suffragii*, 1 September 1914, p. 168.

10. *New York Times*, 6 August 1914, p. 8. In 1918 the antisuffragists charged Catt with being unpatriotic because she had crossed the Atlantic on a German liner. A few years later, during the season of the Red Scare in the United States in the 1920s, Catt's sailing on this ship in wartime was used as evidence of her dangerous anti-American (i.e., pro-peace) proclivities.

11. Minutes of the Peace Parade Committee, 12 August 1914, pp. 10–17, Villard papers, Houghton Library.

12. Catt, "Woman and War," Empire State Campaign Committee, August 1914. While some neo-feminists of the 1970s and 1980s criticized the suffragists for clinging to the nineteenth-century idea of woman the nurturer, the idea that peace depends on the leadership of women has never completely disappeared. This does not imply that no men were working for peace, indeed, Catt and Addams were agreed that the peace societies were dominated by men. It does suggest that if more women had leadership roles in the peace movement and if they had the political clout of the vote, war could be abolished.

      The idea of women's vital role in peace has recently been revivified and once more speakers are insisting that because women better understand the sanctity of life they are the natural peacemakers. Dr. Helen Caldicott, a Boston pediatrician and critic of nuclear arms, is a popular speaker on this theme.

13. *New York Times*, 15 September 1914, p. 5; ibid. 19 September 1914, p. 2; ibid. 22 September 1914, p. 3; *Woman's Journal*, 26 September 1914, p. 264; *Jus Suffragii*, 1 October 1914, pp. 174–79.

14. Catt to Schwimmer, 28 October 1914, Catt papers, LC.
15. Catt in her introduction of Emmeline Pethick-Lawrence at the Woman's Peace Party organization meeting in January 1915. WPP papers, SCPC.
16. Catt to Addams, 14 December 1914, Catt papers, LC.
17. Addams to Catt, 21 December 1914, Addams papers, SCPC.
18. Although Catt knew the suffragettes had ceased militant activities in England when war began, she also recognized that it is not uncommon for public opinion to lag behind what was actually happening. In August 1914 the suffragists and suffragettes had united behind their government's war effort. They believed that in doing so women would reinforce their demand for votes by demonstrating that they were participating, contributing, patriotic citizens. Thus, the militant Pankhurst and the constitutional Fawcett contingents were agreed on wartime tactics, while others, like the Pethick-Lawrences, who were antipathetic to any excuse for violence, devoted themselves strenuously to opposing the war.
19. Catt to Addams, 4 January 1915, Catt papers, LC.
20. The Swarthmore College Peace Collection has the most complete records of the Woman's Peace Party. Marie Louise Degen, *The History of the Woman's Peace Party* (Baltimore: Johns Hopkins Press, 1939), is the only detailed treatment of the organization although it is discussed in most books about peace movements in the United States. Reorganized after World War I, its successor continues work as the Women's International League for Peace and Freedom.

    Fanny Garrison Villard to Frank Garrison, 10 January 1914 [sic], and 16 January 1915, Villard papers, Houghton Library. The first letter was misdated by Fanny Villard but internal evidence and comparison with her diary entry of January 10, 1915 establish the year as 1915.
21. "Dog snarling at my heels," Mary Gray Peck notes on August 4, 1929 after a long talk she had with Catt that day, Catt papers, LC; Catt and Shuler, *Woman Suffrage and Politics*, pp. 288–89. Although the Women's Political Union did not join the Empire State Campaign Committee, it was active in the campaign and was responsible for many of the successful publicity stunts and for increasing interest.
22. Inez Haynes Irwin, *Angels and Amazons* (Garden City, N. Y.: Doubleday, Doran & Co., 1934), p. 319.
23. Francis Sheehy Skeffington to Hanna Sheehy Skeffington, 23 October 1915. Personal collection of Andree Sheehy Skeffington, Dublin, Ireland.
24. Catt and Shuler, *Woman Suffrage and Politics*, pp. 290–91. Catt attributed the quotation to Dr. Baruch in some notes in her papers at the LC.
25. Catt at Senate Hearing, 15 December 1915, Harper, *Woman Suffrage*, 5: 753.
26. Gertrude Brown, *On Account of Sex*, Chapter 4, pp. 3–4. Unpublished manuscript, Brown papers, SSC.

CHAPTER 14. WAR (pp. 130–141)

1. Gertrude Brown, *On Account of Sex*, Chapter 11, p. 3.
2. The federal amendment was called the Sixteenth Amendment from its introduction in the Senate in 1878 until 1909 when the income tax amendment took the number. When the Seventeenth, dealing with popular election of senators, became law in 1912, suffragists gave up trying to call the number and began speaking of it as the federal amendment. It was also called the Susan B. Anthony Amendment, especially by members of the Congressional Union, who wanted to imply their organization was the true heir of the revered pioneer. The NAWSA properly insisted it was no more Anthony's amendment than that of the other early suffragists and officially referred to it as the federal amendment although the more popular name, Anthony Amendment, crept into even some official NAWSA reports.
3. Anthony and Harper, *Woman Suffrage*, 4: 248–49. Differences of opinion between Catt and Paul on strategy are mentioned in Susan W. Fitzgerald, ed., *Proceedings of the Forty-seventh Annual Convention, 1915*, (New York: National Woman Suffrage Publishing), pp. 155–56; also some letters in the National Woman's Party papers, for example, Dora Lewis to Paul, 14 July 1916; Paul to Lewis, 26 July 1916, Smith College Microfilm 437; Catt and Shuler, *Woman Suffrage and Politics*, p. 248. The Congressional Union members from suffrage states met in June 1916 and formed the National Woman's Party headed by Anne Martin of Nevada. The names Congressional Union and National Woman's Party were for awhile used interchangeably by the public and press even after March 1917, when the two were officially amalgamated. Alice Paul was elected chairwoman and Anne Martin vice chairwoman at that time.
4. *Woman's Journal*, 24 June 1916.
5. The Executive Board also agreed on sending a telegram to President Wilson asking for clarification of his stand. He replied, although he said he thought his position had been made clear: "The plank received my hearty approval before its adoption and I shall support its principle with sincere pleasure. I wish to join with my fellow Democrats in recommending to the several States that they extend the suffrage to women upon the same terms as to men." Catt to Wilson, 16 June 1916; Wilson to Catt, 19 June 1916, Catt papers, NYPL. Wilson said he had been away from the city and her telegram did not get to him promptly, hence the delay in replying.
6. Hanna J. Patterson, ed., *Proceedings of the Forty-eighth Annual Convention, 1916*, (New York: National Woman Suffrage Publishing), pp. 48–68. The speech was widely reported, printed as a pamphlet by the NAWSA, and the *Woman's Journal*, 16 September 1916, published it in full. Some of the examples of the problems of getting referenda passed in state legislatures were used in a book Catt compiled in January 1917, *Woman Suffrage by Federal Constitutional Amendment* (New York: National Woman Suffrage Publishing, 1917). An appendix gives a summary of

the thirty-six male suffrage states grouped according to the degree of difficulty met in amending the state constitutions.

7. Peck, *Carrie Chapman Catt*, p. 257, attributed a version of the statement to Kate Gordon of New Orleans. Catt dated the animosity of the two leading southern women, Kate Gordon and Laura Clay of Kentucky, toward her from this time. Catt said they were the only women who got to the point where they would not speak to her. When the convention "voted to go back to the old federal amendment they withdrew from the association and joined in the opposition to the Federal Amendment. When we went to Tennessee for our last ratification, those two women were there sailing around with the antisuffragists and working to keep Tennessee from ratifying. They wouldn't speak to me" (Catt to Alice Stone Blackwell, 18 November 1930, Catt papers, LC).

8. Catt, "A National Survey," 1916, typescript, sixteen pages, Catt papers, NYPL; Minutes of the Executive Council meeting, 10 September 1916, NAWSA papers, LC; Carrie McCord Parke, President, Alabama Equal Suffrage Association, in *Proceedings of the Forty-ninth Annual Convention, 1917*, ed. Nettie Rogers Shuler (New York: National Woman Suffrage Publishing), pp. 188–89; Maud Wood Park, "The Winning Plan," in *Victory—How Women Won It*, pp. 123–24. Park's statement was often quoted and she used it again in *Front Door Lobby*, pp. 15–17. She told about the convention at a Westchester, New York observance of Catt's fifty years in suffrage work reported in *Standard-Star*, New Rochelle, New York, 22 May 1936. The story was repeated at Catt's eightieth birthday celebration, 9 January 1939, typescript, three pages, Catt papers, LC.

9. William Howard Taft had made a ten-minute speech of welcome to Washington in 1910 but had not committed himself to woman suffrage. The four noted public workers were Margaret Dreier Robins, President, National Trades Union League, Chicago; Julia Lathrop, Chief, National Children's Bureau, Washington, D. C.; Dr. Katherine Bement Davis, Chief, Parole Commission, New York; and Dr. Owen Lovejoy, Head, Child Labor Committee.

10. Harper, *Woman Suffrage*, 5: 499–500. Most newspapers carried reports of his speech the next day, of course. The "Chatauqua salute"—waving handkerchiefs but not applauding—was a popular method of demonstrating appreciation, admiration, and support among the suffragists and other groups.

11. Some of the organizations formed prior to 1916 to urge the United States to prepare for war included the National Security League (December 1914), the League to Enforce Peace (June 1915), the American Defense Society (August 1915), and the American Rights Committee (December 1915). Senator Henry Cabot Lodge, Republican from Massachusetts, and Henry L. Stimson, Secretary of War from 1911 to 1913, both antisuffragists, were prominent in the increasingly strong preparedness movement.

12. This was an attitude with precedence in Catt's lifetime. In the 1860s the American Peace Society, established in 1828 and strongly abolitionist in membership, refused to condemn the Civil War.

13. *New York Times*, 12 October 1916, p. 10. 14. Harper, *Woman Suffrage*, 5: 721.
15. Abridged Minutes of the Executive Council of the National American Woman
    Suffrage Association, held in Washington, D.C., February 23–24, 1917, pp. 2–3,
    NAWSA papers, LC; Harper, *Woman Suffrage*, 5: 723–25. Wilson wrote to the
    NAWSA "to express my very great and sincere admiration of the action taken"
    (*Woman's Journal*, 10 March 1917, p. 55).
16. Forbes comment, *Woman's Journal*, 17 March 1917, p. 63; Blackwell, ibid., 10
    March 1917, p. 58. The fluttering in the dovecotes began in February 1917, when
    the National Board of the Woman's Peace Party appealed to Catt to show
    patriotism "by refraining from any action tending to increase the war spirit"
    (letter signed by Jane Addams, chair, and other members of the board, 23
    February 1917, WPP papers, SCPC).
        There was considerable comment after the fact, for example: *New York
    Times*, 7 March 1917, p. 11; Jane Addams to Harriet P. Thomas, 14 March 1917,
    WPP papers, SCPC; Catt to Mrs. Owen Kildare, 26 September 1917, Catt
    papers, NYPL. In 1919 a message from the Hungarian Communist women was
    relayed to Catt by a friend: "Tell Mrs. Catt that even if she is an imperialist
    reactionary we would go far to meet her again and shall always love and admire
    her greatness" (Alice Riggs Hunt to Catt, 17 June 1919, Catt papers, LC).
    Mildred Scott Olmsted, for many years a leader in the Women's International
    League for Peace and Freedom, was in Bavaria with a relief organization imme-
    diately after the war when a woman asked her, "Why did Mrs. Catt desert us?"
    (Olmsted interview with the author, 23 March 1976). It has been generally
    overlooked that Catt did not act independently but with the approval of the
    Council of One Hundred who ostensibly reflected the consensus of the nation-
    wide suffragist network it represented.
17. To Mary Gray Peck from Clara Hyde, 3 February 1917, NAWSA papers, LC.
18. *Woman's Journal*, 31 March 1917; 7 April 1917; 13 April 1917; Harper, *Woman
    Suffrage*, 5: 523, 632–33. Catt and Helen Gardener were guests of Senator
    Champ Clark and his wife, both strong suffragists, for the historic event.
19. "To the Presidents," 9 April 1917, Laura Clay papers, University of Kentucky
    Libraries, Special Collections.
20. Emily Newell Blair, *The Woman's Committee United States Council of National
    Defense, An Interpretative Report, April 21, 1917, to February 27, 1919* (Wash-
    ington, D.C.: Government Printing Office, 1920), p. 21. Blair was scornful of
    the conditions under which women were organized and were expected to be
    effective without status.

> There seems to be a general acceptance of the idea that when you deal with women,
> you go to their organizations, when you deal with men you go to the governor or a
> legislature. Theoretically governors are supposed to represent women as well as men
> but the very appointment by the Council [of National Defense] of an Advisory
> Committee on Women's activites showed that in effect, it was recognized that

women must function through their organizations, since they could not, under the
political system, function directly through the Government (p. 24).

21. *Woman's Journal*, 14 April 1917; *International Woman Suffrage News*, 1 May 1917.
22. Catt's rationale was one many liberals espousing various causes in the United
States adopted during these difficult years. For an excellent discussion of this
point see Sidney Kaplan, "Social Engineers as Saviors: Effects of World War I on
Some American Liberals," *Journal of the History of Ideas* 17, no. 3, (June 1956):
346–69, and George Creel, *How We Advertised America* (New York: Harper &
Brothers, 1920), p. 4. Phillip Knightley in his enlightening book describing how
truth is always *The First Casualty* in war wrote of the equally successful sales pitch
made to the British (New York: Harcourt Brace Jovanovich, 1975, p. 12). "As
dangerous as madness . . ." Justin Kaplan, *Lincoln Steffens* (New York: Simon &
Schuster, 1974), p. 225.
23. Jane Addams, *Peace and Bread in Time of War* (New York: Macmillan, 1922), pp.
132–33, 142. John Dewey discussed changing public opinion in his introduction
to the 1945 edition of Addams's book (New York: King's Crown Press): "The book
takes us through the period when the war seemed remote and unreal, and the
American public reacted in incredulity and exasperation; through the phase of
gradual hardening into sullen acceptance of war as a fact; to the time, when, after
a delay of two and a half years, we responded to the declaration of war with
enthusiastic participation in which the earlier all but universal pacifism was
treated as cowardly retreat or as actively treasonable" (p. ix).

Helen Michalowski, "The Roots of American Nonviolence," in *The Power of
the People*, ed. Robert Cooney and Helen Michalowski (Culver City, Calif.: Peace
Press, 1977), pp. 14–15, makes distinctions of principles held by various kinds of
pacifists. This is a valuable, liberally illustrated history of active nonviolence in
the United States.
24. Catt to Lucy E. Anthony, 2 April 1940 and 12 April 1940; Catt to Daniels, 10
April 1940, Catt papers, NYPL. Catt wrote to Anne Martin about an incident
she and Shaw found amusing: "Mr. [Herbert] Hoover was rather toplofty about his
orders to women and upon one occasion Miss Shaw issued rather a sharp
challenge to the Food Administration Department. That brought his chief
assistant over to the Woman's Division immediately and by way of apology he
stated that both he (Dr. Wilbur of California) and Mr. Hoover were strong
advocates of suffrage. He seemed to think that if this were true they could snub
the women all they liked." Catt to Martin, 22 March 1920, Bancroft Library,
University of California, Berkeley.
25. Catt to Josephus Daniels, 2 February 1940, Catt papers, NYPL. Daniels had
written Catt to get information about the Woman's Committee for a book he was
writing; she in turn asked Lucy Anthony for any records she might have. Catt
reminded her "he was the head of the Council of National Defense part of the

time, hence the director of the Woman's Commttee." Lucy Anthony and Catt exchanged a few letters about it.

CHAPTER 15. THE WINNING PLAN WORKS (pp. 142–152)

1. Jeannette Rankin intended to introduce the federal suffrage amendment the first day of the session but it was upstaged by the more dramatic events; it was introduced the second day. Lobbying and some committee work continued; Catt testified at a Senate hearing on April 20, 1917.
2. *Woman's Journal*, 3 February 1917, p. 25, printed the letter that concluded: "As you know, I have a very real interest in the extension of the suffrage to the women, and I feel that every step in this direction should be applauded." Also, Maud Wood Park, "Supplementary Notes about Helen Gardener," Equal Rights Collection, SL.
3. *New York Times*, 28 March 1917, p. 8; Catt and Shuler, *Woman Suffrage and Politics*, p. 295; Gertrude Brown, *On Account of Sex*, Chapter 16, p. 8.
4. Brown details the fundraising in *On Account of Sex*, Chapter 17, titled "High Finance."
5. Clara Hyde to Mary Gray Peck, 22 January 1922, NAWSA papers, LC. Mrs. Frank Leslie, then Miriam Squier, had met Frank Leslie through her second husband, an editor of one of Leslie's journals. She herself was editor at different times of three of his twelve periodicals. She and Leslie each obtained a divorce and were married in 1874. She then divided her time between society and magazines. Leslie had overextended his publishing enterprises and when he died in 1890 was bankrupt. She took control, paid off creditors, revitalized the business, made herself rich, and indulged in marriages that the tabloid editors relished, one of them to the brother of Oscar Wilde.
6. *Woman's Journal*, 17 March 1917.
7. Rose Young, *The Record of the Leslie Woman Suffrage Commission, Inc., 1917–1929* (New York, 1929), pp. 61, 85–86; Mildred Adams, *The Right to Be People* (Philadelphia: J. B. Lippincott, 1967), p. 138.
8. The Leslie Bureau also edited and published the *Woman Citizen* (merger of *Woman's Journal*, *Woman Voter*, and the *National Suffrage News*) as well as books and pamphlets on suffrage. Some money went to NAWSA's Congressional Committee, and a little to state referenda campaigns. After the war the IWSA and struggling suffrage organizations in other countries were helped. At home the new League of Women Voters received some money but the bulk was spent on publicity and publications.

　　　The incorporators of the Leslie Suffrage Commission, Inc. were Catt, Alice Stone Blackwell, Harriet Taylor Upton, Margaret Dreier Robins, and Mrs. Winston Churchill. Their first meeting was held on March 29, 1917. Four other women were added immediately to the board of directors: Mary Garrett Hay, Anna Pennybacker, Mrs. Thomas B. Wells, and Mrs. Arthur L. Livermore. The commission met regularly for the next twelve years. In the 1920s two women were added to fill vacancies, Caroline McCormick Slade and Eleanor Roosevelt, to whom Catt wrote and said she had been "nominated and seconded by two 'black Republicans'" (probably Catt and Hay). A biographer of Eleanor Roosevelt suggested it was a great honor to be elected to "the holy of Holies" (Catt to Eleanor Roosevelt, 7 July 1926, Eleanor Roosevelt papers, FDR Library, Hyde Park, New York; Joseph Lash, *Eleanor and Franklin* [New York: Signet, 1971], p. 416).

Rose Young's *Record* was the official and complete report and brought the history up to the last meeting in 1929, but Catt headed a continuing committee to disburse a remaining $30,000. The final report, dated May 28, 1941, showed $939,751.26 was the total received and spent. Under cover of a letter of June 14, 1941, Catt sent a copy of the last statement to Eleanor Roosevelt and other members of the Leslie Commission (Eleanor Roosevelt papers, FDR Library, Hyde Park, New York).

9. Brown, *On Account of Sex*, Chapter 21, p. 9.
10. *New York Times*, 14 May 1917, p. 6. Catt was speaking at the three-day Mississippi Valley Conference in Columbus, Ohio. It was not a new theme. At the beginning of the European war, Catt wrote in a long letter to the *New York Times*, "Our protest is against the imperialism which makes the Kaiser and the Czar hold that they have a divine right to rule over men in their respective realms, and which in an attenuated form, persuades men as a whole to think they have a divine right to rule over women as a whole" (8 October 1914, p. 10).
11. Mary Garrett Hay, an adroit politician, was credited with bringing Tammany around to giving suffrage a chance in the election. "Mollie Hay is an A#1 politician of the Tammany variety," wrote Clara Hyde to Peck (neither of whom was particularly fond of Hay). "She plays up the common people.' She has got the city party machine solidly behind her. Moll has pounded and pounded at the statement that New York City won the victory. Of course it did. And it never would have won if the organization had not been so nearly perfect as it was" (5 December 1917, NAWSA papers, LC.)
12. Brown, *On Account of Sex*, Chapter 18, pp. 3–4. Catt wrote to Edna Giles Fuller, 30 October 1946: "There are certain states that were important because it happened that they did something which made a turn in the tide, for example, Wyoming, the first state, and the immediate states that followed are. Illinois which adopted a new kind of law, which was followed quickly by other states; certain states which were lost because there was political criminality in the last vote; New York because it was the greatest public vote obtained anywhere in the world" (Catt papers, NYPL).
13. Catt and Shuler, *Woman Suffrage and Politics*, p. 299.

14. Ibid.
15. "An Address to the Congress of the United States," *Proceedings of the Forty-Ninth Convention, 1917*, ed. Nettie Rogers Shuler, pp. 50–67. This speech was already printed in pamphlet form when the convention met and each senator and representative was given a copy. The pamphlet is in several libraries, including the Sophia Smith Collection at Smith College. The pamphlet cover is a cartoon depicting an American soldier saying to Uncle Sam, "She has given me to democracy; give democracy to her," as he points toward a motherly figure. The cover cartoon was originally used by the *Woman Citizen*, 29 September 1917. See also the *Woman Citizen*, 22 December 1917, p. 69.

Years later Catt told a graduate student that this was one of the two most important speeches she ever made; the other was "An Address to the Legislatures of the United States" (New York: National Woman Suffrage Publishing, February 1919) in preparation for the ratification campaign (Ima Fuchs Clevenger, "Invention and Arrangement in the Public Address of Carrie Chapman Catt" [Ph.D. diss., University of Oklahoma, 1955], pp. 77–78, quotes a letter from Catt, 1 June 1945).
16. Catt to presidents, 11 January 1918, Park papers, SL; Park, *Front Door Lobby*, p. 160. This posthumously published book is a detailed and insightful account of the work of the Congressional Committee in the last crucial years. Park's reports are also in the NAWSA *Proceedings, 1917*, pp. 107–13, and in Justine Leavitt Wilson, ed., *Proceedings of the Jubilee Convention, 1919* (New York: National Woman Suffrage Publishing), pp. 119–51. In addition she contributed two chapters to *Victory—How Women Won It*.
17. "War Aims," *Woman Citizen*, 22 June 1918, p. 75.
18. Hyde to Peck, 26 June 1918, NAWSA papers, LC.
19. Catt to Park, 20 July 1918, Catt papers, SSC.
20. Catt to Hyde, 20 September 1918, Catt papers, LC.
21. Park, *Front Door Lobby*, p. 212.
22. *Woman Citizen*, 5 October 1918, p. 375.
23. *Woman Citizen*, 14 September, 21 September, 28 September, and 5 October 1918 covered the Senate action in detail as did the daily papers. The *Congressional Record* carried the complete debates. Ida Husted Harper described the vote in the *International Woman Suffrage News*, of October and November 1918. See also Park, *Front Door Lobby*, pp. 192–213.
24. Catt to Mrs. John G. Pyle, 16 August 1918, Richardson Archives, University of South Dakota, Vermillion.

CHAPTER 16. VICTORY (pp. 153–165)

1. Catt to Katherine Boyles, 3 May 1925, Huntington Library, San Marino, California.

2. As the years went on, Catt began articulating in detail her idea of what the League of Women Voters would do. In 1915 she wrote, "We shall reorganize [the suffrage association] for the purpose of training women in the new duties of citizenship, we shall teach them something of American history [including] the evolution of woman suffrage in America" (Catt, "If We Win in New York," *Woman's Journal*, 30 October 1915).

   The first course in women's history in a university curriculum was announced in the *Woman's Journal*, 9 May 1891, p. 148: "Professor James H. Canfield, in whose department of American History and Civics this new work falls, has been striving to secure this new departure for several years," the *Journal* reported, detailing his plan scheduled to begin in the fall at the University of Kansas in Lawrence. "The goodly sum of one hundred dollars" was donated by friends in Topeka to buy books for the "Woman's Alcove" in the library, Laura Johns reported in the *Journal*, 18 July 1891. Canfield was the father of the writer Dorothy Canfield Fisher.

3. Catt to Mrs. Robert A. Dean, 6 June 1919, Edson papers, University of California, Los Angeles.

4. Part of the call to the Jubilee Convention read: "NAWSA invites the women voters of the fifteen full suffrage states to attend this anniversary convention, and there to join their forces into a League of Women Voters." The fifteen were Wyoming (1869), Colorado (1893), Idaho (1896), Utah (1896), Washington (1910), California (1911), Kansas (1912), Oregon (1912), Arizona (1912), Montana (1914), Nebraska (1914), Nevada (1914), New York (1917), Michigan (1918), Oklahoma (1918), and South Dakota (1918). Although a popular phrase in the League of Women Voters is that it was "conceived in St. Louis and born in Chicago [1920]" it had an earlier conception and longer gestation. See also *Proceedings, 1919*, pp. 199–248; Harper, *Woman Suffrage*, 5: 570, 683–88. Mrs. Charles H. Brooks of Kansas chaired the new League.

5. Because it was a new Congress, the House had to vote again on the amendment in spite of their favorable vote of January 10, 1918. New Hampshire Congressman Edward H. Wason was credited by Maud Wood Park for persuading Mann to chair the committee. Wason himself said he had been converted to woman suffrage by Catt when he heard her address the Constitutional Convention in his state years before (Park, *Front Door Lobby*, p. 241).

6. *New York Times*, 23 May 1919, p. 12.

7. Hyde to Peck, 5 June 1919, NAWSA papers, LC. The letter continued:

   As you may suppose CCC is very happy. Moll came in like a conquering bull this P.M. hot off the amendment trail. She said there were anxious moments at 2 P.M. when amendments to the amendment were offered. Reid of Missouri spoke 5 hours in an attempt to filibuster. This is confidential (told me by one who had it from Moll [Catt?]). She said the Repubs were under wonderful discipline. Watson the Repub whip had given orders that no matter what the Dems might say they were not to answer!! The Dems made the most of their opportunity and the Repubs busted a button but kept silent!! Lodge said not a word tho he voted No.

Park thought the decisive factor was the success of Catt's winning plan presented at Atlantic City in 1916. The state suffrage associations had kept their pledges and followed the program of action outlined. Park detailed the successes in thirty-one states, which raised the total of presidential electors for whom women were eligible to vote from 91 to 339 (Park, *Front Door Lobby*, pp. 270–71).

8. The plans had been ready for over a year. Catt wrote to Park on April 25, 1918: "We are going ahead with our preparations for ratification. We are getting the petitions ready and the literature" (Catt papers, SSC). At the NAWSA Executive Council meeting the same month, plans for the ratification campaign were completed and approved, and the work of state committees was outlined and perfected in detail, reported the *Woman Citizen*, 27 April 1918, p. 428.

9. Reilly to Shaw, 11 June 1919, Shaw papers, SL. Shaw was touring the country with former President Taft and President Lowell of Harvard University on behalf of the League of Nations when she came down with pneumonia in Springfield, Illinois. She was able to go home to Moylan, Pennsylvania, but she never recovered and died there July 2, 1919, at the age of seventy-two. Catt spoke at her funeral held three days later, placing on her breast the flag pin given her by the NAWSA with diamonds marking the suffrage states and the Distinguished Service Medal from the United States government for her work in the war, which she had received just six weeks before her death.

10. The committees and their heads during 1919 were: (1) Committee on American Citizenship, Mrs. Frederick P. Bagley of Massachusetts, who was also on the National Republican Party platform and program committee; (2) Women in Industry, Mrs. Raymond Robins, head of the National Women's Trade Union League; (3) Unification of Laws for Women, Mrs. Catharine Waugh McCulloch, attorney-at-law; (4) Improvement of Election Laws and Methods, Mrs. Jacob Baur of Illinois; (5) Food Supply and Demand, Mrs. Edward P. Costigan; (6) Child Welfare, Mrs. Percy V. Pennybacker of the Woman's Division of the National Democratic Party; (7) Social Hygiene, Dr. Valeria H. Parker; (8) Committee on Research, Mrs. Mary Sumner Boyd (*Woman Citizen*, 21 February 1920, p. 906; Harper, *Woman Suffrage*, 5: 686–87).

11. Many of the women present had worked with Susan B. Anthony, and her presence was strongly felt so much did the victory owe her. Fittingly, her one hundredth birthday fell midway in the convention, February 15, 1920, as was noted affectionately and often. Details of the convention are from Nettie Rogers Shuler, ed., *Proceedings of the Victory Convention National American Woman Suffrage Association (1869–1920) and First National Congress League of Women Voters*, (New York: NAWSA, 1920). Catt made two major addresses, one to the National Convention on February 13 and one to the League of Women Voters on Febrary 14.

12. *Woman Citizen*, 28 February 1920, p. 921. On her death she willed the pin to the League of Women Voters. It was sold and the $3,000 it brought was used as seed money for the Carrie Chapman Catt Memorial Fund, which was begun in April 1947. Its purpose was to spread the practical knowledge and the underlying theory of how a democracy works, and why. Over the years it has accomplished this by having exchanges of women to and from dozens of countries, old and new. For the last thirty years there have been programs with Latin American women, in recent years there has been emphasis on the newly independent nations as well. The Memorial Fund is now called the Overseas Education Fund, a name that more accurately describes its work.

13. 22 March 1920, Martin papers, Bancroft Library, University of California, Berkeley.

14. Catt to Alicia Moreau, 13 September 1920, Catt papers, LC; Hyde to Peck, 20 July 1920, NAWSA papers, LC; Hyde to Catt, 22 July 1920, Catt papers, LC.

    On Catt's urging, Tennessee governor Albert H. Roberts had called a special session of the legislature to meet in early August. Tennessee had not acted before because of a clause in the state constitution that required the legislature voting on a federal amendment to be elected after the amendment was submitted for ratification. A similar clause in Ohio's constitution had been declared unconstitutional by the U.S. Supreme Court in June so it appeared that the way was opened for Tennessee. After several legal opinions, the governor called the special session to vote on the Nineteenth Amendment, the suffragists' last hope for getting the thirty-sixth state in time for all women to vote in the presidential election in November. The other two possible states, Vermont and Connecticut, had governors who refused to call special sessions, in spite of pressure by the suffragists. Connecticut, especially, had seen an all-out effort in May which had brought women there from forty-six states for a week of intensive work as an Emergency Suffrage Corps. Governor Holcomb could see no emergency.

15. Catt to Peck, 15 August 1920, Catt papers, LC.

16. *Woman Citizen*, 4 September 1920, p. 364.

17. Another friend in Tennessee was the speaker of the Senate in 1920, Andrew Todd of Murfreesboro, who was ostracized by many of his local supporters after he favored ratification. Sarah Spence DeBow, formerly of his home town, wrote a small pamphlet she called, "The History of the Case," about his "cruel persecution." She was in Murfreesboro when "the enormous Indignation Meeting [was] held in the Court House yard to denounce Andrew Todd for voting for Ratification and to pledge themselves that he should never again be elected to office. I believe if Mr. Todd had appeared that day he would have been lynched and while I dared to walk around the Square while it was going on I was thankful I did not feel called upon to enter the Court House yard" (NAWSA papers, LC).

18. An editorial in the *New York Times* on the occasion suggested that the private signing of the proclamation was a wise diplomatic move on the part of Secretary Colby. By so doing he was tactfully declining to say whether the NAWSA or the

Woman's Party should be given the greater part of the credit for the amendment ("With Neither Dear Charmer," 28 August 1920, p. 6).

Various legal means were tried to have the ratification invalidated. Anticipating the possibility that if it were successfully overturned in only one state it would cause enormous legal complications, Connecticut ratified the amendment on September 14, 1920 and Vermont on February 9, 1921. The final word came on February 27, 1922, when the U. S. Supreme Court declared that the federal amendment had been legally ratified August 26, 1920. Catt in "A Postscript to Victory," *Woman Citizen*, 25 February 1922, briefly reviewed the several challenges to the ratification.

Counting the two that came late, thirty-eight states ratified the amendment; nine—Alabama, Georgia, Maryland, Mississippi, South Carolina, Virginia, Delaware, Louisiana, and North Carolina—voted against ratification. Florida, under Governor Catts, was the only state in which there was no action.

19. Park, *Front Door Lobby*, p. 276.
20. *Woman Citizen*, 4 September 1920, p. 364.
21. Ibid., pp. 362–63.
22. Catt to Peck, 12 October 1920, and 6 September 1920, Catt papers, LC. Park said that Wadsworth "considered woman's quixotic tendency to place the interests of persons above the interest of property was sufficient reason to oppose the amendment. He believed not in democracy but in oligarchy for the well-to-do" (Park, *Front Door Lobby*, p. 177).

Catt bought the estate (seventeen acres and twenty-room house) in Briarcliff in the spring of 1919 and she and Hay lived there until they moved to New Rochelle nine years later. Catt loved "the farm," as she called it, which gave her scope for her passion of gardening, in spite of the fact it was an hour and a half commute to her office in New York. Hay never did like living so far from the city and hated Juniper Ledge from the beginning.

23. *New York Times*, 21 October 1920. One can only imagine the private arguments Catt and Hay had on the subject of the presidential candidates. After the election in a letter to Peck, Clara Hyde flippantly noted, "CCC is sick in bed today from a heavy cold. Moll blames it on the fact that she came out for Cox" (10 November 1920, NAWSA papers, LC).
24. "World Politics and Women Voters," *Woman's Home Companion*, November 1920, p. 4.
25. *New York Times*, 17 November 1920, p. 18; Hyde to Peck, 20 November 1920, NAWSA papers, LC.
26. *New York Times*, 20 November 1920, p. 19.
27. 22 November 1920, Catt papers, LC.
28. *New York Times*, 28 January 1921, p. 1; 29 January 1921, p. 1; *Woman Citizen*, 5 February 1921, pp. 949, 950–51, 959.

CHAPTER 17. THE ALLIANCE RESUMES (pp. 169–183)

1. At the 1916 NAWSA convention, Jennie Roessing, president of the Pennsylvania State suffrage association, assumed the leadership of a campaign to raise $5,000 for the Alliance, which she did with the help of Clara Hyde, Millicent Garrett Fawcett, Adela Coit, and Chrystal Macmillan. The headquarters work during the war is detailed in IWSA, *Report, 1920*, pp. 27–36.
2. "Greeting to the IWSA," *International Woman Suffrage News*, February 1919.
3. Clara Hyde to Mary Gray Peck, 26 January 1919, NAWSA papers, LC. Actually the war was not officially ended until July 2, 1921, with final ratification of treaties October 18, 1921.
4. As a result of the war, the Austro-Hungarian Empire was fragmented, with the new states of Czechoslovakia, Austria, and Hungary carved from it; the northeast section (including Galicia, which had had representation in the IWSA) had been incorporated into Poland; a section in the southeast had gone to Rumania, another section to Yugoslavia, yet another to Italy. Serbia was enlarged to become the Serb-Croat-Slovene kingdom, later known as Yugoslavia; new states, including Estonia, Latvia, and Lithuania had been established.
5. "Mrs. Catt to the Women of Europe," *Woman Citizen*, 12 June 1920, p. 43; Josephine Schain, 6 November 1939, Schain papers, SSC. Cf. Lysistrata's explanation to the Commissioner: "It's rather like yarn. When a hank's in a tangle, we lift it—so—and work out the snarls by winding it up on spindles, now this way, now that way. That's how we'll wind up the War, if allowed: We'll work out the snarls by sending Special Commissions—back and forth, now this way, now that way—to ravel these tense international kinks" (*Lysistrata*, in *Aristophanes' Four Comedies*, ed. William Arrowsmith, trans. Douglass Parker [Ann Arbor: University of Michigan Press, 1975], p. 44).
6. On Catt's recommendation, Addie Daniels, wife of the Secretary of the Navy, was appointed by President Wilson to be the official U. S. representative to the IWSA congress. She often spoke of it as "one of the happiest experiences of her life" (Josephus Daniels to Catt, 4 March, 1940, Catt papers, NYPL).
7. Schreiber and Mathieson, *Journey towards Freedom*, p. 28.
8. *Report of the Eighth Congress*, pp. 222–23.
9. *Woman Citizen*, 12 June 1920, p. 45.
10. Ibid., 25 December 1920, pp. 818–28; clipping in Iowa State University archives, bylined Margaret Walter, dated London, 24 Jan., Reciprocal News Service. Internal evidence makes it clear Walter is describing Catt and other leaders at the London meetings in November 1920. "Her single jewel" was the star sapphire given her at the NAWSA victory convention in 1920.
11. *The Vote*, 10 December 1920, p. 293.
12. Details of the conference are in *Year Book of the National League of Women Voters and Proceedings of the Third Annual Convention and Pan-American Conference of*

Women Held at Baltimore, Maryland, April 20–29, 1922. The *Woman Citizen* throughout the spring of 1922 ran many articles on the meetings and they were discussed in the *Bulletin of the Pan American Union,* July 1922. There are several letters of appreciation to Catt from delegates to the conference in the Catt papers at the Library of Congress, for example, from Esther N. de Calvo, 5 July, 1922.

13. Catt kept a diary of her travels in Europe and South America from October 8, 1922 to March 17, 1923. It had apparently been started in 1917 (although she later misdated it 1916) but had only three days' entries. Catt had come across it when she was cleaning out her apartment and decided to keep it on this trip. Diary entries in the text that follow are from this source; the diary is in the Catt papers, LC.

     "The Fascisti in Italy," *Woman Citizen,* 16 December 1922, pp. 8–9, 28; Catt to Nettie R. Shuler, 28 November 1922, Catt papers, LC.

14. The Committee on Woman Suffrage had been replaced by a Women's Association for Political Interest, which at the time Catt was there was working for prohibition; "Austria Revisited," *Woman Citizen,* 30 December 1922, pp. 7–8, 29; also Catt travel diary.

15. "The Bright Spot of Europe," *Woman Citizen,* 24 February 1923, pp. 7–8, 29; also Catt travel diary. The Alliance friend was Frantiska Plaminkova who was later a senator in the Czechoslovak Parliament. At the IWSA conference in Copenhagen in 1939 she was urged by her friends not to return to Prague but she was determined to be with her own people. In November Catt wrote the U. S. State Department seeking information about her. By that time she had been murdered by the Nazis.

16. The only thing Catt wrote about her Reichstag speech was the one line quoted from her travel diary, 12 November 1922. Medicated with opium and strychnine, she probably remembered little about it. In her report to the *Woman Citizen* she did not mention it at all and the only notice in that journal was a dreadful picture of her taken in front of the building. The note about Lord d'Abernon was from a letter written to Catt by Christopher Garrett, Millicent Garrett Fawcett's nephew, and was included in her travel diary.

17. "A Glimpse of Germany," *Woman Citizen,* 27 January 1923, pp. 26–27.

18. Elizabeth Babcock was an American woman who had left Smith College in 1910 after her junior year for health reasons. She had campaigned actively for suffrage in upper New York State and worked with the YMCA in Germany during the war. She died November 12, 1925, after a long illness contracted in the winter of her South American trip (Dorothy Kenyon to William Allan Neilson, 16 November 1925, Neilson papers, Smith College Archives).

     Anita Trumbull van Lennep was born in Valparaiso, Chile, attended Wellesley College, married a New York banker, and lived in that city for forty years. It is surprising that she accompanied Catt on this trip because she was an antisuffragist. Apparently she was asked along because of the Chilean background and her fluency in Spanish, also she had enough money to pay her own way. Rosa Manus did not like her at all; Catt did not complain then or later, but when they returned home she would never accept invitations or meet her anywhere although Anita van Lennep considered Catt her close friend (Manus to Clara Hyde, 2 December and 11 December 1922, Catt to Manus, 4 August 1939, Catt papers, LC, *New York Times*, 17 March 1938).

19. Catt, "Busy Women in Brazil" *Woman Citizen*, 24 March 1923, pp. 9–10, "Mrs. Catt in Brazil," *International Woman Suffrage News*, March 1923, pp. 81–82. An interesting profile of Bertha Lutz is Roy F. Nash, "The Brains of Brazil's Woman Movement," *Woman Citizen*, 25 March 1922, pp. 9, 16; see also Alice Morgan Wright to Margaret Grierson, 18 April 1950, Wright papers, SSC.

20. Catt, "South American Contrasts," *Woman Citizen*, 7 April 1923, pp. 10–11, 32; Catt, "Argentina and Uruguay," *International Woman Suffrage News*, April 1923, pp. 97–98, 103.

21. Catt to Mary Garrett Hay, 28 January 1923, Catt papers, LC.

22. Catt, "Anti-Feminism in South America," *Current History*, September 1923, pp. 1033–34; "Report of Carrie Chapman Catt on South American and European Trip, 1922–1923," Catt papers, LC. This last was made to the Leslie Commission and marked "Confidential." The *Current History* article is similar to the report but Catt tempered her criticisms about the church and tried to be positive about the women's movement in South America in the magazine.

23. Catt to Hay, 18 January 1923, Catt papers, LC.

24. Mussolini's address was not given in the official report of the congress but it was printed in many newspapers with slight variations. The quotations here are from *The Vote*, 25 May 1923, p. 165.

25. "Address of the President," *Report of Ninth Congress* (Dresden: B. G. Teubner, 1923), pp. 28–29.

26. L. de Alberti, "How Rome Welcomed the Great Congress," *International Woman Suffrage News*, July 1923, p. 146.

27. Peru joined in 1926, bringing to four the number of South American countries in the Alliance (Argentina and Uruguay were both 1920 affiliates; Brazil, 1923). There had been a delegate from Chile at the 1902 IWSA meeting in Washington but at no subsequent congress until this one in 1923.

28. Another controversial subject was what in the United States after 1922 came to be known as the Equal Rights Amendment, covered at the congress by a declaration that all work should be open to women and that men and women should be paid at the same rate in the same occupation or grade. No one argued the equal pay aspect; what split the feminists at Rome in 1923 and for over thirty years afterward was the question of protective legislation. The Dutch and Scandinavian delegates were leaders of those who stood for abolition of special laws for women; those from the United States supported the hard-won protections needed by women in industry. At the time, women were making headway in labor

legislation in spite of the predominantly male-controlled, male-oriented, and male-priority labor unions. It seemed to laboring women in the United States and to liberal humanists like Catt that it would be retrogressive to relinquish the rights women had worked so hard to get, including laws concerning minimum wages, suitable hours, safety, and sanitary conditions. The National Women's Trade Union League and other women of the American Federation of Labor, the National Consumers' League, and dozens of others sided with the National League of Women Voters on the issue in the United States; abroad the International Federation of Trade Unions and the International Conference of Labour and Socialist Women took similar stands.

29. Catt to Margaret Sanger and Juliet Rublee, 24 November 1920, Sanger papers, LC. Although this referred to Catt's refusal to get involved in the birth control movement, it is characteristic of her attitude to concentrate on one reform at a time. Aletta Jacobs had worked on birth control for many years before Sanger discovered the cause but had never been able to proselytize Catt. "We quarreled all around the world about it," Catt told Clara Hyde, "and I haven't changed my mind—nor she hers. I don't mind how much they control the births but I do not like nor think necessary all the talk about it" (9 March 1924, Catt papers, LC).

30. *New York Times*, 6 June 1923, p. 20; *Woman Citizen*, 16 June 1923, p. 28; Catt to Peck, 20 September 1923, Catt papers, LC.

31. *Report of the Twelfth Congress of the International Alliance of Women for Suffrage and Equal Citizenship, Istanbul, 1935*, p. 12. In 1926 the Paris congress changed the name to the International Alliance of Women for Suffrage and Equal Citizenship. At the meeting in Geneva in October 1945 of the International Committee, the name was again changed to International Alliance of Women. Equal Rights, Equal Responsibilities. It is generally abbreviated to IAW.

The Turkish government issued a series of stamps in honor of the women's congress, one had Catt's picture, others the six women Nobel Prize winners— Marie Curie, Grazia Deledda, Selma Lagerlof, Sigrid Undset, Jane Addams, and Bertha von Suttner. There were stamps depicting activities of women, the Alliance logo, the Yildiz Palace where their meetings were held, and one with a portrait of Kamal Ataturk, president of the Turkish Republic. Catt's picture was on the highest denomination, the 100 Kurus, but after a trial proof, it was realized the honor was reserved for Kamal Pasha Ataturk himself so the value of her stamp was lowered, but not before she received the set that included the only Catt 100 Kurus. She was no collector and sent her set to the most famous philatelist she knew, Franklin D. Roosevelt (Catt to Eleanor Roosevelt, 17 June 1935, Catt papers, NYPL). The stamps were sold at auction along with the rest of FDR's personal collection by his direction after his death.

32. The eight were Bahrain, Kuwait, Nigeria (in six states), Oman, Qatar, Saudi Arabia, United Arab Emirates, and Yemen. In some of these men do not have voting rights either so the comparison becomes fuzzy (United Nations, *Everyone's*

United Nations, p. 256).

The Alliance published a small pamphlet to commemorate its twenty-fifth anniversary in 1929 written by Regine Deutsch, *The International Woman Suffrage Alliance, Its History from 1904 to 1929* (London, 1929). A more ambitious and useful book marked the fiftieth: Adele Schreiber and Margaret Mathieson, *Journey towards Freedom*. Fittingly, publication was subsidized by the Carrie Chapman Catt Memorial Fund. The most recent and complete history, particularly good on the later years, is Arnold Whittick, *Woman into Citizen*. The best records of all are the reports of the proceedings of the congresses, most of which are very detailed. The *International Women's News* (previously the *International Woman Suffrage News* and earlier *Jus Suffragii*) is the most useful printed source for following the movement.

CHAPTER 18. DECISION FOR PEACE (pp. 184–197)

1. Statement made to Mary Gray Peck, Peck manuscript, p. 629, Catt papers, LC. There are pages of manuscript of Peck's *Carrie Chapman Catt* in this collection. The biography was drastically cut for publication and although there are only odd sections of the draft they often contain Peck's reports of conversations with Catt, hence have material otherwise unavailable and of considerable interest. There are sometimes several consecutive, numbered pages, but by no means the entire typescript.
2. *New York Times*, 14 April 1921, p. 16; *Woman Citizen*, 21 April 1921, p. 1184.
3. Harper, *Woman Suffrage*, 5: 98.
4. C. Roland Marchand, *The American Peace Movement and Social Reform, 1898–1918*, p. 78. This is an excellent book with a fine bibliography.
5. *Woman Citizen*, 23 November 1918, p. 531.
6. Ibid., p. 530.
7. Quoted by Joseph P. Lash, *Eleanor and Franklin*, p. 356.
8. Quoted by Inez Haynes Irwin, *Angels and Amazons*, p. 418.
9. *New York Times*, 14 April 1921, p. 16; *Woman Citizen*, 23 April 1921, p. 1184.
10. Elizabeth Hauser, "Eight Months' War against War," *Woman Citizen*, 17 December 1921, p. 23.
11. 20 September, 14 November, and 25 November 1923, Catt papers, LC.
12. 28 December 1923, Catt papers, NYPL.
13. Josephine Schain, "Memorandum to the Sophia Smith Collection on the formation of the Committee on the Cause and Cure of War," National Committee on the Cause and Cure of War papers, SSC. Schain (1886–1972) served first as secretary and later as chair of the National Committee. In 1935 she resigned her

position as national director of the Girl Scouts to devote more time to the NCCW.

14. Catt to Maud Wood Park, 21 January 1924, Schain papers, SSC; Schain, "Memorandum." Catt undertook the new job with enthusiasm in spite of the fact that just a few days before she had turned down a request from Eleanor Roosevelt to serve on the Democratic National Platform on Social Legislation on the grounds she was too busy. In September Eleanor Roosevelt wrote her again asking her to speak for Democratic Presidential candidate John W. Davis, and Catt said "no" again. "While Mr. Davis has outspokenly advocated the League of Nations," Catt wrote, "it does not follow that the way to get this country into the League is necessarily through public support of his election" (Roosevelt to Catt, 14 April 1924; Catt to Roosevelt, 22 April 1924; Roosevelt to Catt, 17 September 1924; Catt to Roosevelt 20 September 1924, Catt papers, NYPL).

    The League of Women Voters convention proceedings throughout the 1920s and 1930s have details about the Women's Joint Congressional Committee. An early article was Charles A. Selden, "The Most Powerful Lobby in Washington," *Ladies Home Journal*, April 1922, pp. 5, 93, 95–96; see also, Elizabeth Eastman, "The Front Door Lobby," *Woman's Journal*, February 1931, pp. 20–21, 40. An excellent summary discussion is Dorothy E. Johnson, "Organized Women as Lobbyists in the 1920s," *Capitol Studies*, Spring 1972, pp. 41–58.

15. *Report of the Third Conference on the Cause and Cure of War Held in Washington, D.C., January 15–19, 1928*, p. 224. The first eight conferences published proceedings in detail; beginning in 1934, as an economy measure, there were daily worksheets for the delegates printed during the conference. Hereafter the 1925–1933 publications will be referred to as *Report of the Conference on the Cause and Cure of War*, followed by the year.

16. Clayton R. Lusk, *New York (State) Legislature Joint Committee Investigating Seditious Activities* filed 24 April 1920. Lusk was the chair of the committee of six appointed in March 1919.

17. *Our Threatened Heritage* (Cambridge, Mass.: DAR Committee of Protest, 1928), p. 5.

18. Stanley Coben's insightful biography of A. Mitchell Palmer focuses on what Coben calls the arresting enigma of Palmer: "How can we reconcile the progressive reformer of pre-World War I years—the champion of the underprivileged—with the militant Attorney-General who violated civil liberties to an extent unprecedented in American history?"

    Palmer had been a friend of suffrage when on grounds of party loyalty he had urged ratification of the Nineteenth Amendment in appeals to legislatures in Delaware, Mississippi, Virginia and Maryland. He had also written to each of the Democratic legislators in New Jersey urging support (Harper, *Woman Suffrage*, 6: 257, 430).

19. Louis F. Post, *The Deportations Delirium of Nineteen-Twenty*, p. 92. Post was the

husband of Alice Thacher Post, pacifist editor of a Swedenborgian paper, who was on the first Executive Board of the Woman's Peace Party in 1915 and later active in the Women's International League for Peace and Freedom.

20. Catt to Schwimmer, 22 October 1921, Catt papers, LC. Pan-American conference: *Woman Patriot,* 1 May 1922; Catt, "Polluted Sources," *Woman Citizen,* 4 October 1924, p. 11. Collecting facts: Catt wrote to twenty-five college organizations on December 26, 1924, sending a questionnaire asking about their groups. In the Catt papers at the Library of Congress are replies from students in several colleges, including Barnard, Dartmouth, Harvard, Radcliffe, Rockford, Vassar, and Wellesley.

21. *Verbatim Report of Address made by Mrs. Carrie Chapman Catt before Ramsey County League of Women Voters and St. Paul Association, St. Paul, Minnesota, November 10, 1923,* pp. 9–10, Catt papers, SSC. Catt strongly suspected the publicist was J. C. Eichelberger who had been a force in the persistent campaign to discredit suffragists in the last years. "In a subtle but not in libelous manner the impression was given that they were socialists and free-lovers and dangerous. After Russia went into the hands of the Communists, suffragists immediately became Bolsheviki. The headquarters for this campaign was an anti-suffrage association whose general manager seemed to be one J. C. Eichelberger" (Catt, "Confidential memorandum," 18 August 1924, four typed pages, Catt papers, SSC).

22. The *Dearborn Independent* articles were published anonymously "By an American Citizen," but it was soon known that the author was Mrs. Haviland Lund, who highly praised herself in the second article. The worst things the women were accused of doing were promoting pacifist and welfare propaganda. The spider web chart appeared without the author's name in the Dearborn paper, although apparently it was signed when it was first circulated in 1923.

23. Leonard L. Cline, *New York World,* 8 June 1924. To illustrate his article, the top of the spider web chart was printed, and in this printing authorship was admitted: "Compiled by Lucia R. Maxwell, 1922–1923."

24. "Poison Propaganda," *Woman Citizen,* 31 May 1924, p. 14; Catt to Addams, 27 May 1924, Catt papers, LC.

25. "Conspiracy vs. Conspiracy," *Woman Citizen,* 20 November 1924, p. 13.

26. "Much Ado about Nothing," *Woman Citizen,* 30 May 1925, p. 30.

27. Johnson, "Organized Women as Lobbyists," p. 47; Affidavit of Mary W. Miller, Marshall, Michigan, p. 4, Bailie papers, SSC.

28. "An Open Letter to the D.A.R.," *Woman Citizen,* July 1927, p. 11; *Congressional Record,* 69th Congress, 1st session, p. 12947.

29. *The First Fifty,* League of Women Voters of Massachusetts, 1970, pp. 29–30; *Congressional Record,* 69th Congress, 1st session, p. 12951.

30. Catt to Florence Kelley, 11 June 1927, Catt papers, LC.

31. A copy of the pamphlet, dated August 1927, is with the Bailie papers, SSC.

Schwed had previously attacked Jane Addams at a convention of the Massachusetts DAR with such virulence that it "brought a gasp from the women present" (Norman Hapgood, Sidney Howard, and John Hearley, eds., *Professional Patriots* [New York: Albert and Charles Boni, 1927], p. 169. Catt reviewed this book for the *Woman Citzen*, July 1927, pp. 36–37).

32. Allen quotation: *New York Times*, 10 April 1928; Villard: *Fighting Years*, p. 247. Catt was so outraged by Villard's being listed she wrote asking if he didn't want to sue for defamation of character. "In order to understand how severely your character and standing have been attacked, you must read the pamphlet ['Our Common Enemy']." Villard replied, "I certainly do want to sue." However, he was later advised by his attorney there was nothing he could do on the basis of evidence submitted (Catt to Villard, 21 January 1928, Villard papers, Houghton Library, also Catt papers, LC; Villard to Catt, 23 January 1928, Villard papers, Houghton Library; Villard to Catt, 11 February 1928, Catt papers, LC).

33. *Literary Digest*, 21 April 1928, p. 9; White to Bailie, 15 May 1928, Bailie papers, SSC.

34. Roosevelt to Katherine Carter, 22 May 1939, Eleanor Roosevelt papers, FDR Library, Hyde Park, New York.

35. William Shirer, *Twentieth Century Journey* pp. 203–4; Hapgood et al., *Professional Patriots*, pp. 170–71.

CHAPTER 19. CAUSE AND CURE OF WAR   (pp. 198–210)

1. This was not the first cooperative venture of the nine sponsoring organizations; six of them had been among the original ten members of the Women's Joint Congressional Committee in 1920.

2. The meeting Catt referred to was probably the Women's Conference on National Defense as Peace Insurance, which opened a four-day convention on February 22, 1925. One hundred women representing sixteen national patriotic societies met to study the National Defense Act. There were other meetings in the next few months along the same lines, for example, the fourth annual convention of the American War Mothers, which declared for defense and preparedness. The keynote speaker, Captain George A. Darte, criticized the recent Cause and Cure conference because not a single constructive suggestion for preventing war was made, and he repeated the current accusation that many women's organizations were "unknowingly the instruments of the radical element." Rear Admiral Fiske made several speeches during these years blaming woman suffrage, with its "effeminization of the country," for the national lack of war preparedness (*New York Times*, 23 February 1925, p. 32; 24 February 1925, p. 18; 16 April 1925, p. 9; 17 April 1925, p. 20; 24 April 1925, p. 18; 27 April 1928, p. 29).

3. *Report of the Conference on the Cause and Cure of War, 1925*, pp. 29, 31.

4. Ibid., pp. 21–26. Senator Borah had introduced a resolution proposing the outlawry of war as early as 1923; it was a subject of wide debate in the following years.

5. Ibid., p. 31.

6. Ibid., p. 97. To Americans who knew Dulles only in his later years as Secretary of State in the 1950s this is a surprising call for governmental flexibility although it anticipated to some extent his 1939 book, *War, Peace and Change* (New York: Harper).

7. Grace Abbot was appointed as consultant in 1920 to the League of Nations Committee on the Traffic in Women and Children. Since 1902 the subject had been the focus of international conferences by men; it took eighteen years before women's voices were represented. The International Woman Suffrage Alliance, which had discussed and condemned the international traffic in women at its first congress, was instrumental in finally getting three women on the League of Nations Committee.

8. *Report of the Conference on the Cause and Cure of War, 1925*, pp. 211–12. One of the first influential articles on the subject was S. O. Levinson, "The Legal Status of War," *New Republic*, 9 March 1918, pp. 171–73. Wars were fought under the sanction of international law, hence "outlaw war and militarism is out of a job," he argued. The difficulties lay in enforcement. How could it be done? by moral suasion? by economic sanctions? by a court of international justice?

   Catt had first heard the phrase perhaps when it was used by Rachel Howland of New Bedford, Massachusetts in a series of resolutions Howland presented at a Council of Women meeting about 1900 (Anna Garlin Spencer, "The History of Woman's Work for Peace," *Pax Special*, April 1925, Peace papers, SSC.)

9. *Report of the Conference on the Cause and Cure of War, 1925*, pp. 32, 35, 358. The idea was not original with Catt but was the major point of a plan submitted in the Bok competition by David Starr Jordan in 1924. As late as 1945, two years before her death, Catt was urging that the United Nations consider a Department of Peace for each country.

10. Ibid., p. 151. Catt's comment on nations "have stolen everything they could stick a flag" was made in a letter to Linley V. Gordon, 15 October 1925, CRIA papers, Rare Book and Manuscript Library, Columbia University. She was preparing to talk in Detroit for the World Alliance for International Friendship through the Churches, and wondered if her idea might "be a little stiff for these timid times." Her criticism of the hotels for not accommodating blacks was made in a letter to the Arrangements Committee, 11 November 1924, Schain papers, SSC.

11. *Report of the Conference on the Cause and Cure of War 1925*, pp. 348–52. There were forty-two subclauses under the four divisions of the causes summary: (1) psychological causes were fear, suspicion, greed, lust of power, hate, revenge, jealousy, and envy; (2) economic causes included territorial aggression; rivalries for markets, energy resources, and essential raw materials; government protection

of private interests abroad without reference to the general welfare; disregard of the rights of undeveloped countries; population pressure; and profits in war; (3) political causes involved the principle of balance of power, secret treaties, unjust treaties, violation of treaties, disregard of minorities' rights, organization for war, ineffective or obstructive political machinery; (4) social and contributory causes included exaggerated nationalism, competitive armaments, religious and racial antagonisms, general apathy, ignorance, war psychology created through the press, motion pictures, textbooks and home influence, social inequalities, social sanctions of war, and lack of spiritual ideals.

12. Robert H. Ferrell, *Peace in Their Time*, p. 45. Coolidge, who was scornful of even his wife's education, could not by any stretch of the imagination be called a feminist. In his forty-seven-minute inaugural address on March 4, 1925, six weeks after his reception of the Committee on the Cause and Cure of War delegates, his single reference to women was in the last paragraph. "Here it [our country] will continue to stand, seeking peace and prosperity, solicitous for the welfare of the wage-earner, promoting enterprise, developing waterways and natural resources, *attentive to the intuitive counsel of womanhood,* encouraging education, desiring the advancement of religion, supporting the cause of justice and honor among the nations" (italics added). William Allen White, *Puritan in Babylon,* p. 315, quotes the paragraph and remarks that it was "Coolidge at his zenith." The statement about Grace Coolidge's education was made by her in *Good Housekeeping,* June 1935, p. 42.

13. *Delegates Worksheet No. 1,* CCCW 1935, p. 3; *National Bulletin,* February 1925, p. 12.

14. Mildred Olmsted, interview with author 23 March 1976; Rosika Schwimmer, "The Cause and Cure of Peace," *World Tomorrow,* 22 February 1933, pp. 181–82.

15. *New York Times,* 27 November 1926, p. 36.

16. Schwimmer, "Cause and Cure," p. 182; Mildred Adams, "For the Healing of the Nations," *Woman Citizen,* January 1927, p. 48.

17. Devere Allen, "Women on the Job of Peace," *Christian Leader,* 18 December 1926, p. 13; *Report of the Conference on the Cause and Cure of War, 1926,* pp. 19–24 (Zimmern), pp. 234–35 (Bliven), pp. 64–65 (Angell).

18. Allen, "Women on the Job," p. 15. Beals had been principal of the American High School in Mexico City and was the author of *Mexico—An Interpretation.* Beals added, "That 17 per cent represents the largest and most powerful companies, it represents companies with fraudulent titles to the lands; it represents the investment of men who have attempted to rob the American people of their birthright and who have corrupted the highest offices of the government." The official *Report* of the conference, edited by Catt, Schain, and other members of the Committee on the Cause and Cure of War, tempers the remarks somewhat, for example, changing "fraudulent titles" to "doubtful titles" (*Report of the Conference on the Cause and Cure of War, 1926,* pp. 196–97).

The specific cause of the tense situation south of the border was the continuation of the land redistribution policy of the revolution that began in 1910. It advocated the breakup of the huge haciendas and return to the nation of many of the subsoil rights granted to foreigners, mainly for oil exploration and extraction. After his election in 1924, President Calles accelerated the social and economic aims of the revolution. U. S. Secretary of State Frank B. Kellogg and President Coolidge wanted to assure fair recompense for American citizens.

There was sabre rattling on both sides; journals of the persuasion that war sells papers did their best to stir up the American public. Most people were confused about the situation, many thought the Mexican government had refused to reason. The perennial bogey of Bolshevism was raised with little basis, and the possibility of conflict with Mexico seemed real.

One of the scholars of the period who gave credit to CCCW was Merle Curti, *Peace or War*, pp. 290–91.

19. Catt, "Peace and Pacific Relations," *Woman Citizen*, September 1927, pp. 18–19; *Report of the Conference on the Cause and Cure of War, 1928*, pp. 40–41.

20. Catt, "The Status Today of War vs. Peace," *Report of the Conference on the Cause and Cure of War, 1928*, pp. 32–44.

21. The suggestion by Briand is credited to Professor James. T. Shotwell of Columbia University (Ferrell, *Peace in Their Time*, pp. 67–69). Shotwell was a regular speaker at CCCW conferences—he addressed eight of the fifteen conferences.

    Catt, "A Proposal from France," *Woman Citizen*, June 1927, p. 28; Catt to the delegates of the Second Conference on the Cause and Cure of War, 29 April 1927, Anne Martin Papers, Bancroft Library, University of California, Berkeley. Catt was careful to point out that the delegates had to act as individuals, the Committee on the Cause and Cure of War had no authority to ask its cooperating organizations to take action, and the presidents of the organizations had themselves little authority for new action that had not been endorsed by their conventions.

22. *New York Times*, 8 April 1928, p. 18; Catt, "The National Committee on the Cause and Cure of War Proposes a Campaign. Its Slogan Is Build Friendships, Not Warships, for National Defense,'" *Woman's Journal*, May 1928, p. 28. (In January 1928, the *Woman Citizen* changed its name back to the original *Woman's Journal* and published under that name until it ceased publication with the June 1931 issue.) There were several non-affiliated organizations that helped the CCCW publicize the drive for resolutions. The National Council for the Prevention of War was one; see, for example, *News Bulletin*, 1 June 1928, p. 4.

23. Catt, "The Outlawry of War," *Annals of the American Academy of Political and Social Science*, July 1928, pp. 1–7. This was a speech at the American Academy of Political and Social Science annual meeting on May 12, 1928. See also, *New York Times*, 13 May 1928, p. 6, and 14 May 1928, p. 8.

24. "Our Foreign Policy," *Foreign Affairs*, July 1928, p. 585.

25. White, *Puritan in Babylon*, p. 410. The pact was variously referred to as the Briand-Kellogg Treaty, the Kellogg-Briand Treaty, the Kellogg Treaty, the Briand Treaty, the General Treaty for the Renunciation of War, the Anti-War Treaty, and the Multilateral Peace Treaty, as well as the Pact of Paris. *The Woman's Journal*, October 1928, p. 20, has a report from Mary M. Morrisson of Chicago, former first vice-president of the National League of Women Voters, who was one of the twenty-odd women who were included in the United States' group to witness the signing.

26. On December 28, 1928, Catt and CCCW Secretary Josephine Schain sent Senator Borah, chair of the Senate Committee, a staggering list of particulars accomplished by their campaign, including the fact that 10,057 resolutions had been adopted. "The mere list of these resolutions weighs 1 pound and 9 ounces and the resolutions themselves, if placed end to end, would measure nearly 2 miles." The letter was printed in the *Congressional Record*, 3 January 1929, p. 1022, followed by petitions filed by senators from twelve states in support of the pact.

    Nearly four closely printed columns of the *Congressional Record* were devoted to reporting some of the petitions before the vice-president, apparently overwhelmed by the numbers with no end in sight, announced that senators could file the petitions later. Vandenberg presented petitions of 70,000 citizens and 896 organizations from Michigan; Dale offered 440 resolutions adopted by civic, fraternal, and religious organizations in Vermont; Frazier had 20 from North Dakota; Shipstead "numerous resolutions" from Minnesota; Idaho, Maryland, Texas, Delaware, Colorado, West Virginia, Wisconsin, Missouri, Connecticut, Arkansas, Ohio, Montana, North Carolina, Tennessee, and Virginia were all recorded that morning with more to come later (*Congressional Record,*) 15 January 1929, pp. 1709–10).

27. Ferrell, *Peace in Their Time*, p. 232.

28. Peck manuscript, pp. 627–28, Catt papers, LC. Hay had never liked living at Juniper Ledge—it was too far from the city, she wasn't the gardener Catt was and had little interest in the land. Catt sold Juniper Ledge in the fall of 1927 but the new owner did not take possession until May. In March 1928 Catt bought the house at 120 Paine Avenue, New Rochelle, which was her home for the rest of her life.

29. Hyde to Peck, 30 November 1929, NAWSA papers, LC.

30. Ibid., 25 January 1929. The "international conversation" referred to was the featured event on the evening of January 15. It was a discussion of the Paris Pact using the format of six speakers, each presenting the opinions of an assigned country, after which "Mr. and Mrs. International Public Opinion" (Raymond T. Rich and Catt) asked questions. After considerable persuasion those who agreed to participate were: Great Britain, Arthur Bullard; France, James T. Shotwell;

Germany, Reinhold Niebuhr; Italy, James G. McDonald; Japan, Sidney L. Gulick; United States, Bruce Bliven.

31. *Report of the Conference on the Cause and Cure of War, 1929*, pp. 190, 198–99.
32. Catt, "The Story of the World Court," *Woman's Journal*, August 1929, p. 13.

CHAPTER 20. THE SHADOWS DARKEN (pp. 211–219)

1. *Woman's Journal*, February 1930, p. 19.
2. *Report of the Conference on the Cause and Cure of War, 1930*, p. 189. Catt's major speech at the conference, "Gaps in the Machinery of Peace," *Report, 1930*, pp. 89–96, was printed as a separate pamphlet and widely circulated. A slightly different version under the same title was published in the *Christian Advocate*, 6 November 1930, pp. 1211–14; "The End of War—2000 A.D.," *Woman's Journal*, March 1930, pp. 20–21, 34, was a close reproduction of the speech. Ruth Morgan in *International Women's News*, March 1930, p. 81, wrote, "Mrs. Catt realized its immense difficulty, but was, nevertheless, persuaded that in this century the cause of war having been discovered, its cure would be accomplished."
3. Report of the Conference on the Cause and Cure of War, 1930, pp. 24–25; *New York Times*, 17 January 1930, p. 9; *New York Herald Tribune*, 24 January 1930, p. 6; letter from Josephine Schain to Ruth Woodsmall, 28 November 1932, Schain papers, SSC. A pamphlet, "Women and Disarmament. The Deputation of American, British, French and Japanese Women received by the Chairman of the London Naval Conference at St. James's Palace on February 6th, 1930," was published by the Women's Peace Crusade, the organization under which the drive for signatures was conducted in England. It has many details including lists of associations involved, names of the delegation, and a summary (Peace papers, SSC).
4. Catt, "London—and Tomorrow," *Woman's Journal*, March 1930, p. 24.
5. *Report of the Conference on the Cause and Cure of War, 1931*, pp. 26–27.
6. Ibid., pp. 40, 206.
7. Ibid., pp. 203–6. The month before the conference she had resigned from the National World Court Committee because she was disappointed in the calibre of the work done (Catt to James McDonald and Everett Colby, 31 December 1930, Schain papers, SSC).
8. *Report of the Conference on the Cause and Cure of War, 1932*, pp. 15–24. Caroline Slade, who had been in Mukden on September 18, 1931, gave an eyewitness account of the Japanese coup (Ibid., pp. 135–38).
9. Ibid., pp. 42–46.
10. Ibid., pp. 258–59. Her last speech as chair was titled, "How Long, O Lord, How

Long?" wherein she did try to inject some optimism: "Why after fifty thousand years of war did anyone expect a wholly new method be adopted in fourteen years?" She warned about "red herrings" drawn across their path toward peace to led them into false trails and drew on suffrage memories to illustrate what she meant. Invariably before a suffrage speech she was instructed, "We want you to tell the audience that when women get the vote, they will not divorce their husbands, neglect their children, or fail to mend the family stockings." It was never possible to talk much about what seemed the higher possibilities of the enfranchisement of women.

11. Catt to Gertrude Baumer, editor of *Die Frau*, 4 August 1931, Catt papers, NYPL; *Official Record of the Declarations and Petitions presented by the Disarmament Committee of the Women's International Organisations to the Disarmament Conference, Geneva, February 6, 1932* (Geneva: Tribune de Geneve, 1932), Tuttle papers, SSC, is the complete report. It includes the text of the four authorized petitions and a detailed analysis of the number of signatures from each country, which ranged from 5 from Madagascar to 2,146,062 from Great Britain.

Mary E. Woolley was the first woman appointed an official member of the U. S. delegation to these meetings. Jeannette Marks, *Life and Letters of Mary Emma Woolley*, prints many of Woolley's letters from the conference, pp. 139–53, and details the ceremony of petition presentation, pp. 136–38. See also, Anna Mary Wells, *Miss Marks and Miss Woolley*, pp. 213–22.

12. Catt, "An Extraordinary Session of the Eighth Annual Conference on the Cause and Cure of War, Interlude, Mars Takes a Sabbatical," Catt papers, NYPL. It was printed and distributed to the Cause and Cure organizations. She poked sly fun at the skit's heroines about whom she was ambivalent; they were women of achievement, yet much of their fame had come from war. In her play each woman declared for one of the member organizations of the CCCW: Semiramis joined the YWCA; Hatshepsut the League of Women Voters; Deborah, who had held a World Court in 1296 B.C., opted for the Council of Jewish Women; Zenobia thought she would like the American Association of University Women; Boadicea, the General Federation of Women's Clubs; Jingo, an unsung Japanese queen of 200 A.D. who conquered Korea, was unplaced; but Maria Theresa, who said she never enjoyed one happy second when she had wealth and power, preferred the Women's Trade Union League because the noblest service in the world is work; Rani of Jhansi, who had found riding elephants to war much too hot and unpleasant decided on the Business and Professional Women's Association; and Catherine the Great, acknowledging she got drunk whenever there was a nasty job to do, chose the WCTU.

Catt's health: There is no indication what her specific ailment was; she had pernicious anemia for several years before her death in 1947, suffered at least one heart attack (in 1929), and experienced increasing difficulty walking. Since she had recovered from a broken leg and ankle in 1931 she generally used a cane when she was away from her own home.

13. There are several letters during this time to and from Catt and Manus in the Catt papers, LC; see also Catt to Schwimmer, 26 July 1933, Catt papers, LC. Rosa Manus's sister, Anna, and her husband, Dr. Felix Jacobi, left Germany and lived in New York where Catt saw them frequently in the 1930s. She often mentioned them in letters to Manus. In 1934 Manus was decorated by Queen Wilhelmina for her devoted work as chair of the Holland Committee for Refugees fleeing from Germany.

14. Petition and covering letter dated June 1933, from Catt to Dear Friend of Human Justice, Catt papers, LC. The text of the petition was subsequently printed in journals and newspapers, including the *New York Times*, 14 August 1933, p. 5; *American Hebrew and Jewish Tribune*, 18 August 1933, p. 203.

15. *American Hebrew and Jewish Tribune*, 17 November 1933, p. 3; *New York Times*, 24 November 1933, p. 23.

16. The women of the Committee of Ten were, besides Catt, Mary Dreier, Elizabeth Eastman, Mrs. Kendall Emerson, Mrs. John H. Finley, Mrs. Alexander Kohut, Mrs. James Lees Laidlaw, Mrs. Jacob A. Riis, Mrs. Charles Cary Rumsey, and Mrs. F. Louis Slade. The appeal was endorsed by many more, including Jane Addams, Margaret Culkin Banning, Ella A. Boole, Dorothy Canfield Fisher, Zona Gale, Ellen Glasgow, Isabel Bacon LaFollette, Belle Sherwin, and Lillian D. Wald. The pamphlet, sent to Roosevelt in March, was titled, *Asylum for Refugees under Our Immigration Laws*, a copy is with the Catt papers, LC; see also *New York Times* 19 March 1934, p. 11.

17. *Why Wars Must Cease* (New York: Macmillan, 1935).

18. Peck, *Carrie Chapman Catt*, p. 451.

19. Catt to Eleanor Roosevelt, 16 February 1935, Eleanor Roosevelt papers, FDR Library, Hyde Park, New York.

20. Catt to Mabel Vernon, 29 August 1935, Martin papers, Bancroft Library, University of California, Berkeley. Mabel Vernon was National Campaign Director of the Women's International League for Peace and Freedom (WILPF or WIL). The People's Mandate Committee was an offshoot of a League of Nations Union campaign in 1934 in which the British WIL had been very active. A "Peace Ballot" had been circulated in many countries, but it was unsatisfactory as it sought answers to five loaded questions. However, it gave an American member, Lola Maverick Lloyd, the idea for "a People's Mandate to Governments." The plan was adopted by the Internationl Executive of the WIL in April 1935, and recommended to national sections as their major work for the year. The campaign extended to twenty-five countries. For details see Margaret Tims, "United for Peace," *The WILPF, 1915–1965* (London: George Allen & Unwin, 1965), pp. 144–48; Marks, *Life of Mary E. Wooley*, pp. 157–58; a letter from Katherine Devereux Blake to Mary E. Woolley, 9 October 1936, tells of her unsuccessful

efforts to get Alexandra Kollontai to take up the mandate with Russia, and also her failure to get petition circulation in China (Marks papers, Wellesley College Library, Special Collections).

21. For maximum publicity, the mandate was presented in two stages, on September 26, 1936 to the League of Nations in Geneva, and in March 1937 to Dr. Lamas, President of the Assembly, in Argentina.

This was only one of the dozens of efforts being made throughout the world. In 1936 there were over three hundred peace organizations in the United States alone according to Mary Ida Winder, *Organizations in the United States that Promote International Understanding and World Peace*, (Washington, D. C.: National Council for Prevention of War, 1 April 1936).

NCCCW reprinted a descriptive article that provides an excellent summary of the various methods different organizations were promoting by Elton Atwater, *Organized Efforts in the United States toward Peace* (Washington, D.C.: Digest Press, American University Graduate School, 1936).

22. The letter from President Roosevelt reads:

> My dear Mrs. Catt, Our old friendship dating back to the days when I was a very young State Senator in 1911, would be sufficient reason for me to write you on your completion of half a century of public service. But there is a greater reason—because the whole country applauds you and your very great contributions to our well-being.
>
> The many years of devoted work which you gave to the cause of woman's suffrage have long since been justly rewarded, not only by the passage of the Nineteenth Amendment to the Constitution in our own country, but also by marked improvement in the status of women throughout the world.
>
> Those of us who are directly concerned with the maintenance and encouragement of peace between nations are also grateful to you for the splendid leadership you give to the cause of peace and the furtherance of the prevention of war.
>
> May you continue for many years to come as the strong and active captain in these noble objectives of a better civilization (FDR Library, Hyde Park, New York).

Many honors came to Catt in the last decades of her life. In addition to Ripon College she also received honorary degrees from Iowa State College (1920), the University of Wyoming (1921), Smith College (1925), and Moravian College (1940). She was on dozens of "greatest American women" lists and received gold medals from the New York City Federation of Women's Clubs, the National Institute of Social Sciences, Chi Omega, and the American Woman's Association. For her work with refugees she was awarded the American Hebrew Medal and the Order of the White Rose was conferred by the government of Finland. A 1930 award from the *Pictorial Review* magazine as the outstanding woman of the year brought the then considerable sum of $5,000; with the money she made donations to several peace societies and sent a hundred dollars each to eleven suffragist friends whose incomes had dwindled with the depression.

23. Catt to Schain, 25 August 1936, Schain papers, SSC.

24. *Delegates Worksheet No. 3*, CCCW 1937, pp. 10–11.
25. *Delegates Worksheet No. 3*, CCCW 1938, p. 2.
26. Beth Campbell, "Mrs. Catt Still Can Win Audience," *Washington Post*, undated clipping, probably 21 January 1938, Catt papers, LC.
27. *Delegates Worksheet No. 3*, CCCW 1940, pp. 4–5.
28. Catt to Jennie Bradley Roessing, 4 June 1941, Roessing papers, Archives of Industrial Society, University of Pittsburg Libraries; Catt to Vera Beggs, 26 February 1941, Beggs papers, SSC.
29. Catt, "To the Representatives of the United States at the San Francisco Conference," draft sent to Gertrude Brown, 13 April 1945, Catt papers, SSC.
30. Catt to Cordell Hull, undated (ca. 20 February 1945), File 740.00116/1939/787, National Archives, Washington, D. C. Attached are resolutions passed by the Liaison Committee of Women's International Organizations protesting war crimes being committed. Also is a seven-page pamphlet, "The Ghetto Speaks," 1 January 1943. This report published in New York by the Polish government in exile was the first authentic account in English of the events in Warsaw in July and August 1942. Its shocking details are accurate as confirmed by postwar accounts.

    Until after the war, Catt knew only that Rosa Manus had been taken from her home by the gestapo in August 1941. Her family had last heard from her from Berlin where she was imprisoned. It was presumed she died there (Catt to Friends of Rosa Manus, 10 July 1942, Catt papers, SSC). In February 1946, the *International Women's News* reported hearing from a woman who was imprisoned with Manus in Scheveningen and then in the concentration camp of Ravenbruck, from which in March 1942 Manus was transferred to Auschwitz. That was the last her friend saw of her; it is not known if she survived the trip or died en route.
31. Catt, "How Far Have We Come in Suffrage," *Union Signal*, 5 May 1945, p. 268.

    The Catt papers at the Library of Congress include many condolence letters and resolutions from dozens of organizations with which she had been associated or had befriended. The public felt as President Truman did that "an era in our national life comes to a close." Her obituary was carried nationwide by the major papers; it was front pages news in the *New York Herald Tribune*. Many journals printed editorials and articles about her, including the *New York Times* and the Raleigh, North Carolina *News & Observer*, whose tribute was written by Josephus Daniels: "She died before her dream [of peace] came true, but she builded on a strong foundation, and died in the faith that the vision splendid would bless mankind."

Bibliography

Sources consulted are listed in this order: books, general-interest articles, articles by Carrie Chapman Catt, pamphlets, reports and proceedings, and newspapers and other periodicals. The listing of articles in both categories is highly selective. No effort has been made to list the countless articles and speeches that appeared in the major suffrage journals of the day, such as Woman's Journal, Woman Citizen, *and* Jus Suffragii.

BOOKS

Adams, Mildred. *The Right to Be People.* Philadelphia: J. B. Lippincott, 1967.

Addams, Jane. *Peace and Bread in Time of War.* New York: Macmillan, 1922. 2nd ed. New York: King's Crown Press, 1945.

Anthony, Susan B., and Harper, Ida H., eds. *History of Woman Suffrage.* 4 vols. Rochester, N.Y.: Susan B. Anthony, 1902.

Ashe, Geoffrey. *Gandhi.* New York: Stein and Day, 1968.

Blatch, Harriot Stanton, and Lutz, Alma. *Challenging Years.* New York: G. P. Putman's Sons, 1940.

Boeckel, Florence Brewer. *The Turn toward Peace.* New York: Friendship Press, 1930.

Breckinridge, Sophonisba P. *Women in the Twentieth Century: A Study of Their Political, Social, and Economic Activities.* New York: McGraw-Hill, 1933.

Brown, Gertrude. *On Account of Sex.* Typescript. SSC.

Brown, Mrs. Raymond [Gertrude Brown]. *Your Vote and How to Use It.* Foreword by Mrs. Carrie Chapman Catt. New York: Harper & Brothers, 1918.

Brown, Olympia. *Acquaintances, Old and New, among Reformers.* N.p., 1911.
————, ed. *Democratic Ideals: A Memorial Sketch of Clara B. Colby.* New York: Federal Suffrage Association, 1917.

Burnett, Constance Buel. "Carrie Chapman Catt." In *Five for Freedom.* New York: Abelard Press, 1953.

Bushman, Claudia L., ed. *Mormon Sisters: Women in Early Utah.* Cambridge, Mass.: Emmeline Press, 1976.

Bussey, Gertrude, and Tims, Margaret. *The Women's International League for*

Peace and Freedom, 1915–1916: A Record of Fifty Years Work. London: George Allen & Unwin, 1965.

Calkin, Homer L. *Women in the Department of State.* Washington, D.C.: Department of State, 1978.

Calkins, Gladys G. *Follow These Women.* New York: National Council of Churches of Christ U.S.A., 1961.

Catt, Carrie Chapman. *The Ballot and the Bullet.* Philadelphia: Alfred J. Ferris, 1897.

————. "Evolution of Women"s Careers" and "I Speak for American Women." In *Woman's Centennial Congress.* New York: Mail & Express, 1940.

————. Foreword to *Once upon a Time and Today,* by Maud Nathan. New York: G. P. Putnam's Sons, 1933.

————. Foreword to *The Subjection of Women,* by John Mill. New York: Frederick A. Stockes, 1911.

————. Foreword to *Woman Suffrage in Practice, 1913,* by Chrystal Macmillan, Marie Stritt, and Maria Verone. London: National Union of Women's Suffrage Societies, 1913.

————. Foreword to *Women's Suffrage in Many Lands,* by Alice Zimmern. London: Francis & Co., Athenaeum Press, 1909.

————. Foreword and "Wyoming: The First Surrender." In *Victory How Women Won It: A Centennial Symposium, 1840–1940.* National American Woman Suffrage Association. New York: H.W. Wilson, 1940.

————. "Foreward or Backward?" In *Changing Standards.* New York: New York Herald Tribune, 1934.

————. Introduction: "Passing the Federal Suffrage Amendment" to *The Woman Citizen,* by Mary Sumner Boyd. New York: Frederick A. Stokes, 1918.

————. Introduction: "The Vote and the Voter" to *The Woman Voter's Manual,* by S. E. Forman and Marjorie Shuler. New York: Century, 1918.

————. *Mars Takes a Sabbatical.* Play presented at the Eighth Annual Conference on the Cause and Cure of War, 1933. New York, 1933.

————. "Only Yesterday." In *Our Common Cause Civilization: Report of the International Congress of Women, July 16–22, 1933, Chicago.* New York: National Council of Women of the United States, 1933.

————. *The Woman's Century Calendar.* New York: NAWSA, 1899.

————. *A World Review of Woman Suffrage.* Part 1. The Woman Citizen's Library, edited by Shailer Mathews. Chicago: Civics Society, 1913.

————; Boyd, Mary Sumner; and Rogers, Henry Wade. *Woman Suffrage by Federal Constitutional Amendment.* New York: National Woman Suffrage Publishing, 1917.

————; Roosevelt, Eleanor; Woolley, Mary E.; Addams, Jane; Meloney, Mrs.

William Brown; Boeckel, Florence Brewer; Blair, Emily Newell; Allen,
Florence E.; Hamilton, Dr. Alice; and Fisher, Dorothy Canfield. *Why Wars
Must Cease*. New York: Macmillan, 1935.
————, and Shuler, Nettie Rogers. *Woman Suffrage and Politics: The Inner
Story of the Suffrage Movement*. New York: Scribner's, 1923.
Chafe, William H. *The American Woman: Her Changing Social, Economic, and
Political Roles, 1920–1970*. New York: Oxford University Press, 1972.
Chafee, Zechariah, Jr. *Free Speech in the United States*. Cambridge: Harvard
University Press, 1941.
Chugerman, Samuel. *Lester F. Ward: The American Aristotle*. Durham: Duke
University Press, 1939.
Clements, Barbara Evans. *Bolshevik Feminist: The Life of Aleksandra Kollantai*.
Bloomington: Indiana University Press, 1979.
Clevenger, Ima Fuchs. "Invention and Arrangement in the Public Address of
Carrie Chapman Catt." Ph.D. dissertation, University of Oklahoma,
1955.
Coben, Stanley. *A. Mitchell Palmer: Politician*. New York: Columbia Univer-
sity Press, 1963.
Cole, Wayne S. *Senator Gerald P. Nye and American Foreign Relations*. Min-
neapolis: University of Minnesota Press, 1962.
Cook, Blanche Wiesen, ed. *Crystal Eastman on Women and Revolution*. New
York: Oxford University Press, 1978.
Cooney, Robert, and Michalowski, Helen, eds. *The Power of the People: Active
Nonviolence in the United States*. Culver City, Calif.: Peace Press, 1977.
Creel, George. *How We Advertised America*. New York: Harper & Brothers,
1920.
————. *Rebel at Large*. New York: G. P. Putnam's Sons, 1947.
Curti, Merle. *Peace or War: The American Struggle, 1636–1936*. New York: W.
W. Norton, 1936.
————. *The Growth of American Thought*. New York: Harper & Brothers,
1943.
Daniels, George, ed. *Darwinism Comes to America*. Waltham, Mass.: Blaisdell
Publishing Co., 1968.
Daniels, Josephus. *The Wilson Era: Years of Peace, 1910–1917*. Chapel Hill:
University of North Carolina Press, 1944.
Degen, Marie Louise. *The History of the Woman's Peace Party*. Baltimore: Johns
Hopkins Press, 1939.
de Iongh, Jane. "Letters from Dr. Anna Howard Shaw to Dr. Aletta Jacobs."
In *Yearbook International Archives for the Women's Movement*. Vol. 2.
Leiden: E. J. Brill, 1938.
de Palencia, Isabel. *I Must Have Liberty*. New York: Longmans, Green, 1940.

Dewey, John. Introduction to *Peace and Bread in Time of War*, by Jane Addams. New York: King's Crown Press, 1945.

Dixson, Miriam. *The Real Matilda: Woman and Identity in Australia, 1788 to 1975*. Victoria: Penguin Books Australia, 1976.

Dorr, Rheta Childe. *Susan B. Anthony: The Woman Who Changed the Mind of a Nation*. New York: Frederick A. Stokes, 1928.

Dreier, Mary E. *Margaret Dreier Robins*. New York: Island Press Cooperative, 1950.

Duniway, Abigail Scott. *Path Breaking: An Autobiographical History of the Equal Suffrage Movement in Pacific Coast States*. Portland, Oreg.: James, Kerns & Abbott, 1914.

Earhart, Mary [Dillon]. *Frances Willard: From Prayers to Politics*. Chicago: University of Chicago Press, 1944.

Egan, Maurice. *Ten Years near the German Frontier*. New York: George H. Doran, 1919.

Evans, Richard J. *The Feminist Movement in Germany, 1894–1933*. London: Sage, 1976.

Fawcett, Millicent Garrett. *What I Remember*. London: T. Fisher Unwin, 1924.

Ferrell, Robert H. *Peace in Their Time*. New Haven: Yale University Press, 1952.

Flexner, Eleanor. *Century of Struggle: The Woman's Rights Movement in the United States*. Cambridge: Belknap Press of Harvard University Press, 1959.

Forman, S. E., and Shuler, Marjorie. *The Woman Voter's Manual*. New York: Century, 1918.

Fuller, Paul E. *Laura Clay and the Woman's Rights Movement*. Lexington: University Press of Kentucky, 1975.

Gage, Matilda Joslyn. *Women, Church, and State: A Historical Account of the Status of Woman through the Christian Ages; With Reminiscences of the Matriarchate*. New York: Truth Seekers, 1893.

Gallaher, Ruth A. *Legal and Political Status of Women in Iowa: An Historical Account of the Rights of Women in Iowa from 1838 to 1918*. Iowa City: State Historical Society of Iowa, 1918.

Garland, Hamlin. *A Spoil of Office*. Boston: Arena Press, 1892.

Gilman, Charlotte Perkins. *The Living of Charlotte Perkins Gilman*. New York: Harper & Row, 1935.

———. *Women and Economics: A Study of the Economic Relation between Men and Women as a Factor in Social Evolution*. Boston: Small, Maynard, 1898.

Goodwyn, Lawrence. *The Populist Moment: A Short History of the Agrarian Revolt in America*. New York: Oxford University Press, 1978.

Graber, Kay, ed. *Sister to the Sioux: The Memoirs of Elaine Goodale Eastman, 1885–1891.* Lincoln: University of Nebraska Press, 1978.

Grant, Madison. *The Passing of the Great Race.* New York: Scribners, 1916.

Gray, Madeline. *Margaret Sanger.* New York: Richard Marek, 1979.

Grimshaw, Patricia. *Women's Suffrage in New Zealand.* Auckland: Auckland University Press, 1972.

Gripenberg, Alexandra. *A Half Year in thè New World: Miscellaneous Sketches of Travel in the United States (1888).* Translated and edited by Ernest J. Moyne. Newark: University of Delaware Press, 1954.

Hapgood, Norman; Howard, Sidney; and Hearley, John. *Professional Patriots.* New York: Albert and Charles Boni, 1927.

Harper, Ida Husted. *The Life and Work of Susan B. Anthony.* 3 vols. Indianapolis: Hollenbeck Press, 1898, 1908.

————, ed. *History of Woman Suffrage.* 2 vols. New York: NAWSA, 1922.

Harriman, Mrs. J. Borden. *From Pinafores to Politics.* New York: Henry Holt, 1923.

Higham, John. *Strangers in the Land: Patterns of American Nativism, 1860–1925.* New Brunswick: Rutgers University Press, 1955.

Huxley, Julian. *Essays of a Humanist.* New York: Harper & Row, 1964.

Huxley, Thomas Henry. *Darwiniana.* New York: Appleton, 1898.

International Council on Women. *Women in a Changing World: The Dynamic Story of the International Council of Women since 1888.* London: Routledge & Kegan Paul, 1966.

————. *Women's Position in the Laws of the Nations.* Karlsruhe i.B.: G. Braunsche Hofbuchdruckerei und Verlag, 1912.

Irwin, Inez Haynes. *Angels and Amazons: A Hundred Years of American Women.* Garden City, N.Y.: Doubleday, Doran, 1934.

————. *The Story of the Woman's Party.* New York: Harcourt, Brace, 1921.

Ishimoto, Baroness Shidzue. *Facing Two Ways.* New York: Farrar & Rinehart, 1935.

James, Edward T., ed. *Notable American Women.* 3 vols. Cambridge: Belknap Press of Harvard University Press, 1971.

Kaplan, Justin. *Lincoln Steffens.* New York: Simon & Schuster, 1974.

Knightley, Phillip. *The First Casualty.* New York: Harcourt Brace Jovanovich, 1975.

Kraditor, Aileen S. *The Ideas of the Woman Suffrage Movement, 1890–1920.* New York: Columbia University Press, 1965.

Krupskaya, Nadezhda K. Preface to *The Emancipation of Women,* from the writings of V. I. Lenin. New York: International Publishers, 1966.

Lash, Joseph P. *Eleanor and Franklin.* New York: W. W. Norton, 1971.

Lemons, J. Stanley. *The Woman Citizen: Social Feminism in the 1920s.* Urbana: University of Illinois Press, 1973.

Lessing, Doris. Introduction to *The Story of an African Farm*, by Olive Schreiner. New York: Schocken, 1976.

Luxemburg, Rosa. *Rosa Luxemburg Speaks*. Eited with an introduction by Mary-Alice Waters. New York: Pathfinder Press, 1970.

————. *Selected Political Writings*. Edited and with an introduction by Dick Howard. New York: Monthly Review Press, 1971.

————. *Theory and Practice*. Translated by David Wolff. Detroit: News & Letters, 1980.

Macmillan, Chrystal; Stritt, Marie; and Verone, Maria. *Woman Suffrage in Practice, 1913*. Foreword by Carrie Chapman Catt. London: National Union of Women's Suffrage Societies, 1913.

Marchand, C. Roland. *The American Peace Movement and Social Reform, 1898–1918*. Princeton: Princeton University Press, 1972.

Marks, Jeannette. *Life and Letters of Mary Emma Woolley*. Washington, D.C.: Public Affairs Press, 1955.

Martin, George. *Madam Secretary Frances Perkins*. Boston: Houghton Mifflin, 1976.

McKenna, Marian C. *Borah*. Ann Arbor: University of Michigan Press, 1961.

Mill, John Stuart. *The Subjection of Women*. Foreword by Carrie Chapman Catt. New York: Frederick A. Stokes, 1911.

Montefiore, Dora. *From a Victorian to a Modern*. London: E. Archer, 1927.

Morrison, Joseph L. *Josephus Daniels*. Chapel Hill: University of North Carolina Press, 1966.

Murray, Robert K. *Red Scare: A Study in National Hysteria, 1919–1920*. Minneapolis: University of Minnesota Press, 1955.

Nathan, Maud. *Once upon a Time and Today*. Foreword by Carrie Chapman Catt. New York: G. P. Putnam's Sons, 1933.

National American Woman Suffrage Association. *Victory How Women Won It: A Centennial Symposium, 1840–1940*. New York: H. W. Wilson, 1940.

National Council of Women. *Our Common Cause—Civilization*. New York: National Council of Women of the United States, 1933.

Nitti, Francesco. *The Decadence of Europe*. New York: Henry Holt, 1923.

Noun, Louise R. *Strong-Minded Women: The Emergence of the Woman-Suffrage Movement in Iowa*. Ames: Iowa State University Press, 1969.

O'Neill, William L. *Everyone Was Brave: The Rise and Fall of Feminism in America*. Chicago: Quadrangle Books, 1967.

Pakenham, Thomas. *The Boer War*. London: Weidenfeld & Nicolson, 1979.

Pankhurst, Emmeline [and Dorr, Rheta Childe]. *My Own Story*. New York: Hearst's International Library, 1914.

Pankhurst, E. Sylvia. *The Suffragette Movement: An Intimate Account of Persons and Ideals*. London: Longmans, Green, 1931.

Park, Maud Wood. *Front Door Lobby.* Edited by Edna Lamprey Stantial. Boston: Beacon Press, 1960.

Peck, Mary Gray. *Carrie Chapman Catt: A Biography.* New York: H. W. Wilson, 1944.

Pethick-Lawrence, Emmeline. *My Part in a Changing World.* London: Victor Gollancz, 1938.

Pethick-Lawrence, F. W. *Fate Has Been Kind.* London: Hutchinson, [1942].

Post, Louis F. *The Deportations Delirium of Nineteen-Twenty.* Chicago: Charles H. Kerr, 1923.

Raeburn, Antonia. *The Militant Suffragettes.* London: Michael Joseph, 1973.

Reed, Dorinda Riessen. *The Woman Suffrage Movement in South Dakota.* Vermillion: State University of South Dakota, 1958.

Richardson, Mary R. *Laugh a Defiance.* London: George Weidenfeld & Nicolson, 1953.

Richmond, Rebecca. *A Woman of Texas: Mrs. Percy V. Pennybacker.* San Antonio: Naylor, 1941.

Robins, Elizabeth. *The Convert.* New York: Macmillan, 1907. Reprint. Introduction by Jane Marcus. Old Westbury, N.Y.: The Feminist Press, 1980.

Roosevelt, Eleanor. *The Autobiography of Eleanor Roosevelt.* New York: Harper & Row, Barnes & Noble Books, 1978.

Ross, Ishbel. *Power with Grace: The Life Story of Mrs. Woodrow Wilson.* New York: G. P. Putnam's Sons, 1975.

Rover, Constance. *Women's Suffrage and Party Politics in Britain, 1866–1914.* London: Routledge & Kegan Paul, 1967.

Schirmacher, Dr. Kathe. *The Modern Women's Rights Movement: A Historical Survey.* Translated by Carl Conrad Eckhardt. New York: Macmillan, 1912.

Schreiber, Adele, and Mathieson, Margaret. *Journey towards Freedom.* Copenhagen: International Alliance of Women, 1955.

Sewall, May Wright, ed. *Genesis of the International Council of Women and the Story of Its Growth, 1888–1893.* Indianapolis, 1914.

———. *National Council of Women of the United States, Report of Its Tenth Annual Executive and Its Third Triennial Sessions.* Indianapolis: Hollenbeck Press, 1898.

———, ed. *The World Congress of Representative Women.* Chicago: Rand, McNally, 1894.

———. *Women, World War, and Permanent Peace.* San Francisco: John J. Newbegin, 1915.

Shirer, William. *Twentieth Century Journey.* New York: Simon & Schuster, 1976.

Sicherman, Barbara, and Green, Carol Hurd. *Notable American Women: The Modern Period.* Cambridge: Belknap Press of Harvard University Press, 1980.

Squire, Belle. *The Woman Movement in America.* Chicago: A. C. McClurg, 1911.

Stanton, Elizabeth Cady. *Eighty Years and More.* New York: T. Fisher Unwin, 1898.

———; Anthony, Susan B.; and Gage, Matilda Joslyn, eds. *History of Woman Suffrage.* 6 vols. New York: Fowler & Wells, 1881–Vol. 1, 1881–Vol. 2, 1882–Vol. 3, 1899–Vol. 4, edited by Susan B. Anthony and Ida Husted Harper. Rochester, N.Y.: Susan B. Anthony, 1902. Vols. 5 and 6, edited by Ida Husted Harper. New York: NAWSA, 1922.

———, and the Revising Committee. *The Woman's Bible.* 2 parts. New York: European Publishing, 1895 (Part 1), 1898 (Part 2).

Stern, Madeleine B. *We the Women.* New York: Schulte Publishing, 1963.

Stevens, Doris. *Jailed for Freedom.* 1920. Reprint. Introduction by Janice Law Trecker. New York: Schocken, 1976.

Stites, Richard. *The Women's Liberation Movement in Russia: Feminism, Nihilism, and Bolshevism, 1860–1930.* Princeton: Princeton University Press, 1978.

Strachey, Ray. *The Cause: A Short History of the Women's Movement in Great Britain.* London: G. Bell & Sons, 1928.

Swiney, Frances. *The Awakening of Women or Woman's Part in Evolution.* London: George Redway, 1899.

Taylor, A. Elizabeth. *The Woman Suffrage Movement in Tennessee.* New York: Bookman Associates, 1957.

Terrell, Mary Church. *A Colored Woman in a White World.* Washington, D.C.: Ransdell, 1940.

Torre, Susanna, ed. *Women in American Architecture: A Historic and Contemporary Perspective.* New York: Whitney Library of Design, 1977.

Tracey, Lee. *Rosa Luxemburg: Revolutionary Theoretician.* Detroit: News & Letters, n.d.

Trowbridge, Lydia Jones. *Frances Willard of Evanston.* Chicago: Willet, Clark, 1938.

United Nations. *Everyone's United Nations.* 9th ed. New York: United Nations, 1979.

United Nations Centre for Social Development and Humanitarian Affairs. *Law and the Status of Women: An International Symposium.* Edited by Columbia Human Rights Law Review, Columbia University School of Law. New York: United Nations, 1977.

Van Voris, Jacqueline. *Constance de Markievicz: In the Cause of Ireland.* Amherst: University of Massachusetts Press, 1967.

Villard, Oswald Garrison. *Fighting Years: Memoirs of a Liberal Editor.* New York: Harcourt, Brace, 1939.

Wells, Anna Mary. *Miss Marks and Miss Woolley.* Boston: Houghton Mifflin, 1978.

White, William Allen. *Puritan in Babylon.* New York: Macmillan, 1938.

Whittick, Arnold. *Woman into Citizen.* London: Athenaeum Press, Frederick Muller, 1979.

Willard, Frances E. *Woman and Temperance.* Hartford, Conn.: Park Publishing, 1884.

Wiltz, John E. *In Search of Peace: The Senate Munitions Inquiry, 1934–36.* New Orleans: Louisiana State University Press, 1963.

Women's Centennial Congress, November 25, 26, 27, 1940. New York: Mail & Express, [1940].

Wright, Mary Clabaugh, ed. *China in Revolution: The First Phase, 1900–1913.* New Haven: Yale University Press, 1968.

Young, Rose. *The Record of the Leslie Woman Suffrage Commission, Inc., 1917–1929.* New York: Leslie Commission, 1929.

Zimmern, Alice. *Women's Suffrage in Many Lands.* London: Francis and Co., Athenaeum, 1909.

GENERAL-INTEREST ARTICLES

Adams, Mildred. "All the Americans Meet at Baltimore." *Woman Citizen,* 6 May 1922, pp. 10–13.

———. "Carrie Chapman Catt. *Nation,* 22 March 1937, pp. 330–31.

———. "Carrie Chapman Catt, Leader of Women—Pioneer for Peace." *Pictorial Review,* January 1931, pp. 14–15.

———. "The Distaff Side of Cuba." *Woman Citizen,* 22 March 1924, pp. 13–14.

———. "For the Healing of the Nations." *Woman Citizen,* January 1927, pp. 7–9.

———. "Mrs. Catt, at 75, Still Faces Forward." *New York Times Magazine,* 7 January 1934, p. 3.

———. "The Real Mrs. Catt." *Woman Citizen,* 6 September 1924, pp. 8–9.

Allen, Devere. "Women on the Job of Peace." *Christian Leader,* 18 and 25 December 1926.

Allen, Florence E. "The First Ten Years." *Woman's Journal,* August 1930, pp. 5–7.

Anthony, Susan B. "Woman's Next Step as Women See It." *New York Times Magazine,* 12 January 1941, p. 11.

Arndt, Jessie Ash. "Centennial Honors Carrie Chapman Catt." *Christian Science Monitor,* 9 January 1959, p. 13.

———. "Mrs. Catt Says Peace Depends on Morality." *Christian Science Monitor,* 11 January 1944, p. 17.

Ashby, M. Corbett. "Carrie Chapman Catt." *International Women's News,* April 1947, p. 83.

Beahan, Charlotte L. "Feminism and Nationalism in the Chinese Women's Press, 1902–1911." *Modern China,* October 1975, pp. 379–416.

Beard, Mary R. "Feminism as a Social Phenomenon." *Woman's [sic] Press Magazine,* November 1940, pp. 5–10.

———. "Women and the War Habit." *Woman's Journal,* May 1930, p. 5.

Bent, Silas. "Women of America Can Yet Save Europe, Says Mrs. Catt." *New York Times,* 17 June 1923, part 8, p. 3.

[Blackwell, Alice Stone.] "Mrs. Carrie Chapman Catt." *Woman's Journal,* 3 February 1900, p. 1.

Blair, Emily Newell. "Putting Women into Politics." *Woman's Journal,* March 1931, pp. 14–15.

———. "Why I Am Discouraged about Women in Politics." *Woman's Journal,* January 1931, pp. 20–21.

Boeckel, Florence Brewer. "The Steps that Lead to Peace." *Good Housekeeping,* December 1929, pp. 20–21.

Booth, Alice. "Carrie Chapman Catt." *Good Housekeeping,* October 1931, p. 34.

Boyle, Ruth. "Let Us Have No More Wars." *Good Housekeeping,* April 1928, p. 65.

Brown, Gertrude Foster. "Why the League [of Women Voters] Objected." *Woman Citizen,* July 1926, p. 24.

Brown, Margaret W. "Medals Awarded Mrs. Carrie Chapman Catt, Leader in the Woman Suffrage Movement." *The Numismatist,* February 1952, pp. 114–24.

Burnett, Constance Buel. "Carrie Chapman Catt." *American Girl,* April 1945, pp. 5–7.

Canning, Hazel. "'Can't Oust Us from New Rights,' Says Famous Suffragist." *Boston Sunday Post,* 11 February 1945, p. 5.

"Carrie Chapman Catt." *Current Biography 1940,* pp. 150–52.

"Carrie Chapman Catt Remembered." *Pi Beta Phi Arrow,* Spring 1961, pp. 10–11.

"Carrie Lane Chapman Catt, 1859–1947." *A Century of Friendship in Pi Beta Phi* [St. Louis, Mo., Pi Beta Phi, n.d.], pp. 386–88.

"China's Suffragists Ready to Use Force." *New York Times,* 23 June 1912, part 5, p. 8.

Clark, Adele. "The Second Conference." *Woman Citizen,* February 1927, p. 30.

Conway, Jill. "Women Reformers and American Culture, 1870–1930." *Journal of Social History,* Winter 1971–72, pp. 164–77.

Creel, George, and Lindsey, Ben B. "Measuring Up Equal Suffrage, An Authoritative Estimate of Results in Colorado." *Delineator,* February 1911, pp. 85–86.

Cruickshank, Sandra. "She Cleared the Way for Women's Rights." *Iowa Homemaker*, January 1961, p. 11.

Duryea, Florence Spencer. "A Convention in Three Languages." *Woman Citizen*, 30 May 1925, p. 12.

Eager, Harriet Ide. "A Farm Girl Who Leads Two Million." *Woman's Magazine*, October 1919, p. 5.

Eastman, Elizabeth. "The Front Door Lobby." *Woman's Journal*, February 1931, pp. 20–21.

Flexner, Eleanor. "Carrie Chapman Catt." In *Notable American Women*. Vol. 1. Edited by Edward T. James. Cambridge: Belknap Press of Harvard University Press, 1971.

———. "Changing Tactics in the Woman Suffrage Movement." Speech given at American Historical Association meeting, 28–30 December 1960.

Foster, Helen Herbert. "Women Forge ahead in Politics." *Brooklyn Eagle Magazine*, 26 June 1932.

Graves, John Temple. "One of the World's Great Women." *Cosmopolitan*, February 1916, pp. 445–46.

"A Great Suffragist Leader Mrs. Chapman Catt." *The Vote*, 26 November 1920, p. 579.

Hackett, Catherine I. "Today's Business-Peace." *Woman's Journal*, February 1930, pp. 18–19.

———. "Your Business in Washington." *Woman's Journal*, May 1928, pp. 26–27.

Harper, Ida Husted. "The Winning of the Vote." *Woman Citizen*, 8 August 1925, pp. 7–8.

——— "Woman Suffrage throughout the World. *North American Review.* September 1907, pp. 55–71.

———. "The World Movement for Woman Suffrage." *American Review of Reviews*, December 1911, pp. 725–29.

Harrington, W. P. "The Populist Party in Kansas." *Collections of the Kansas State Historical Society, 1923–1925*, pp. 403–50.

Haskell, Oreola Williams. "Carrie Chapman Catt." *Today's Housewife*, April 1923, p. 8.

Hauser, Elizabeth J. "Eight Months' War against War." *Woman Citizen*, 17 December 1921, pp. 22–24.

Higham, John. "The American Party, 1886–1891." *Pacific Historical Review*, 1950, pp. 37–46.

Ingham, Harvey. "Carrie Chapman Catt—Eightieth Birthday Today." *Mason City Globe Gazette*, 9 January 1939.

Irwin, Will. "Talking War to Death." *Our World*, May 1922, pp. 3–7.

————, and Milholland, Inez. "Two Million Women Vote." *McClure's Magazine*, January 1913, pp. 241–51.

Jacobi, Anna Manus. "Carrie Chapman Catt." *International Women's News*, April 1947, pp. 83–84.

Jensen, Joan M. "All Pink Sisters: The War Department and the Feminist Movement in the 1920s." Paper read at the Fourth Berkshire Conference, 24 August 1978. Mimeographed.

Johnson, Dorothy E. "Organized Women as Lobbyists in the 1920s." *Capitol Studies*, Spring 1972, pp. 41–58.

Kaplan, Sidney. "Social Engineers as Saviors: Effects of World War I on Some American Liberals." *Journal of the History of Ideas*, June 1956, pp. 346–69.

Kenneally, James J. "Catholicism and Woman Suffrage in Massachusetts." *Catholic Historical Review*, April 1967, pp. 43–57.

————. "Woman Suffrage and the Massachusetts Referendum' of 1895." *Historian*, August 1968, pp. 617–33.

————. "Women and Trade Unions, 1870–1920: The Quandary of the Reformer." *Labor History*, Winter 1973, pp. 42–55.

Kenyon, Dorothy. "The Place of Women." Smith Alumnae College Lecture, 1946, Smith College, Northampton, Massachusetts. Mimeographed.

Keyes, Frances Parkinson. "A Dinner. A Conference. A Wedding." *Good Housekeeping*, April 1925, p. 75.

Larson, T. A. "Dolls, Vassals, and Drudges—Pioneer Women in the West." *Western Historical Quarterly*, January 1972, pp. 5–16.

————. "Woman's Rights in Idaho." *Idaho Yesterdays*, Spring 1972, pp. 2–4.

Lasch, Christopher. " 'Selfish Women': The Campaign to Save the American Family, 1890–1920." *Columbia Forum*, Spring 1975, pp. 24–31.

Lawton, Alice. " 'There Is Nothing in Suffrage Propaganda that May Be Regarded as an Indorsement of Free Love': Mrs. Carrie Chapman Catt Answers an Accusation Frequently Made by the Antis." *Evening Sun*, 27 May 1914.

Levinson, S. O. "The Legal Status of War." *New Republic*, 9 March 1918, pp. 171–73.

Maddux, Edith Walker. "The Pacific and Peace." *Woman Citizen*, September 1925, p. 16.

Malcolm, Isabel. "Women's War on War." *Woman's Journal*, February 1928, pp. 8–9.

Marshall, Edward. "Worldwide Awakening to Woman's Place in Affairs." *New York Times*, 1 December 1912, part 5, p. 4.

McCann, Anabel Parker. "Ten Years of Woman Suffrage—Mrs. Catt Talks of Results of Enfranchisement." *New York Sun*, 26 March 1930.

McCulloch, Rhoda E. "Carrie Chapman Catt." *Woman's Press*, June 1947.

McGovern, James R. "Anna Howard Shaw: New Approaches to Feminism."
    Journal of Social History, Winter 1969–70, pp. 135–53.
———. "The American Woman's Pre-World War I Freedom in Manners and
    Morals." *Journal of American History,* 1 September 1968, pp. 315–33.
McIlvaine, Beth. "Where Women Vote." *Woman Citizen,* June 1926, pp. 20–
    21.
McLaughlin, Kathleen. "What Women Have Done with the Vote." *New York
    Times Magazine,* 24 November 1940, p. 5.
McMullen, Frances Dewry. "The W.C.T.U." *Woman Citizen,* 27 June 1925,
    p. 13.
Mende, Clara. "A Visit to Mrs. Chapman Catt." *International Woman Suffrage
    News,* January 1926, p. 53.
[Mill, Harriet Taylor.] "Enfranchisement of Women." *Westminster Review,*
    July 1851, pp. 149–61.
Morain, Thomas. "The Entry of Women into the School Teaching Profession
    in Nineteenth Century Iowa." Paper read at Conference on the History of
    Women, 21 October 1977, College of St. Catherine, St. Paul, Minnesota.
    Mimeographed.
"Mrs. Ben Hooper of Oshkosh: Peace Worker and Politician." *Wisconsin
    Magazine of History,* Winter 1962–63.
"Mrs. Carrie Chapman Catt—Constructive Decisionist." *Everybody's,* No-
    vember 1916, pp. 639–40.
"Mrs. Catt Fights for Peace." *Literary Digest,* 1 February 1936, p. 8.
"Mrs. Catt to Name New Federal Department." *Woman Patriot,* 1 April 1922,
    p. 1.
Niebuhr, Ursula M. "The Nature and Function of Woman." *Womans Press
    Magazine,* October 1940, pp. 17–21.
Notestein, Ada Comstock. "An Eminent Citizen." *Yale Review,* September
    1944, pp. 151–53.
O'Neill, William L. "Carrie Lane Chapman Catt." *Encyclopedia of American
    Biography.* New York: Harper & Row, 1974.
Onken, Amy Burnham. "Achievement Award." *Pi Phi Arrow,* December
    1941.
Page, Charles Hunt. "Lester Frank Ward." *Class and American Sociology: From
    Ward to Ross.* New York: Dial Press, 1940, pp. 29–72.
Patterson, Ada. "Mrs. Carrie Chapman Catt '80." *Iowa State Alumnus,*
    February 1910.
[Paul, Alice.] "Woman Suffrage and Congress." *Independent,* 27 December
    1915, p. 522.
Peabody, Anne. "Tribute to Carrie Chapman Catt." *First Wisconsin Con-
    ference on the Cause and Cure of War,* June 16, 1937, pp. 3–10. Mim-
    eographed.

Peck, Mary Gray. "Biographical Sketch: Carrie Chapman Catt." [1914?] Mimeographed.

———. "Carrie Chapman Catt's Eightieth Birthday." *Elmira College Bulletin,* March 1939, pp. 13–14.

———. "Changing the Mind of a Nation, The Story of Carrie Chapman Catt." *World Tomorrow,* September 1930, pp. 358–61. Slightly different version in *Adventurous Americans,* edited by Devere Allen. New York: Farrar & Rinehart, 1932.

———. "Great Promulgator." *International Women's News,* January 1939, pp. 26–27.

———. "Mrs. Catt at College: 1880–1930." *Woman's Journal,* September 1930, p. 21.

Read, Jessie Stringfellow. "The Story of the Biennial." *Good Housekeeping,* September 1924, p. 85.

Reed, Evelyn. "Is Biology Woman's Destiny?" *International Socialist Review,* December 1971.

Reynolds, Minnie J. "Carrie Chapman Catt: The Acknowledged Leader of Women Who Has Made a World-Wide Appeal for Political Equality." *New Idea Woman's Magazine,* November 1909.

Richardson, Anna Steese. "God Send a Leader of Women." *Colliers,* 27 October 1923, p. 7.

———, and Shuler, Marjorie. "We Women Want Peace." *Woman's Home Companion,* September 1928, p. 4.

Rosenberg, Rosalind. "The Dissent from Darwin: The New View of Woman among American Social Scientists, 1890–1915." Paper read at the Second Berkshire Conference on the History of Women, October 1974, Radcliffe College. Mimeographed.

Ross, Myrna. "A Woman Who Is Serving Her Country." *Fashion Review,* January 1918.

Roszak, Theodore. "The Hard and the Soft: The Force of Feminism in Modern Times." In *Masculine/Feminine,* edited by Betty Roszak and Theodore Roszak. New York: Harper & Row, 1969, pp. 87–104.

Schwimmer, Rosika. "The Cause and Cure of Peace." *World Tomorrow,* 22 February 1933, pp. 181–83.

Selden, Charles A. "The Most Powerful Lobby in Washington." *Ladies Home Journal,* April 1922, p. 5.

Shuler, Marjorie. "All the World at Rome." *Woman Citizen,* 16 June 1923, p. 7.

———. "All the World's Women at Paris." *Woman Citizen,* July 1926, pp. 5–7.

———. "Preserves Versus Politics: A Glimpse into the Home and Career of Carrie Chapman Catt, Crusader for Women's Social Freedom, Who Says the Cause of World Peace Is Their Greatest Challenge." *Christian Science Monitor Weekly Magazine*, 26 September 1930, p. 3.

Smith, Myra A. "Seek Peace and Pursue It." *Womans Press*, March 1935, pp. 126–27.

Snowden, Mrs. Phillip. "The Woman Suffrage Movement in Great Britain." *Chautauquan*, March 1910, pp. 98–108.

Sporborg, Mrs. William Dick. "Mrs. Catt, Nearing Seventy Seven, Looks Back on Fifty Years' Service to Women." *New York Herald Tribune*, 5 January 1936.

Stanton, Elizabeth Cady. "The Solitude of Self." *Woman's Journal*, 23 January 1892, p. 25.

Straus, Dorothy. "Champion of Women." *Saturday Review of Literature*, 26 August 1944, p. 22.

Strauss, Anna Lord. Columbia Oral History Interviews, 1971–72.

Strom, Sharon Hartman. "Leadership and Tactics in the American Woman Suffrage Movement: A New Perspective from Massachusetts." *Journal of American History*, September 1975, pp. 296–315.

Taylor, Antoinette Elizabeth. "South Carolina and the Enfranchisement of Women: The Early Years." *South Carolina Historical Magazine*, April 1976, pp. 115–26.

———. "The Woman Suffrage Movement in Arkansas." *Arkansas Historical Quarterly*, Spring 1956, pp. 1–36.

———. "The Woman Suffrage Movement in Florida." *Florida Historical Quarterly*, July 1957, pp. 42–60.

———. "The Woman Suffrage Movement in Mississippi, 1890–1920." *Journal of Mississippi History*, February 1968, pp. 1–34.

Thomason, Mrs. R. E. "Toast to Carrie Chapman Catt." *Woman Citizen*, 19 March 1921, p. 109.

Thompson, Dorothy. "Who Wants Peace?" *Survey Graphic*, February 1937.

Toombs, Elizabeth. "The Convention at Des Moines." *Good Housekeeping*, July 1923, p. 48.

Van Zile, Edward S. "'America's Women Must Give Organized Aid to the Nation to Enable It to Wage Successful War,' Says Mrs. Carrie Chapman Catt." *New York Sun*, [ca. 28 March 1917].

Wheaton, Anne Williams. "A Suffrage Hearing." *Woman's Journal*, March 1928, p. 27.

———. "The Status of the World Court." *Woman's Journal*, March 1928, pp. 26–27.

Wood, Marjorie. "Lives of America's Twelve Greatest Women: Carrie Chapman Catt." *Woman's Viewpoint*, November 1924.

Woolf, S. J. "Mrs. Catt, at Eighty, Calls Women to War on War." *New York TImes Magazine*, 8 January 1939, p. 10.

ARTICLES BY CARRIE CHAPMAN CATT

"Anti-Feminism in South America." *Current History*, September 1923, pp. 1028–36.

"Applied Democracy." *Crisis*, November 1917, pp. 19–21.

"Are You a Normal?" *Christian Advocate*, 6 November 1924, pp. 1359 60.

"Can the Church Stop War?" *World Tomorrow*, June 1931, p. 189.

"College Women as Citizens." *Pi Beta Phi Arrow*, June 1922, pp. 613–20.

"Con: The Equal Rights Amendment." *Congressional Digest*, April 1943, p. 118.

"Crisis in Suffrage Movement." *New York Times Magazine*, 3 September 1916, p. 5.

"Disarmament." *Missionary Review of the World*, December 1931, pp. 934–36.

"Domestic Economy." *Iowa Homestead*, 16 March 1883.

"An Eight-Hours Day for the Housewife—Why Not?" *Pictorial Review*, November 1928, p. 2.

"Elements in a Constructive Foreign Policy." *Annals of American Academy of Political and Social Sciences*, July 1927.

"Feminism and Suffrage." *New York Times*, 15 February 1914, part 5, p. 4.

"Friction in International Opinion." *Annals of American Academy of Political and Social Science*, July 1926, pp. 49–50.

"Gaps in the Machinery of Peace." *Christian Advocate*, 6 November 1930.

"The History [of woman suffrage in the United States]." *Eleusis of Chi Omega*, September 1941, pp. 293–99.

"How Far Have We Come in Suffrage?" *Union Signal*, 5 May 1945.

"It Is Folly to Be Sick in America." *Good Eating*, March 1934, pp. 12–13.

"Joining Hands for Peace." *Union Signal*, 17 October 1931, p. 630.

"Let's Talk It Over." *Good Housekeeping*, March 1928, pp. 36–37.

"Looking Forward." *General Federation Clubwoman*, January 1945, p. 14.

"Mary Church Terrell, An Appreciation." *Oberlin Alumni Magazine*, June 1936.

"Men, Women, and War." *Standard* [New York Society for Ethical Culture], November 1925, pp. 69–73.

"The National Outlook for the Suffrage Cause." *San Francisco Examiner*, [ca. 5 November 1899].

"The New Christmas Spirit." *Today's*, December 1913, p. 3.

"On the Wings of the Dollar." *Christian Advocate*, 31 May 1928, pp. 680–82.

"The Outgrown Doctrine of Monroe," *World Tomorrow*, November 1926.

"The Outlawry of War." *Annals of the American Academy of Political and Social Science*, June 1928.

"Ready for Citizenship." *Public*, 24 August 1917, pp. 817–18.

"Short Skirts and French Dictators." *Forum*, April 1927, pp. 578–85.

"A Survival of Matriarchy." *Harper's Magazine*, April 1914, pp. 738–48.
"Thanksgiving and Hard Times." *Christian Century*, 18 November 1931, pp. 1455–56.
"Too Many Rights." *Ladies Home Journal*, November 1922, p. 31.
"Unite Women by Vote." *Boston American*, 17 April 1915.
"Wake Up, Nevada!" *Out West*, August 1914, pp. 70–71.
"What Next?" *American Legion Weekly*, 6 September 1920, p. 5.
"What Right Has Woman to Be Free from Political Duties?" *New York Sun*, 16 September 1915.
"What Women Have Done with the Vote." *Independent*, 17 October 1925, pp. 447–48.
"Why I Have Found Life Worth Living." *Christian Century*, 29 March 1928, pp. 406–8.
"Why Suffrage Fight Took Fifty Years." *New York Times Magazine*, 15 June 1919, p. 3.
"Why We Did Not Picket the White House." *Good Housekeeping*, March 1918, p. 32.
"The Will of the People." *Forum*, June 1910, pp. 595–602.
"The Woman Suffrage Movement." *Public*, 12 June 1914, pp. 568–70.
"Woman's Place." *New York Tribune*, 22 August 1914.
"Woman Suffrage Must Win." *Independent*, 11 October 1915, p. 58.
"Woman Suffrage Only an Episode in Age-Old Movement." *Current History*, October 1927, pp. 1–6.
"Woman Suffrage: The First Ten Years." *New York Times Magazine*, 24 August 1930, p. 3.
"Women in Politics." *Collier's Weekly*, 30 October 1900, pp. 18–19.
"Women Voters at the Crossroads." *Public*, 31 May 1919, pp. 569–70.
"World Politics and Women Voters." *Woman's Home Companion*, November 1920, p. 4.
"The Years I Like Best." *Good Housekeeping*, October 1923, p. 17.

PAMPHLETS

Atwater, Elton. *Organized Efforts in the United States toward Peace*. New York: National Committee on the Cause and Cure of War, 1936.
Bailie, Helen T. *Our Threatened Heritage*. Cambridge: D.A.R. Committee of Protest, 1928.
Britt, George. *Rumors (made in Germany)*. New York: Council for Democracy and National Committee on the Cause and Cure of War, 1942.
DeBow, Sarah Spence. *The History of the Case*. N.p. [Tennessee, 1920.]

Deutsch, Regine. *The International Woman Suffrage Alliance: Its History from 1904 to 1929.* London, 1929.

League of Women Voters of Massachusetts. *The First Fifty.* Boston: LWV, 1970.

Miller, Helen Hill. *Carrie Chapman Catt: The Power of an Idea.* New York: Carrie Chapman Catt Memorial Fund, 1958.

Schwed, Hermine. "The Strange Case of Mrs. Carrie Chapman Catt." N.p., n.d.

"Study of Patriotic Propaganda." Federal Council of the Churches of Christ in America, New York, 5 May 1928.

Winder, Mary Ida. *Organizations in the United States that Promote International Understanding and World Peace.* Washington, D.C.: National Council for Prevention of War, 1 April 1936.

Zetkin, Clara. *Woman Suffrage.* Translated by J. B. Askew. London: Twentieth Century Press, [1906].

REPORTS AND PROCEEDINGS

Aberdeen, Ishbel, ed. *International Council of Women Report of Transactions of the Fourth Quinquennial Meeting Held at Toronto, Canada, June, 1909.* London: Constable & Co., 1910.

Blair, Emily Newell. *The Woman's Committee United States Council of National Defense: An Interpretative Report April 21, 1917 to February 27, 1919.* Washington, D.C.: Government Printing Office, 1920.

Conference on the Cause and Cure of War, Report on: 1st, Washington, D.C., 1925; 2nd, 1926; 3rd, 1928; 4th, 1929; 5th, 1930; 6th, 1931; 7th, 1932; 8th, 1933; Delegates Worksheet, Nos. 1–4, 9th, 1934; Delegates Worksheet, Nos. 1–4, 10th, 1935; Delegates Worksheet, Nos. 1–4, 11th, 1936; Delegates Worksheet, Nos. 1–4, 12th, Chicago, 1937; Delegates Worksheet, Nos. 1–4, 13th, Washington, D.C., 1938; Delegates Worksheet, Nos. 1–4, 14th, Washington, D.C., 1939; Delegates Worksheet, Nos. 1–4, 15th, Washington, D.C., 1940.

International Woman Suffrage Alliance, Report of Congress: 1st, Washington, D.C., 1902; 4th, Amsterdam, 1908; 1st quinquennial, London, 1909; 6th, Stockholm, 1911; 7th, Budapest, 1913; 8th, Geneva, 1920; 9th, Rome, 1923.

National American Woman Suffrage Association, Proceedings of annual conventions from the 32nd, Philadelphia, 1900 through the *Proceedings of the Victory Convention and First National Congress League of Women Voters,*

Chicago, 1920. Variously titled, usually *Handbook of the National American Woman Suffrage Association Proceeding of [Number] Convention.*

National League of Women Voters, Yearbook and Proceedings of the Third Annual Convention and Pan-American Conference of Women held at Baltimore, Maryland, 20–29 April 1922.

Official Record of the Declarations and Petitions Presented by the Disarmament Committee of the Women's International Organisations to the Disarmament Conference. Imprimatur de la Tribune de Genève, 1932.

United States Congress, Senate, Committee on the District of Columbia, Hearing under S. Res. 479, March 4, 1913. Senate Report No. 53, 63rd Cong., 1st sess., Congressional Serial Set No. 6512.

NEWSPAPERS AND OTHER PERIODICALS

Cerro Gordo Republican. Mason City, Iowa, 1883. Name changed to *The Republican,* Mason City, 24 August 1883.

Charles City Intelligencer. Iowa, 1880–93.

Far and Near. New York, 1891–October 1894 (ceased publication).

Floyd County Advocate. Charles City, Iowa, 9 January–25 December 1886; 1 May–25 December 1890.

International Woman Suffrage News. London, 1 May 1917–September 1947.

Interocean. Chicago, 1874–90.

Jus Suffragii. International Woman Suffrage Alliance, London, 15 September 1906–1 April 1917. Name changed to *Internatioal Woman Suffrage News.*

Mason City Republican. Iowa, 3 April 1884– 30 December 1886.

National Suffrage Bulletin. New York, September 1895–April 1901. Edited by Carrie Chapman Catt.

New Citizens. New Orleans, December 1912–April 1914.

New Southern Citizen. New Orleans, October 1914–May 1917.

New York Suffrage Newsletter. Syracuse, 1900–1912.

New York Times. 1900–1947.

Republican. Mason City, Iowa, 24 August 1883–27 March 1884. Name changed to *Mason City Republican,* 3 April 1884.

The Vote. London. Women's Freedom League, 30 October 1909–31 December 1926.

Western Woman Voter. Seattle, January 1911–January 1913.

Woman Citizen. New York, 2 June 1917–December 1927. Name changed back to *Woman's Journal.*

Woman Voter. New York, 1910—1916.

Woman's Column. Boston, 1887–1917.

Woman's Journal. Boston, 1870–1917. Name changed to *Woman Citizen,* became *Woman's Journal* again January 1928.

Woman's Journal. New York, January 1928–June 1931.

Woman's Standard. Des Moines and Waterloo, Iowa, September 1886–November 1911.

Index

The Feminist Press at The City University of New York offers alternatives in education and in literature. Founded in 1970, this nonprofit, tax-exempt educational and publishing organization works to eliminate stereotypes in books and schools and to provide literature with a broad vision of human potential. The publishing program includes reprints of important works by women, feminist biographies of women, multicultural anthologies, a cross-cultural memoir series, and nonsexist children's books. Curricular materials, bibliographies, directories, and a quarterly journal provide information and support for students and teachers of women's studies. Through publications and projects, The Feminist Press contributes to the rediscovery of the history of women and the emergence of a more humane society.

New and Forthcoming Books

Always a Sister: The Feminism of Lillian D. Wald, a biography by Doris Groshen Daniels. $12.95 paper.

Among the White Moon Faces: An Asian-American Memoir of Homelands, by Shirley Geok-lin Lim. $22.95 cloth.

The Answer/La Respuesta (Including a Selection of Poems), by Sor Juana Inés de la Cruz. Critical edition and translation by Electa Arenal and Amanda Powell. $12.95 paper, $35.00 cloth.

Australia for Women: Travel and Culture, edited by Susan Hawthorne and Renate Klein. $17.95 paper.

Black and White Sat Down Together: The Reminiscences of an NAACP Founder, by Mary White Ovington. Edited and with a foreword by Ralph E. Luker. Afterword by Carolyn E. Wedin. $19.95 cloth.

Changing Lives: Life Stories of Asian Pioneers in Women's Studies, edited by the Committee on Women's Studies in Asia. Foreword by Florence Howe. Introduction by Malavika Karlekar and Barbara Lazarus. $10.95 paper, $29.95 cloth.

Carrie Chapman Catt: A Public Life, by Jacqueline Van Voris. $13.95 paper

The Castle of Pictures and Other Stories: A Grandmother's Tales, Volume One, by George Sand. Edited and translated by Holly Erskine Hirko. Illustrated by Mary Warshaw. $9.95 paper, $23.95 cloth.

Challenging Racism and Sexism: Alternatives to Genetic Explanations (Genes and Gender VII). Edited by Ethel Tobach and Betty Rosoff. $14.95 paper, $35.00 cloth.

China for Women: Travel and Culture. $17.95 paper.

The Dragon and the Doctor, by Barbara Danish. $5.95 paper.

Japanese Women: New Feminist Perspectives on the Past, Present, and Future, edited by Kumiko Fujimura-Fanselow and Atsuko Kameda. $16.95 paper, $45.00 cloth.

The Maimie Papers, by Maimie Pinzer. Historical editor: Ruth Rosen. Textual editor: Sue Davidson. Foreword by Florence Howe. Introduction by Ruth Rosen. $17.95 paper.

Memories: My Life as an International Leader in Health, Suffrage, and Peace, by Aletta Jacobs. Edited by Harriet Feinberg. Translated by Annie Wright. Afterword by Harriet Pass Freidenreich. $18.95 paper, $45.00 cloth.

Music and Women, by Sophie Drinker. Afterword by Ruth A. Solie. $16.95 paper, $45.00 cloth.

No Sweetness Here, by Ama Ata Aidoo. Afterword by Ketu Katrak. $10.95 paper, $29.00 cloth.

Paper Fish, by Tina De Rosa. Afterword by Edvige Giunta. $9.95 paper, $20.00 cloth.

A Rising Public Voice: Women in Politics Worldwide, edited by Alida Brill. Foreword by Gertrude Mongella. $17.95 paper, $35.00 cloth.

Seeds 2: Supporting Women's Work around the World, edited by Ann Leonard. Introduction by Martha Chen. Afterwords by Mayra Buvinic, Misrak Elias, Rounaq Jahan, Caroline Moser, and Kathleen Staudt. $12.95 paper, $35.00 cloth.

The Slate of Life: More Contemporary Stories by Women Writers of India, edited by Kali for Women. Introduction by Chandra Talpade Mohanty and Satya P. Mohanty. $12.95 paper, $35.00 cloth.

Solution Three, by Naomi Mitchison. Afterword by Susan Squier. $10.95 paper, $29.95 cloth.

Songs My Mother Taught Me: Stories, Plays, and Memoir, by WakakoYamauchi. Edited and with an introduction by Garrett Hongo. Afterword by Valerie Miner. $14.95 paper, $35.00 cloth.

Streets: A Memoir of the Lower East Side, by Bella Spewack. Introduction by Ruth Limmer. Afterword by Lois Elias. $19.95 cloth.

The Tree and the Vine, by Dola de Jong. Afterword by Lillian Faderman. $9.95 paper, $27.50 cloth.

Women of Color and the Multicultural Curriculum: Transforming the College Classroom, edited by Liza Fiol-Matta and Mariam K. Chamberlain. $18.95 paper, $35.00 cloth.

Prices subject to change. Individuals: Send check or money order (in U.S. dollars drawn on a U.S. bank) to The Feminist Press at The City University of New York, 311 East 94th Street, New York, NY 10128-5684. Please include $4.00 postage and handling for the first book, $1.00 for each additional. For VISA/MasterCard orders call (212) 360-5794. Bookstores, libraries, wholesalers: Feminist Press titles are distributed to the trade by Consortium Book Sales and Distribution, (800) 283-3572.